The Agrarian
Origins of
American Capitalism

The Agrarian
Origins of
American Capitalism

Allan Kulikoff

UNIVERSITY PRESS OF VIRGINIA

Charlottesville and London

THE UNIVERSITY PRESS OF VIRGINIA
Copyright © 1992 by the Rector and Visitors
of the University of Virginia

First published 1992

An earlier version of portions of Chapter 1 and Chapter 2 appeared as "The Transition to Capitalism in Rural America." *William and Mary Quarterly*, 3d Ser. 46 (1989): 120–44. An alternative version of Chapter 4 will appear as "Was the American Revolution a Bourgeois Revolution?" in Ronald Hoffman and Peter J. Albert, eds., *"The Transforming Hand of Revolution": Reconsidering the American Revolution as a Social Movement*, forthcoming. An alternative version of Chapter 6 will appear in John Murrin, ed., *War and Society in Early America from the Aztecs to the Civil War*, forthcoming. An earlier version of parts of Chapter 7 appeared as "Migration and Cultural Diffusion in Early America, 1600–1860" in *Historical Methods* 19 (1986): 153–69, reprinted with permission of Heldref Publications, a division of the nonprofit Helen Dwight Reid Educational Foundation. An earlier version of parts of Chapter 8 appeared as "Uprooted Peoples: Black Migrants in the Age of the American Revolution," in Ira Berlin and Ronald Hoffman, eds., *Slavery and Freedom in the Age of the American Revolution*, pp. 143–71, reprinted with permission of the University Press of Virginia, 1983.

Printed in the United States of America

Library of Congress Cataloging-in-Publication Data
Kulikoff, Allan.
The agrarian origins of American capitalism/Allan Kulikoff.
p.   cm
Includes bibliographical references and index.
ISBN 0–8139–1388–8
1. United States—Economic conditions—To 1865. 2. United States—Rural conditions. 3. Agriculture—Economic aspects—United States—History. 4. Capitalism—United States—History. I. Title
HC 105.K87 1992
338. 1'0973—dc20   92–11395
                                                                     CIP

For Xie Lihong

Contents

Rural Migration and Capitalist Transformation

Preface

THESE ESSAYS have their origin in my long search to understand early American society in general and rural life in particular. Works of synthesis rest on large bodies of literature. This book is no exception. I am indebted to innumerable historians, beginning with Karl Marx. But my struggle to comprehend how American society changed can be understood as the result of an intense historical education. The publication of these essays gives me an opportunity to explain my intellectual odyssey.

My viewpoint has changed markedly since 1969 when I entered graduate school. When I began my graduate training, I knew that I wished to study poorer people in early America. Everywhere I looked in contemporary America, from campuses to urban ghettos, ordinary people were rising up, demanding equality, racial justice, an end to poverty, war, and oppression. How, I wondered, had similar people lived in the past? I examined Boston in the 1780s and 1790s, intent on researching, in the cliché of the time, "history from the bottom up." The result of that inquiry reflected the then very new "new social history," with its quantitative methodology. Notwithstanding the mass of fresh data I presented, I came to see flaws in my work. I knew how much Bostonians were worth (according to the tax assessor) and what jobs they held, but other than dividing my population arbitrarily into "classes" based upon wealth, I could not explore their social lives (family, kinship, class struggles, and the like).

I turned to study of the Chesapeake region for my dissertation, in part, to escape New England and examine a place then ignored by social historians. Possessing an intense desire to learn about slaves, I began work on Prince George's County, Maryland. Little did I realize then that it would take fourteen years of detective work and writing to complete the project that evolved from the dissertation. Much of that time was spent collecting, coding, and analyzing quantitative data. I found myself in the middle of a remarkable group of historians at the Maryland Hall of Records (especially Lois Green Carr, Russell R. Menard, and Lorena Walsh), each intent on analyzing similar data. We shared data, ideas, and methods.

My struggle to find a mode of explanation proceeded slowly. Like my Maryland colleagues, I placed data in a demographic and economic framework that emphasized how the demand for tobacco and the realities of mortality and fertility explained social change. As I completed work on the manuscript of *Tobacco and Slaves*, I became dissatisfied with this demographic and economic model. It permitted one to use quantitative data to distinguish periods in Chesapeake history. But the social conflict inherent in any slave society was pushed to one side. Influenced by women's history and labor history, I added chapters on women and the household and on class politics to go along with my detailed reconstruction of the slave community. Still, it was difficult to tell precisely what the manuscript argued, other than illuminating the demographic and economic basis of social relations. Readings of the manuscript by Elizabeth Fox-Genovese and Sean Wilentz persuaded me that the formation of a peculiar class system that flowered in the Old South constituted the theme of the book, and I rewrote it to reflect this vision.

This desire to understand rural class formation, which developed from my Chesapeake research, has framed my work since the mid 1980s. I have struggled to clarify the dynamics of class relations in rural America, both in teaching and research. When I began teaching agrarian history, I discovered few signposts to aid my inquiry. Most literature failed to address questions of capitalist transformation, which were at the center of my interest. My search for a better framework led me to European work on agrarian and economic history, especially to Marxist debates over the transition from feudalism to capitalism.

Seven of the chapters in this volume were previously published or will soon appear. I began writing the first essay in 1979, and three were published before 1990. In their original form, they reflected my understanding of capitalism at the time of composition. Authors of such collections often reprint the essays as they first appeared, perhaps adding headnotes to illuminate changes in their thinking. I have chosen, however, to substantially revise earlier essays to make a more coherent whole, focusing upon the rural origins and development of American capitalism. Although the book opens with a theoretical inquiry, it is not a book of theory, but instead uses theory to frame empirical questions in American agrarian history.

These essays, the first fruits of my interest in capitalism, not only came out of my reading and research but from intensive discussion within communities of scholars at Northern Illinois University, Princeton University, the Philadelphia Center for Early American Studies, and the annual meetings of the Social Science History Association. As well, extraordinary individuals, deeply committed to understanding the development of capitalism, immeasurably strengthened this book.

Elizabeth Fox-Genovese has supported and nurtured this project from the outset, offering advice, reading chapters, and strengthening theoretical formulations. Always willing to discuss Marxist and literary theory at great length, she pushed me to write with the clarity that such works rarely achieve. She read the penultimate draft of the book with care, elucidating complex theoretical issues and encouraging greater accuracy, precision, and conciseness.

Stanley Engerman not only shared his vast knowledge of economic and social history with me but read every version of every chapter of the book with the perseverance for which he is renowned. Skeptical of the Marxist framework of the book, he suggested alternative formulations and read every sentence twice and thrice, searching for errors.

Sean Wilentz, who read the penultimate draft of the book, vigorously contested some of my key ideas, continuing intensive discussions we had for five years at Princeton. Alfred Young not only read the chapters on the American Revolution but edited chapter 5 with extraordinary diligence, paying attention to argument, clarity, style, and sources. Otto Olsen read the first half of the manuscript and provided valuable alternative readings of numerous issues. Mary Furner read an early version of chapter 3 and suggested ways to understand the problem of language in a social context. John Murrin edited chapter 6 and frequently commented on my work in progress while I was at Princeton. And I am indebted to William Beik for intensive discussion of topics of mutual interest, especially capitalist transformation and bourgeois revolution.

In addition, I received valuable comments at seminars or in writing from Peter Albert, James Barrett, Ira Berlin, Michael Bernstein, Lois Green Carr, Kathleen Conzen, Edward Cook, Richard Dunn, Robin Einhorn, Herbert Erschowitz, James Farley, Aaron Fogelman, Eugene D. Genovese, C. H. George, the late Herbert G. Gutman, P. M. G. Harris, Ronald Hoffman, Francis Jennings, James McPherson, Robert Margo, Jacqueline Miller, Carl Parrini, Edward Pessen, Daniel Rogers, Marvin Rosen, Steven Rosswurm, Susan Rugh, Darrett Rutman, Robert St. George, Rima Schultz, Daniel Scott Smith, Lawrence Stone, Thad Tate, Peter Thompson, Sue Sheridan Walker, Lorena S. Walsh, David Weiman, Eli Zaretsky, and Michael Zuckerman.

I have learned much from my students. My graduate seminars, especially my American Rural History seminar in 1988, provided essential feedback on my ideas about capitalist transformation. Not only have Susan Branson, Michelle Gillespie, Lucy Murphy, Marcia Sawyer, Michael Smuksta, Terry Sheahan, and other graduate students permitted me to read and use works in progress, thereby enriching my scholarship, but they have often disagreed with me, forcing yet new considerations of my theoretical position.

I presented versions of chapters at the Shelby Cullom Davis Seminar, the Philadelphia Center for Early American Studies, the Capital Historical Society, Princeton University, Millersville University, Northern Illinois University, the Newberry Library, Colgate University, the University of Chicago, Chicago Area Labor History Seminar, and the Chicago Area Early American History Seminar. I would like to thank all the participants for their valuable comments.

My editor John McGuigan not only read the manuscript with care, suggesting ways to streamline the arguments but pushed me to complete the final version of the book. Gerald Trett conscientiously copyedited the final manuscript.

I began this book at Princeton University, where summer grants and graduate research assistance made initial research possible. Fellowships from the National Endowment for the Humanities and the Newberry Library (through their Lloyd-Lewis and NEH funds), and the American Council for Learned Societies were instrumental in completing the book. Northern Illinois University provided two summer stipends and the dean of the College of Liberal Arts, James Norris, furnished sufficient funds to permit me to take off an academic year to complete the manuscript. Dean Norris and Dean Jerrold Zar of the Graduate School funded a publication subsidy.

Works of synthesis demand the talents of many librarians. I have used library resources at Bryn Mawr College, University of Pennsylvania, Princeton University, Northern Illinois University, and the Newberry Library. The interlibrary loan departments at Princeton and Northern Illinois have been especially important, providing materials from far-flung places needed to complete the book.

There is no way of adequately thanking Xie Lihong. She read the final draft of the manuscript, not only making stylistic suggestions but pushing me to clarify my arguments. She cheered me up when I was blue, listened to my tirades on history, Marx, and capitalism, shared with me her passion for her own work in literature, taught me — from her firsthand experience — about modern socialism in China. To her this book, and indeed the rest of my life, is dedicated.

The Agrarian Origins of American Capitalism

Introduction:
Capitalist Transformation
and Agrarian Society

THE AGRARIAN HISTORY of the British colonies and the United States is
at a crossroads. The vast outpouring of economic and ecological histories,
ethnohistories of Indian communities, analyses of class, racial, and ethnic
strife, studies of rural women, and regional and community studies reach
such contradictory conclusions that they defy synthesis.[1] We need a model
of rural development that links time and place in various regions. The capitalist transformation of rural America—the making of independent smallholding farmers and artisans and dependent women and slaves into
capitalists and wage laborers—provides such a synthesis. Beginning in the
countryside, long before the explosive growth of cities, monopoly capitalism, and heavy industry, capitalism changed our entire society—its class
structure, gender relations, rural ideologies, migration patterns, distribution
of resources, organization of the state and of knowledge.

This process was complex, multifaceted, differentiated, contested. It
took centuries, not decades, to complete. The growth of the world market,
increasingly organized around capital accumulation and predicated upon
the expropriation of surplus value by capitalists from wage laborers, im-
pinged upon Americans, whatever their class.[2] Struggles over capitalism involved women and men, old classes and new, masters and journeymen,
laborers and capitalists, yeomen and land speculators, Indians and whites,
Catholics and Protestants, immigrants and native-born, Whigs and Democrats, North and South, city and countryside, settled areas and frontiers.
Conflicts within classes could be as great as those between them. Sometimes
conflicts, like those between capitalists and urban workers, focused on pro-

1. Recent works include Hahn and Prude, eds., *Countryside in Age of Capitalist
Transformation*; G. Wright, *Old South, New South*; Faragher, *Sugar Creek*; Atack and
Bateman, *To Their Own Soil*; Limerick, *The Legacy of Conquest*; Fox-Genovese, *Within
the Plantation Household*; Innes, ed., *Work and Labor in Early America*; C. Clark, *Roots of
Rural Capitalism*; Merchant, *Ecological Revolutions*; S. Burns, *Pastoral Inventions*.
2. Surplus value, in Marxist thought, defines how exploitation occurs in a capitalist economy. Surplus value, created at the point of production and expropriated from
wage laborers, is the difference between capital needed to produce the product and its
final value. See Bottomore, ed., *Dictionary of Marxist Thought*, s.v. "Surplus Value."

ductive relations; more often, like those between Protestants and Catholics, they embedded class struggle in ethnic or cultural rivalry. Although colonial America developed out of England's capitalist economy, the United States was not born capitalist but *became* capitalist. Capitalist transformation had its origin in the rural American North during the century after 1750. It occurred within both the macroeconomics of regional, national, and world economies and the microeconomics of household, market, and ideology. Rural class struggles over control of land, credit, and the division of labor stand at the center of capitalist transformation, influencing culture, religion, and gender relations.

Asserting the primacy of capitalist transformation invites controversy. Historians disagree on where and when capitalism began, its causes, and the class identity of supporters and opponents. Since any position one takes precludes others, scholars need to state precisely the premises of their arguments. Influenced by Marx and Marxist writings, my arguments are embedded within a framework of historical materialism. Marxists emphasize the social relations of production, class formation, and class struggle. Culture, language, ideology, and religion are all rooted in class relations but, at the same time, each profoundly influences the ways classes relate to each other. Although historical materialism is a theory of determination, constraining human choices, it nonetheless insists upon human agency. Marx captured the ambiguity of human agency in a world of structural determination. "Men make their own history," he wrote, "but they do not make it as they please; they do not make it under circumstances chosen by themselves, but under circumstances directly encountered, given and transmitted from the past."[3]

These premises raise thorny problems of definition. How the origin of capitalism is understood depends, to a degree, upon choice of contested definitions of class and capitalism used in the analysis. The term *class* is central to our inquiry. Because the meaning of class is hotly contested, we need to define the term carefully.[4] E. P. Thompson's conception of class provides a starting point. Class relations, he insists, grow out of history and are contingent on human agency. "Class happens," he writes, "when some men, as a result of common experiences, . . . articulate the identity of their interests . . . against other men whose interests are different from (and usually opposed to) theirs." Although "class experience is largely determined by the productive relations into which men . . . enter involuntarily," their understanding of class is "embodied in traditions, value systems, ideas, and insti-

3. K. Marx, *Eighteenth Brumaire*, 97.
4. Ossowski, *Class Structure in Social Consciousness*, brilliantly describes debates over class.

tutional forms."[5] Classes emerge at the end of a long process of class struggle. "People find themselves in a society structured in determined ways"; especially "in productive relations, they experience exploitation . . . (or the need to maintain power over those whom they exploit), they identify points of antagonistic interest, they . . . struggle around those issues," slowly discovering "themselves as classes." These struggles are protracted; "class and class-consciousness," Thompson insists, "are always the last, not the first, stage in the real historical process."[6]

In Thompson's hands, class becomes a dynamic, historical process, changing as productive relations develop, framed by the cultures of the contending classes. Nonetheless, his model unwisely conflates class and class consciousness. People enter class relations, Thompson argues, only when they "articulate" differences between themselves and an antagonistic class. Although he admits that class can be used "to organize historical evidence," he warns against any "tendency to read back subsequent notions of class" into societies where people "saw themselves and fought . . . in terms of 'estates' or 'ranks' or 'orders.'" Following this definition it would be difficult to find classes in rural America until the late nineteenth century. Since farmers had a determinative, if changing, place in the class structure and understood their place in the productive order, class analysis must include them.[7]

The relation between class formation and consciousness is a major issue for Thompson. In classless societies, he argues, class formation took place through endemic class struggle. By invoking widespread class struggle, Thompson makes it clear that class society was not preceded by a placid world without conflict. The idea of "class struggle without class," however, raises serious problems. If "class struggle" does not involve classes, structurally defined, then it might be called "social conflict," thereby avoiding class analysis altogether. Class struggle should be embedded in class structures of exploitation, between existing classes, always in the process of formation and reformation.[8]

5. E. P. Thompson, *Making English Working Class*, 9–11, and "Eighteenth-Century English Society," 147–48. Thompson's ideas are contested: So and Hikam, "'Class' in Writings of Wallerstein and Thompson," 457–62; Sewell, "Thompson's Theory of Class Formation," 50–77; and E. M. Wood, "Politics of Theory," 45–75; all vehemently disagree about Thompson's class theory.

6. E. P. Thompson, "Eighteenth-Century English Society," 149–50.

7. E. P. Thompson, "Eighteenth-Century English Society," 147–49, and "Thompson Interview," 17–20. Compare G. A. Cohen, *Marx's Theory of History*, 73–77, and Sewell, "How Classes Are Made," 57–66, with Dawson, "Revamping Sociology of Class," 419–23. E. M. Wood, "Politics of Theory," 50–52, 59–61, insists Thompson has been misunderstood on this point.

8. Thompson, "Eighteenth-Century English Society," 149–50; P. Anderson, *Arguments within English Marxism,* chap. 2; So and Hikam, "'Class' in Writings of Wallerstein and Thompson," 462–66.

How, then, can one embed class in determinative structures yet retain the centrality of human agency? Analytic Marxists provide signposts. A structural understanding of class begins with productive property. Classes can be distinguished by their ownership, control, or use of property — the land, livestock, labor, and tools — whose reproduction perpetuates a social order. Ruling classes maintain their power by controlling production and exploiting producers. Exploitation, defined as the expropriation "of the fruits of the labour of one class by another," can take the form of profit, rent, or interest. Ruling-class exploitation of subordinate classes should be distinguished from other forms of oppression (sexual harassment or enslavement, for instance) which do not encompass expropriation of surpluses; slaves suffered greater oppression but lower rates of exploitation than early wage laborers. Subordinate classes "produce for others who do not produce for them." Relations between classes involve class struggle and interclass alliances. Through class struggle, classes become aware of their place in the productive order and seek to change or sustain it.[9]

This framework raises a key question for students of American agrarian life. Neither exploiter nor exploited, most farmers owned land and equipment and worked their farms with family labor. They seemed to lie outside of class society, yet they struggled with great planters, land speculators, or capitalists to maintain control of their productive property. Erik Wright's conception of contradictory class locations helps resolve this dilemma. He argues that such classes as farmers do not fit into a two-class schema because they resemble both proletarians and bourgeoisie, and are thereby located in "more than one class simultaneously." Members of such classes can be dominant and subordinate, exploited and exploiter. They make complex interclass alliances, tying themselves to capitalists, hoping to join that class, or to workers to regulate capitalist property.[10]

The idea of contradictory class locations suggests a way to understand American farmers. Small producers in early America owned the means of production but depended on merchants or planters for credit. As capitalism expanded, farmers' class location became even more contradictory. They owned, but did not hire, labor power; small capitalist farmers, they struggled

9. For sometimes contradictory versions of these points, see E. O. Wright, *Classes*, chaps. 1–4 (quote on 77); G. A. Cohen, *Marx's Theory of History*, chap. 3 (quote on 69), 183–93; Roemer, "New Directions in Marxian Theory," 81–113; Brenner, "Social Basis of Economic Development," 23–53; Poulantzas, *Classes in Contemporary Capitalism*, introduction; Elster, *Making Sense of Marx*, 319–31; Fox-Genovese and Genovese, *Fruits of Merchant Capital*, 151–56; Neale, *Class in English History*. For a critique of analytic Marxists, see So, "Class Struggle Analysis," 39–59, esp. 39–45.

10. E. O. Wright, *Classes*, chaps. 1–4 esp. 37–51 (quote 43–44), 124–26. For the class identity of American farmers, see chap. 2.

with financial and monopoly capitalists to maintain their farms in a world characterized by industrial consolidation, allying themselves with noncapitalist farmers in an agrarian crusade that lasted a generation at the end of the nineteenth century.[11]

Defining class entails combining the insights of the structural propositions of the analytical Marxists with Thompson's class-struggle framework. Class identity or location is determined by one's relation to the means of production and is outside of human volition. The engine of change in productive relations — capitalist transformation, for instance — is found in struggle between classes over control of productive property. Such struggles are mediated by the cultures of the participants and entail rising class consciousness by dispossessed classes.

Analysis of agrarian transformation is further complicated by disagreement between neoclassical economists and Marxists over defining capitalism. Capitalism, in non-Marxist accounts, refers to a system of exchange "in which goods are bought and sold," where individuals produce "for the market," purchasing goods from the market in return. Capitalists maximize profits, accumulating wealth for investment.[12] Differences in the *extent* of trade, specialization, and profit-maximization distinguish capitalist from noncapitalist economies. Such definitions make it difficult to find noncapitalist economies; land and labor markets and foreign trade, for instance, developed rapidly in medieval Europe.[13] American economic historians, unsurprisingly, find the word *capitalism* so imprecise that they refuse to use it, but call the United States an entrepreneurial, commercial, or business society. Rather than focus on capitalism, they examine commercialization and market-embeddedness among householders.[14]

Marxists understand capitalism as a mode of production in which capitalists, who own the means of production, expropriate surplus value from proletarians, who own only their labor power. A few Marxists, like Paul Sweezy and Immanuel Wallerstein, make exchange central to their understanding of capitalism, explaining the commodification of everything, espe-

11. Goodwyn, *Democratic Promise*, and McNall, *Road to Rebellion*, are contrasting class analyses of the agrarian uprising.

12. Dobb, *Studies in Development of Capitalism*, chap. 1, remains unsurpassed as an analysis of possible meanings for capitalism. But see Lane, "Meanings of Capitalism," 5–13, quotes on 6–7; E. O. Wright, *Classes*, 106–7; Haskell, "Capitalism and Humanitarian Sensibility," 339–42.

13. For markets in medieval Europe, see Parker and Jones, eds., *European Peasants and Their Markets*, pt. 1; Hilton, "Capitalism — What's in a Name?" 145–52.

14. Rothenberg, "Markets, Values, and Capitalism," 174–78; E. J. Perkins, "Entrepreneurial Spirit," 163–69; Bruchey, *Roots of American Economic Growth*, chap. 2; Robertson, *America's Business*, 11–19, esp. 8.

cially labor power, by increasing commerce, rather than by class struggle.[15] For most Marxists, an understanding of capitalism begins with free labor. Capitalism creates a class of free laborers (proletarians) who are endowed with so few of the tools needed for production that they can subsist only by working for wages. Proletarianization results from class struggle between peasants and capitalists over control of productive property. As capitalists gain control of the economy, a labor market, where workers sell their labor power to the highest bidder and capitalists buy labor power at the lowest price, develops.[16]

The purpose of capitalism is the accumulation of capital. The most efficient way for capitalists to accrue resources is to expropriate surplus value from free wage laborers. Wage earners become free laborers only when their work creates surplus value. North American slaves were sometimes paid an implicit wage, but they did not enjoy self-ownership; the hired hand of American yeomen farmers worked only to increase family subsistence; strawhat outworkers, early factory workers, post–Civil War cowboys, and late nineteenth-century California migrant laborers and Great Plains threshing crews, in contrast, all created surplus value for their capitalist bosses and therefore must be counted as free wage laborers.[17]

In a capitalist economy, the state serves to ensure the sanctity of labor contracts, to protect the productive value of private property, and to facilitate trade. To increase productivity, the capitalist state appropriates tax or public resources to capitalist enterprises (land grants to American railroads) and allows entrepreneurs to violate the property rights of original owners in the name of development (large water mills for early factories that flooded farmland).[18]

Capitalism, as a labor system, progressively separated home from work, "productive" market labor from "unproductive" subsistence labor, thereby devaluing the domestic work of married women but encouraging female market production on the farm, in the factory, and at the schoolhouse. In order to revalue their labor, women devised an ideology of domesticity, turning child nurture and housekeeping into tools needed to make republican

15. Wallerstein, *Historical Capitalism*; Sweezy, "A Critique." For responses to this view, see Hilton, ed., *Transition from Feudalism to Capitalism*, and Fox-Genovese and Genovese, *Fruits of Merchant Capital*, 15, 190–93.

16. My understanding of capitalism is informed by Fox-Genovese and Genovese, *Fruits of Merchant Capital*, 3–26, 189–92; Bottomore, ed., *Dictionary of Marxist Thought*, s.v. "Capitalism"; Hilton, "Capitalism — What's in a Name?" 144–58.

17. G. A. Cohen, *Marx's Theory of History*, 67–70, 180–93; Wallerstein, *Historical Capitalism*, chap. 1.

18. Wallerstein, *Historical Capitalism*, chap. 2; Horwitz, *Transformation of American Law*.

citizens. But, at the same time, radical women demanded full bourgeois rights of property and franchise.[19]

Capitalism, defined in this way, raises problems for historians examining rural America. Most farmers were small producers who used family labor, only occasionally employing outsiders; rather than hire wage labor, they mechanized planting and harvesting. The Marxist distinction between a mode of production and a social formation helps explain this seeming contradiction. Although the capitalist mode of production tends to reduce middle classes to wage labor, other types of productive relations (between independent producers and capitalists, for instance) are embedded in capitalist societies ("social formations"). One can identify a capitalist social formation by its central tendency, by the dominance of wage labor and expropriation of surplus value by capitalists, not by absolutely uniform capitalist social relations of production.[20]

Moreover, even in the most capitalist of societies, proletarianization is incomplete, with many households able to grow some of their food on property they control. Not only did rural folk seek to maintain as much economic autonomy as possible, but sometimes capitalists — who wanted to hire seasonal wage laborers — found the perpetuation of such semiproletarian households desirable. The greater the quantity of food the semiproletarian might produce, the lower the wage the capitalist would have to pay and the less likely the state would have to support workers during the off-season. The growth of cottagers in eighteenth-century Pennsylvania and the struggle over sharecropping in the postbellum South are examples of semiproletarian classes in the United States.[21]

Before the final victory of capitalism in the United States, several centuries of struggle passed. The British North American colonies were born in a capitalist Atlantic economy. However antagonistic to capitalism they were, they should not be called *precapitalist* but *noncapitalist* social formations. Some — colonial slaveowners, for example — distanced themselves from capitalism by extending private property to human beings. Others — antebellum slaveowners, for instance — were *anticapitalist*, devising modern economies

19. I have been influenced by Fox-Genovese, "Property and Patriarchy," 36–59; Cott, *Bonds of Womanhood*; Kerber, "Separate Spheres, Female Worlds," 9–39.

20. See chap. 1 for the debate over the class position of American farmers. For rural wage labor, see G. Wright, "American Agriculture and Labor Market," 193–209; for California, see Daniel, *Bitter Harvest*. For theory, see E. O. Wright, *Classes*, 11, 17, 109–11; G. A. Cohen, *Marx's Theory of History*, 77–79.

21. Wallerstein, *Historical Capitalism*, 22–28, 36–37; G. Wright, *Old South, New South*, chaps. 2–4; Woodman, "Post-Civil War Agriculture and the Law," 319–37; Clemens and Simler, "Rural Labor and the Farm Household in Pennsylvania," 106–43.

based upon collective cooperation or explicitly defending unfree labor systems.

To determine when an area became capitalist, one needs to look at the broader society, beyond the farm community. The growth of wage labor in a region, along with a bourgeois ideology, and state support for development suggest rapid development of capitalism even if wage laborers (including cottagers and sharecroppers) and capitalists constitute a minority of the farm population. In such areas, like the nineteenth-century American North, farmers and their children were often enticed into temporary or permanent wage labor, thus accelerating capitalist development. As the cost of land, labor, and machinery rose, more farmers were pushed into rural wage labor or forced to move to the city, thereby greatly reducing the proportion of farmers in the American population.

Looking at class and capitalism this way suggests that the emphasis of American social historians upon human agency, the ways women and men make their own histories and struggle with those who would deny them the fruits of their labor, is overdrawn. While they have enriched our understanding of class, gender, and racial relations, and given the dispossessed a voice,[22] these historians concentrate so much upon human agency that they play down conflicts between different groups of the dispossessed and the structural constraints upon choice. Ruling classes, by their power, limited the choices of the poor and of small property-holding classes. Poorer groups themselves had contradictory goals: if the state protected the human property of small slaveholders, slaves cold never gain their freedom; if working-class men earned the family wage so many desired, they could increase the subordination of their own wives.

By highlighting the decades between the Revolution and the Civil War, a century of vigorous class struggles over capitalism, the essays in this volume will illuminate several key elements of rural capitalist development. Chapter 1 delineates debate over the transition to capitalism in rural America while chapter 2 examines the history of the American yeoman classes. As the third chapter shows, rural struggles over capitalism engendered their own self-conscious languages of class that farmers, whether sympathetic to capitalism or not, made to explain the new relations of production in which they were embedded.

The American Revolution may have been the most crucial event in the creation of capitalism. It was a bourgeois revolution, chapter 4 argues, because it accelerated capitalist development. Chapter 5 shows how revolutionary ferment led to the making of the American yeoman classes,

22. Representative examples include Gutman, *Black Family in Slavery and Freedom*; L. W. Levine, *Black Culture and Black Consciousness*.

opponents of capitalism, supporters of a hierarchical household system. The final chapter in this section, a case study of yeomanry in the Revolutionary era, examines military manpower procurement in Virginia.

The last section of the book turns to regional differences in capitalist development in North and South. At the same time as a northern free labor society emerged, white southerners created a modern, anticapitalist slave society. To gain insight into this vast topic, we will focus on migration. Chapter 7 examines white migration, North and South, from 1600 through the 1880s, suggesting the links between economic development, the flight from capitalism, and western migration. The last chapter places the forced movement of slaves from the old to the new South in the early nineteenth century in the context of the growth of world capitalism, especially the English textile industry.

Perspectives on Rural Capitalism

Chapter 1

The Transition to Capitalism in Rural America

In 1904 MAX WEBER read a paper comparing European and American agrarian society at the International Congress of Arts and Sciences, held as part of the Louisiana Purchase Exposition in St. Louis. Weber, who had traveled across America for three months before the meeting, visiting both cities and farms, contrasted the feudal social relations still found in parts of Europe with capitalist agriculture in the United States. European peasants had traditionally produced to support a seigniorial class and to supply their own needs. "The past two thousand years," he concluded, "did not train the peasant to produce in order to gain profit." In contrast, "the American farmer is an entrepreneur like any other" and had become "a rationally producing small agriculturist" long ago. The Civil War had destroyed the "aristocratic, social, and political centers of the rural districts," thereby consolidating capitalist agriculture. This was especially true in northern wheat-producing areas where a farmer was "a mere businessman" who believed in "absolute economic individualism."[1]

The issues Weber raised have been a mainstay in agrarian history for over half a century. The earliest commentators believed that northern farmers practiced subsistence agriculture on self-sufficient farms and placed the timing of the development of commercial agriculture in the nineteenth century. Using aggregate statistical data, colonial historians in the 1950s and 1960s described a dominant commercial economy. A second debate, over the extent of capitalist economic relations in the South, began in the 1960s with Eugene D. Genovese's challenge to the easy identification of staple agriculture with capialism.[2]

---

1. M. Weber, "Capitalism and Rural Society in Germany," 363–85 (quotations on 364, 365, 369, 383, 385). Weber's American travels are detailed in Brann, "Max Weber and the United States," 18–30, and the exposition congress is examined in Coats, "American Scholarship Comes of Age," 404–17.

2. Rothenberg, "Market and Massachusetts Farmer," 283–85, and Headlee, *Political Economy of Family Farm*, 1–42, provide opposing summaries of the earlier northern debate; for the southern debate contrast Genovese, *World Slaveholders Made*, esp. part

During the past decade, American historians and historical economists have participated in a reinvigorated discussion of the temporal and agrarian origins of American capitalism. Focusing on family farmers in the Northeast and upland South, these scholars have emphasized the meaning of capitalism, the character of rural economic exchange, and the degree of market participation — issues often missing in the early northern debate. Participants have not only borrowed theories from neoclassical economics, Marxian economics, and cultural anthropology but they have produced a substantial body of empirical research based on systematic examination of individual data (like account books) neglected by earlier scholars.[3]

This chapter seeks to explain this new debate over the transition to rural capitalism, assess its achievements, and evaluate its deficiencies. The subject should have a central place in early American social and economic history because it illuminates broader patterns of class conflict and social cohesion in the countryside, where the vast majority of Indians, settlers, and slaves lived. Whether one contends that capitalism arrived with the first colonists or that it came to dominate the countryside only after much struggle depends upon how that term is defined, and the definition in turn structures debate about economic exchange.

Problems of Definition

At the risk of oversimplification, it can be said that participants in the debate on the transition to capitalism in rural America have formulated two contradictory visions, one influenced by neoclassical economics and economic history and the other by social history and anthropology. Whether economists or historians, those influenced by neoclassical economics stress the impact of market forces on human behavior and seek to explain how market

1, and Fox-Genovese and Genovese, *Fruits of Merchant Capital*, chaps. 2, 5–6, 9, 12, with Oakes, *Ruling Race*.

3. Among key works in the debate are Merrill, "Cash Is Good to Eat," 42–71; Mutch, "Yeoman and Merchant," 279–302; Henretta, "Families and Farms," 3–32, and "Transition to Capitalism," 213–38; C. Clark, "Household Economy, Market Exchange, and Rise of Capitalism," 169–89, and *Roots of Rural Capitalism*; Jaffee, "Peddlers of Progress," 511–35; Hahn and Prude, *Countryside in Age of Capitalist Transformation*, 3–21; Nobles, "Capitalism in Countryside," 163–77; Vickers, "Competency and Competition," 3–29; Gross, "Culture and Cultivation," 42–61; R. L. Bushman, "Opening the American Countryside," 239–56; Headlee, *Political Economy of Family Farm*, 1–42; Rothenberg, "Market and Massachusetts Farmers," 283–314, and "Emergence of a Capital Market," 781–808; Lemon, "Early Americans and their Social Environment," 115–31; Appleby, "Commercial Farming and 'Agrarian Myth,'" 833–49; Pruitt, "Self-Sufficiency and Agricultural Economy," 333–64; E. J. Perkins, "Entrepreneurial Spirit," 160–86.

processes spread through rural society. Despite borrowing from a wide range of theories — including the "new" social history, the cultural Marxism of E. P. Thompson, structural Marxist theories, and various anthropological frameworks — those influenced by social history all seek to uncover patterns of economic and social behavior of ordinary rural people and to relate their behavior to the social relations of production and to social and political consciousness. I will use the terms *market historians* and *social historians* for the two groups, but readers should understand how imprecise the terms are and how broad disagreements within each group can be.

Market historians insist that America developed out of vigorous commercial expansion and that early American farmers were entrepreneurial. They implicitly measure capitalism by commercial expansion and household participation in commodity markets. As markets developed and became more integrated (as measured by price convergence), farmers participated in them more fully. Market historians do disagree about change within a capitalist economy. Some insist that colonists came with a capitalist (or acquisitive) ideology and see change as further embeddedness in the system; others see substantial changes within capitalism at the end of the eighteenth century.[4]

Social historians start with Marx's distinction between production for use (use-value) and production for exchange (exchange-value). In economies where use-value predominates, householders control the means of production and sell some goods at markets but use most of what they produce in their households or exchange it in their local communities. The value of the goods is not determined by market prices but by their utility to those who make or use them. Markets in such economies are *places*, regulated by the state or custom, where people trade goods or labor and where merchants facilitate commerce over local hinterlands. Rural areas in the North and upland South, far from urban markets, these scholars believe, shared characteristics of noncommercial economies until the mid-nineteenth century. In commercial economies, dominated by exchange-value, goods are commodities that have market prices and exchanges are always made through the abstract medium of money. Markets in commercial economies become both places and *processes* that set prices and distribute goods over vast regions. A capitalist economy is a commercial economy, where profits are divided between the original producers (petty capitalists, artisans, wage laborers) and a class of capitalists who own and control the means of production. Capitalists expropriate part of the value of goods made by the original producer. Work-

4. Compare Rothenberg's description of change in "Market and Massachusetts Farmers," 283–314, with Lemon's "Early Americans and Their Social Environment," 115–31, and E. J. Perkins's "Entrepreneurial Spirit," 160–86.

ers in capitalist economies sell their labor power in labor markets. Capitalist transformation is not an automatic process but one fraught with conflict and violence, as capitalists attempt to reduce independent farmers to dependent wage workers. Agrarian historians who share such views can point to planters and sharecroppers in the postbellum South or migrant workers in California as examples of capitalist rural areas.[5]

While admitting that rural Americans frequently exchanged goods on local and even regional and international commodity markets, social historians contend that most exchange was for the immediate use of the farm household or its neighbors. Prizing independence, farmers sought land, some of them argue, not to gain profit (or even to maximize utilities) but to make a competency in order to maintain complex lineages and to sustain a traditional communal and noncapitalist mentalité. Others emphasize the dominance of noncommercial exchange of labor and goods between local households, nearly all of whom owned some land and were able to partially feed and clothe themselves by their own labor.[6]

This debate over the definition of capitalism is, in part, a controversy over the utility of two different classical economic models, originating in the interpretations of Karl Marx and Adam Smith. Where one side, looking through Marxian lenses, sees some of the social relations embedded in such documents as account books as evidence of noncommercial exchange, the other decries a lack of precision, demands testable definitions of capitalism, or prefers that the term not be used. Such critiques sometimes lead to reiteration of theory and brusque rejection of evidence proffered by the other side.[7]

Nonetheless, the debate over the definition and utility of capitalism has a broader significance. It suggests confusion over the nature of American economic development from initial colonization through the nineteenth

5. Capitalism is defined on pp. 5–6. For use-value and exchange-value, and commercial economies, see K. Marx, *Capital*, 1: chap. 1, esp. 125–39, and *Pre-Capitalist Economic Formations*; Hobsbawm, "Introduction," 12–16, 67–68, 94–96, 110–17; Bottomore, ed., *Dictionary of Marxist Thought*, s.v. "Exchange" and "Use Value." The best analysis of markets and the market from this perspective is Agnew, "Threshold of Exchange," 99–118.

6. For the first version, see Henretta, "Families and Farms," 3–32; R. B. Bushman, "Family Security in Transition to Capitalism," 238–56; and Vickers, "Competency and Competition," 3–29. For the second see Merrill, "Cash Is Good to Eat," 42–71.

7. See especially the exchanges over Henretta's "Families and Farms" (Lemon with a reply by Henretta, "Comment on Henretta's 'Families and Farms,'" 688–700) and over Rothenberg's "Market and Massachusetts Farmers" (Weiss, "Market and Massachusetts Farmers: Comment," and Rothenberg, "Market and Massachusetts Farmers: Reply," 475–80, plus Bernstein and Wilentz, "Marketing, Commerce, and Capitalism," and Rothenberg, "Markets, Values, and Capitalism," 171–78).

century. Only with great difficulty can historians present an unambiguous description of early American social and economic relations. It is clear that settlers in British North America never established feudalism. Not only had much of rural England become fully capitalist by the mid-seventeenth century, with classes of entrepreneurial landlords, capitalist tenants, and wage laborers, but settlers understood that feudal social relations would no longer protect their rights-in-land. The "feudal revival" of the mid-eighteenth century in New York was an attempt by increasingly capitalist landlords to impose capitalist ground rent; local residents resisted these capitalist economic relations in feudal forms. But English peasants had protested the expropriation of their land by capitalists, tearing down enclosures or reflooding fens. Colonists, often the urban descendants of peasants or rural folk who feared displacement, migrated in part to escape capitalist landlords who had deprived or would deprive them of land. They gained sufficient land to reject the dependence of wage labor and sought, however incoherently, to devise social formations within capitalist world markets that preserved some of the communal and hierarchical ethos characteristic of local communities in feudal England. As capitalism expanded in the nineteenth century, these attempts continued, especially in places most isolated from commodity markets.[8]

The rural economy of early America was clearly commercial. It can be described as undergoing either an intensification of capitalist production or a transformation from noncommercial or at least noncapitalist social formation to a capitalist one. For instance, those who insist on the early emergence of capitalism can point to individual landownership and the substantial rights of alienation that it entailed, while those who describe noncapitalist social formations can point to initial communal control over land in New England and the persistence of primogeniture and entail in the southern colonies. Where one scholar examining account books sees intricate exchanges of labor and goods between kindred and neighbors, another insists that these exchanges are commercial and documents that assertion by comparing prices found in the account books with prices in urban markets.

One's definition of capitalism structures one's vision of American society. Market historians reject any idea of a "transition to capitalism" or of "capitalist transformation" and implicitly hold that economic conflicts are

8. K. Marx, *Capital*, 1: chaps. 26–33 (chap. 33 gives perceptive comments about colonies in a capitalist world); Aston and Philpin, eds., *Brenner Debate*; Lachmann, *From Manor to Market*; D. Levine, *Reproducing Families*. For riots and unrest, see Charlesworth, ed., *Atlas of Rural Protest in Britain*, 8–41, 63–83; R. B. Manning, *Village Revolts*. Social characteristics of migrants are sketched in chap. 7 below. For tenancy, see Berthoff and Murrin, "Feudalism, Communalism, and the Yeoman Freeholder," 256–88; Kim, *Landlord and Tenant in Colonial New York*, chaps. 5–8.

concerned with the distribution of profits rather than being struggles between antagonistic classes. The social historians' vision of a precapitalist and noncommercial economy implies great conflict over the development of capitalism and struggle between noncommercial farmers and capitalist entrepreneurs (whether land speculators, capitalist farmers, or financial, industrial, or monopoly capitalists) over economic relations.

A Marxian definition possesses substantial advantages for the study of rural America. It gives the agrarian critics of capitalism a new voice, capturing their noncapitalist familial relations and intense nonmarket gift exchanges of goods and labor with neighbors. It suggests that violence preceded the victory of capitalists and thereby provides a powerful explanation for intermittent agrarian uprisings of independent landholding farmers (or those seeking that status) as diverse as New England–born New York tenants in the mid-eighteenth century and the late nineteenth-century Populists of the cotton South and northern plains. And it points to cooperation and internal struggles within households over the sexual division of labor and exchanges between households.

The Debate over Exchange Relations

The most exciting part of the American debate over agrarian capitalism is the controversy over the nature of economic exchange between households in the Northeast and in the upland South. This emphasis distinguishes the American debate from those on England and Europe over the transition from feudalism to capitalism. Participants in the European debates emphasize class conflict and structural change that led to the decline of feudalism and the coming of agrarian capitalism. They ignore exchange relations within individual households or communities, for whatever vestiges of use-values persisted, they influenced neither feudal nor capitalist class relations. Seeking the origins of capitalist economic and class relations, Marxist and anti-Marxist scholars alike pay little attention to the noncommercial world of peasants.[9] Where European historians emphasize structural change, American scholars often privilege cultural issues or combine culture and structure. To delineate cultural and ideological change, the American debate, unlike the European, has accentuated the behavior of individual households at home, in the local community, and in various local and national markets. Economists and market historians seeking explanations of economic development within a capitalist world face social historians who wish to understand farmers who resist capitalist advance. To sustain these conflicting

---

9. Hilton, ed., *Transition from Feudalism to Capitalism*; Aston and Philpin, eds., *Brenner Debate*.

views, scholars have plumbed hundreds of farm and store account books, thousands of probate inventories, and innumerable tax lists and censuses searching for forms and patterns of exchange.

As this work has proceeded, a remarkable convergence on the substance of social and economic change has occurred among those who follow the neoclassical and Marxist branches of classical economics. Granted, the theoretical explanations of the meaning of forms of exchange conflict, but descriptions of economic patterns and economic change themselves are often similar. Both groups deny familial self-sufficiency, describe patterns of economic exchange between households or within markets (and argue about the relative importance of the two patterns), and struggle to understand the timing and significance of economic transformation. When taken together, these differing visions of the meaning of economic exchange and transformation raise new questions that neither alone poses.

Both sides deny the development of either subsistence agriculture (an economic level achieved with a nearly complete absence of exchange) or self-sufficient farms (nearly total production of a farm's own food and clothing). Market historians have documented extensive exchange between households and at markets; farmers in much of eastern New England in the mid-eighteenth century, for example, not only sold goods on local markets but depended on imports from outside the region for much of their grain. Occasional charges by market historians to the contrary notwithstanding, social historians also deny the existence of self-sufficient households and subsistence agriculture. While they contend that farm households participated in few commercial market exchanges, they have described complex systems of local exchange of goods and labor that permitted households to procure food and cloth that they could not make themselves. Families with insufficient resources to participate in exchanges had to sell their labor or personal goods to feed and clothe themselves. The two sides contend over the *degree* of local self-sufficiency and the *extent* of market exchange rather than the *fact* of exchange.[10]

Both sides document nonmarket exchange outside of competitive commodity markets. The key issues here are how frequently the price of goods was set competitively and how the balance between gift and market exchange changed. Social historians contend that most exchanges of goods and labor took place between households apart from competitive markets

10. Pruitt, "Self-Sufficiency and Agricultural Economy," critiques left scholarship for insisting upon self-sufficiency; Weiman, "Families, Farms, and Rural Society," argues for a life-cycle view of relative self-sufficiency, exchange, and the sale of capital goods; Vickers, "Working the Fields," documents exchanges of goods but the dominance of family and hired labor (rather than labor exchanges) in colonial New England.

and that these exchanges were noncommercial because merchants did not charge explicit interest, farmers rarely even implicitly charged interest in accounts with each other, book credit predominated, accounts stayed on the books for years without a reckoning, and farmers did not create negotiable commercial paper. Market historians deny the economic significance of such nonmarket, "gift" exchanges, pointing to the ubiquity of market exchange and the fact that shopkeepers charged implicit interest (in different "cash" and "credit" prices). Yet the ubiquity of nonmarket exchange is implied in their work. To write of increasing market embeddedness and increasing price convergence as Rothenberg does, suggests, after all, a time (perhaps a frontier stage) when market exchange was less common. James T. Lemon argues that "between a third and a half or more" of the produce of Pennsylvania farmers was sold on local or international commodity markets; the rest was part of a "subsistence" economy that presumably included reciprocal local exchanges hidden in Lemon's aggregate data on trade, production, and consumption.[11]

In a similar way, both sides document substantial commercial exchange in developing commodity markets. Market historians have detailed patterns of eighteenth-century international commodity trade from registers of the Board of Trade and have examined farm account-book transactions at local stores. They argue that commercial exchange predominated from the outset of settlement or that farmers became increasingly enmeshed in it. Those social historians who insist upon the preeminence of noncommercial exchange admit that farmers sometimes sold goods on commodity markets but argue that such sales were of minimal importance. In a calculation based upon the circulation of money in early America, Michael Merrill has suggested that in 1800 perhaps a quarter of the monetary value of all exchanges took place in commercial markets. But, he adds, as commercialization permeated the countryside, the proportion of market exchanges jumped to three-quarters by 1870.[12]

A judicious synthesis of these two visions of economic exchange better describes American reality than either of them alone. American farmers lived within a dynamically growing capitalist world economy that encompassed the entire North Atlantic rim. Nearly all of them participated more or less regularly in commodity markets, to procure money to pay taxes and buy imported manufactured goods. Nonetheless, a system of noncommercial exchange developed in most rural communities based on male householder reciprocity (and, as these scholars ignore, upon exchanges between women)

11. Rothenberg, "Market and Massachusetts Farmers," 281–314; Lemon, *Best Poor Man's Country*, chap. 1, esp. 27–29.
12. Merrill, "Survey of the Debate over Exchange in Early America," 9–10.

rather than on competitively set market prices. This system was imbued with great cultural significance by farm families, for it sustained their independence, their ability to live "competently" without being forced into abject financial dependence on creditors.

Examination of the relationship between reciprocal local exchange and market exchange not only resolves difficulties in both market and social interpretations but potentially opens up significant new questions about both economic behavior and political and economic ideology. The perpetuation of local exchange between households, outside of markets, when local and regional commodity markets expanded, shows the need to look beyond utility-maximizing behavior (defined as understanding tradeoffs between production and leisure and as ordering economic preferences) of farmers to the goals that lay behind this kind of behavior.[13] In the early stages of commercial expansion, farm families may have used the proceeds of commercial exchange to create and sustain new social networks outside the marketplace. How and when such exchanges waxed and waned and their precise relationship to frontier development, commercial exchange, and capitalist advance need further analysis. The perpetuation of gift exchange and neighborliness on the farm in the era of monopoly capitalism suggests examination of its transformed function, especially its ability to sustain commercial farms in times of low crop prices. And the growing importance of commercial exchange in settled areas of the Northeast during the late eighteenth and early nineteenth centuries and its immediate development in northern parts of the Midwest suggest that capitalism was generated by commercial farm families within rural communities. Opponents of commercial advance and capitalist exploitation struggled with these small capitalist farmers.[14] How farmers made decisions, perhaps unconscious of their effect, to employ farm labor, agree that their daughters work in factories, purchase mechanized farm equipment, or buy negotiable commercial instruments that thrust them into capitalist economic relations should be added to analyses of the perpetuation of old ways.

This vision of a complex economic order, filled with a confusing amalgam of forms of exchange, also clarifies the political economy of the new nation. During the Revolutionary era farmers devised a new ideology to legitimate their increasing political participation. That ideology grew in part from Adam Smith's arguments about the willingness of small farmers to innovate; it was reflected in the economic thought of such founding fathers as Thomas Jefferson and John Adams. As Merrill has recently shown, these men espoused a form of "agrarian realism." They insisted that a society organized

13. See Rothenberg, "Bound Prometheus," 628–37.
14. Smuksta, "Work, Family, and Community," chaps. 1, 3–4.

around independent small proprietors was the best possible social order, one likely to sustain prosperity. Jefferson, for one, believed that small farmers were superior citizens, not because they worked the earth, but because they avoided complete dependence upon markets by making some of their own subsistence and selling surpluses on commodity markets to buy what they could not acquire locally. Such an ideology presumed the growth of commercial markets within a system in which men could make economic and political decisions because they retained both ownership and control of the means of subsistence. To maintain independence, farmers had to stay clear of heavy indebtedness or deep involvement in the market to prevent creditors from determining the economic behavior of the household. Those who fed and clothed their families mostly from the produce and labor of their farms could decide what crops to grow, what commodities to bring to market, which candidates to support without undue pressure from anyone.[15]

Both sides of the debate, finally, agree that both North and South experienced major economic transformation. This transformation, which began in the rural Northeast in the third quarter of the eighteenth century, spread slowly across the country but did not reach more isolated regions (or former slave societies) until nearly the end of the nineteenth century. Market and social historians, however, describe these transformations quite differently. Where a student influenced by social history sees a "transition to capitalism" that entailed great class struggle, a market historian searches for structural economic change that occurred when farmers chose to participate in markets.

Focusing on Massachusetts, Winifred Rothenberg has provided the most elaborate structural analysis of economic transformation. Before the mid-eighteenth century, the rural New England economy was more isolated from the North Atlantic economy than it was to become. Farmers participated irregularly in regional commodity markets (shown by relatively low levels of convergence between rural farm prices and urban wholesale prices); they paid farm laborers a set wage unaffected by labor markets; and the book debts they accumulated could not be sold on financial markets. The Revolution, however, was a great watershed: galloping inflation made older forms of investment precarious; the need to feed armies and cities created more integrated regional markets; and ideas of systematic individualism led men to question older labor relationships. Rapid price convergence of agricul-

---

15. See Merrill, "Political Economy of Agrarian America," chaps. 3, 5. Merrill would probably not accept the spin I put on his arguments. For views that connect agrarianism to aristocratic nostalgia or American mythology, see H. N. Smith, *Virgin Land*, part 3, and Hofstadter, *Age of Reform*, chap. 1. This issue is more fully explicated in chaps. 3 and 5.

tural products after the war suggests that Massachusetts farmers participated with increasing regularity in regional commodity markets. Fearing renewed inflation, middling farmers began to invest in commercial paper, exchangeable in financial markets, and began to pay market wages to the laborers they hired, giving close attention to seasonal needs and local supplies of workers.[16]

While Rothenberg describes grand economic changes, she refuses to link them together as "a transition to capitalism," preferring to analyze each change in terms of the growth and transformation of markets. Unlike historians influenced by Marx, she sees little struggle in the development of these markets; rather, she implicitly argues, middling and wealthy farmers chose to participate in labor, commodity, and finance markets because they increased opportunity for economic advancement and provided income for an improved standard of living. The key issue here is economic development; struggles — when they occurred — were between groups of capitalists over the allocation of resources. This vision makes it difficult to explain such agrarian uprisings as Shays's Rebellion, because it misses the ambiguities of farmers who participated in markets *and*, at the same time, sought a kind of household autonomy. Moreover, it ignores the class struggles between these small producers and a rapidly growing class of capitalists who dominated the courts.[17] But it does point to the enthusiastic reception of capitalist economic and class relations by large numbers of middling farmers, men and women who were major players in the struggle over rural capitalism.

Steven Hahn's examination of upcountry Georgia yeomen, 1850–90, provides a Marxist analysis of transformation. During the antebellum era, Hahn argues, this noncapitalist society was free from substantial commercial exchange. Most exchange occurred between households, and farmers sold little produce on commodity markets; few farmers either owned slaves or grew cotton. Although cotton production and slaveholding increased in the boom years after 1850, most farmers resisted commercialization. They maintained an egalitarian economic order (for white male landowners) by keeping the range (land not under cultivation) open to the animals of poorer men and by electing numerous poorer men to public office. The destruction of slavery led to the formation of a new class of capitalists, insistent upon development. Because the southern infrastructure was heavily damaged, cotton prices rose immediately after the war, and more and more upcountry

16. Rothenberg, "Market and Massachusetts Farmers," 283–314, "Emergence of a Capital Market in Rural Massachusetts," 781–808, and "Emergence of Farm Labor Markets," 537–66.

17. For rural revolts in the eighteenth century, see R. M. Brown, "Back Country Rebellions and the Homestead Ethic," 73–99; Szatmary, *Shays' Rebellion*; Slaughter, *Whiskey Rebellion*; and chap. 5 below.

farmers produced the crop on small farms. But, like the ex-slaves before them, they were sometimes forced into sharecropping and debt peonage. The enclosure of the open range (justified by the need for greater productivity) not only increased inequality but, along with crop liens and sharecropping, threatened to thrust more farmers into wage labor.[18]

Hahn's vision of a transition to capitalism, unlike Rothenberg's, stresses economic and class struggle over control of economic resources. Political conflict, moreover, was a forum for regulating class struggle. If markets seem nearly autonomous in the neoclassical version of transformation, in this version they are the consequence of political conflict between contending classes of yeomen and merchants as well as of economic forces. And like many left historians, Hahn recaptures the behavior and ideology of the losers in the adoption of capitalism. But his work may underestimate antebellum commercial exchange, misidentifying as a noncommercial society what was actually a frontier economy slowly embedded in commodity markets, and thereby exaggerating the postbellum conflict.[19]

When these two versions of the transition to capitalism are placed side by side, they raise new questions and new possibilities for research. The impact of changing commodity prices, levels of market embeddedness, and the growth of monopoly capitalism on farmers' movements and other class struggles, for example, might be examined. The timing of farmers' decisions to participate more fully in the market or to pull back from commercial agriculture might well be related to farm income, to national prosperity (as measured by the construction of canals or railroads), or to the demands of creditors. A full study might describe, with equal sympathy, the behavior and viewpoints of both agrarian capitalists and their neighbors who struggled against capitalist advance. And economists or historians interested in institutional change might well examine statute and common law and see what impact, if any, they had on the market relations of production.

Explicating the American Transition Debate

The debate over the transition to capitalism in rural America has generated substantial new historical evidence, insight, and questions. Yet it has created as many problems as it has resolved. First, the social and economic relations that preceded capitalism are not at all clear nor has the meaning of rural

18. Hahn, *Roots of Southern Populism.*
19. Such a critique of Hahn's work may be inferred from Shirley, "Market and Community Culture," 219–48; Ford, "Yeoman Farmers in the South Carolina Up-country," 17–37, and "Rednecks and Merchants," 294–318; Weiman, "Families, Farms, and Rural Society," 255–77; "Farmers and the Market in Antebellum America," 627–48, and "Economic Emancipation of the Non-Slaveholding Class," 71–94.

capitalism after the transition been adequately described. Second, the conceptual framework narrows discussion of economic change, focusing upon exchange in local communities and ignoring production and regional and national agricultural trade. Third, it presumes that the household is the most fundamental and elementary element of social and class organization, thereby precluding examination of internal household processes, especially of gender roles and the sometimes conflicted relation between husbands and wives. Theories generated in the European debate over the transition to capitalism, recent Marxist rural sociology, and feminist writings, usually ignored by participants in the American transition debate, begin to resolve these issues.

Where the European debate is conceptually clear, dealing with the transition *from* feudalism *to* capitalism, the American debate is confused. European historians place the origins of capitalism in the decline of serfdom or in class struggles surrounding feudal production. The transition to capitalism came when the extraction of peasant surplus by extraeconomic compulsion disintegrated and then — in order to retain their wealth — landlords succeeded in undermining peasant property rights and hiring ex-peasants as wage laborers. Before 1700, capitalists in England had, with state support, gained control of most peasant land and then hired improving tenants who worked the land with wage laborers.[20]

Although all agree that feudalism did not reach these shores, the economic system, social formation, or mode of production that preceded capitalism in America is rarely specified. A few social historians like Michael Merrill have envisaged a third economic system — a "household" or "domestic" mode of production — that predominated in rural communities until the 1840s, in opposition to the commercial or capitalist society of the cities and the North Atlantic rim. In the household mode of production, exchanges of labor and goods among households were "controlled by need rather than price." The goods and labor farmers exchanged, the debits and credits found in their accounts, are gifts, rather than commodities exchangeable at markets or interest-bearing securities. Cash does not "mediate the exchange of products," but is merely another product available for exchange as "good to eat" as corn or milk.[21]

20. K. Marx, *Capital*, 1: chaps. 12–15, 26–33, is the classic statement. Dobb, *Studies in the Development of Capitalism*; Hilton, ed., *Transition from Feudalism to Capitalism*; Aston and Philpin, eds., *Brenner Debate* are the most important recent contributions to the debate. These comments follow Brenner's essays in the *Brenner Debate*. For England, see also chap. 7.

21. Sahlins, *Stone Age Economics*, analyzes a "domestic mode of production"; Merrill, "Cash Is Good to Eat," 42–71 (quotes on 53), and "So What's Wrong with the 'Household Mode of Production?'" 141–46, posit a "household mode of production."

While such a conception illuminates exchange relations, pointing to networks of noncommercial exchange found on American farms even in the twentieth century, it denies the importance of commercial exchange (and the merchants who organized it) found everywhere in early America. It comes close to conflating commerce, common in slave and feudal societies, with capitalism, a special form of commerce in which free workers sell their labor power. Moreover, it ignores the relation of noncommercial exchange to commercial exchange; even the least commercial farms were greatly influenced by commodity prices and interest rates set by those within commodity markets in an era when world capitalism greatly expanded. It also obscures struggles within the household, leading implicitly to romanticizing a noncommercial "world we have lost."[22]

One might alternatively argue that the transition was *within* capitalism from a rudimentary form of exploitation to a more mature system. Ideas of "stages" of capitalism have merit. Proponents acknowledge the capitalist transformation of England, pay attention to the bourgeois property relations dominant in the American countryside, relate colonial development to the expansion of international commodity markets, and delineate the process of rural class formation. Immanuel Wallerstein, for instance, argues that colonial social formations grew out of the capitalist world system. As industry rose in the core capitalist countries (like England), town populations grew, creating new demands for grain that could not be met locally. The periphery, American colonies of the European powers, provided raw materials for core countries, especially silver and food (grain, sugar, rice, tobacco).[23]

These models cannot accommodate the ambiguities and contradictions of early capitalism in either England or America. English opponents of capitalism, found in the most developed parts of the realm, accepted some elements of capitalist production while rejecting others. In England such opposition took place within the context of the growth of a landless working class. But in the colonies migrants — some of them radical opponents to the dispossession of the peasantry by English capitalists — could find abundant land. Isolated from capitalists and sometimes even commodity markets, they devised strikingly noncapitalist and occasionally even anticapitalist social formations. To see struggles over ownership, development, and use of land

22. C. Clark, "Household Mode of Production," 166–71; Wessman, "Household Mode of Production," 129–39; Mutch, "Colonial America and Debate about Transition to Capitalism," 852–59. Merrill has rethought the concept, dropped the language of "mode of production," and admitted the interpenetration of noncommercial and commercial exchange ("Political Economy of Agrarian America," chap. 3).

23. Wallerstein, *Modern World-System I*, chap. 2; see S. J. Stern, "Feudalism, Capitalism, and the World-System," 829–45, for a critique. The best American example is Hacker, *Triumph of American Capitalism*.

between small farmers and capitalists as conflicts between petty or failed capitalists and their more successful brothers obscures the profound difference between the contending classes.[24]

Early American class relations, then, grew from agrarian capitalism in England and from reactions against it. Settlers and their descendants could hardly survive outside the North Atlantic system, with its trade and credit networks, but many refused to fully accept the commodification of land, goods, trade, and labor that capitalism inspired. Instead they created — through the development of staple agriculture or the search for marketable goods, through the formation of labor systems that would permit both economic independence and commerce, through complex class struggles over the use of land — dynamic and modern social formations tied to the world market but not fully of it. Southern planters devised a noncapitalist and increasingly anticapitalist slave regime in the colonial and antebellum eras; northern farmers relied on petty commodity production and local exchange to keep capitalist class relations at bay.[25]

While southern slavery hindered the spread of capitalism, the hybrid nature of the economic order of the early American North provided a porous defense at best against capitalist advance. Small producers rejected feudal hierarchy but wanted the fruits of capitalism without the large-scale agriculture and wage labor that went with it. Frontier conditions and accidents of geography allowed northern farmers to establish semiautonomous farms and create noncapitalist social formations that survived for generations. But wherever capitalists (even the early hand "manufacturing" capitalists before the machine age) invested their profits and created new markets, an important minority of farmers rushed to invest and participate, and soon entire communities found themselves dependent on markets and forced to share profits with distant capitalists.[26]

The State, the Household, and Capitalist Development

By focusing the debate on economic exchange rather than on the means of production and productive relations, historians almost automatically ignore fundamental change within the Western capitalist economy, such as the development of international commodity markets in tobacco, rice, cotton, and

24. For the transfer of radical traditions see Linebaugh, "All the Atlantic Mountains Shook," 87–121, and A. F. Young, "English Plebeian Culture," 185–212; Hahn, *Roots of Southern Populism*, is an evocative examination of rural revolt.

25. This point is most fully developed in Genovese, *World Slaveholders Made*, pt. 1, and Fox-Genovese and Genovese, *Fruits of Merchant Capital*, chaps. 1–3, 9–10.

26. Cayton and Onuf, *Midwest and Nation*, chaps. 2–3; and n. 22 above. I am indebted to Elizabeth Fox-Genovese, who greatly strengthened this formulation.

wheat or the later rise of monopoly capitalism. New labor systems — slavery, migrant wage labor — grew out of transformations within capitalism and influenced levels of production, social relations, the mix of commercial and noncommercial exchange, and the willingness of ruling and subordinate classes to accept capitalist class relations. Moreover, warfare or depressions affected household economic and demographic behavior even in places with little commercial exchange by reducing credit below that needed to establish farms, buy livestock, pay taxes, and sustain local exchange.[27]

There may have been a dynamic relation between production and exchange, the one affecting the other. For example, the rise of industrial capitalism in New England in the middle third of the nineteenth century created demands for a new, semiskilled labor force, thereby encouraging young women to leave home and work for wages. Their wages, and those provided by outwork, encouraged commercial exchange and challenged male authority in the household. As rural industry grew, new cities appeared in the countryside, creating increased demands for grain, vegetables, and fruit and encouraging rural capitalist production. And consumer demands of urban workers and farmers (in part to replace goods produced by farm wives making straw hats or by adolescents working in factories) increased industrial production.[28]

All participants in the debate, even those most influenced by neoclassical economics, have focused upon local communities, and usually on places presumed to have relatively low levels of commercial exchange, at least at the outset of settlement. They have ignored the fully commercial staple economies of the slave South, Great Plains, and California.[29] Study of the relationship of commercial and noncommercial exchange in these places illuminates the importance of changes in production. For instance, local markets and exchange networks of labor and goods developed most fully in the eighteenth-century Chesapeake after the adoption of slavery and the disappearance of booming tobacco prices.[30] If this pattern was duplicated in other staple economies, it suggests one should look at the *creation* of a tradi-

27. Wallerstein, *Modern World-System I*, elucidates these points. McCusker and Menard, *Economy of British North America*, chaps. 4, 13–14; G. Wright, *Political Economy of Cotton*; and Williamson, "Greasing Wheels of Export Engines," 189–214, provide American examples.

28. Prude, *Coming of Industrial Order*; Dublin, *Women at Work*; D. S. Brady, "Consumption and Style of Life," 73–78.

29. For an analysis close to the terms of this chapter, see Daniel, *Bitter Harvest*, chaps. 1–2; for the South see Fox-Genovese and Genovese, *Fruits of Merchant Capital*; Genovese, *World Slaveholders Made*, pt. 1; for the Plains, Friedmann, "Simple Commodity Production and Wage Labour," 71–100.

30. Kulikoff, *Tobacco and Slaves*, 99–104; Carr and Walsh, "Economic Diversification and Labor Organization," 166–75.

tional form of exchange as a response both to developing value systems *and* to constricted commodity markets within a capitalist world economy.

By examining communities, analysts of capitalist transformation have underplayed the significance of the nation-state in the creation of commercial and capitalist economic relations *and* in the perpetuation of nonmarket relations of production. The United States Constitution mandated a national legal system, a continental common market, and free migration (except for slaves). During the nineteenth century, moreover, capitalists developed a transportation system that linked local, regional, and national markets. These changes transformed exchange relations in local communities. Two examples illustrate the pattern. When migration reduced the agricultural labor force of New England at the same time as cheap western grain underpriced local farmers, thereby eliminating agricultural markets, New England farmers either had to find new commodities to sell in order to maintain noncommercial exchange networks or search for industrial employment. When a railroad or canal linked previously isolated locales in New York or the Midwest to regional markets, middling farmers increased market participation while those too poor to compete or too wedded to noncommercial exchange had to leave for a more isolated area.[31]

National economic development, however, generated class conflicts between farmers who sought just enough development to ensure access to markets, economic independence, and absolute control over their households and capitalists who wished to devise a fully integrated national market. The kind of farmers who urged rejection of the Constitution on these grounds later supported the Jeffersonian Republicans and Jacksonian Democrats, fighting their Federalist and Whig opponents over national land policy, internal improvements, credit and banking. Both the persistence of noncapitalist exchange systems and the triumph of monopoly capitalism at the end of the nineteenth century must be seen within the context of these struggles.[32]

Just as the debate over capitalist transformation has ignored productive relations, it has downplayed the dynamics of exchange within the household. Participants in the debate all assume that the household was an indivisible unit. Farm households, of course, were income-pooling units of

---

31. A stream of work deals with such national issues, often linking them to regional development (see G. R. Taylor, *Transportation Revolution*; P. W. Gates, *Farmer's Age*; Pred, *Urban Growth and Circulation of Information*; Grossberg, *Governing the Hearth*), but most participants in this debate spend little space discussing such issues.
32. Handlin and Handlin, *Commonwealth*; Hartz, *Economic Policy and Democratic Thought*; Gunn, *Decline of Authority*; Wallenstein, *From Slave South to New South*; Horwitz, *Transformation of American Law*; Ashworth, *Agrarians and Aristocrats*, are very suggestive of the general issues.

production that had to sustain themselves, and husbands and wives had to cooperate in the productive enterprises (planting, harvesting, household manufacturing) of the farm. However tasks were divided, the wife had to know enough to take over the farm in the absence or death of her husband.[33] Nonetheless, the presumption of household unity assumes not only cooperation but almost egalitarian agreement, thereby precluding the possibility of conflict and tension within households, especially between husbands and wives, over reproduction, household authority, the sexual division of household labor, and the distribution of goods produced by members for consumption, reciprocal exchange, or sale. Such conflicts probably existed even in communities most isolated from commercial markets. Moreover, the sexual and age division of labor within households itself influenced capitalist transformation and bourgeois ideology, and in turn household gender relations influenced economic development. One does not need to find violent confrontations to examine the structural basis of conflicts within both non-capitalist and capitalist social formations. Such "cooperative conflicts" were janus-faced, involving rudimentary cooperation and sometimes heated struggles. If the farm household was to prosper, husband and wife had to resolve conflicts by "negotiations" over the division of labor or resources and cooperate in daily labor.[34]

Strangely, historians who examine economic exchange ignore the exchange *within* the household of goods individually produced by husband or wife, petty commodities later traded in the local community. As men cultivated wheat or tobacco or corn, women grew vegetables and tended chickens and cows. The vegetables, eggs, and butter wives traded with neighbors or at local markets provided essential income, especially when grain crops were poor or prices low. The domestic labors of farm women were particularly difficult on western frontiers; their subsistence-oriented, import-replacement production took precedence over local exchange. Arriving on a frontier farm, women had to plant new gardens, milk cows, make soap and candles, spin flax and wool, churn butter and collect eggs for local sale, as well as keep house in tiny, barely furnished houses, cook over an open hearth, and sew clothing. Many frontier women helped their husbands build structures, clear brush, and plow fields, tasks they had to take over when their husbands fell ill.[35]

33. For contrasting theoretical views about households, see Fox-Genovese, "Antebellum Southern Households," 215–53, and Folbre, "Logic of Patriarchal Capitalism." J. M. Jensen, *Loosening the Bonds*, and especially Fox-Genovese, *Within the Plantation Household*, are valuable case studies. For widows' mastery of farmwork (and their husbands' gender roles), see Waciega, "'Man of Business,'" 43–49, 54–61.

34. Sen, "Gender and Cooperative Conflicts," 123–49.

35. Faragher, "History from the Inside Out," 542–50, *Sugar Creek*, chaps. 11–12, and *Women and Men on the Overland Trail*, 49–65; Riley, *Frontierswomen*, 29–40, 58–

Production of home manufactures required complex local exchanges wherever it occurred. Making a piece of homespun cloth in the colonies required complex cooperation among husbands, wives, and daughters as well as complex labor exchanges among neighboring women. Men cultivated the family's patch of flax and herded and sheared the family's sheep; women carded fiber (with the help of their children) and spun yarn; men (often local craftsmen) or sometimes wives wove the cloth, and women sewed the garments. But since few families cultivated flax and owned sheep, flax and wool cards, spinning wheels, and looms, there must have been substantial local exchange of goods for labor among farm and mechanic families. The cloth produced by these complex exchanges replaced some, but not most, of the imported cloth families needed for their annual household needs. Even when women made homespun, they sometimes traded it for imported cloth.[36]

The romantic imagery that can sometimes be found in descriptions of noncommercial economies stems from a failure to understand the household dynamics of patriarchal families. Notwithstanding the productive activities of farm wives, under the common law they had neither a political role outside the household nor much authority within their families but much responsibility for child care and domestic production. Since wives did not own the goods they produced in the farm enterprise, husbands customarily owed them financial support. In the best marriages, a wife served as a "deputy husband," working with her spouse in shop or field and taking over when he was away, thereby achieving a bit of autonomy and some personal satisfaction. Given the contradiction between the work wives completed and their lowly legal status, male abuse or violent conflicts over the proper roles of husbands and wives sometimes ensued. Even when women accepted the constraints imposed by law and their husbands, courts rarely backed them if husbands became abusive or failed to support them.[37]

Under the common law, married women had no rights to property, even to the land and chattels they brought into marriage. Such an inequitable distribution of ownership within the family reduced the authority of the wife while increasing that of the husband. However much husband and wife

68; McMahon, "'Indescribable Care Devolving upon a Housewife'"; Buley, *Old Northwest* 1:202–25; Smuksta, "Work, Family, and Community," chaps. 3–4.

36. Hood, "Organization of Textile Manufacture," is the most thorough account, but see also Kulikoff, *Tobacco and Slaves*, 100–103, 179–80, 431; Ulrich, "Housewife and Gadder," 21–34; Fox-Genovese, *Within the Plantation Household*, 120–29, 434; J. M. Jensen, *Loosening the Bonds*, 46–50; E. A. Perkins, "Consumer Frontier," 497–506.

37. Salmon, *Women and the Law of Property in Early America*, is the best introduction to the status of women under the common law. For deputy husbands, see Ulrich, Good Wives, chap. 2.

cooperated, ultimate authority over subsistence decisions belonged to him. The "magic of property" gave men the rights to fruits of their labor and the authority to direct children and wives in their daily labor. To add to the collective enterprise and increase the value of property was a goal for all farmers, whether they sought market embeddedness or the maintenance of the family lineage. For traditional farmers, the addition of family labor was crucial to the farm's success.[38]

By underestimating struggle within the household, social historians exaggerate resistance in the North to capitalists during the first half of the nineteenth century. Whatever the reality, some middling farm women welcomed opportunities when male capitalists created expanded markets, opened textile mills, or encouraged education. Wives of wealthy farmers made products such as butter for sale as well as for home consumption, using the proceeds to supply their own larders. Daughters who earned factory wages or taught school and wives who earned money from outwork gained a small measure of financial independence from their fathers and husbands. Although rural women failed to win the social and political rights guaranteed to men by bourgeois individualism, they manipulated bourgeois ideas of the proper role of women to their own advantage, insisting that ideals of domesticity and child nurture gave them rights within the household and rights over their own reproductive organs. Such behavior sometimes led to conflicts with husbands satisfied with older forms of household authority, struggles that can be clearly seen in passive resistance by wives when husbands insisted that they leave bourgeois comforts for western frontiers.[39]

If changing gender roles played an important role in the development of capitalism in rural America, then we may have to revise our understanding of the timing of the coming of capitalism. Devaluing the impact of changing gender roles on capitalist transformation might lead to overemphasis on the perpetuation of noncapitalist relations of production. Christopher Clark's important work on the Connecticut River Valley illustrates the problem. Clark shows how farmers in that region readily incorporated numerous changes, including the beginnings of small factories and workshops and the rise of tobacco cultivation, into preexisting patterns of local, reciprocal exchange. For much of the nineteenth century, these farmers seemed to prevent a full transition to capitalism. Yet at the same time, Clark shows how the internal roles of women and men in the household were transformed — changes that he fails to connect with any broader process of capitalist expan-

---

38. W. N. Parker, "Magic of Property," 480, 486–87.

39. J. M. Jensen, *Loosening the Bonds*; Dublin, *Women at Work*, and "Women and Outwork," 51–70; Nelson, "Vermont Female Schoolteachers," 5–29; Faragher, *Women and Men on the Overland Trail.*

sion. If arguments made here are correct, then Clark has documented an ambiguous and partial capitalist transformation, one that left some earlier forms of economic exchange in place, while revolutionizing relations within the household.[40]

There is no ideal solution for resolving problems raised by the American transition debate. North America experienced no transition from feudalism to capitalism, for the world around it was already capitalist. But for three centuries many local societies found themselves not yet embedded in a fully capitalist social formation. What is needed is a framework that encompasses regional differences *and* national processes, economic exchange in markets (both commercial and noncommercial) *and* in the household, changes within both the small producer *and* the capitalist classes, and the subtleties of both class *and* gender relations and struggles.

One can envisage rural America as containing a succession of historically specific social formations, each with its characteristic internal contradictions and class struggles, embedded in particular places and times. Each social formation embodied noncapitalist and capitalist relations of production, small producers and merchants or capitalists. In each society, either noncapitalist or small capitalist relations of production predominated, but alternative class relations could be found. Notwithstanding these variations, American agrarian societies changed from varied noncapitalist social formations, often somewhat isolated from commodity, credit, and labor markets, toward more and more fully commodified and capitalist productive systems.

Examination of contending social formations resolves, or at least evades, the problem of defining alternative modes of production in noncapitalist economies embedded in capitalist world markets. Modes of production — the class relations and productive systems encompassing multination regions — define dominant class relations over centuries. By the seventeenth century, capitalism was clearly in the ascendency, and no other mode of production rose to challenge it. Instead, the growing North Atlantic capitalist economy threw off competing modern — if sometimes noncapitalist — societies, more or less dependent upon international commerce and capitalism for their perpetuation.

40. C. Clark, "Household, Market and Capital"; Clark's more recent work, *Roots of Rural Capitalism*, comes much closer to the view expressed here.

Chapter 2

The Rise and Demise of
the American Yeoman Classes

FOR A CENTURY, from the mid-eighteenth century to the Civil War, yeomen who, in Thomas Jefferson's words, "labor in the earth," depending upon "their own soil and industry . . . for their subsistence," predominated in much of the country.[1] The yeoman classes, in both their northern small-farmer and southern slave versions, gave way after much struggle to rural social formations dominated by small competitive capitalists or by monopoly capitalists. Relating the struggle of these social classes, and their contradictory relationship to the capitalist world economy, illuminates the confused history of rural America.

One must admit that the term *yeoman* can be misleading. English yeomen were defined differently than their nominal counterparts in the American colonies and new nation. In England they were commercial farmers and sometimes tenants near the top of a complex agricultural hierarchy; in America, they were small producers who grew most of their own food. The term, moreover, evokes a romantic myth of the American past, one uninvolved in class relations, class struggle, gender conflict.[2] Carefully defined, however, it can be used to address a wide range of significant questions about class and gender, exchange and production.

Yeoman is a class term, relating to farmers who owned the means of production and participated in commodity markets in order to sustain familial autonomy. From the mid-eighteenth century to the end of the nineteenth, such men decided what crops to produce, how to divide farm tasks among family members, when to send crops to distant markets. Practicing "safety-first" agriculture, they grew much of the food they consumed and bartered with neighbors for the rest. To sustain familial subsistence, they occasionally hired hands. Within their households, yeomen denied female individualism and insisted that women bend to their authority. The wives of yeomen (or

---

1. Jefferson, *Notes on State of Virginia*, 157–58.
2. Contrast H. N. Smith, *Virgin Land*, and Folbre, "Logic of Patriarchal Capitalism."

"yeoman women?") were precisely that, *wives*, without separate political or social identities.[3]

The ownership of land was essential for the reproduction across generations of the yeomanry. A majority of rural family heads could expect to own land, sufficient to practice safety-first agriculture, by the time they reached their early thirties. The sons of farmers considered land ownership an entitlement, due them when they reached maturity. They understood land as a means to sustain themselves and their families, not to accumulate capital, even if they acquired substantial wealth and capital.[4]

The behavior of yeoman farmers was influenced by their relations with other classes, such as capitalists or great planters, slaves or wage laborers. The strategies they pursued to achieve economic independence — how deeply they committed themselves to market production, how often they hired hands — were shaped by capitalist expansion. However much yeoman classes of North and South resembled each other, they were structurally different: in the North, yeomen struggled with capitalists to retain any semblance of economic autonomy but faced increased market embeddedness; in the commercial economy of the slave South, they contended with planters over control of the state, but planter and yeoman shared visions of local sufficiency and united to keep "wage slavery" at bay.[5]

Yeomen lived in an ambiguous world, where inequalities of sex, class, race, and wealth persisted and even strengthened. While upholding these inequalities, they nonetheless thought that there should be no differences among men, that all should aspire to the life of a yeoman. Knowing that the world was divided between producers and nonproducers, yeomen supported political democracy, interpreted as rule by propertied freeholders, and urged the widest possible franchise because nearly all men would ultimately own land. Only such a democratic polity could protect their economic rights to land and subsistence.[6]

Moreover, the story of yeomen may have been unique among groups

3. H. N. Smith, *Virgin Land*, chaps. 11–15; Eisinger, "Freehold Concept in Eighteenth-Century American Letters," 42–59; M. E. Young, "Congress Looks West," 78–83, 94–97, 105–8. For female individualism, see Fox-Genovese's brilliant essay "Property and Patriarchy," 36–59, and for a different viewpoint, Folbre, "Logic of Patriarchal Capitalism."

4. Weiman, "Families, Farms, and Rural Society," 255–77; Vickers, "Competency and Competition," 3–29; Henretta, "Study of Social Mobility," 165–78.

5. C. Clark, *Roots Rural Capitalism*; Faragher, *Sugar Creek*, chaps. 18–20; Hahn, *Roots of Southern Populism*, chaps. 1–3; Fox-Genovese and Genovese, *Fruits of Merchant Capital*, chap. 9. One can speak of a yeoman social formation in the North but of yeoman classes within a slave social formation in the South.

6. Ashworth, *Agrarians and Aristocrats*, chap. 1; Hatch, *Democratization of American Christianity*. This vision was nearly the opposite of Tocqueville's in *Democracy in America*, 2:32–41, 99–108. See Wilentz, "Many Democracies," 207–28, esp. 225.

and classes in the United States. The struggles of yeomen and capitalists bear only superficial similarities to conflicts between Indians and whites or between workers and manufacturers. Indians shared with yeomen the goal of local self-sufficiency in food and extensive gift exchange, but Indian dependence grew as whites destroyed their means of independent subsistence and seized their lands, forcing them into extensive trade relations.[7] Urban workers shared with yeomen a republican producer ideology, an insistence on looking at themselves as economically independent, and struggles to control their own labor. But capitalists owned the workplace and soon the tools used in production; workers became increasingly dependent on a market wage set in unequal competition with capitalists.[8] Unlike either Indians or the urban proletariat, yeomen owned land, the means of production, property that ensured their independence and endowed their skills with great economic meaning.

Yeomen were embedded in capitalist world markets and yet alienated from capitalist social and economic relations. They participated in commodity markets with regularity—but only to sustain noncommercial neighborhood networks. They sought absolute ownership of landed property like the bourgeoisie—but used it to nourish patriarchal power at home. They moved west to maintain the class they had devised—but the sale and ready alienation of land was a powerful solvent of any noncapitalist social formation. The revolutionary ideals that legitimated their political participation sustained an ideology of individualism that privileged capitalist economic development and gave their wives authority that destroyed their power in the home. One is less surprised at the victory of capitalists, whether farmers, financiers, or farm women over yeomen, than at the intensity and great length of the struggle.

Yeoman farmers can be contrasted with capitalist farmers who sought greater market embeddedness, concentrated on staple crops, and bought financial instruments. Seeking greater profits and a bourgeois life-style, they bought machinery and hired wage laborers to increase their output and profits. They owned their land but often transferred control over its use to financial capitalists who determined which market crops to grow. The more risks they took, the more they had to buy food from storekeepers. Often they had been yeomen, but slowly, imperceptibly, unconsciously, they became petty capitalists while continuing to espouse ideals of independence long after such ideals had ceased to have economic meaning for them.[9]

7. Among many fine works, see Merchant, *Ecological Revolutions*, chaps. 1–3; Cronon, *Changes in the Land*; Jennings, *Invasion of America*, pt. 1; Unser, "Food Marketing and Interethnic Exchange," 279–310.

8. The most important works include Wilentz, *Chants Democratic*; Gutman, *Work, Culture, and Society* and *Power and Culture*; Stansell, *City of Women*.

9. For an example of the process see Daniel, *Bitter Harvest*, chaps. 1–2.

This chapter sketches the history of the American yeoman classes. Notwithstanding regional differences in the persistence of yeoman classes, based upon contrasting labor systems and availability of cheap land, the formation and disintegration of the yeoman class was everywhere similar. Adapting to American conditions, English migrants and their children began to form yeoman classes, but that class was not consolidated until the time of the American Revolution. As capitalism permeated the northern countryside between the Revolution and the Civil War, yeomen struggled with rural and urban capitalists to retain their independence. Northern victory in the Civil War presaged the spread of capitalist agriculture and wage labor to every part of the South and West it had not previously penetrated. By the late nineteenth century yeomen predominated in only small, isolated pockets of rural America.

The Formation of the Colonial Yeoman Classes

The yeoman class formed out of complex struggles during the seventeenth century: English class conflicts that continued in the colonies, warfare with Indians, and conflicts among colonists over who should rule at home. Despite these conflicts, settlers made thousands of new homes on American frontiers. Both these struggles and the reality of landownership slowly led yeomen to become conscious of their role as citizens and to create a class ideology. A yeoman class thereby slowly developed over the eighteenth century.

Our analysis begins in England. The first migrants to our shores — husbandmen, former husbandmen, new urban workers — had lived through the birth of English capitalism. Although feudal lords had coerced peasants into making extraeconomic payments, in return peasants had controlled most of England's lands. During the sixteenth and seventeenth centuries, capitalist landlords had expropriated the peasants' land and rented it to improving tenants. Forced into agricultural labor or into the urban work force, they fought rearguard actions where they could, tearing down hedges that enclosed common lands, flooding drained swamp lands, rioting for a fair price for bread. Believing wage labor to be debased, they dreamed of regaining land they or their parents had lost.[10]

Leaving England behind, white Americans of the seventeenth century carried with them a mass of contradictory goals, none of which meshed very well with the undeveloped American environment. Migrating to escape religious persecution or dispossession, these husbandmen, agricultural and ur-

10. K. Marx, *Capital*, 1: chaps. 26–30; B. Manning, "Peasantry and the English Revolution," 133–58; Clark, *Working Life of Women in the Seventeenth Century*, chaps. 3–4; C. Hill, "Pottage for Freeborn Englishmen," 219–38.

ban laborers, and artisans rejected the capitalists' demand that they sell their labor power on free markets. Yet a majority of white migrants to the seventeenth-century South and the eighteenth-century middle colonies were indentured servants or redemptioners who had to sell themselves into temporary servitude to pay their passage to America. Though often possessing craft skills, migrants still yearned for the independence and security that only land provided. Insisting upon respect from their betters, they repudiated possessive individualism, the only possible basis for mutual respect in a capitalist society.[11]

Seventeenth-century colonists, seeking such contradictory goals, enmeshed themselves in innumerable struggles. Indian villages could be found everywhere in the early seventeenth-century colonies. Demanding Indian land, colonists defeated them in battle and sent them into exile far beyond the limits of white settlement. And they fought incessantly among themselves over who would rule their communities. The search for secure land sometimes lay behind these conflicts. Bacon's Rebellion in Virginia in 1676 illustrates the complex relation between political conflicts and struggles for land. Indentured servants, demanding rights masters ignored, had defied their masters by running away and refusing to obey orders since the beginning of settlement. As long as ex-servants could eventually get land, they more or less willingly worked as agricultural laborers. But access to land was critical. When Nathaniel Bacon, an English gentleman, fomented rebellion and Indian warfare in 1676 to obtain political power, he gained adherents among the freedmen of frontier counties, who feared that unless the Indians were massacred, there would be no land for them.[12]

Settlers came, in part, to find land of their own, but they had no reason to expect that they could gain landownership easily. After all, gentlemen, the class of men who had taken their land in England, sometimes migrated with them. Even more important, contrary to the American myth of opportunity, until the end of the seventeenth century there was great land *scarcity* in America. So much land—but no capital to develop it; so much land—but much of it in settlers' minds a "howling wilderness"; so much land— but hostile Indians seemed to control much of it and threatened to force them off the rest. What little land colonists could develop had to be carefully exploited. Living in scarcity in the midst of abundance, seventeenth-century

11. Galenson, *White Servitude in Colonial America*; E. S. Morgan, *American Slavery, American Freedom*; Cressy, *Coming Over*, esp. chaps. 2–3, 7; Innes, *Labor in a New Land*; for individualism, see chap. 4 below.

12. Cronon, *Changes in the Land*, and Jennings, *Invasion of America*, are excellent studies of Indian-white contact. For conflicting views of Bacon's Rebellion, see Washburn, *Governor and the Rebel*; E. S. Morgan, *American Slavery, American Freedom*, chaps. 11–14; and S. S. Webb, *1676*, book 1.

colonists rejected the complex system of land tenure in England but did not immediately create a capitalist land market, where all land had a price and anyone could buy or sell it. New England communities that held land in common for a generation and then slowly distributed it to the sons of early settlers acted prudently, given the wilderness and hostile Indian neighbors. In contrast, southern colonies gave land away to anyone who financed his own voyage to the colonies. Individual southern settlers farmed on isolated homesteads, scattered over a larger area, but they had the good sense not to venture far from populated areas.[13]

Events at the end of the seventeenth century increased land supplies and created a capitalist land market. Over the seventeenth century, most New England and the Chesapeake colonists had become used to owning land. Capitalist land markets developed in these places after lands were distributed to the initial settlers. By the early eighteenth century these colonists had conquered sufficient land from the Indians to meet the needs of several generations. Similar events soon occurred in most of the other colonies. When he founded Pennsylvania in the 1680s, William Penn made peace with Indians, thereby opening much new land to white settlement, which he immediately sold to speculators and settlers, creating a capitalist land market.[14]

This new American reality of plentiful land combined with the inherited goals of the descendants of settlers led ordinary white families to forge a new class system in rural America based upon widespread landownership. During the last half of the eighteenth century, between two-thirds and three-quarters of householders were freeholders who owned land in places as disparate in social structure as Connecticut, eastern Massachusetts, Long Island, eastern New Jersey, and Tidewater Virginia — a far greater proportion than in England. As population grew, land became scarce, and sons of yeomen migrated to new frontiers, taking up unimproved land rather than falling into tenancy.[15]

Thus, pioneer farmers, on their way to becoming yeomen, had to re-

13. The classic essay on land abundance in America is Turner, *Frontier in American History,* chap. 1, but see also H. N. Smith, *Virgin Land.* For land law and distribution see Konig, "Community Custom and the Common Law," 148–64; E. S. Morgan, *American Slavery, American Freedom,* 94, 171–73, 218–23; C. Earle, *Evolution of a Tidewater Settlement System,* chaps. 1, 5, 7.

14. See n. 13 for land systems. For the impact of Indian warfare on white settlement, see E. S. Morgan, *American Slavery, American Freedom,* chap. 13, and L. K. Mathews, *Expansion of New England,* chap. 3. Pennsylvania's land system is described in Nash, *Quakers and Politics,* chaps. 1–2, esp. 15–19, 52–53.

15. Main, *Society and Economy in Colonial Connecticut,* 123–25, 160–61; Pruitt, "Agriculture and Society," 112, map 8; Kulikoff, *Tobacco and Slaves,* 86–90; A. F. Young, *Democratic Republicans of New York,* 585–88; D. P. Ryan, "Landholding, Opportunity, and Mobility," 571–92.

make their class on every new frontier, recreating the material base necessary to sustain familial autonomy, local exchange, and market agriculture. At the outset of settlement, few pioneers owned land. Instead, they squatted on land owned by others. Once large numbers of families arrived, however, residents either registered ownership of land or left the area. Since land remained abundant, the proportion of landowners rose to high levels. For example, just over half the heads of households in frontier Lunenburg County, Virginia, owned land in 1750, a decade after the first settlers arrived, but by the 1760s between three-quarters and four-fifths of them had land. Within a decade of initial settlement, three-quarters to four-fifths of householders owned land in Piedmont Virginia, in egalitarian and poor agricultural towns in Massachusetts, and in thinly settled parts of Lancaster County, Pennsylvania, and northeastern New York.[16]

When landownership spread, labor shortages on the farm inevitably grew. Men who knew they could farm their own land married at youthful ages, in their early to mid twenties, rather than work on their parents' farms. Northern farmers relied upon exchanges of labor with neighbors, an occasional hired hand, and particularly upon their own families, especially the large numbers of children their wives bore. In contrast, southern farmers, even yeomen, solved the problem of farm labor with slaves. The high demand for tobacco and rice in England gave wealthy southerners access to slave markets, and yeomen often owned a slave or two, critical additions to scarce family labor.[17]

Yeoman expectations of land ownership were not fulfilled everywhere in the eighteenth-century colonies. Great landlords, who rented as much as several hundreds of thousands of acres to tenants, dominated counties in the Hudson River Valley, southern Maryland, and the Northern Neck of Virginia. During the early years of settlement, Dutch landlords enticed few farm families, for they could procure land on nearby frontiers. Only low rents and long terms — often for several lives — that were almost the equivalent to freehold land tenure, attracted yeomen. As settlement proceeded and land became scarce, landlords adapted income-generating tenancies at will and by the 1750s granted only annual leases at high rents.[18]

16. Kulikoff, *Tobacco and Slaves*, 156; A. F. Young, *Democratic Republicans*, 585–88; Pruitt, "Agriculture and Society," 112 and maps 9, 11; Lemon, *Best Poor Man's Country*, 92–96; Nicholls, "Origins of the Virginia Southside," chaps. 2–3.

17. Dunn, "Servants and Slaves," 157–94; Rediker, "'Good Hands, Stout Heart, and Fast Feet,'" 123–44; Vickers, "Competency and Competition," 3–29, and "Working the Fields in a Developing Economy," 49–69; Clemens and Simler, "Rural Labor and Farm Household," 106–43.

18. Kim, *Landlord and Tenant*, vii, chaps. 3–6; Countryman, *People in Revolution*, chap. 1; Stiverson, *Poverty in a Land of Plenty*, chaps. 2–4, 144–45; Bliss, "Rise of Tenancy in Virginia," 427–41; and Kulikoff, *Tobacco and Slaves*, 132–35.

Most farmers, however, seeking economic independence, avoided tenancy and dependency. Whenever rich men threatened secure land tenure, yeomen and their sons resisted reduction to a state of dependency, sometimes with violence. In 1730 in Virginia, for example, when the Assembly passed a tobacco inspection act that diminished tobacco output of yeomen, small planters (yeomen and tenants) in several counties burned down the inspection warehouses. In the 1750s and 1760s Massachusetts farmers who had moved to Hudson Valley land owned by New York landlords revolted several times, rejecting tenancy and seeking freehold land tenure, and Massachusetts sovereignty over lands they farmed. Such resistance led yeomen to greater self-definition as a class.[19]

Gentlemen, whose connections to English capital and complex marriages within their class assured their wealth and continued political prominence, procured millions of acres of undeveloped land through land speculation, grants from provincial governments, or inheritance. They learned that secure land tenure for farmers ensured the social peace they desired. With land abundant, most of them sold off undeveloped acres to yeomen, retaining economic power by granting credit. By the second third of the eighteenth century, gentlemen in settled parts of New England, the Chesapeake region, and Pennsylvania guaranteed the security of the land and slaves of yeomen and control over their own households, but in turn expected social and political deference. New England gentlemen provided credit for sons in older towns to buy land, formed land companies and sold off land cheaply, and gave credit to worthy neighbors. In the South they imported enough slaves to supply the needs of many poorer planters, thereby creating a great class barrier between white free men and all people of color.[20]

Yeomen were active agents in this process of class formation. Within the constraints of the capitalist world market, they devised a traditional household economy. Wanting to sustain a competency, they made sufficient goods to keep the family free from demeaning wage labor. Notwithstanding the cooperation among family members necessary for economic independence, they assumed authority over their wives and children. Wives of yeomen, whose labors in garden and dairy and exchanges with neighbors made the

19. For Virginia, see Kulikoff, *Tobacco and Slaves*, chap. 3; for New York, see the contrasting views of Kim, *Landlord and Tenant*, chaps. 7–8, and Countryman, *People in Revolution*, chap. 1. Chaps. 3 and 5 delineate this yeoman ideology.

20. Kornblith and Murrin, "Making and Unmaking of the American Ruling Class"; Kulikoff, *Tobacco and Slaves*, chaps. 3, 4, 7; Cook, *Fathers of the Towns*; and Zuckerman, *Peaceable Kingdoms*, esp. chaps. 5–6, provide opposing views of this process. Grant, *Democracy in the Connecticut Frontier Town*, chaps. 2–5, examines land speculation and sales.

farm viable, had neither separate political nor legal identities. Yeoman families produced most food they consumed and tried to obtain the rest by trading with neighbors. To ensure familial autonomy and finance the exchange of labor, food, and home manufacturers with neighbors, they sold surpluses at local markets connected to commodity markets. Participation in these markets mandated certain payment and impersonal credit relations; local exchange was informal, based upon friendship or kinship, and characterized by barter over long periods of time.[21]

Yeomen lived in the capitalist world economy as well. An important minority of northern farmers, who lived near cities or along rivers, turned to commercial agriculture, sending large surpluses to market, lending money at interest, and renting land near towns to increase their profits. Grain deficits in southern Europe particularly propelled an important minority of Delaware Valley farmers into international grain commodity markets. Local exchange networks, for these farmers, diminished in importance. In the Chesapeake colonies, where nearly every farmer sold tobacco for foreign markets, yeomen felt these constraints especially severely. Although the largest planters created nearly self-sufficient plantations based on slave labor, smaller slaveowners and planters without slaves had to participate in staple markets without such advantages. Over the eighteenth century, however, they grew more food crops and devised local exchange networks as intensive as those of their northern neighbors.[22]

A traveler to the colonies in 1750 would have found peaceful class relations and intensive exchange networks in New England, the Chesapeake colonies, and parts of the middle colonies. By contrast, Hudson River Valley landlords and men who financed backcountry settlement from Pennsylvania to Georgia sought greater political control. There numerous land wars ensued, beginning in New Jersey in the 1730s and touching Vermont, the Hudson River Valley, backcountry Pennsylvania, western North Carolina, and western South Carolina by the 1770s, variously pitting Eastern land speculators, landlords, or merchants and their many local allies against yeomen farmers seeking to protect their property from the burdens of debt, the lack of government, bandits, or unfair taxation.[23]

The American Revolution played a role both in consolidating the yeo-

---

21. For alternative visions of the behavior of small farmers and their relation to capitalism, see chap. 1; Merrill, "Cash Is Good to Eat," 42–71; Henretta, "Families and Farms," 3–32; Rothenberg, "Market and Massachusetts Farmers," 283–314; Vickers, "Competency and Competition," 3–29.

22. Rothenberg, "Market and Massachusetts Farmers," 283–314; Doerflinger, "Farmers and Dry Goods in the Philadelphia Market Area," 166–95; Carr and Walsh, "Economic Diversification and Labor Organization," 144–88.

23. Chap. 5 describes these conflicts in detail.

man class of small producers and in legitimating rural capitalism. Yeomen, who constituted a majority of the "people" needed to fight the war, demanded an active role in the formation of public policy. They used their newfound power to sustain their independence; as a result, a "traditional" producer ideology became more deeply embedded in local consciousness. But the ideology of the Revolution pointed to possessive individualism, to the political rights of each person abstracted from family and community. For increasing numbers of farmers, rural merchants, and country manufacturers, independence meant freedom to make binding contracts and to use property as they saw fit, even at the cost of disturbing traditional common rights to unimproved land or water.[24]

Land, the Yeomanry, and Capitalists in the New Nation, 1780–1860

The reproduction of yeoman farms required easy availability of inexpensive land. Yeomen, both in North and South, managed to buy frontier land, either from the state or speculators. Once on the land, they built productive farms with family labor, sustaining a yeoman-dominated social formation or finding a place in southern slave society. But the dynamic spread of capitalism constricted yeoman success in the North, and by the 1850s, if not earlier, competitive small capitalist farms had replaced those of the yeomanry in much of the region.

Since state and federal governments enforced private property rights, selling off nearly all land they held and guaranteeing that owners could alienate it, only landownership could provide farmers with familial security. After the conquest of Indian land, but before it was surveyed, squatters claimed it, treating forests and range as common property, regulated by their community. The sale of land created private property, destroying common rights. Squatters might sell their improvements, but if they wished to stay on the land, they had to pay for it. A father and adult sons might work the land together, but only the owner of the property enjoyed legally secure rights. Inheritance transferred landownership to heirs, contingent upon satisfying demands that they pay portions to those, usually daughters, without a landed bequest. Small farmers, lacking sufficient land to graze animals or procure wood for heat, fences, or buildings, had to rely upon open access to privately held land.[25]

24. For the issues raised here, see chaps. 3–5; Gates, *Farmer's Age*, chap. 3; Kulik, "Dams, Fish, and Farmers," 25–50.

25. See Alchian and Demsetz, "Property Rights Paradigm," 16–27; Swaney, "Common Property," 451–62; Liebcap, "Property Rights in Economic History," 227–52, esp. 231–35, for meanings of private property. Hahn, *Roots of Southern Populism*, chap. 2; Ditz, *Property and Kinship*; Arrington, Fox, and May, *Building City of God*, chaps. 2–4, 7–12, are case studies of private property and collective rights.

State and federal policies for disposal of land structured yeoman opportunity to own farms. Until the 1820s most pioneers may have settled on lands owned by the states. State land policies varied, from private development by speculators in New York to land lotteries in Georgia. But the effect was the same everywhere. The proprietors of the 3.3 million-acre Holland land track in western New York subdivided their domain into parcels between 1800 and 1820, selling each at current market prices. Georgia land lottery certificates were negotiable, and most winners sold their shares. In upcountry Georgia, at best a fifth of landowners had gained land through the lottery; the rest bought from speculators.[26]

Buffeted by capitalists seeking development and farmers wanting free land, Congress tried to regulate settlement by ensuring that farmers had capital to develop their land yet keeping prices affordable. In 1820, after an experiment in granting credit to purchasers, Congress instituted cash sales by auction but lowered the price from $2.00 to $1.25 an acre. Nearly all federal land placed on the market between 1820 and 1860, except land warrants given to veterans of the War of 1812, was sold at auction. Speculators not only purchased much land at auctions but bought nine-tenths of the warrants given to veterans. Settlers with capital purchased federal land directly, but most bought on credit from speculators, thus being forced into market production to pay for their land.[27]

Conflict over land policy in antebellum America, not surprisingly, was constant, both in Congress, where partisan debates over disposal of land were endemic, and between speculators and frontier settlers. Antebellum squatters regularly organized claims clubs to enforce (sometimes with violence) their right to buy at auctions land they had developed or at least to recoup the value of their improvements from the purchasers. Squatters struggled with land companies and absentee owners as well. In Iowa in the 1840s, for instance, settlers clashed with the New York Land Company, refusing to recognize its title to land they farmed.[28]

Federal and state policy led to highly concentrated land ownership. The wealthiest 5 percent of landholders owned between a third and two-fifths of all land in both 1798 and 1860. There were, of course, regional variations: southern property, especially in cotton regions, was more concentrated than that of the rural North. Such inequality in landholding, with the differential access to credit it implied, attests to the perpetuation of classes of wealthy

26. Wyckoff, *Developer's Frontier*, chaps. 3–6; Weiman, "Peopling the Land by Lottery," 837–42, 849–56.

27. P. W. Gates, *History of Public Land Law Development*, chaps. 7–9; Bogue, *From Prairie to Cornbelt*, chap. 3; Oberly, *Sixty Million Acres*, esp. chaps. 4–6.

28. P. W. Gates, *History of Public Land Law Development*, 152–60, 203–8; Bogue, "Iowa Claims Clubs," 231–53, provide many examples.

farmers at the top of an income hierarchy and of tenants, sharecroppers, or wage laborers unable to get land, at the bottom.[29]

Nonetheless, state and federal allocation of land sustained a large class of smallholders. At the end of the eighteenth century, before migration to the transapplachian West, about two-thirds of white household heads owned land in places as different as Pennsylvania and Virginia. Such high levels of landownership persisted: about half the adults over twenty-one held land in 1798, and similar proportions owned land in early nineteenth-century Tennessee and Ohio. (These figures include sons still living at home.) During both the early and mid-nineteenth century, from about two-thirds to four-fifths of farm operators owned their own farms. Many of these families possessed too few acres to grow all their own food, much less send substantial surpluses to market, but all of them attained some degree of security from reliance upon the market or wage labor.[30]

Land accumulation among small producers came at the intersection of frontier land development and land acquisition across the life cycle. The first pioneers usually began farming before land was put on sale. Since squatters lacking legal title and speculators waiting until they could get a good price held much of the land, few household heads could claim ownership. As few as one in six household heads owned land in the frontier South during the late eighteenth century and that pattern persisted later in frontier Arkansas. Once development proceeded, small producers bought land, and the proportion of landowners increased. A similar pattern can be seen in the American North in 1860. Over four-fifths of the farm operators owned land, but only two-thirds of them held land in frontier Kansas and Minnesota.[31]

Sons of small producers gradually accumulated small quantities of land from their wives' dowries, inheritance, and purchase. The proportion of landholders among householders or farm operators increased dramatically

29. Soltow, *Wealth and Income*, chap. 2, "Kentucky Wealth," 620–33, and "Progress among Ohio Propertyholders," 405–26; Atack and Bateman, *To Their Own Soil*, chap. 6; G. Wright, *Political Economy Cotton South*, chap. 2, document land distributions. For those who failed to get land, see J. M. Marshall, *Land Fever*; C. Bushman, "Wilson Family," 27–39, and works in n. 30.

30. Simler, "Tenancy in Colonial Pennsylvania," 554–57; Kulikoff, *Tobacco and Slaves*, 131–35, 153–57; D. P. Ryan, "Landholding, Opportunity, and Mobility," 573–78; Swierenga, "Quantitative Methods in Rural Landholding," 791–800; Atack, "Tenants and Yeomen," 17–20; Bode and Ginter, *Farm Tenancy*, 1–6, chap. 6; Soltow, "Inequality amidst Abundance," 134–44, and "Land Inequality on the Frontier," 276–85; Ilisevich, "Class Structure," 97–107.

31. Fischer, *Albion's Seed*, 751–53; Bolton, "Economic Inequality in Arkansas," 619–33, and "Inequality on the Southern Frontier," 57–61; Weiman, "Peopling the Land by Lottery," 837–42, 849–56; Bode and Ginter, *Farm Tenancy*, 1–6; Atack, "Tenant and Yeoman," 19.

from age twenty-one through the mid-forties. As few as half of farm operators owned land in their twenties, but nine-tenths or more of them held land
by the time they reached age fifty. Such life-cycle acquisitions of land could
be found in late eighteenth-century New Jersey, the mid-nineteenth-century
North, and late antebellum Tennessee. This accumulation permitted the reproduction of yeoman farms across generations, but it hardly reduced the
high levels of inequality found throughout American rural society. Sons of
small farmers usually acquired land, if they persisted in agriculture, but they
owned 50 to 200 acres, not the 1,000 acres of the richest landowners.[32]

Such acquisition of farms depended upon the ready availability of frontier land. Poorer families could attempt to increase their capital by squatting
and selling improvements and might—if they were lucky—eventually have
sufficient resources to buy land. Young families with some capital could
avoid expensive land in settled areas and attain landownership at somewhat
younger ages. And fathers with adolescent children might sell expensive
land and buy a larger quantity of land in a newly settled region in order to
provide farms for his sons.[33]

Access to land, of course, did not guarantee that yeomen could attain
ascendancy or even survive as a class. Antebellum northern yeomen, unless
they lived in the southern portions of the Old Northwest, were either pushed
from older rural areas to the newest frontiers or accommodated to capitalist
agriculture. The luckiest capitalist farmers paid off their mortgages and sold
frontier acres to newcomers, reaping high capital gains; others—unable to
pay their loans—transferred mortgages to neighbors. Latecomers or poor
families had few opportunities to buy land in barely colonized frontier counties. Southern yeomen in staple-producing regions, like their colonial ancestors, were tied to a large-slaveholding planter class; yeomen predominated
in the upcountry South, readily attaining local sufficiency through safety-
first agriculture, home manufactures, and exchange with neighbors.[34]

Encouraged by growing demand for food in eastern and midwestern cities, an important minority of northern farmers competed vigorously in commodity markets. Early nineteenth-century farmers in the Northeast began to
specialize in garden crops and dairy products; mid-nineteenth-century upper

32. Atack and Bateman, *To Their Own Soil*, 99–100; Atack, "Agricultural Ladder
Revisited," 9–23; D. P. Ryan, "Landholding, Opportunity, and Mobility," 576–78;
Winters, "Agricultural Ladder in Southern Agriculture," 36–52; Newell, "Inheritance
on the Maturing Frontier," 261–303.
33. These speculations are consistent with Easterlin's "bequest model" in "Population Change and Farm Settlement," 63–70, but I do not accept the implications
about family government that might be drawn from it.
34. Chap. 7 examines aspects of this issue, but see Atack and Bateman, *To Their
Own Soil*, chaps. 9–14; Faragher, *Sugar Creek*; Hartnett, "Land Market on the Wisconsin
Frontier," 41–53; Fox-Genovese and Genovese, *Fruits of Merchant Capital*, chap. 9;
Hahn, *Roots of Southern Populism*, chaps. 1–3.

midwesterners sent wheat to distant markets and dairy products to nearby towns. Men with some capital might expect to improve their family's standard of living. Like urban manufacturers, these farmers ran small businesses, investing two or three thousand dollars in the farm. In the 1850s they bought reapers, thereby reducing their labor costs, increasing their productivity, and forcing yeomen unable to buy reapers or hire reaping crews out of business.[35]

As capitalism spread through the North, yeomen saw their sons and neighbors fall into wage labor. Less than two-fifths of the household heads in the rural Northeast in 1860 owned or leased farms; most of the rest were laborers, domestic servants, or artisans. Seasonal and temporary laborers built canals and railroads, harvested lumber from forests, and worked in mines. With the growth of capitalist and proletarian classes, the predominance of social formations the yeomanry dominated had evaporated, and large northern yeoman classes were more and more left to isolated corners of the free labor North.[36]

Labor, Farm Women, and the Reproduction of Yeoman Households, 1800–1880

The reproduction of the yeoman farms required childbearing on the part of the wife. To build viable farms, household labor was ultimately necessary; in a society where wage labor was relatively scarce and machinery nearly nonexistent, the farmwork of children was essential. Children provided for the old age of parents; in return, parents bequeathed land to children, thereby perpetuating the lineage. Uncontrolled fertility reflected both power relations within the household and a familial ideology, sustained by strong communal norms, that valued the lineage over the individual and insisted that each member of the household fulfill his or her role. The perpetuation of the household itself and the family through generations therefore became the foremost value. However much women may have objected to constant childbearing, cultural norms in yeoman societies combined with their husbands' power were too strong to overcome.[37]

During the nineteenth century, childbearing was a key issue in family

35. Atack and Bateman, *To Their Own Soil*, chaps. 10–11; David, "Mechanization of Reaping," 3–28; Bogue, *From Prairie to Cornbelt*, chap. 10; Headlee, *Political Economy of the Family Farm*, chaps. 1–4.

36. Atack and Bateman, *To Their Own Soil*, 43–46; Tobin, "Lowly Muscular Digger," chaps. 2–5, 9; G. R. Taylor, *Transportation Revolution*, chaps. 3, 5, 13; Dublin, *Women at Work*; Prude, *Coming of Industrial Order*; Goldin and Sokoloff, "Women, Children, and Industrialization, 741–74.

37. This section interprets the demographic findings using a feminist theoretical framework outside of the demographic mainstream. See Folbre, "Of Patriarchy Born," 261–84, and Kulikoff, "Why *Men* Stopped Bearing So Many Babies," 1–5.

politics. Notwithstanding increased knowledge of contraception before the mid-nineteenth century, uncontrolled "natural" fertility continued strong among many free women, including most southern women, Mormons, rural immigrants, and — for a while — northern frontier women. Such high marital fertility, often coupled with early female marriages, led to large families. But when capitalist agriculture and bourgeois culture spread, first to the rural Northeast and then to the Midwest, fertility declined, with great consequences for the organization of farm households.[38]

Southern white women, embedded in a paternalistic slave society, continued to bear large numbers of children even when population pressure on land rose or when slaves, more than family labor, provided family subsistence and income. Only a quarter of interregional differences between the Southeast and the Southwest in the fertility of southern white women can be explained by abstinence, abortion, or contraception. Notwithstanding complaints from wealthy women about the dangers of repeated pregnancies, high fertility was firmly entrenched in Southern culture, especially among planters, who wanted sons and considered suffering in childbirth the fate of women. Only after 1830 did a few wealthier Virginia women begin to limit fertility, reducing conceptions in their thirties perhaps by practicing abstinence.[39]

In the frontier Northwest, the link between production and reproduction was clearer. Childbearing was a necessary part of women's work. The fertility of white women was greatest just behind the newest frontiers, where farm-making activities reached their peak. The needs of farm labor, low population density, and male assertions of patriarchal control all raised the birthrate. Frontier women who married young to westering men bore children every two-and-a-half years until menopause, giving birth to five to eight children. Such male assertiveness must have led to innumerable conflicts, especially after birth control became established in the Northeast.[40]

38. D. S. Smith, "'Early' Fertility Decline in America," 73–84; Reed, *From Private Vice to Public Virtue*, chap. 1; Yasuba, *Birth Rates*, chap. 2; Easterlin, "Population Change and Farm Settlement," 45–75; Sundstrom and David, "Old-Age Security and Farm Family Fertility," 164–76; Bean, Mineau, and Anderton, *Fertility Change on the American Frontier*, chaps. 1–2, 4–6; Bash, "Differential Fertility," 162–77; M. J. Stern, *Society and Family Strategy*, chap. 3; Fliess, "Fertility, Nuptiality, Family," 254–60. Wahl, "New Results in Decline in Household Fertility," 405–18, and Ewbank, "Marital Fertility," 141–70, suggest persisting high marital fertility on the farm through the nineteenth century.

39. Steckel, "Antebellum Southern White Fertility," 337–40; Lewis and Lockridge, "'Sally Has Been Sick,'" 5–19; McMillen, *Motherhood in the Old South*, chap. 4, esp. 107–9.

40. Atack and Bateman, *To Their Own Soil*, chap. 4; Easterlin, "Population Change and Farm Settlement," 45–75; M. Ryan, *Cradle of Middle Class*, 21–43, 267; Faragher, *Women and Men on the Overland Trail*, 57–59. For an example of a conflict over contra-

The embourgeoisment of farm women accelerated the spread of capitalism in the North. The incorporation of the northern countryside into urban culture and economy was predicated on the growth of cities (and the consumer demand they created) and the desire of bourgeois rural women for increased amenities in their homes. To purchase more manufactured goods, farmers increased market production; rising market embeddedness required them to hire more wage laborers, including women to help in the fields and with household production. Growing rural demand fed urban growth, as city workers rushed to supply new goods and services. Textile manufacturing provides an example of this process. Colonial families probably made little cloth, preferring to buy cheap imported cloth. But when wars from the 1770s to 1815 disrupted cloth imports, home manufacture soared. These new demands placed added pressure on overworked women, who either established ever more complex exchange networks with neighborhood women or accepted outwork employment for wages. Women so disliked this added work that they encouraged their daughters to work in textile mills as soon as they were established. Mill towns grew into small cities, setting into motion even more intense urbanization and proletarianization.[41]

The doctrine of child nurture, which quickly became embedded in the culture of the bourgeois Northeast (and then Midwest) was predicated upon small families, a desire bourgeois farm husbands shared with their wives. Although older siblings or hired girls could provide custodial care, only a mother could nurture her children. Such intensive care was time-consuming, adding markedly to other farm tasks. Repeated pregnancies risked illness or death and took wives away from child nurture. In order to provide high-quality care, bourgeois rural women deemed it essential that they bear fewer children, spaced sufficiently far apart to permit intensive training of infants and toddlers. While women believed that controlling their fertility was a key component of their individual identity, men sought smaller families for economic reasons. As land became scarcer and more expensive, farm holdings dropped, and men could no longer ensure security in old age by promises of bequests. At the same time, men sought to reduce the added costs of childrearing imposed by the increased schooling that cut the number of hours sons and daughters worked on the farm.[42]

---

ception and abortion in a frontier setting, see Lerner, ed., *Female Experience*, 425–28 (excerpt from Henry C. Wright, *The Unwelcome Child* [1858]).

41. For a provocative restatement see Fox-Genovese, *Within the Plantation Household*, chap. 1. Simler, "Landless Worker," 163–99, describes early proletarianization; for textiles, see Tryon, *Household Manufacturers*, chaps. 4–8; Henretta, "War for Independence and Economic Development" 45–87; J. M. Jensen, *Loosening the Bonds*, 87–88; Dublin, *Women at Work*.

42. Folbre, "Of Patriarchy Born," 260–77; D. S. Smith, "Family Limitation," 222–45; Cott, *Bonds of Womanhood*, chap. 2; Degler, *At Odds*, chap. 8; Leavitt, "Under the

Abstinence, contraception, and abortion together helped reduce family size. A farm couple wed in the rural Northeast in the 1830s probably began married life without practicing contraception, save for extended lactation or short intervals of abstinence to stretch out births. Once they reached a targeted number of children, the men practiced coitus interruptus and the women douched after intercourse. Since these methods often failed, the wife may well have traveled to a nearby town to have one or two abortions. Taken together, these methods reduced births. A white Protestant farm woman, born in 1770, who married in her mid-twenties, gave birth to six or seven children; her granddaughter, born in 1825 and married at the same age, bore only three or four children. Wealthy and middling farm women, in families where child nurture took on great importance, had fewer children than poorer freeholders, tenants, farm laborers, or rural industrial workers, all of whom needed child labor to augment family income.[43]

Despite the patriarchal desires of male migrants, bourgeois ideals of domesticity and child nurture, carried by northeastern missionaries, soon spread among northwestern farm families. As early as the 1790s Yankee denominations mailed thousands of evangelical tracts to western frontier communities, began churches, and sent missionaries — preachers, preachers' wives, school teachers — to spread the gospel of evangelicalism and temperance. Female teachers sent west by evangelical groups between 1830 and 1860 were particularly influential. Imbued with a mission to evangelize the West and thereby make middle-class homes possible, these women taught sexually mixed classes, established Sunday schools, and usually married and stayed in the West, making bourgeois homes and raising families.[44]

Only New England–born women, well practiced in the ways of child nurture, successfully resisted husbands in the early decades of settlement of the Old Northwest. Influenced by female missionaries and their own experience, they wanted to make bourgeois homes, practice child nurture, and reduce the size of their families as soon as the necessities of farm making had

---

Shadow of Maternity," 130–54; Parkerson and Parkerson, "'Fewer Children of Greater Spiritual Quality,'" 56–67.

43. Reed, *From Private Vice to Public Virtue*, chaps. 1–2; Mohr, *Abortion in America*, chaps. 1, 3–4; Yasuba, *Birth Rates*, chaps. 1–2, 4; Atack and Bateman, *To Their Own Soil*, 61–70; Vinovskis, *Fertility in Massachusetts*, chaps. 1, 3; Osterud and Fulton, "Family Limitation and Age at Marriage," 481–94; Temkin-Greener and Swedlund, "Fertility Transition in the Connecticut Valley," 30–41; M. J. Stern, *Society and Family Strategy*, chap. 3; Bash, "Differential Fertility," 161–86.

44. Bloch, "Battling Infidelity," 39–60; M. Ryan, *Cradle of Middle Class*, 52–55, 101, 116–24; Buley, *Old Northwest*, 2:428–61; Sweet, *Minister's Wife*, 123–26; Kaufman, *Women Teachers on the Frontier*, xvii-xxii, 5–49, 226–29; Boylan, "Evangelical Womanhood in the Nineteenth Century," 62–80, esp. 71–73.

passed. Wives of the richest farmers had new three- or four-room houses built, with wood or carpeted floors and cook stoves. As soon as country stores opened, they bought kitchen utensils and cloth, in order to cook more varied meals and to make changes of clothes for their families.[45]

New England–born farm mothers, who had been forced by their husbands' perception of economic necessity to raise large families in the Midwest, taught their daughters that as autonomous individuals they had a right to control their bodies. At the same time, the supply of cheap land that had permitted men in their early twenties to marry and begin farming diminished, and as a result, the marriage age for both men and women rose. The total number of children these women bore naturally diminished. But midwestern Protestant farm women convinced their husbands that smaller farm families were necessary for child nurture and their own peace of mind. These women began using douches and getting abortions about a decade after northeastern farm women. As a result, peak fertility was lower and fertility declined progressively more rapidly in northwestern states settled in the 1830s and 1840s than states further to the east. The average number of children born to women living in older midwestern states may have declined from seven or eight to three or four by 1860.[46]

The decline in childbearing reshaped the division of labor on farms. With fewer children, families could no longer count on the increased farm production that had come to earlier generations when children reached adolescence. Nor were there excess youths (at least in the Northeast) willing to serve as farm hands for those without older children, for many of them worked in factories or moved west. As the labor force available to northeastern farmers diminished in size, farmers had to find profitable tasks, like providing eggs and dairy products to nearby cities, or adapt the least labor-intensive or most easily mechanized crops to survive. Many apparently could no longer make a living in farming; as early as 1837, only a third of Massachusetts families earned a living from agriculture.[47]

Schooling, as much as reduced fertility, diminished the labor time children could work on the farm. Endemic conflicts over establishing common

---

45. Riley, *Frontierswomen*, 67–77; McMurry, *Farmhouses in Nineteenth-Century America*, chap. 3; Atherton, *Frontier Merchant in Mid-America*, chap. 2.

46. Parkerson and Parkerson, "'Fewer Children of Greater Spiritual Quality,'" 52–68; Easterlin, "Population Change and Farm Settlement," 45–75; Atack and Bateman, *To Their Own Soil*, chap. 4; Leet, "Fertility Transition in Antebellum Ohio," 359–78. For an example of mother-daughter communication on control over their own bodies, see Austin, *Early Horizon*, 142–43; for contraception, see M. Ryan, *Cradle of Middle Class*, 155–57; Myres, *Westering Women*, 154–56, 316–17; Mohr, *Abortion in America*, 49, 79–81, 89, 94, 98–101.

47. L. A. Craig, "Northern Antebellum Household Labor," 67–81; Siracusa, *Mechanical People*, 32–37.

schools in the Midwest illuminate differences between yeomen and capitalist farmers over commercial agriculture and the allocation of farm labor. Because land the Northwest Ordinance set aside for education did not cover
the costs of schooling, farmers had to pay taxes for common schools. Capitalist farmers, land speculators, merchants, and educated clergymen who
saw universal education as necessary for moral improvement and economic
growth stood on one side of the conflict. Arrayed against the reformers were
a majority of cash-poor farmers without income to pay high taxes. These
men functioned well in small producer societies with the most rudimentary
literacy skills; education for them needed only to inculcate morality. Many
yeomen paid a teacher to instruct their children a few weeks a year, but they
wanted them home to work for most of the year, building capital by their
labor. As reformers continued to lobby, schooling slowly increased. By the
1850s, after mostly-urban bourgeois reformers succeeded in allocating state
tax dollars for common schools, educational levels, as measured by both the
proportion of children in school and the number of days they attended,
jumped to high levels even in regions of the Midwest dominated by upland
southern yeomen.[48]

Monopoly Capital and the Demise of the Yeomanry, 1860–1900

The development of capitalist agriculture and bourgeois culture in the North
notwithstanding, yeoman classes dominated large parts of the South, lower
Midwest, and transmississippi northern frontier in 1860. Yeomen wanted to
perpetuate the independent farms and local networks that had sustained a
competence, and once they were freed, blacks — with their demands for forty
acres and a mule — clearly shared the yeoman ideal of local self-sufficiency
and familial independence.

Yet the Civil War, with its destruction of slavery, presaged the demise of
the yeomanry. Postbellum capitalists destroyed the yeomanry as a class, even
in those places (like the upcountry South) where it had been most secure.
Without slavery, ex-planters no longer supported yeoman aspirations but
took up capitalist development. Planters and their allies, for instance, successfully challenged the open range, and its protection of smallholders, in
state legislatures. Yeoman predominance disappeared in the North as well,
its decline accelerated by the behavior of small capitalist farmers and their
children as well as railroad and grain elevator owners. By the turn of the

48. Richardson, "Town versus Countryside," 407–16; Kaestle, "Public Education
in Midwest," 60–74, and *Pillars of the Republic*, 182–92; Fuller, *Old Country School*,
chap. 2; Fishlow, "Common School Revival," 49–66; Soltow and Stevens, *Rise of Literacy*, chaps. 3–4; E. W. Stevens, "Dimensions of Literacy," 157–86; Faragher, *Sugar
Creek*, chap. 13.

century the countryside had become the home of small capitalists, who struggled with their wealthier counterparts over the distribution of farm output while subjecting wage laborers to ever-greater labor discipline.[49]

Government land policy encouraged capitalism, in less ambiguous ways than before the war. Although the Homestead Act gave free land to farmers with the capital to develop it, farmers could neither send crops to market nor buy manufactured goods without the aid of railroads. During the twenty years after the Homestead Act, most newly surveyed lands were still sold, often to lumbermen or other large capitalists, and the federal government gave millions of acres to railroads along their rights-of-way to help finance construction. To procure land near transportation routes, settlers often had to buy from railroads or speculators.[50]

Rapid farm creation on remaining lands confiscated from Indians reduced opportunities for rural Americans to acquire land. Land values jumped, especially at the end of the century, suggesting increasing land scarcity. Everywhere during the late nineteenth century, cash tenancy and sharecropping increased, even in the Midwest and northern plains where they had barely existed before the Civil War. Although farm ownership continued to grow over the life cycle, as the price of land increased and population grew, the relative number of freehold farms diminished. Far from providing new opportunities, tenanted farms probably replaced farms made by squatters, who — unlike tenants — might have gained income from selling improvements they made. Men unable to buy land after years of agricultural wage labor, sharecropping, or cash tenancy may have left agriculture altogether, rather than remain in rural dependency.[51]

Proletarianized wage labor — in agriculture, ranching, mining, railroad construction, textiles — grew rapidly in nineteenth-century rural America, attracting the sons and daughters of farmers and dispossessed tenants and sharecroppers. Seasonal labor and a tramping system had developed in the antebellum decades, with laborers working in the country a few months a year, planting and harvesting crops, and then moving on to cities or forests to find employment. Most were young men who found other employment after marriage. As the proportion of work done by wage laborers in the North grew from a quarter in 1860 to over a third early in the twentieth century,

49. Hahn, *Roots of Populism*, chaps. 4–6; Ransom and Sutch, *One Kind of Freedom*, chaps. 4–5, 8–9; Shannon, *Farmer's Last Frontier*, chaps. 6–9.

50. P. W. Gates, *History of Public Land Law Development*, chaps. 14–17, and "Homestead Law in Incongruous Land System," 652–81; Mann and Dickerson, "State and Agriculture," 283–301.

51. Lindert, "Land Scarcity and American Growth," 855–64; Bogue, "Farm Tenants," 103–19; Ransom and Sutch, *One Kind of Freedom*, chaps. 4–5; Winters, "Tenancy as an Economic Institution," 382–408; Atack, "Agricultural Ladder Revisited," 21–25.

laborers became increasingly marginal—Irish and later Asian and Mexican immigrants, the poor, blacks. A majority of ex-slaves and their descendants fell into agricultural wage labor. The level of proletarianization varied among types of agriculture. Fruit and vegetable farming relied extensively on wage labor and over half the work on some early twentieth-century midwestern corn and dairy farms was done by wage laborers. Even on wheat farms, where over four-fifths of the workers were family members, wage laborers in hired threshing crews harvested grain precisely when it ripened.[52]

As monopoly capitalism dominated more and more industries—railroads, steel, oil—in the post–Civil War era, a variety of systems of wage labor on labor-intensive capitalist farms developed. Highly capitalized bonanza wheat farms and small but intensely developed fruit and vegetable farms, concentrated in the Northeast and California, set the capitalist owners against their proletarian (and often migrant) labor force, on the one side, and eastern capitalist railroad owners and finance capitalists, on the other. Semiproletarian agriculture predominated in the cotton South and parts of the West. Cotton sharecroppers lived and worked independently but the landlord owned land, equipment, implements, seeds, and the crop in the ground; croppers had no rights to land, nor even to the crop, but received a half-share from the landlord as an annual "wage." Cowboys in the era of the long drive, and on the closed range, were wage laborers, who worked independently on the range but struggled against their capitalist bosses for fair remuneration and the rights to own guns and cattle as well as farm their own homestead lands.[53]

By the late nineteenth century, these classically capitalist, wage labor–intensive units had become an important minority of American farm operations, but family farms that combined ownership and labor and therefore needed only to sustain the household and renew the means of production to reproduce themselves dominated American agriculture. In 1900 three-quarters of American farmers, outside the South, owned farmland. The per-

---

52. G. Wright, "Agriculture and Labor Market," 193–99, and Friedmann, "Simple Commodity Production and Wage Labour," 71–100, argue for the diminishing importance of wage labor. But evidence found in Atack and Bateman, *To Their Own Soil*, 43–46; Earle and Hoffman, "Foundation of Modern Economy," 1055–94; Cox, "American Agricultural Wage Earner," 95–114; G. Wright, *Old South, New South*, chaps. 3–4; J. D. Hall et al., *Like a Family*, chaps. 1–3; Irwin, "Farmers and Laborers," 53–60; Lenin, "Capitalism and Agriculture in the United States," 131–203; Isern, *Bull Threshers and Bindlestiffs*, chap. 4; Daniel, *Bitter Harvest*, chaps. 1–3; and Frauendorfer, "American Farmers and European Peasantry," 166–68, suggests its increasing importance.

53. Buck, *Granger Movement*, chaps. 4–7; Isern, *Bull Threshers and Bindlestiffs*, chap. 4; Daniel, *Bitter Harvest*, chaps. 2–3; Lenin, "Capitalism and Agriculture in the United States," 165–79; Ransom and Sutch, *One Kind of Freedom*, chaps. 4–8; G. Wright, *Old South, New South*, chaps. 2–4; Weston, *Real American Cowboy*, chaps. 2–4.

sistence of family farms suggests that economic obstacles prevented the development of wage-labor plantations. Living in a capitalist society, however, most farmers were capitalists. Even if they failed to hire wage labor, they did own the means of production. They considered themselves businessmen and participated in commodity, finance, and land markets. A growing majority of farms had become capital-intensive units that sold staples or sent produce to American cities. The independence, the ability of farm families to make day-to-day decisions or to produce their own subsistence, was increasingly reduced on owner-operated units by bankers and other capitalists. Despite occasional conflicts with monopoly capital, their identity as small capitalists cannot be doubted.[54]

The flexibility of family farms—their efficient use of family labor and machinery, their low labor costs, their ability to weather low prices through increased subsistence production—can be seen in the rapid replacement of labor-intensive bonanza farms by family farms on the Great Plains after 1880. These family farmers sold wheat on increasingly integrated world commodity markets and combined occasionally in business cooperatives. They mostly used family labor, but threshing crews, operated by capitalists, harvested their crops. Far from being independent yeomen, they were increasingly constrained by capitalists, having no control over railroad rates, the grading (and therefore price) of their wheat by grain elevators, or the operation of Chicago futures markets.[55]

The development of capitalism brought new tensions and conflicts to rural gender relations. Urban capitalists, farm men, and farm women had somewhat different interests. Monopoly capitalists sought to attain surplus value from higher railroad rates, interest (on mortgages or advances), or profits from the sale of new machinery and consumer durables. In a system where labor and property were increasingly commodified, where the ideology of systematic individualism reigned supreme, household authority became problematic, and farm wives and husbands needed to renegotiate the gender division of labor on the farm and the relation of each to the state. These negotiations resulted in remarkably varied gender relations on the farms, depending upon crop-and-region specific relations of production

54. Llambi, "Small Modern Farmers," 350–72; Rome, "American Farmers as Entrepreneurs," 37–49; U.S. Bureau of Census, *Historical Statistics*, 1:459, 465. Friedmann, "Simple Commodity Production and Wage Labour," 71–100, "World Market, State, and Family Farm," 545–86, and "Household Production and National Economy," 158–84; and Mann, *Agrarian Capitalism*, argue that late nineteenth- and early twentieth-century family farmers were not capitalist because they hired few wage laborers.

55. I follow the description, but not the theory, of Friedmann's articles, cited in n. 54 above. Isern, *Bull Threshers*, examines wage labor on wheat farms. For urban capitalists, see Cronon, *Nature's Metropolis*, 120–42.

(quantity of wage labor used in production; relation between market and nonmarket production; income and ability to procure consumer durables).[56]

The embourgeoisement of the wives of farmowners, defined to include the retirement of wives from market production, was incomplete and often contested in decades following the Civil War. Childrearing, domesticity, and household management took on new significance for middle-class farm women, as seen in their desire to build efficient farmhouses appropriate for both market and domestic labor.[57] Women, however, still participated in production on most grain, dairy, and cotton farms, and with the growth of urban or small-town markets extended their sales of eggs or butter. Many also continued subsistence activities — cultivating gardens, canning vegetables, sewing clothes — essential for the reproduction of the farm unit. Time spent on market and domestic labor varied among regions and might entail complex conflicts like those among freedwomen who wanted to reduce (but not end) their market activities and landlords who counted on their continued participation. Only on farms dominated by wage labor (California vegetable and fruit farms, cattle ranches) or by a single staple traditionally produced by men (wheat bonanza farms) did the market participation of women plummet. If capitalism reduced the productive, market labor of these women, it increased that of others. In the Southwest, where Mexican and Indian men left the village to become migrant workers, women took over farms, subsistence and market production alike.[58]

Under the impact of capitalist development, farm women came to support fuller conceptions of female citizenship. If the market for commodities and labor determined value, there was no reason to vest married women's property rights in their husbands. Radical women, insisting on their rights as individuals, began a long fight to retain control over their own property and wages and to gain the right to vote in the antebellum decades. Farm wives and farm daughters had actively participated in the antislavery and suffrage movements of the 1830s and 1840s, signing abolitionist petitions and attending the woman's rights convention in Seneca Falls. Over the last decades of the nineteenth century, women from farm backgrounds increas-

56. My general perspective is informed by Deutsch, "Confronting Capitalism"; for technology, see K. Jellison, "Rural Technological Change."

57. McMurry, *Families and Farmhouses*, chaps. 3–5, 7.

58. Osterud, *Bonds of Community*, chaps. 6–9; Schwieder, "Labor and Economic Roles Iowa Farm Wives," 152–68; Flora and Flora, "Structure of Agriculture," 195–205; Jerde, *From Peasants to Farmers*, 193–201; May, "Women, Farm Production and the Meaning of Land"; Mercier, "Women's Role in Montana Agriculture," 50–61; Deutsch, *No Separate Refuge*, chaps. 1–2; Jones, *Labor of Love*, chaps. 2–3; Ransom and Sutch, *One Kind of Freedom*, 45–47, 232–36; and Jaynes, *Branches without Roots*, 228–39, 322–25.

ingly supported women's rights and the vision of female equality it encompassed: they attended lectures, read newspaper articles and tracts, joined the Grange and Farmers' Alliances, argued about their rights at the dinner table, insisting that full citizenship actually accentuated their special roles as mothers. Female lobbying, along with substantial male support, led legislators in the transmississippi West, capitalist since settlement, to consider and even support women's rights decades before the eastern-dominated feminist movement managed to gain national victory.[59] Farm women with full citizenship rights could negotiate about the distribution of labor and resources on the farm from a new, more individualistic position of formal equality, perhaps making cooperation more reciprocal than in the past.

Monopoly capital—with its control of railroads, grain elevators, and farm prices—threatened the survival of the yeoman way of life where it persisted and the solvency of capitalist farmers. Between 1870 and 1900 farmers repeatedly challenged the hegemony of monopoly capitalists, organizing regional and national movements to reign in their power. The Grange, with 750,000 members in every state in 1875, as much a business and social organization as a political movement, nonetheless lobbied for state regulation of railroad rates to reduce transportation costs. The Farmer's Alliance and the Populist party, the largest political movement of farmers in our history, was a cross-class alliance, temporarily unifying small capitalist wheat farmers, southern cotton growers and small producers, bourgeois and traditional farm women in a crusade against monopoly capital. As the Alliance and Populists attempted to satisfy all the interests in its coalition, its goals became intensely contradictory, at once looking backward to yeoman independence and forward to a cooperative commonwealth (with farmer-run stores), organized production, and state regulation of agriculture. Its failure symbolized the demise of the yeomanry as a widespread and viable class and the triumph of capitalism in the agricultural sector.[60]

The Legacy of the Yeoman Classes: The Twentieth Century

Notwithstanding continuing expansion of yeoman farms into the early twentieth century, the rising proportion of output on highly capitalized

59. Chused, "Married Women's Property Law," 1359–1425; Wellman, "Women and Radical Reform," 113–31, and "Seneca Falls Women's Rights Convention," 9–37, esp. 14–17; DuBois, *Feminism and Suffrage*; Jeffrey, "Women in Southern Farmers' Alliance," 72–91; Marti, "Sisters of the Grange," 247–61; Moynihan, *Rebel for Rights*, chaps. 4–6; Matsuda, "West and Legal Status of Women," 47–56; Beeton and Edwards, "Anthony's Woman Suffrage Crusade in West," 5–15; Holley, *Samantha Rastles the Woman Question*, chaps. 1, 4.

60. Nordin, *Rich Harvest*; Goodwyn, *Democratic Promise*; Pollock, *Just Polity*.

farms and the increasing number of farms hiring migrant labor document the growing dominance of capitalist relations of production in the country-side. Even as the number of small farms on the plains grew after 1900, capitalist farmers marginalized yeoman production. Pockets of a yeoman social formation persisted — especially in Appalachia — into the twentieth century, but even there commodity production, mining, and industrial development disrupted older patterns early in the century.[61]

Even as the number of farms rose to a historical peak between 1890 and 1910, family farming became increasingly precarious. Although one (or more) children of farmers usually followed their parents' calling, farming became an almost closed system, requiring prior family landownership for entry. Reproduction of the farm unit, then, mandated access to inherited land. But such access diminished substantially by the late nineteenth century. Iowa farmers did not get land from parents but usually purchased the land they first farmed; farmers in Bucks County, Pennsylvania, often ordered that their land be sold rather than bequeathed to their children. Although such instrumental views of land as a commodity probably permeated agrarian America, some farmers like Germans in Illinois planned their estates carefully to ensure that at least some of their children could continue in farming. As the number of farms declined, relative to population, and inter-generational access to farms diminished, migration off the farm accelerated. The children of small owners, then, became wage workers in country or city or used education to enter professional occupations. After 1900 farm de-population quickened and soon only capitalist farmers (whether highly capitalized family units or corporate farms) and wage laborers remained.[62]

Yeoman agriculture, however, left an enduring legacy. The ideology of agrarian independence, translated into the idea of the family farm, remains embedded in American ideology. Nonmarket exchange of labor and commodities, household production, communal cooperation, and woman's production of petty commodities (eggs, butter) for local sale persisted on capitalist farms. But such practices no longer aimed at achieving communal

61. Lenin, "Capitalism and Agriculture in the United States," 131–203. For opposing views of Appalachia, see Pudup, "Boundaries of Class in Preindustrial Appalachia," 139–62; Eller, *Miners, Millhands, and Mountaineers*, chap. 1; Billings and Blee, "Family Strategies in a Subsistence Economy," 63–88.

62. G. Wright, "American Agriculture and the Labor Market," 201–4; Friedburger, *Farm Families and Change*, chap. 5; Shammas, Salmon, Dahlin, *Inheritance in America*, 104–8; Carroll and Salamon, "Share and Share Alike," 219–32; Landale and Guest, "Generation, Ethnicity, Opportunity," 280–99; Florey and Guest, "Coming of Age among U.S. Farm Boys," 233–49; Lansdale, "Opportunity, Movement, and Marriage," 365–86; Shover, *First Majority, Last Minority*, chap. 1; U.S. Bureau of Census, *Historical Statistics*, 1:457–59; Rohrer and Douglas, *Agrarian Transition*, chap. 5.

self-sufficiency; rather, they helped sustain family income of capitalist farmers in times of dearth or low prices.[63]

The history of the American yeoman classes, as we have told it, does not point to the exceptionalism of the American frontier but, rather, to different roads to capitalist development. Settlers in the English colonies left a dynamically growing capitalist economy but rejected the commodification of labor already occurring there. Controlling their own labor, they became independent producers, the sturdy yeomanry. Another yeoman class developed in Ontario, settled by English and Loyalist migrants who, like Americans, had experienced early capitalist development. Other colonies in the Americas, settled by Europeans from seigniorial societies, had no similar class. Quebec, which was similar in many ways to New England (population growth was as rapid; a mixture of subsistence production and trade of surpluses was common), developed a seigniorial society with vestiges of feudal relations of production similar to that of France. What was exceptional about the rural United States, then, was not the development of capitalism, but the formation and long history of regional classes of yeomen, living in a capitalist world but not of it.[64]

The demise of yeoman social formations and the rise of capitalist ones entailed a complex series of processes, at the same time regional and national, involving household and market, gender and class relations. Contemporaries, using the social languages they had inherited, had few words to understand these remarkable changes. To comprehend change, as we shall see in chapter 3, they devised new — and contested — languages of rural class. These languages, in turn, helped to structure social reality, class conflict, and economic change.

63. Sachs, *Invisible Farmers*, chap. 1; Fink, *Open Country Iowa*, chaps. 1–2, 6.
64. For Quebec, see R. C. Harris, *Seigniorial System in Early Canada*; Greer, *Peasant, Lord, and Merchant*. For Ontario, see L. F. Gates, *Land Policies of Upper Canada*, and Gagan, *Hopeful Travellers*.

Chapter 3

The Languages of Class
in Rural America

GEORGE CALEB BINGHAM, Missouri artist and Whig politician, evokes contrasting images of rural life in two oil paintings. In *Family Life on the Frontier*, completed before 1845, he portrays evening activities of an idealized frontier family, one consistent with Whig virtues of good order and rational, market agriculture (fig. 1). While the father sits in his humble cabin reading by the dim light of the fireplace (perhaps intent on becoming an educated "book" farmer), his wife nurses her baby and his daughters prepare the evening meal. A clock above the fireplace suggests the importance of time in raising productivity. The image meshes well with antebellum ideas of the role of men as breadwinners and women as nurturers. *The Squatters*, painted in 1850, portrays a far different scene, of "a family [that] has built its log cabin in the midst of a clearing and commenced housekeeping" (fig. 2). The rude cabin, lacking even a fireplace, stands in the background. The farm wife labors, washing clothes as food cooks (or, perhaps, boils water for the laundry) on an open, outside hearth, but her husband leans on a stick, searching the horizon, perhaps fearing dispossession, and their son sits, apparently relaxing. Two youths, maybe their sons, relax in the background. Nor do the men work much, for the ground seems barren and uncultivated.[1]

By evoking approval of the bourgeois father intent upon improvement and disapproval of the lazy squatter, Bingham's paintings articulate and extend a language of rural class over half a century in the making. He made his position clear in a letter to the New York Art-Union, where he consigned *The Squatters* to be sold. "The Squatters as a class," he argued, "are not fond of the toil of agriculture, but erect their rude cabins upon the remote portions of the National domain, when abundant game supplies their physical

1. S. Burns, *Pastoral Inventions*, is the best analysis of rural images in ideological terms. For Bingham, see Johns, "'Missouri Artist' as Artist," 111–18; R. Tyler, "Bingham, Native Talent," 25–49; Demos, "Bingham: Artist as Social Historian," 218–28 (esp. 222); Groseclose, "'Missouri Artist' as Historian," 53–92 (esp. 62–66); Rash, *Paintings and Politics of Bingham*, chaps. 1–2 (esp. 58–61); and McDermott, *Bingham: River Portraitist*, 75 (quote).

Fig. 1. George Caleb Bingham, *Family Life on the Frontier*, before 1845.
(Private collection courtesy of the New Orleans Museum of Art)

wants." But when the game thins, "they usually sell out their slight improvement, with their *'preemption title'* to the land, and again follow the receding
footsteps of the savage."[2] His painting illuminates one side of a multidimen-
sional, class-centered debate on the place of farmers in American society.
This position, as we shall see, was attacked by Democrats, who had a radically different vision of rural life.

Explicating such class languages, whether embedded in images or texts,
has become problematic in recent scholarship.[3] Social classes, writings on
language suggest, built class languages upon words (*democracy, individual,
yeoman, producer*, for instance) that were ambiguous, contested, and given
meaning only within political debate. The rhetorical building blocks of class

2. McDermott, *Bingham: River Portraitist*, 75.
3. For critical examinations of these theories from a historical context, see B. D.
Palmer, *Descent into Discourse*, esp. chap. 1, and Watts, "Idiocy of American Studies,"
625–60. P. Burke, Introduction, 1–20; Belsey, *Critical Practice*, chaps. 2–3; Eagleton,
Literary Theory, chaps. 3–4; and P. Smith, *Discerning the Subject*, provide simple intro-
ductions.

Fig. 2. George Caleb Bingham, *The Squatters*, 1850. (Courtesy, Museum of Fine Arts, Boston, bequest of Henry L. Shattuck in memory of the late Ralph W. Gay)

language were shared by all classes. Evangelical, liberal, and republican languages, for instance, were widely diffused in the United States during the half-century after independence. Everyone understood the dominant meaning of words elucidated by the ruling class, but when combined into ideologies, such words became ways for subordinate classes to express discontent. Subordinate classes and groups — workers, poor farmers, blacks, women — contested the meaning their rulers put on words, thereby forging new, class-conscious languages. To protest injustice, they became bilingual, appealing to the ruling class in their common language while insisting on the new, class-based meanings of words.[4]

Gareth Stedman Jones's essay on the class language of nineteenth-century English Chartism has been the most influential attempt to create a historically informed Marxist theory of language. His comments about the

4. D. T. Rogers, *Contested Truths*; Eagleton, "Ideology and Scholarship," 114–25; Fox-Genovese, "American Culture and New Literary Studies," 11–12, 26–28, for bilingualism. This paragraph is informed by Bakhtin, *Dialogic Imagination*, 259–300.

relation between class consciousness and language can be broadly applied. Though denying that he seeks to replace "a social interpretation by a linguistic" one, he argues that ideology "cannot be constructed in abstraction from its linguistic form." If one frees language from a necessary class interpretation, giving it "some autonomous weight," one can "establish a far closer . . . relationship between ideology and activity." Developed in political debate, often independently from class struggle, class language becomes "a complex rhetoric binding together . . . shared premises, analytical routines, strategic options, and programmatic demands," capable of mobilizing a class or coalition of classes. Such a language succeeds until "a gulf [is] opened up between its premises and the perceptions of its constituency."[5]

Languages of class with their contested rhetoric are public, refined in political debate, especially in bourgeois societies. Bourgeois societies provide forums — taverns, schools, newspapers, political rallies — open to all groups. Class languages legitimate state authority, both by sustaining its policies and by providing a forum for dissent, a way of changing state policy without disrupting the goals of the state and its ruling class. Even though rudimentary class languages appear in day-to-day struggle between social classes, they blossom only in public political conflict.[6] One sees rural class language, then, in rural revolts (Shays's Rebellion, the Whiskey Rebellion), debate over land policy, stump speeches, political canvassing, newspaper articles.

This chapter traces the history of contested languages of rural class in America, from their colonial origins to the Civil War era.[7] Coming to America after capitalist English landlords had expropriated the peasants' land, colonists brought with them a confusing array of class words. Until the mid-eighteenth century, rural class conflicts, however severe, were local, intermittent, and unconnected to broader public life. Colonists, for this reason, did not turn political words into a class-conscious language. Incensed by demands of colonial officials or landlords, eighteenth-century colonists, however, did slowly make a class ideology, based on landownership and a version of the labor theory of value. Rural class languages developed in the Revolutionary era. New class struggles, embedded in Jeffersonian and Jacksonian politics, intensified conflicts over class language in the mid-

5. G. S. Jones, *Languages of Class*, 90–108, quotes on 94–95, 101, 107.

6. This paragraph is informed by Habermas, *Structural Transformation of the Public Sphere*, chaps. 1–3, though his purpose is quite different from mine.

7. Work on class language in America is in its infancy. Wilentz, *Chants Democratic*, is a valuable model; M. J. Burke, "Conundrum of Class," is the best full-scale inquiry; D. T. Rogers, *Contested Truths*, prologue, chaps. 2–3, is a sophisticated analysis of political language as contested. Discussions of rural class language often see it as hegemonic rather than contested: Hofstadter, *Age of Reform*, chaps. 1–2; H. N. Smith, *Virgin Land*; L. Marx, *Machine and Garden*, chap. 3; M. E. Young, "Congress Looks West," 74–112; Berthoff, "Independence and Attachment," 99–124.

nineteenth century. But as proletarianization and debates over slavery heightened, new and radical groups turned rural class language to abolitionist or proletarian uses, disrupting older debates. No longer able to agree over the terms of the debate, violent struggle replaced contests over class language.

The Languages of Rural Class in Early America

American colonists borrowed rural language from England, and despite the migration of Scots, Irish, Germans, and Africans in the eighteenth century, English words continued to predominate. If the words were the same, the social meanings to which they were put were quite different. Because colonists failed to replicate the complex system of land tenure found in England, they could neither maintain the status distinctions such words as *yeoman* suggested nor use the labels to build class ideologies.

An examination of rural occupational labels (*farmer, yeoman*) and their relation to rural classes illuminates the embryonic development of class language in the colonies. When embedded in political struggle, with citizens molding words to fit ideological frameworks, occupational labels can provide class identity, distinguishing rural and urban, owner and renter. The meaning of colonial occupational terms, even as designations of status, was at best confused; when farmers wished to express hostility toward rulers, they used English concepts of equity and justice, rather than making a language directly connected to their class position.

Colonists understood the class language of rural England. The late sixteenth-century English used the same words to label occupations, indicate status, and symbolize class relations. Tenants and freeholders were called husbandmen. Mostly without political rights, their control of land depended upon manorial tradition. Yeomen, freeholders whose land earned at least forty shillings a year, were "deemed to be the strength and riches of the kingdom," and gained voting rights from the independence that freehold land tenure provided. Political thinkers believed that the militia, manned by the yeomanry, would protect England against invasion or tyranny. Although cottagers rented a small plot and had access to common land, they worked for wages to supplement what they could grow or gather. Laborers, who worked by the day and lived at the edge of subsistence, deemed their work servile, and their betters looked upon them as debased.[8]

8. *Oxford English Dictionary*, s.v. "Yeoman"; H. Higgs, ed., *Palgrave's Dictionary*, s.v. "Yeoman"; Thirsk and Cooper, eds. *Seventeenth-Century Economic Documents*, 160 ("Arguments for Repeal of the Irish Cattle Act, 1666," quote), 765–90 (Gregory King excerpts); Wrightson, *English Society, 1580–1680*, 31–36; E. S. Morgan, *Inventing the People*, chap. 7; C. Hill, "Pottage for Freeborn Englishmen, 219–38.

Economic development profoundly changed the English countryside during the seventeenth century. The proportion of cottagers and laborers, already a third early in the century, rose to half of the rural populace by 1700. At the same time, only a fifth of rural householders were husbandmen. Often the chief tenants of lords and the employers of farm laborers and cottagers, yeomen increasingly became well-off commercial farmers, defined by the quantity of land farmed and income received, rather than the form of tenure held.[9]

In this era of transformation, English husbandmen, cottagers, cloth workers, and laborers protested frequently, rioting against men who enclosed land or drained fens to preserve their rapidly disappearing common rights to water, wasteland, and forest. Mostly laborers, whose cottage gardens provided a hedge against low wages, rioters protested to maintain common rights, tearing down hedges, reflooding fens, and filling in ditches. Using a rudimentary class language, they justified their behavior. Their enemies, enclosing gentlemen and nobles, large-scale tenants and yeomen, had to be stopped. Rioters in the Midlands revolt of 1607, one report suggested, sought not only to "throw downe enclosures" but to "kill up Gentlemen, and . . . levell all states as they levelled bankes and ditches." However harsh the words, their goals were clear: *levelling* referred to common rights, equally open to everyone. They placed themselves precisely in the class order. A leader of the 1596 Enslow Hill Rebellion insisted that his followers "were no base fellows, but husbandmen who possessed plough lands of their own." The 1607 rioters revolted "only for reformation of thos late inclosures which made them of the porest sorte reddy to pyne for want." They struggled to avoid complete reliance upon wages, but enclosures, a pamphleteer argued in 1656, "have made farmers cottagers, and cottagers beggars," leaving these poor families with no recourse but to move to "market towns and open field towns hoping they may find some employment."[10]

Colonists brought English class language with them and tried to apply it in settler communities. But English class language poorly reflected the colo-

9. M. Campbell, *English Yeoman under Elizabeth and the Early Stuarts*. Numerical estimates were calculated from Thirsk and Cooper, eds., *Seventeenth-Century Economic Documents*, 768–69, 780–81 (King's work); Lachmann, *From Manor to Market*, 16–19; Lindert and Williamson, "Revising England's Social Tables," 385–99; Lindert, "English Occupations," 701–7.

10. Little record seems to have survived of the participants' political language but see R. B. Manning, *Village Revolts*, chaps. 2–4, 9 (quotes 224, 230, 235); J. E. Martin, *Feudalism to Capitalism*, chaps. 9–10; B. Manning, "Peasantry and the English Revolution," 133–58 (quote 176); Thirsk and Cooper, eds., *Seventeenth-Century Economic Documents*, 147–50 (John Moore, *Scripture Word against Enclosure*, 1656, quote 150); Underdown, *Revel, Riot, and Rebellion*, chap. 5; B. Sharp, *In Contempt of All Authority*, chaps. 4–6.

nial situation: while a diminishing proportion of Englishmen were freeholders, as many as two-thirds of eighteenth-century white adult male colonists
owned land. Reflecting greater opportunities found in the colonies, Americans used status-tinged words (*husbandman, yeoman*) interchangeably to
indicate landownership. Nonetheless, when they experienced political
oppression, whether from landlords or lawyers, the tax man or bandits, they
understood their plight in terms remarkably similar to rural folk in seventeenth-century England.[11]

English class terms took on new meaning in the colonies. Lacking a resident nobility and a legally imposed system of status, colonists used the word
gentleman to refer to wealthy farm operators. In England, the word *farmer*,
when used at all, denoted a tenant; in the colonies it encompassed *owners*
and *tenants*, "not only the men who rent lands of others, but also the little
freeholders who live upon their own property." *Planter*—a term used in the
southern colonies to denote staple producers—had been used in England to
describe anyone who planted crops.[12]

By the early eighteenth century, the words *farmer, yeoman, planter*, and
husbandman all commonly referred to both landowners and tenants. Such a
usage suggests a perceived lack of class distinctions among farmers beyond
the gulf between gentlemen and everyone else. Notwithstanding differential
use of occupational terms in the colonies, the same lack of distinctive class
labels could be found everywhere. During the first half of the eighteenth
century, Plymouth County, Massachusetts, court clerks recorded over two-
thirds of farm operators as *yeoman* and the rest as *husbandman*. There was
little difference in the wealth of the two groups, at least as measured by the
size of debt suits in which they engaged. By the 1770s, New England farm
operators were universally called yeomen.[13] Although early Pennsylvania
settlers either retained craft labels (*carpenter, weaver*) or were called husbandmen, by the early eighteenth century, most farm operators were labeled yeomen. By the 1770s, however, court clerks used the words *farmer* and *yeoman*

11. For landholding, see Kulikoff, *Tobacco and Slaves*, 135, 156; Main, *Society and
Economy in Colonial Connecticut*, chap. 6; Simler, "Tenancy in Colonial Pennsylvania,"
542–69; for transatlantic radical traditions, see Linebaugh, "All the Atlantic Mountains Shook," 87–121; A. F. Young, "English Plebeian Culture," 185–213.

12. *American Husbandry*, 49 (quote); Soltow and Keller, "Pennsylvania in 1800,"
30–31; *Oxford English Dictionary*, s.v. "Farmer," "Planter."

13. V. D. Anderson, *New England's Generation*, 124–25; Konig, ed., *Plymouth Court
Records*, 1:241–56, 358–72, 6:3–12, 358–72, 10:3–12 (16 yeomen and 4 husbandmen
in 1700–1702; in May 1736, 32 yeomen and 11 husbandmen; in May 1743, 47 yeomen, 24 husbandmen and 1 farmer; in Dec. 1785, 46 yeomen and 3 husbandmen). In
1774 A. H. Jones, *American Colonial Wealth*, 2:607–1096, finds 72 explicitly labeled
yeoman decedents, 7 husbandmen and 5 farmers.

interchangeably for farm operators, poor and wealthy. After the Revolution *farmer* gradually replaced *yeoman* as the preferred label.[14]

Southern tobacco and rice producers called themselves planters, but southern farm operators who exported no staples referred to themselves as farmers. Tobacco growers distinguished among gentleman planters, planters, and poor planters, thereby linking wealth and status to occupational labels. In Prince George's County, Maryland, in the 1730s, for instance, clerks labeled almost three-quarters of men in public records as planters. Half of gentlemen, one-quarter of craftsmen, and almost two-thirds of poor tenants who owned no adult slaves were called planters. The use of the word persisted into the early nineteenth century in tobacco-growing areas, but as general farming expanded, the proportion of farm operators labeled planter declined: three-fifths of a sample of Chesapeake farm-operating decedents in 1774 were labeled farmers and the rest planters.[15]

Yeoman classes formed throughout the colonies by the mid-eighteenth century, sustained by expectations of landownership. Notwithstanding this rapid yeoman class formation, the vague use of occupational terms suggests that colonial farmers lacked a class- or craft-conscious language. Participants in rural revolts against New York landlords or Carolina great planters, whose actions threatened secure land tenure, struggled for a class voice, borrowing seventeenth-century English imagery ill-suited to their status as freeholders. To justify their actions, they adapted a labor theory of value, arguing that their improvement of their holdings was all that gave land value. But the occupational labels they used in their protests were either inappropriate or lacked class specificity. Even as farmers slowly became conscious of themselves as a class, they focused upon particular grievances, not upon broader political rights.[16]

14. Soltow and Keller, "Pennsylvania in 1800," 30–31; Schweitzer, *Custom and Contract*, 64–73 (Chester County inventories, 1717–51, show 116 decedents called yeomen but only 5 husbandmen and 5 farmers); Lucy Simler, work in progress on Chester Country, Pennsylvania; A. H. Jones, *American Colonial Wealth*, 1:69–401. Inventories from six Middle Atlantic counties show 33 yeomen, 43 farmers, and 9 called farmers and yeomen.

15. Isaac, *Transformation of Virginia*, 16; Black Books, 2:110–24 (1733 Prince George's County tithables lists) linked to Prince George's deeds, wills, court records, and inventories, Maryland State Archives; A. H. Jones, *American Colonial Wealth*, 2:1155–1403 (26 planters, 38 farmers in Maryland and Virginia counties, 1 farmer-planter; 1 farmer-merchant; 1 farmer-justice), 3:1473–1619 (Charleston District, 26 planters, 3 esquires); Lorena Walsh research in progress.

16. In addition to chap. 2 above and chap. 5 below, see R. L. Bushman, "Massachusetts Farmers and the Revolution," 77–124; Countryman, "'Out of the Bounds of the Law,'" 39–69; R. M. Brown, "Back Country Rebellions," 73–99; A. Taylor, "Backcountry Conclusion to the American Revolution."

Protesters labeled themselves *the poor*, or *settlers*, or *inhabitants*, not farmers, or yeomen, or planters distinctive in their calling. In a long 1767 petition to the provincial Assembly, the South Carolina Regulators, fighting the refusal of lowcountry planters to suppress banditry, most often referred to themselves as settlers, but also called themselves *inhabitants*, *free men* — *British Subjects*, *the poor Planter*, or *freeholders*, terms they considered synonyms. Complaining about heavy taxes and autocratic government, North Carolina Regulators of 1768–71 usually labeled themselves *poor Inhabitants*, or *poor oppressed* and *suffering people*. Occasionally they saw themselves in craft terms, as *poor Industrious farmers* or *planters*. Adapting a political language of oppression rather than an economic language of exploitation, they insisted that lawyers, the "men in power . . . whose interest it was to oppress, and make gain of the Labourer," were their class enemies.[17]

The standard political language of class among gentlemen contrasted greatly with that of dissatisfied farmers. Comparing colonial society to the balanced government of Britain, with its monarchal, aristocratic, and democratic elements, gentlemen divided it into "lower," "middling," and "better" classes or into "meaner," "middling," and "better" sorts. Such natural divisions legitimated the political subordination of lower and middling classes and the superiority of highborn gentlemen.[18] Farmers in this natural order had no rights but those granted by the ruling classes.

Rather than debate about class, farmer and gentleman spoke mutually incomprehensible tongues. Colonial ruling classes, influenced by contemporary ideals of class rule, rejected farmer demands, refused to recognize the legitimacy of public debate over class issues, and insisted upon obedience. Calling upon the North Carolina Assembly to suppress the Regulators, Governor Tryon insisted that the rebels had "broke through all the Bounds of human Society, and trampled under Foot the Laws of their Country." Led by "Seditious Ringleaders," ordinary farmers are but "deluded People" who must be brought back "to the Duty of good Citizens and good Subjects."[19]

Once gentlemen assured themselves of the subordination of farmers, they could wax nostalgic about agriculture, reciting praises of the virtue of farm labor drawn from the classical pastoral tradition. They not only read pastoral poetry but diffused pastoral ideals widely to farm families in almanacs. As in England, disseminators of pastoral writings looked backward to a

17. Hooker, ed., *Carolina Backcountry*, 213–46 (213, 215, 220, 221 for examples); Saunders, ed., *Colonial Records of North Carolina* 7:760, 8:75–76; Husband, *Fan for Fanning*, 356–61; and Powell, Huhta, and Farnham, eds., *Regulators in North Carolina*, 187–89, 268–71. Kay, "North Carolina Regulation," 74–77, describes North Carolina regulators' class language.
18. M. J. Burke, "Conundrum of Class," 23–31; Main, *Social Structure*, chap. 7.
19. Powell, Huhta, and Farnham, eds., *Regulators in North Carolina*, 288–89.

more stable society and forward to improved agriculture. In the filler set between each month's calendar, almanac writers gave advice on farming and praised farmers as "*lords* of the soil" who "may live as genteel, tho' not in such splendour, as lords" by diligent labor.[20]

Almanac publishers liked to reprint pastoral verse. The *American Country Almanac* for June 1751, published in Philadelphia and New York, for instance, waxed poetic about summer farm labor:

> Your Sythes and Hocks ye Husbandmen prepare
> Behold and see the starred Rules Declare
> The Season (in the general) moderate and fair,
> A Harvest well enough, if you'll take care.

Simplicity and innocence, moreover, defined farm life, as the verse for September 1754 in the same almanac illustrates:

> How happy is the rural swain,
> Inur'd to hardships from his natal day.
> He knows no more in life than what he feels:
> His views are all Confin'd within that sphere

The use of the antique word *swain* (which referred to a farm laborer in England) and of the label *husbandman*, rarely found outside of New England, suggests that the almanac publisher wished to invoke ancient verities, rather than virtuous *colonial* farm operators.[21]

Even though pre-Revolutionary almanac writers presented vital data (calendars, solar events, farming advice), they failed to appeal to the political concerns of farm families, avoiding both a labor theory of value and reference to rural struggle over land. Not surprisingly, pastoral images from almanacs played no role in rural protests, nor did farmers identify with the "husbandmen" and "swains" who populated the pastoral poetry found in them.[22]

The Making of Languages of Rural Class

The Revolution prompted great ferment over the persuasive uses of language, both oral and written. Since patriot leaders needed to mobilize the populace, the public sphere, open to the free population, expanded greatly.

20. Eisinger, "Farmer in the Eighteenth-Century Almanac," 106–12 (quote 112); for England, see R. Williams, *Country and City*, chaps. 1–9.
21. See n. 20; for poetry, see More, *American Country Almanack, 1751*, page for June, and *American Country Almanack, 1754*, page for September.
22. Nearly all of Eisinger's examples of a labor theory of value and the "freehold ethic" in almanacs are from the Revolutionary period ("Farmer in Eighteenth-Century Almanac," 106–12). I searched More, *American Country Almanack, 1748–67*, and found no examples.

Tom Paine was the first in a long line of popular pamphleteers; Federalists and Antifederalists alike appealed to growing public opinion. Not only the ruling classes, but farmers and mechanics, women and blacks, began to use language self-consciously for political purposes. The explosion of dissent legitimated by the break with Britain, the rise of political parties, the growth of newspapers and social libraries, the spread of more democratic evangelical denominations, the expansion of subversive genres like the novel, all document a "village enlightenment" in which ordinary folk came to understand the power of words to shape reality, incite resistance, or compel obedience. Common words — *republicanism, democracy, the people, nature, rights, constitution* — became malleable, taking on new and contested meanings. As Thomas Jefferson realized, "the new circumstances under which we are placed call for new words, new phrases, and for the transfer of old words to new objects." This redefining of language led men who upheld the older order and those who sought change to invent political languages of class.[23]

These new languages of class were not simply masks for self-interest but a struggle to understand new circumstances in an American republic. Conflicts over language stood at the intersection of political revolution and economic change. The conventional gentry understanding of class, based upon the balanced English constitution, was disrupted by revolution and by Tom Paine's slashing attack. Reflecting upon the political changes of the Revolution, gentlemen adapted the economic language found in Physiocratic writings and the works of Adam Smith. But the harmonious relations between social classes some of these works portrayed poorly reflected conflicts threatening to tear the new nation apart. Farmers, craftsmen, women, and blacks listened to debates among gentlemen, thought, and created their own, very different understandings of the meaning of the Revolution.[24]

Underneath the debate between Federalist and Republican on the definition of and appropriate relations between classes stood profound disagreement about American society. If most commentators agreed that economic divisions — the few and the many, the poor and the wealthy, productive and unproductive classes — reflected social reality, they vehemently disagreed about class relations. Where Republicans saw conflict between aristocrats

23. D. T. Rogers, *Contested Truths,* chap. 2; E. S. Morgan, *Inventing the People,* chaps. 10–11; C. Jordan, "'Old Words' in 'New Circumstances,'" 491–513 (Jefferson quote on 491); Simpson, *Politics of American English,* chaps. 1–2; Jaffee, "Village Enlightenment," 327–46; Davidson, *Revolution and the Word,* esp. chaps. 3–4; Cmiel, *Democratic Eloquence,* chap. 1; L. H. Cohen, "Mercy Warren: Politics of Language," 481–98; Rollings, "Words as Social Control," 415–30; Richey, "Four Languages Early American Methodism," 155–71.

24. For philosophical influences on the development of class language, see M. J. Burke, "Conundrum of Class," chap. 2, and Simpson, *Politics of American English,* chap. 1. See below and chap. 5 for Revolutionary-era debates.

and the common people, Federalists believed that harmonious relations between classes with common interests were essential. Such intense differences led to charges and countercharges of Republican leveling or Federalist
aristocracy.[25]

The property-owning yeomanry, perceived on all sides as a particularly
virtuous middling class, were central to this debate. They participated in the
ferment, creating a rural class language. In the republican polity of the new
nation, use of the word *gentleman* slowly dissipated. In most of the North,
rural farm operators preferred the word *farmer*. Only New Englanders continued to use *yeoman*; as late as 1842, Plymouth County clerks universally
called farm operators *yeoman*. In the South, by the 1820s, poorer staple producers began calling themselves *farmers*. By the 1830s, *planter* had replaced
gentleman throughout the South to refer to wealthy slaveowners, and *farmer*
meant all other farm operators, no matter what crops they produced.[26]

As occupational labels for farm operators narrowed to *farmer* and *yeoman*, these labels became political class terms. Both poorer farmers and their
opponents (capitalists, land speculators) tried to appropriate the words for
their own purposes, thereby turning them into mainstays in the rhetoric of
Republicans *and* Federalists, Democrats *and* Whigs. As a result, two different
though related languages of rural class developed by the 1790s, one by democratic farmers, the other by entrepreneurs.

These two rural class languages were built upon similar images. Everyone knew that the words *farmer* and *yeoman* referred to the independent,
male freeholding small farmers of America. Although politicians used these
images in contrasting ways, each viewed the farmer as a virtuous man, whose
labors increased the wealth of the nation. Despite women's essential farm
labor and Revolutionary patriotism, these languages of male citizenship excluded them, presuming that only men had rights to express political opinions. But emphases in the two languages varied dramatically. Where
democrats protested the power of an "aristocracy" and thought that farmers
should maintain some autonomy from the market, conservatives saw a
union of classes and urged market embeddedness as the guarantor of the
farmers' independence.

The origins of a democratic language of rural class can be traced in part

25. M. J. Burke, "Conundrum of Class," chap. 3, is the best discussion, but see
Kerber, *Federalists in Dissent*, 182–92, and R. K. Matthews, *Radical Politics Jefferson*,
chaps. 2–3, 6.
26. Konig, ed., *Plymouth Court Records*, 15:3–12 (Apr. 1835, 42 yeomen, 1 husbandman), and 15:217–23 (28 yeomen). Demaree, *American Agricultural Press*, 393–
98, shows that 48/73 (66%) of northern farm journals used the word farmer and 14
(19%) used *agriculturalist*. Six of 16 southern farm journals (states that later joined the
Confederacy) used planter in their titles and 5 used *farmer*.

to the politicization of farmers during the 1770s and their participation in debates surrounding the Constitution. Addressed as citizens of the new republic, needed to guarantee victory over Britain, they insisted upon their democratic rights as farmers, their ability to influence public policy. But the new states tried, often successfully, to suppress their demands, and many of them saw the Constitution as a victory for aristocracy.[27]

Antifederalist writers deliberately appealed to farmers by writing in their name. The "Letter from the Yeomanry of Massachusetts" addressed the "publick," "the disinterested part of the community." The newspaper letter distinguished between the virtuous opponents of the Constitution and its supporters "chiefly made up of civil and ecclesiastical gown men," "who are turning our republican government into a hateful aristocracy." The author of the "Federal Farmer" chose the title intentionally, seeking to appeal not only to farmers but to all who identified with them. The author insisted, for instance, that representation "must be considerably numerous" if all classes — "professional men, merchants, traders, farmers, mechanics" — are to share in running the country.[28]

Such views of farmers spread widely in the 1790s and became part of a fully articulated rural ideology. William Manning's *The Key of Libberty* documents the diffusion of this ideology. Written in the late 1790s by a poorly educated but well-read middling Massachusetts yeoman, this unpublished essay called "Republicans, Farmers, Mecanicks, & Labourers" to action against "all ordirs of men who git a living without labour." To emphasize the union of all who worked with their hands, he called himself a "labourer."[29]

Conscious of the struggles of laboring classes, "the many," against "the few," professionals, merchants, and other wealthy men, Manning insisted upon equitable taxation. If the "end of Government is the protection of Life, Liberty & property," then "the poor mans shilling aught to be as much the care of government as the rich mans pound," and taxes "aught to be layed equally according to the property each person purses & the advantages he receives from it." Manning related equitable taxation to a labor theory of value: "Labour is the soul parrant of all property — the land yealdeth nothing without it, & there is no food, clothing, shelter, vessel, or any nesecary of life but what costs Labour & is generally esteemed valuable according to the Labour it costs." But "many are so rich that they can live without Labour," and these men support policies that reduce the supply of money, drying up credit, impoverishing the many, and leading to rebellion.

27. The classic account is G. S. Wood, *Creation of American Republic*; for rural life, see chaps. 5–6 below.

28. Storing, ed., *Complete Anti-Federalist*, 4:223–25, 2:230.

29. Morison, ed., "Manning's *Key of Libberty*," 202–54 (quotes on 209, 211). For Manning, see Merrill and Wilentz, "Money and Justice in Revolutionary America."

The remedy, Manning believed, was education. Knowledge could be disseminated by founding an organization of "Republicans & Labourers" open only to "free male persons who are 21 years of age, who Labour for a living." Not only would such an organization oppose the Society of Cincinnati—dominated by the few—but it would hold meetings and publish an educational magazine. This would furnish laborers "with the meens of knowledge" to discover "all impositions of all ordirs of men" and promote "Agruculture, Manifactoryes, Industries & Econimy."[30]

Influenced both by English political economists and Physiocrats and by farmers' demands, Jeffersonian Republicans developed theories of rural democracy. George Logan, a wealthy Quaker gentleman-farmer, provides an example. Although Logan had opposed the democratic Pennsylvania Constitution of 1776, supported recharter of the state bank, and sought to ratify the Constitution in 1787, he listened carefully to his farmer constituents and slowly took up more radical positions, favoring free trade and farm interests. By the late 1780s, he not only began to praise the 1776 state constitution but opposed a bill allowing tax collectors to seize farmers' property for unpaid taxes because it gave them tyrannical power and would reduce farmers, already suffering from low prices, to poverty.[31]

Logan articulated his newfound Jeffersonian views of rural life in three political pamphlets. His *Letters Addressed to the Yeomanry* (1791) attacked the imposition of indirect taxes on consumption goods as inequitable and destructive of the economy, urging instead direct taxes on physical property. "The independent yeomanry of England are almost annihilated," Logan insisted, because of heavy, inequitable taxation. He sought to educate the American yeoman or farmer—words he used interchangeably to refer to America's independent freeholders—to prevent such actions here.

To argue against federal indirect taxes, Logan borrowed Physiocratic ideas about agriculture. "The cultivation of land being the only productive employ," he wrote, "the laborer, the mechanic, the manufacturer" were "occupied in the service of the Farmer." Agriculture, then, was the source of all taxes, even "every indirect tax, however circuitous." If agriculture produced all wealth, then the "independent yeomanry" followed the "most honorable and most useful employ," and "ought to be regarded as the most valuable class of citizens." The farmer, "engaged in the laborious, but honorable, employ of cultivating" his crops should pay "an equitable proportion of the net produce of" his farm as taxes but then "enjoy the free disposal of the remainder."

30. Morison, ed., "Manning's *Key of Libberty,*" 209, 217–18, 252, 250, 242–43.
31. Tolles, *George Logan of Philadelphia,* chap. 4; M. J. Burke, "Conundrum of Class," 87–91.

Examining rural society, Logan saw potential for class conflict. Like Manning, he divided society into the few and the many and feared that a class of monied aristocrats might take over the government. Only alert farmers could prevent that usurpation of power. "How long will you suffer yourselves," he asks farmers, "to be duped by the low cunning and artifice of half-informed Lawyers, and mercenary Merchants," by legislators who "forget that their country is inhabited by an independent yeomanry?" Nonetheless, he was persuaded that "the yeomanry of the United States will certainly never suffer themselves to be reduced to that abject state of servility . . . to the arbitrary opinion of the few."[32]

At the same time as Jeffersonians created a democratic language of rural class, Federalists — using the same words — made a more politically conservative language. Three ideas permeate Federalist discourse on agriculture: use of pastoral images to praise agrarian life; insistence that the intensity of a farmer's labor, not a venal aristocracy, determined his income; and the need for more markets, higher productivity, and agricultural reform. In contrast, Jeffersonians rarely adopted images from pastoral traditions and made improved markets and agricultural reform minor parts of their appeal.[33]

Conservative appeals to farmers began during the 1780s. Federalists often solicited farmer approval of the Constitution. For instance, "A Farmer" wrote "To the Farmers of Connecticut": we farmers "are all groaning under an intolerable burden of public taxes, and at the same time lamenting the scarcity of cash and the difficulty of vending the produce of our farms." The Constitution would solve these problems by replacing state imposts with fair federal taxes and by forcing Great Britain to open the West Indies to American produce. "One of the People," a Pennsylvanian, saw "bankrupt merchants, poor mechanics, and distressed farmers" as "the effects of the weakness of the Confederation." Far from being enemies, he believed that "the interests of these three are intimately blended together," and all should approve the Constitution. But farmers should especially seek "immediate execution [of] this Constitution" because the country could then regulate its foreign trade, thereby finding markets for its produce, which would, in turn, increase the price of land.[34]

Fear of disorder and rebellion, especially among venal "speculators" and illegal "settlers" in the West, permeated Federalist language of rural class. Seeking intensive commercial development of western lands through grad-

---

32. [Logan], *Letters Addressed to the Yeomanry*, 6, 21, 5, 34, 38, 32, 34, 13; Eisinger, "Influence of Natural Rights and Physiocratic Doctrines," 13–23.

33. L. Marx, *Machine and Garden*, 116–44, exaggerates the pastoral imagery in Jefferson's thought, which, in any event, is not found among other Republicans.

34. M. Jensen, ed., *Documentary History of Ratification*, 3:392–94, 2:186–92.

ual settlement, rather than migration of farmers who sold small surpluses, supporters of the Northwest Ordinance wished to keep speculators and squatters off of unsurveyed lands. They put speculators and settlers in the same class; as George Washington wrote in 1783, "to suffer a wide extended country to be over run with Land Jobbers, Speculators, and Monopolisers or even with scatter'd settlers" would be unwise policy that would produce conflict with Indians, scatter the population too widely, and "aggrandize a few avaricious Men to the prejudice of many."[35]

Philadelphia Federalist reformer Benjamin Rush even denied that frontier settlers were farmers. "The *first* settler in the woods is generally a man who has outlived his credit . . . in the cultivated parts of the state." Emulating the Indians, "he revolts against the operation of the laws. He cannot bear to surrender up a single natural right for all the benefits of government." Not until such Indian ways disappeared and settlers established "schools and churches" to promote "order and happiness in society" could "the term *farmers*" be applied to them.[36]

Federalists continued to appeal to farmers through pastoral poetry, didactic novels, and almanacs after 1789. The pastoral poetry of the Federalist Connecticut Wits linked American democratic laws and prolific land supplies to the prosperity and independence of farmers, especially in comparison to the English and Europeans. As David Humphreys wrote:

> Columbians! say, what happiness is yours?
> Say, ye who, not as tenants, till the soil,
> The joys that freemen find in rural toil?

Such independence, he added, made farmers more productive:

> In clearing fields, and adding farms to farms;
> 'Tis independence prompts their daily toil,
> And calls forth beauties from the desert soil

Timothy Dwight expressed similar ideas in *Greenfield Hill*:

> Through the whole realm, behold convenient farms
> Fed by small herds, and gay with cultur'd charms;
> To sons in equal portions handed down,
> The sire's bold kindling in the son;

35. Fitzpatrick, ed., *Writings of Washington*, 27:133 (quote, Washington to James Duane, 7 Sept. 1783), 28:107–8, 137–38 (Washington to Hugh Williamson, 15 Mar. 1785, and to William Grayson, 25 Apr. 1785). The best guide is Onuf, *Statehood and Union*, esp. chaps. 1–3; Onuf quotes Federalists more extensively than Republicans on ideological issues, whom he assumes represent Americans in general.

36. Rush to Thomas Percival, 26 Oct. 1786, quoted by Berkhofer, "Northwest Ordinance and the Principle of Territorial Evolution," 50–51.

No tyrant riding o'er the indignant plain;
A prince, a king, each independent swain.

And an anonymous poet linked democracy to a labor theory of value. In the United States, with "Democratick laws," without a "tyrant Lord," "he who sows enjoys the product of his toil."[37]

Federalists placed pastoralism, a labor theory of value, and praise of farmers, into a developmental vision of America. Dwight, for one, saw the frontier transformed by the "beauties of cultivation" in which "flocks and herds will frolic over the pasture, and fields will wave with harvests of gold." *Farmer's Friend*, a didactic novel published in 1793 by Enos Hitchcock, a Congregational minister in Providence, exemplifies this approach. He dedicated the novel "To All Farmers, through the United States," by telling the story of Charles Worthy, a poor orphan who through his own diligence "does honor to his Occupation."

Hitchcock paints Worthy as an ideal modern farmer. After choosing fertile frontier land to farm, he "first felt himself a freeholder, and independent of the caprice of others both for his exertions and his enjoyments." His knowledge of the secrets of plants and animals "assisted him in making progress in his business as a farmer." And "the property he enjoyed was the fruit of his own labor; and his improvements were the effects of his own experience." After reading the latest agricultural literature, "he pursued his occupation with great industry; and every spring" he saw "his grass grow thicker by means of the manure and tillage he bestowed upon the ground." Because he directed his hired men well and paid them promptly, "his fields and meadows were put into the best order, his fences were seasonably repaired."

Hitchcock's comparison of farmers Worthy and Slack illuminates his insistence that individual initiative, not an inequitable class system, was responsible for failure or success. Just as Worthy's hard labor yielded success, Slack's negligence ensured failure. Slack refused to work in his fields and hired men took on his habits. Soon, "his fences became bad, his cattle destroyed his corn . . . and did great damage to his neighbors' fields." His poor working habits led to "the contempt . . . of the most sensible and fashionable people by their affectation of grandeur, and the hatred of many of the poorer but virtuous people by their injustice" for he failed to pay "the wages of the labourer."

Hitchcock's espousal of a labor theory of value must be seen within this context of individual industriousness. Adopting the voice of an urban

37. Eisinger, "Freehold Concept in Eighteenth-Century Letters," 42–59 (quotes on 50–51); Bottorff, ed., *Miscellaneous Works of David Humphreys*, 38; Briggs, "Timothy Dwight Composes a Landscape," 359–77.

gentleman, Hitchcock writes that "by labor every thing is produced; without labor the most fertile fields would soon be overrun with forests, the finest meadows become stagnant waters, or wild and unyielding thickets." Echoing Jefferson, he insists that "if therefore there is any difference between one human being and another, that part of them must be the most valuable who cultivate the ground, and provide necessaries for the rest."[38]

Hoping to gain votes from every class, neither party sharply specified a class constituency. Nonetheless, Federalists appealed most to commercial farmers, ever more fully embedded in capitalist relations of production, while Republicans sought support from poorer farmers who produced small surpluses but wanted to maintain a bit of independence from the market. Fragmentary evidence suggests that voters understood party appeals in this way and responded accordingly. In Hingham, Massachusetts, Republicans achieved that union of the many that Manning wanted. Hingham's yeomen, artisans, and laborers overwhelmingly supported the Jeffersonians in 1806; the wealthy, merchants, and professionals voted Federalist. In early nineteenth-century Frederick County, Maryland, English-speakers tended to vote Federalist and Germans tended to vote Republican, but nonslaveholders among both groups voted for Republicans more often than their slave-owning neighbors. And in several Virginia elections in the late 1780s, non-slaveholders and small slaveholders supported Antifederalist candidates while the wealthiest men usually voted for Federalists.[39]

Jacksonian Debates over Rural Class Language

As political debate over economic issues became more pointed during the Jacksonian period, a confusing multiplicity of class languages emerged, reflecting sharpening knowledge of class antagonisms, commercialized agriculture, industrialization and immigration, and growing fear of urban depravity. Political economists and radical reformers, Whigs and Democrats, editors and artists, spokesmen for farmers and laborers, advocates of slavery or of free labor, struggled to understand changed productive relations, to reinvent the past or create a virtuous future. Debates over class became ever more intensely public and national, permeating congressional proceedings, electoral gatherings, newspaper columns, and imaginative literature. The struggle to create rural class languages was central in these larger conflicts.[40]

38. Briggs, "Timothy Dwight Composes a Landscape," 372–73; Hitchcock, *Farmers Friend*, dedication, 61, 68, 107, 110, 108–9, 116–17.
39. D. S. Smith, "Process, Event, Process"; Bohmer, "The Causes of Electoral Alignments," 251–76, esp. 263–67; Risjord, "How the 'Common Man' Voted," 36–64.
40. Wilentz, *Chants Democratic*, chap. 4; D. T. Rogers, *Contested Truths*, chap. 3; M. J. Burke, "Conundrum of Class," chaps. 4–5; Cmeil, *Democratic Eloquence*, chap. 2;

The words available to educated Americans proliferated in the antebellum era. Democratic visions of equality vied with republican ideals of virtue; evangelicalism coexisted with the economic liberalism of Adam Smith. One could find advocates for all these views in Jeffersonian times, but their appeal broadened with the further diffusion of education, newspapers, and political parties. Those who formed class language borrowed from these conflicting frameworks, building new if contested meanings as they proceeded.[41]

Systematic commentators in the 1820s and 1830s struggled over two contradictory visions of American class relations. Most began with Adam Smith's distinction between productive (farmers and manufacturers or mechanics) and unproductive (lawyers, servants, doctors) laborers and the conflict between those who earned a wage and those who made money from capital. Smith inspired two visions of class. Most American political economists rejected his distinction between productive and unproductive labor, insisting that the interests of working people and owners of capital were identical. Matthew Carey, for one, had a "deep conviction that there is an identity of interest between the farmers and manufacturers," and that rural poverty emanated from "an erroneous policy, predicated on . . . a supposed hostility between the cultivators of the soil and the manufacturers." Heirs of Jeffersonians, still wedded to visions of a new aristocracy, built upon Smith's distinction, seeing substantial conflicts between producers and nonproducers. John Taylor, for one, contrasted the true manufacturers like farmers with "a monied sect, composed of privileged combinations" who were "an aristocratical oppressor."[42]

Political economists struggled to understand changes in relations of production in England and the United States. They slowly came to see two new classes, dubbed capitalists and workingmen or laborers, as components of the new social order. Although Adam Smith did not use the label *capitalists*, he did define capital as property that yields profits or adds to stock of things. By the early 1820s, political economists on both sides of the Atlantic discov-

---

Conkin, *Prophets of Prosperity*; S. Burns, *Pastoral Inventions*, chaps. 1–4; Buell, "American Pastoral Ideology," 1–29; Johns, "Farmers in Works of Mount," 257–81; Heinze, "Yeomanry Transformed," chap. 2; Horlick, *Country Boys and Merchant Princes*, chap. 2; Gross, "'Most Estimable Place in World,'" 1–15.

41. When read together, Appleby, *Capitalism and a New Social Order*; Ashworth, *Agrarians and Aristocrats*; Meyers, *Jacksonian Persuasion*; Berthoff, "Conventional Mentality," 753–84; and A. F. Tyler, *Freedom's Ferment*, suggest the interpenetration of these contested languages.

42. M. J. Burke, "Conundrum of Class," chap. 3; A. Smith, *Wealth of Nations*, 66–71, 314–31, esp. 314–16; Carey, *Essays on Political Economy*, 413–14 (quote), 439–41, 458–60; J. Taylor, *Construction Construed*, 208–9, 233.

ered a new class called capitalists. The term was ambiguous, referring either to anyone possessing capital or to a class of men (entrepreneurs, factory owners, bankers) who made profits off the labor of others. John Taylor, who viewed industrial society with horror, used the term in both ways. On the one hand, "privileged capitalists" were economic aristocrats, bankers and monopolists who enriched themselves unfairly; on the other, he admitted "that capitalists, whether agricultural, commercial, or manufactural, constitute useful and productive classes in society" if their profits had been gained "by fair and honest industry." John McVicker, who lamented the "vulgar prejudice against the rich," defined capitalists more precisely as "holders of land or money, who furnish" laborers "the means of labour, and who live on rent." By the 1830s, economists paired laborers (often including farmers and craftsmen) and capitalists as two antagonistic or complementary classes. "The workingman could not do without the capitalist, nor the capitalist without the working man," Condy Raguet argued in 1831.[43]

Notwithstanding the insistence of early political economists that nearly all men engaged in productive labor, agrarian beliefs of the superior virtue of farmers, in a country still overwhelmingly rural, remained strong. The nearly unitary political struggles over appropriation of rural class language common in the Jeffersonian era broke down into concurrent debates. Antebellum agrarianism, in its conflicting variations, emerged at the confluence of democratized pastoralism and Physiocratic doctrine, the egalitarianism of a redistributive agrarian law and the developmental necessity for agricultural improvement. Agrarianism could be found in such diverse genres as the agricultural press, landscape painting, and writings of agricultural reformers and urban radicals. Farm journals, which mixed paeans to yeomen with advice on improving agriculture, were the foremost repository of agrarianism. Like colonial almanac writers, these publishers insisted that farming was the most virtuous occupation, especially in contrast to the venality of city life. The virtuous farmer, independent of any master but nature, freely labored to add value to the land and feed the country, experimenting in technological innovations while building America. Only slothful behavior — careless farming or heavy drinking — might reduce agrarian independence. Urban radicals jumped on the contradiction in northern farm journals of supporting capitalist innovations while imagining a pastoral present. Admitting the virtues

43. I have used M. J. Burke, "Conundrum of Class," chaps. 2–3, esp. 110–11, 143–59 (Raguet quote 153), 164–73, 193–94, as a guide. R. Williams, *Keywords*, 42–44; A. Smith, *Wealth of Nations*, 262–65, 314–22; J. Taylor, *Construction Construed*, 208–10, 232–34 (quote) and *Arator*, 86–87, 102, 108; C. W. Hill, *Political Theory of John Taylor*, chap. 3; Conkin, *Prophets of Prosperity*, 60–61; McVicker, *Outlines of Political Economy*, 162–63 (quote); Raymond, *Elements of Political Economy*, 98–107; Wayland, *Elements of Political Economy*, book 3, chap. 3, esp. 405.

of farming, a few radicals insisted that only the destruction of private property and the widespread distribution of the use of land to the urban poor could sustain national prosperity.[44]

Debates over federal land policy illuminate the ways rural citizens shaped various class languages to understand their situation. Even if everyone began with agrarian presumptions (themselves contested), Whigs and Democrats constructed opposing languages of rural class to explain their land policies. They disagreed about how to define farmers, what rural activities were legitimate, and what relations farmers should have with other classes. Unlike earlier commentators, antebellum congressmen understood class terms in a rural context, seeing class protagonists as indigenous to rural areas. As capitalist agriculture, spurred on by urban development, spread in the East and frontier settlement filled the West, debates over land policy added the words *pioneer, squatter, settler, speculator,* and *capitalist* to rural class vocabulary.

Notwithstanding chasms between Democrats and Whigs, they agreed on the terms of the debate, each seeking to preserve the small-scale farm, headed by a white man, within a system of private property. Everyone—Democrats and Whigs, radical reformers and conservatives—began by praising the farmer as a male citizen, linking land ownership to political virtue, espousing a labor theory of value. To appeal to farmers with a white male language of citizenship when male and female radicals had begun to seek some citizenship rights for women and agitate against slavery was to take a stand *against* political rights for women and blacks. Such silences about gender and race secured intraparty unity across free labor and slave regions growing further apart. When politicians debated political rights for women or blacks, they vehemently rejected them, pointing to the corruption of the dependent or powerless.[45]

Whigs and Democrats also implicitly agreed upon an exclusionary language of race. Despite the growing class of free blacks and increasing abolitionist sentiment in the 1830s and 1840s, Whigs and Democrats alike presumed that black people were slaves, not citizens, and therefore not an appropriate subject for debate. This strategy permitted northern and southern party members to unify on land issues of interest to farmers. Indians as

44. T. P. Thornton, "Between Generations," 189–211; Heinze, "Yeomanry Transformed," chap. 2; Rossell, "Tended Images," 425–40; Abbott, "Agricultural Press Views the Yeoman," 35–48; S. Burns, *Pastoral Inventions*, chaps. 1–5; Conkin, *Prophets of Prosperity*, chap. 9.

45. Berthoff, "Conventional Morality," 753–84; J. Matthews, "Race, Sex, and Dimensions of Liberty," 275–91; Buell, "American Pastoral Ideology," 9–19, give contrasting views of this point.

well stood outside, rarely mentioned unless as savages preventing settlement by virtuous white farmers.

Consensus on the subservient place of rural women was particularly pronounced. Whigs and Democrats limited their appeal to male citizens, continuing to profess old verities, even as they were breaking down. They ignored the changed status of northern middling women by the late 1830s — appropriation of an ideology of bourgeois domesticity and possessive individualisms by women, growth of female school teaching, beginnings of female reform.[46] White men were citizens, owned farms, bequeathed land; women were wives, dependents, classed with children. Without preemption (giving squatters right of first purchase of land they improved), Democrat William Fulton argued, settlers would be "ruined and their wives and children deprived of a home and shelter"; Thomas Benton found pioneers, "the best of citizens," "raising respectable families of sons and daughters, fulfilling all their duties to society." Whigs agreed: John Calhoun denied that preemption would "benefit the man, with many children but little money, who might desire to emigrate to the West to improve the condition of himself and his family"; William Merrick though it sound policy to "give to the . . . honest . . . poor man, who owns no land . . . the opportunity of acquiring a home, and comfort for himself and family."[47]

Senators identified farms as households, income-pooling economic units of production, headed by male citizens.[48] To perpetuate such households, men needed land. Despite the gradual demise of these households in the North, Democrat James Buchanan of Pennsylvania wanted to sustain them in the West. He amended a bill to limit settlement to settlers "to allow the fathers" of "children between the ages of twelve and twenty-one years, or mothers of such children, whose fathers are dead, to enter a section of land in the name of each child." Lands would not be patented until the child reached adulthood, thereby eliminating speculation. When the child comes of age, "he goes out to the West with his wagons and horses, and farming implements, and becomes the very best settler that the new States can have." Buchanan designed his amendment to increase the authority of fathers over minor children by keeping them at home with a promise of land at adult-

---

46. Kerber, "Separate Spheres, Female Worlds," 9–39; Cott, *Bonds of Womanhood*; J. Matthews, "Race, Sex, and Dimensions of Liberty," 275–91; Ryan, *Cradle of Middle Class*. For rural women, see J. Jensen, *Loosening the Bonds*; Kaye, "Ladies Department of *Ohio Cultivator*," 414–24; Wellman, "Women's Rights, Republicanism, and Revolutionary Rhetoric," 353–84.

47. *Congressional Globe*, 25th Cong., 2d sess., App., 136 (Fulton), 29 Jan. 1838, 143 (Benton), 30 Jan. 1838, 137 (Calhoun), 29 Jan. 1838, 130 (Merrick), 27 Jan. 1838.

48. Fox-Genovese, *Within the Plantation Household*, chap. 1.

hood and, as well, to permit children to create viable frontier households, without demeaning debts to speculators.[49]

Debate over this amendment uncovers tensions created by capitalist transformation of households. John Ruggles, a Maine Democrat, discerned sexual ambiguity in the amendment: it permitted fathers to enter land for daughters, whose husbands controlled it after marriage under common law. Presuming that only men's labor made land valuable, he sought to "restrict the entry by parents to male children only," arguing that "the ladies would not be very desirous of entering on the arduous task of cutting down forests and clearing wild lands." Ruggles implicitly understood that giving land to a daughter provided her husband with *two* tracts and that factories and domesticity had eroded older forms of household government in the Northeast. The Senate, however, overwhelmingly (38 to 3) turned down the amendment. Ruggles gained support only from Democratic Senators from Connecticut and New York, states where capitalist transformation had proceeded most rapidly.[50]

Notwithstanding agreement over the terms of debate, Whigs and Democrats contested land policy, creating opposed languages of rural class. Democratic and Whig views on rural class developed from the debate, each refracting upon the other, the differences they presented to farmers sharpening as debate proceeded. Where Whigs supported industry and banks and saw the fate of farmers and manufacturers intertwined, Democrats — building upon but transforming Adam Smith — distinguished the productive (farmers, artisans, laborers) and unproductive (bankers, merchants, manufacturers) classes and appealed to farmers who wished to maintain some autonomy from full market embeddedness. Democrats called Whigs aristocrats; Whigs labeled Democrats agrarians seeking to retard American development.[51]

Political debates over the distribution of federal land were directly connected to farmers' aspirations, especially of those who lived in or wished to move to the West. In debating land policy, congressmen gave class meaning to such words as *speculator, squatter, pioneer,* and *settler,* embedding them in analyses of frontier class relations. The desirability of preemption, the necessity of graduation (lowering prices if land had been on the market for a number of years), the way to eliminate unnecessary land speculation, all divided Democrats and Whigs. Between 1838 and 1846, 87 percent of House Demo-

49. *Cong. Globe,* 24th Cong., 2d sess., 126, 26 Jan. 1837.

50. *Cong. Globe,* 24th Cong., 2d sess., 152, 3 Feb. 1837.

51. Ashworth, *Agrarians and Aristocrats,* is the best analysis of this ideological conflict, but see P. W. Gates, *Landlords and Tenants,* and Swierenga, *Pioneers and Profits,* for contrasting views of land policy in action.

crats but only 34 percent of Whigs voted for preemption; 76 percent of Democrats but just 13 percent of Whigs supported graduation. During the same years, 85 percent of Senate Democrats but merely 19 percent of Whigs voted for graduation.[52] Such party differences were especially clear in Senate debates in 1837 over limiting land to actual settlers and in 1838 over preemption. Democrats agreed with each other three-quarters of the time and Whigs four-fifths of the time on thirteen votes on amendments to and passage of the bill limiting land to settlers. Party agreement was even higher on the 1838 preemption bill, where nine-tenths of Whigs and Democrats each voted with majorities of their own party. Eastern Democrats sometimes deviated from their party's position when they believed that their western colleagues sought to depopulate the East; western Whigs occasionally voted for preemption to maintain local support.[53]

Democrats began with Physiocratic ideas about agriculture. "Agriculture," argued Thomas Benton (Missouri), "which produces the means of subsistence to man and beast, is always . . . first . . . ; manufacturers, which fashions and prepares these means for use, stands second; and commerce, which exchanges the superfluities of different nations, is third." The primacy of agriculture, he concluded, necessitated preemption, for farmers deserved "the privilege of first purchase, at Government price, in a small tract in the new lands."[54]

If agriculture was primary, farmers' work gave land its value. The "enterprise and perseverance" of pioneers, Clement Clay (Alabama) argued, "has given settlement and cultivation to your remotest wilds." A settler on the public domain seeking preemption rights, John Tipton (Indiana) contended, had "improved" that land "by the labor of his own hands"; James Buchanan would always vote "to protect the poor man in the possession of the land he had rendered valuable by the sweat of his brow."[55]

Democrats admitted that land had a market price, affected by soil fertility and location, once farmers had improved their holdings. But they denied

52. Ashworth, *Agrarians and Aristocrats*, 250–52, 277–78, for roll calls. Two essays reach opposite conclusions about land ideology. Where M. E. Young, "Congress Looks West," 74–112, sees liberals, Berthoff, "Independence and Attachment, Virtue and Interest," 99–124, sees classical republicans.

53. *Cong. Globe*, 24th Congress., 2d sess., scattered from 90 to 172 and App., 115, 167–70, 173–77, 314–17, 321–22, 335–39 (1837 bill limiting settlement); ibid., 25th Cong., 2d sess., App., 129–43 (1838 preemption bill). On bill for limiting settlement, 80% of Whigs agree on average (5.8% standard deviation), 75% of Democrats agree (12.3); ibid., 24th Cong., 2d sess., 115, 121, 139, 143–46, 152, 156, 167, 172 (21 Jan.–9 Feb.); ibid., 25th Cong., 2d sess., App., 1838, 133, 135, 143 (27–30 Jan.).

54. *Cong. Globe*, 25th Cong., 2d sess., App., 143, 30 Jan. 1838.

55. *Cong. Globe*, 25th Cong., 2d sess., App., 140, 29 Jan. 1838, (C. Clay) 134 (Tipton) and 132 (James Buchanan, Pennsylvania), both 27 Jan. 1838.

that unimproved soil, no matter how fertile or favorably located, was anything but wasteland. For that reason, new land almost always sold for the
$1.25 minimum price set by law when first put on the market. "It is only
when waste land was improved," William Fulton (Arkansas) argued, "that its
true value could be known." It is "the honest settler who enhances the value
of the public domain, and assists in bringing it into market." Lucius Lyon
(Michigan) provided an example: "What would any man give for the best
land in the fertile, but wild and uncultivated region west of the Rocky Mountains? . . . Would he give fifty cents, ten cents, or even five cents an acre?"[56]

Democrats saw two antagonistic classes in frontier America, settlers and
speculators. Settlers (also called pioneers, farmers, planters, and yeomen)
had made the country great by improving wastelands. Virtuous men, they
would gladly pay for the land they improved. Positive images repeatedly re-
cur in Democratic descriptions of settlers: "pioneers of the new States — the
cultivators of the soil — the defenders of the country against Indian aggres-
sion"; "hardy and daring race of pioneers and settlers"; "industrious and
worthy citizens"; "honest and hardy yeomanry."[57]

Democrats viewed benignly those who settled on unsurveyed acres, denying the Whig charge that they were criminals, squatters on public land.
John Tipton (Indiana) described the settlement process: farmers enter "the
best public land they could find, building cabins to shield their families . . . ,
cultivating the soil, regardless [of] whether the land had been surveyed or
not, with the . . . intention of paying the Government for the lands whenever they should be brought into market." "They are a law-abiding people,"
William Fulton argued, "except being found on the public lands without a
legal title." Settlers had no choice: "in travelling with their families to the
West, they had exhausted their little means," and — unable to afford surveyed acres — "therefore went beyond lands already in market." Not surprisingly, Democrats bristled at Whig depictions of settler venality. Despite their
honesty, John Robinson (Illinois) lamented, "these men were to be called
repeatedly here, with a sneer, *'squatters, squatters,'*" a negative label Democrats refused to use.[58]

In contrast, Democrats saw land speculators as "organized bands,"
"money speculators," who preyed upon farmers, who would "drive them off
and reap the fruits of their industry." They were, Senator Fulton insisted,
"combinations of speculators, leagued together . . . to enrich themselves by

56. *Cong. Globe*, 25th Cong., 2d sess., App., 136 (Fulton), 138 (Lyon), 29 Jan. 1838.

57. *Cong. Globe*, 25th Cong., 2d sess., App., 129 (John Norvell, Mich., 27 Jan.
1838), 136–37 (William Fulton, 29 Jan. 1838), 141 (Henry Hubbard, N. H., 29 Jan.
1838).

58. *Cong. Globe*, 25th Cong., 2d sess., App., 134 (Tipton), 27 Jan. 1838, 134 (Fulton), 26 Jan. 1838; ibid., 24th Cong., 2d sess., 123 (Robinson), 25 Jan. 1837.

preying on the industrious cultivator." Refusing to compete, they bought the best lands for the minimum price and then held an auction of their own, where they did bid the price up "to ten and twenty dollars" an acre. As Robert Walker (Mississippi) argued, the outcome was clear: "entire States are swept in a single year into the hands of speculators," creating a "monopoly of the public lands by a few individuals."[59]

Democrats identified speculators as monied men, often calling them capitalists. Senator Benton attacked "foreign capitalists, wielding tens of millions of money . . . , pulling up and putting down the price of all property." And Senator Fulton argued that "under the existing system, capitalists, great and small, and borrowers from banks, will send from the old States millions of money annually for land speculations, which they would otherwise invest in some useful business, or in some public improvements, at home." This Democratic emphasis upon finance capital permitted them to distinguish "money speculators," whom they attacked, from "bone and sinew speculators," pioneers who dabbled in land speculation, whom they praised.[60]

Without a legislative remedy, disaster awaited farmers. Senator Walker saw the emergence of a new, more powerful aristocracy. "In vain, shall we have struck down the feudal system, with its . . . relation of lord and vassal, if we . . . continue here this worse than feudal vassalage, this system of American landlords engrossing millions of acres, and regulating the terms of sale." Land distribution will be upended by "landed monopolies . . . by which a few capitalists may engross in a single year the ownership of States, and control the destinies of millions." We will then "create here a landed aristocracy, without the title but more powerful and wealthy than the sinking nobility of England." Then "the occupant will not be the owner of the soil he cultivates, but . . . the tributary of some absentee landlord," creating "a relation of abject dependence, on the one hand, and tyrannical power on the other." Vast class conflict, "a war of capital against labor, of the producer against the nonproducer, of the cultivator against the speculator" will ensue.[61]

Walker's speech illuminates the ways language shaped the meaning of class and class relations. Although himself a wealthy land speculator, Walker had championed the rights of settlers who squatted on the lands he purchased, and considered yeoman farmers a key constituency.[62] The picture he draws of grasping speculators destroying the lives of virtuous producers had

59. *Cong. Globe*, 25th Cong., 2d sess., App., 132 (Buchanan), 27 Jan. 1838; ibid., 140 (C. Clay), 29 Jan. 1838; ibid., 136–37 (Fulton), 29 Jan. 1838; ibid., 24th Cong., 2d sess., App., 168 (Walker), 14 Jan. 1837.

60. *Cong. Globe*, 25th Cong., 2d sess., App., 130 (Benton), 27 Jan. 1838; ibid., 136 (Fulton), 29 Jan. 1838.

61. *Cong. Globe*, 24th Cong., 2d sess., App., 168, 14 Jan. 1837.

62. Shenton, *Robert Walker*, 12–15, 19–20, 24–26.

immediate resonance among farmers fearful of dependency. Struggling to understand land speculation and capitalist agriculture, Walker adapts class words — however contradictory — that might help explain rural life. His protagonists are at the same time "capitalists" and "monopolists," absentee landlords and almost feudal aristocrats. Rather than the United States, the images implicitly refer to a debased Europe containing the worst of feudalism and capitalism.

Horrified at the prospect of violent class conflict, Democrats not only sought legislative protection for squatters but defended their efforts to fend off speculators. They vigorously attacked Whig charges that settlers lawlessly combined to prevent others from getting the best land. Settlers "have, it is true," Senator Lyon related, "formed pre-emption societies" in which members "are to be allowed to purchase each a quarter section . . . , including his improvement, without any competition from members at the public sales." Such "societies," he insisted, "contemplate no resistance, no force, no violence," and any outsider may freely "bid against the settlers."[63]

If Congress passed bills favoring settlers, class conflict would be mitigated. Inexpensive land allowed not only sons of farmers, but even the poor, to own land, thus avoiding dependence. Clement Clay argued that "the poor laboring man, who has no land he can call his own . . . , the lessee, or hireling, of some rich proprietor, or wealthy landlord" hoped to better his condition in the West. He sought "to give every industrious poor farmer of the old States, who was not a freeholder, the opportunity of becoming so, by extending to him the privilege of taking a . . . quarter section of the public land at Government price." That policy would "make every tiller of the soil a freeholder, and thereby render him more independent and useful to his family and as a citizen."[64]

Even though Whigs, in the words of William Merrick (Maryland), agreed with Democrats that the West was "peopled by brave and hardy and patriotic yeomanry," they presumed that settlers pursued self-interest. Where Democrats insisted that labor alone gave land value, Whigs like Henry Clay (Kentucky) asserted that "the fertility of the soil, the natural advantages of the tract, and its capacity to yield a profitable return for the capital and labor expended upon it . . . gave value to land." Whigs wanted settlers to pay market prices. To sell land at the minimum price constituted, Senator Merrick contended, "a large and valuable gratuity," especially when settlers selected the "best and most valuable tracts of land . . . paying for them . . . the paltry sum of one dollar and twenty-five cents per acre, when

63. *Cong. Globe*, 25th Cong., 2d sess., App., 138, 29 Jan. 1838.
64. *Cong. Globe*, 25th Cong., 2d sess., App., 140, 29 Jan. 1838. Other Democratic examples of this "safety-valve" theory can be found in John Tipton, ibid., 134, 27 Jan. 1838; Kirkland, "The West, Paradise of the Poor," 182–90.

in fact the lands . . . are worth, and would command were they fairly brought into the open market, ten or twenty times that sum." To price all unimproved land the same "would be to suppose that there was no difference in value between the most fertile, the best wooded, best watered, and most advantageously located tracts . . . , such as squatters will always seize upon, and those most destitute of these qualities."[65]

Not surprisingly, Whigs viewed land speculators far more positively than Democrats, seeing them as critical to western development. Hugh White (Tennessee) admitted that "large capitalists" sometimes bought the best parcels, forcing settlers to pay high prices. But such "industrious, enterprising, and intelligent" men "enhance" land values and "facilitated migration" by "important improvements, such as railroads, canals, harbors, cities." If "fortunes . . . are made or augmented" by speculation, "it is a just reward of enterprise and public spirit"; if poor men could not afford the best lands, plenty remained on the prairies, and all farmers could take advantage of "a nearer and more extensive market . . . in the new and flourishing cities."[66]

Most speculators, moreover, were not large capitalists but ordinary farmers, seeking security for their families. Thomas Ewing (Ohio) defined speculators as "men who purchase public land either for subsequent sale, or . . . as an investment of money, to rise in value, and become a resource in after life, or an outfit for their children." Such behavior, he added, was a "just and honest mode of acquiring property," one that ill deserved "opprobrious epithets." Democrats, of course, called *these* men settlers, not speculators.[67]

Whigs matched positive Democratic views of settlers with diatribes against men, always labeled squatters, who ventured onto the public domain before surveying. Since laws forbid squatting, they were "trespassers," "*intruders* on the public lands," "law breakers," "idle, profligate," "lawless rabble," "plunderers" who "lawlessly seize upon" public land "and appropriate it to their individual use." Their behavior prevented orderly settlement and led to Indian wars. "By interfering with the Indians," these "disturbers of the public peace," John Davis (Massachusetts) argued, "provoke hostilities, and create the very wars in which they affirm they have suffered."[68]

65. *Cong. Globe*, 25th Cong., 2d sess., App., 130 (Merrick), 27 Jan. 1838; ibid., 139 (Clay), 29 Jan. 1838.

66. *Cong. Globe*, 24th Cong., 2d sess., 148, 2 Feb. 1837. White was a dissenting Democrat who broke with Van Buren. I have counted him in voting analyses as Democratic; Ashworth, *Agrarians and Aristocrats*, 81, identifies him as a Whig in 1841.

67. *Cong. Globe*, 24th Cong., 2d sess., App., 335, 23 Jan. 1837.

68. *Cong. Globe*, 24th Cong., 2d sess., App., 313 (John Davis, Mass.), 9 Feb. 1837, 338 (Thomas Ewing), 23 Jan. 1837, 176 (John King, Georgia); ibid., 25th Cong., 2d sess., App., 134, 139 (Henry Clay), 27 and 29 Jan. 1838, 130 (William Merrick). King was a dissenting Democrat who resigned later in 1837 when he refused to obey instructions.

Squatters often formed societies to monopolize public lands and prevent others from bidding on acreage they held. Each, Thomas Ewing said,
was a "kind of joint stock company or association, who all unite to '*improve*'
and to secure each other in the possession" of land. At auctions they practiced "violence and intimidation . . . to put down competition." Once they
"make themselves masters of the country," John Calhoun insisted, they
"would exact more from the poor and peaceable emigrant for the liberty of
settling" than the minimum price. These men, Senator Davis added, defy
"the title of the United States . . . ; make war on all persons who shall dare to
bid for these lands . . . and by such high-handed violence secure themselves
great tracts of the country." Having gained land through intimidation, they
quickly resell it for a profit, "divide the booty" and move on "like bird of
prey" to another "favored region, to convert it to private property by the
same process of lawless violence."[69]

Squatters, Whigs contended, fraudulently claimed that they occupied
and improved land—as preemption laws required. "If it is prairie, they
merely run a furrow round it," if woods, they chopped down a few trees,
Senator Ewing discovered. Sometimes, according to Senator Davis, they enclosed a thousand acres in this way, and "considered themselves as having
established preemption rights to all inclosed by the furrows." Cultivation is
proved, Ewing added, "by building a little pen of rails, and sowing oats or
turnips or radishes upon ten or twelve square feet of ground."[70]

Whigs claimed that squatters *were* either speculators themselves, their
agents, or their allies. Richard Bayard (Delaware) was certain that many
squatters settled "with a view to speculate on the public domain." And if not,
Henry Clay contended, "they had been hired to claim, and to hold, by speculators, for the purpose of getting these best portions of the public domain
into their hands." According to Senator Ewing, "squatting becomes a regular
profession," with squatters selling their improvements "at an advance of two
or three hundred dollars to large capitalists who have their agents always at
hand."[71]

Squatters and speculators, Whigs suggested, conspired to prevent poor
men from getting land. The poor, "widows and orphans, aged and infirm,"

69. *Cong. Globe*, 24th Cong., 2d sess., App., 339 (Ewing), 23 Jan. 1837; ibid., 25th
Cong., 2d sess., App., 137 (Calhoun), 29 Jan. 1838. Calhoun never belonged fully to
either party; on land issues, he voted with Whigs. Ashworth, *Agrarians and Aristocrats*,
238–50, traces Calhoun's convoluted party history; Ford, "Political Economy of Calhoun," 404–24, is the best recent evocation of his ideology.
70. *Cong. Globe*, 24th Cong., 2d sess., App., 338 (Ewing), 23 Jan. 1837, 315 (Davis),
9 Feb. 1837.
71. *Cong. Globe*, 25th Cong., 2d sess., App., 136 (Bayard), 29 Jan. 1838, 132 (Clay),
27 Jan. 1838; ibid., 24th Cong., 2d sess., App., 339 (Ewing), 23 Jan. 1837.

are as deserving as squatters. "We have many poor, too poor even to journey to your public lands," John Davis lamented. "They are meritorious and they suffer all the privations incident to their unfortunate condition, and I claim for them their share of the public bounty if the public property is to be distributed." Preemption laws were class legislation, favoring squatters. Hugh White would "not consent to pass any law which shall operate against the mass of the community—against the small capitalist, the farmer, the mechanic, *for the special benefit of any class of speculators, however great their power, or democratic their professions."* [72]

Where Democrats evoked a world of socially constrained markets, Whigs presumed that farms were businesses and farmers entrepreneurs, whose success depended upon well-functioning markets and intensive farming. Economic interest not only ruled behavior but, if all had equal access to property, sustained an equitable social order. Attempts to limit markets by guaranteeing economic outcomes created special classes, like squatters, with unfair privileges. Permeated with these class images, Whig language shaped expectations of market-oriented farmers, legitimating vigorous land markets, agricultural reform, and use of agricultural machinery.

Democrats and Whigs used their contrasting appeals to farmers to generate support for economic policies, like tariffs, indirectly tied to agriculture. Democrats lambasted protectionism, insisting that free trade served farmers best. Far from nurturing a large home market, protectionism reduced farmers to poverty and dependence. "Before the construction of the Erie Canal, and the railroads, before the protective system took root," the *Democratic Review* lamented in 1849," the prosperity of New England farmers was great" for they "supplied the old world with produce at fair prices." But as tariffs rose, "farmers lost their markets and become gradually impoverished. Their children, from the position of substantial farmers, supply the labor market." [73]

Whigs like Horace Greeley contended that tariffs protected all producers, including farmers. A vigorous home market, Greeley argued, would increase crop prices. "The ability of the Eastern States to purchase" prairie grain "depends on . . . the market for their manufactures in the Great West." With tariffs, farmers would no longer pay merchants or shippers; urban workers would earn enough to buy grain at good prices, "and the consequent Home Consumption of Agricultural staples would inevitably raise" its price. By creating a home market, tariffs would make an equitable society, "bringing the farmer, the artisan, the manufacturer into immediate contact

72. *Cong. Globe*, 24th Cong., 2d sess., App., 315 (Davis), Feb. 9, 1837; *Cong. Globe*, 24th Cong., 2d sess., 148 (White), 2 Feb. 1837.
73. "Economic Progress," 97–109 (quotes on 103–4); "Free Trade," 291–301.

with each other, and enabling them to interchange their products without the intervention of several non-producers."[74]

Democratic and Whig messages were complex combinations of economic positions, cultural and religious imagery, ethnic and racial biases, personal rivalries and kin loyalties, some of which cut across class appeals parties made. Capitalist and yeoman farmers supported, in various places, each party. Notwithstanding these contradictory influences on partisan support, petty producers tended to vote for Democrats while capitalist farmers tended to vote Whig. In heavily Whig New England towns, poorer farmers (and their kin) from plebeian Protestant churches and younger, less established farmers supported Democrats more often than wealthy farmers (and their kin), especially if they attended the local Congregational Church. Ohio's Democrats garnered backing from farmers in less wealthy, and presumably less market-oriented, counties, distant from transportation; Whigs from wealthy areas near transportation routes. Similarly, nonslaveholders—especially those distant from town—in Prince Edward County, Virginia, and Cumberland County, North Carolina, voted more heavily Democratic than men with commercial or manufacturing interests and farmers who resided near local villages.[75]

The Disruption of Rural Class Languages

Notwithstanding profound regional differences that lurked below the surface, debate on rural issues persisted throughout the 1830s and 1840s, with little regional difference in the class appeals each party made. Only by ignoring the condition of urban workers and growing distinctions between free labor and slavery could either Democrats or Whigs agree among themselves on depictions of rural classes. When the fundamental assumptions of partisan debate—the sanctity of private property, the place of women and blacks in civil society—were challenged, class languages began to disintegrate. As antislavery sentiment grew in the North and southerners defended slavery, the regional meaning of rural ideologies diverged, with northern commentators supporting free labor and southerners insisting that the spread of slavery best protected the yeomanry. By the 1850s the centrifugal force of

74. Greeley, *Hints toward Reforms*, 125–33, 238–47, 252–54 (quotes on 127, 129, 244, 245); see also Basler, ed., *Collected Works of Lincoln*, 1:407–16 ("Fragments of a Tariff Discussion," 1847).

75. Most Jacksonian voting studies deny that wealth or occupation (often called "class") influenced voting, but for reaffirmations of the importance of class, see Wilentz, "On Class and Politics in Jacksonian America," 45–63; Goodman, "Social Basis of New England Politics," 23–58; Ratcliffe, "Politics in Jacksonian Ohio," 6–36; Watson, *Jacksonian Politics and Community Conflict*, chaps. 6–7; Shade, "Society and Politics in Antebellum Virginia's Southside," 163–93.

conflicts over free labor and slavery destroyed the political meanings of rural class language.

Widespread debate over private property and the plight of the urban working class intersected with rural class languages. Proslavery advocates lambasted capitalism for degrading workers and making them dependent; labor leaders drew bleak pictures of the urban landscape and saw the solution in the countryside; communes experimented with collective property as a solution to the decline of virtue; Mormons rejected both democratic church polity and unconstrained private property. These assaults upon private property attacked the basis of rural life itself, its systems of inheritance, land distribution, and household organization.[76]

Appalled by urban suffering during the depression of 1838–44, reformers like radical democrat George Evans and Whig Horace Greeley turned to land reform as a solution to urban poverty. Their ideas pointedly challenged widely shared rural beliefs. If workers could procure land, wages would rise and dependence diminish. Although their *goals* resembled those of Democrats, they went further, seeking land redistribution, abolition of capitalist land markets, and restraints on inheritance. Unable to attain these goals, or the more modest objective of free land to settlers, radicals urged workers to "Vote Yourself a Farm" or joined evangelicals in such quixotic activities as resettling supposedly abandoned children, footloose boys, or urban workers in the west.[77]

George Evans, master polemicist of land reform, meshed Physiocratic and utopian socialist ideas into a searing critique of the American land system. "The use of the LAND is the equal natural right of all," he insisted, "as much necessary to man's free existence as the *light*, the *air*, or the *water*; all are INALIENABLE RIGHTS." But the "land monopoly," "aristocrats," "speculators" raise land prices so high that thousands of oppressed workers are kept pent up in cities. "If the public lands were made free to actual settlers, and all speculations . . . prohibited, . . . the surplus mechanics and other laborers . . . might become independent cultivators of the soil, capable of adding to the national wealth instead of burdening society as paupers or criminals."

Evans sought not only free land for workers but a revolution in rural relations of production. If everyone had a right to *use* land, none could *own* it: since "*property* is anything produced by labor," and "*land* is not the prod-

76. Genovese, *World Slaveholders Made*, 165–94; Pessen, *Most Uncommon Jacksonians*, chaps. 8–11; Horlick, *Country Boys and Merchant Princes*, chap. 2; Arrington, Fox, and May, *Building City of God*, chaps. 2–4; works cited in n. 77 below.

77. Zahler, *Eastern Workingmen and National Land Policy*, chaps. 1–5; Wilentz, *Chants Democratic*, 335–43; Degler, "West as a Solution to Urban Unemployment," 63–84; Lause, "Voting Yourself a Farm in Antebellum Iowa," 169–86; Bellingham, "Waifs and Strays in New York," 130–48.

uct of labor," then "land is *not* property." Since "all men have a natural right
to a portion of the soil," and as many "are deprived of this right," then
"those who now possess it have no equitable title," but "the same right to
their possessions (exclusive of improvements), as a man has to stolen property which he has purchased, not knowing it to be stolen." To ensure that
everyone had land to use, we should "abolish *property in land* in the old
States" and not institute it in the newer ones. The consequences of such a
change were great. Evans sought a government gift of the use of a hundred
acres to every landless citizen. As long as he used the land, he could keep it,
but "if he leaves, any other citizen not possessed of land" would "have the
right to take possession on paying a fair valuation for the improvements."
This system, of course, would abolish "the power of individuals to sell land
and dispose of it by will."[78]

Horace Greeley, influenced by Evans and by Fourierist Socialism, also
espoused land reform as a solution to urban poverty. Unlike Evans, he supported capitalist development and property rights in land. Still, he insisted
that "man has a natural right to such a portion of the earth not already improved . . . as he can cultivate and make fruitful." For that reason he opposed
large Government grants made to an individual "to be held by him and his
heirs for their own use," especially if land was leased to a "tenant class" kept
"poor and subservient." This "Land Monopoly" led to "the frequent lack of
employment, the scanty reward, and the meager subsistence often accorded
to Labor." For as population increased and land prices rose, it became "far
more difficult . . . for a portionless young man to buy a farm," whether an
urban youth or a poor settler.

Greeley's solutions to urban problems — a homestead grant to landless
men, restriction of the quantity of the public domain any man could hold
until all had land, and limitations on (but not abolition of) inheritance of
land — were less radical than Evans's. This program, he contended, would
give *"Equal Opportunities"* to all, would lead to "a continual division and
subdivision of large estates, with a steady increase in the number and proportion of small proprietors, each his own employer and his own laborer,
whereby the mass of landless seekers for work as hirelings or tenants would
be rapidly diminished."[79]

In adapting rural class language for their own use, urban radicals tore it
from its rural context, changing it in ways farmers would find disturbing. If

78. Evans presents his land reform ideas in *The Radical*, especially 1 (1841): 1–10,
19–25. For quotes see 2, 22, 5, 60, 9, 24, 4, 10; extended italics have been eliminated.
79. Greeley, *Hints toward Reforms*, 17–27, 311–18, 322–26 (quotes on 19, 18,
21, 315, 314); R. M. Robbins, "Horace Greeley: Land Reform and Unemployment,"
18–41.

labor gave land value, farmers deserved the profits of the land as well as their improvements. All farmers sought to protect their property and increase its value — small capitalists seeing land as an investment to sell or bequeath, yeomen using it to ensure dynastic control and succession. Outside of these agreements about rural life, radical musings about property helped bring the debate to a breaking point.

As regional tensions accelerated, farmers came to see how different their respective societies had become. Slavery had long divided the nation; during the 1830s, the Senate received antislavery petitions; during the 1840s, abolition societies and small free-soil, antislavery parties appeared in the North and proslavery activity grew in the South. A threatening 1844 letter to Duff Green, a proslavery newspaper editor, from a northern antislavery Democrat suggests the vehemence of sectional disagreement on slavery and freedom and its relation to the language of rural class. The letter writer called Green the "most contemptible of God's creatures," a man who hated northerners and supported government "by a clique who believe that the world was created only for the purpose of raising cotton and the institution of slavery." Northern Democrats "will be gulled no longer," by "such men as you and Mr. Rhett . . . who had the audacity to call the honest and enlightened Yeomanry of New England low peasantry" — a term suggesting dependence and depravity — "in a speech on the floor of the House." [80]

The civil war in Kansas during the mid–1850s illuminates the division of northern and southern yeomen into two antagonistic classes. Superimposed upon squabbles among settlers over land was the momentous choice of slavery and freedom that popular sovereignty legislation gave them. Two groups of settlers, each composed of small, nonslaveholding farmers, seeking the same opportunities as earlier pioneers, reached Kansas, one from the North and the other from the South. The border war that ensued pitted men like unsuccessful abolitionist farmer John Brown against similar proslavery men. They hardly saw each other as virtuous yeomen. "The abolition party," wrote the Missouri-based "Law and Order Party," wished to "flood Kansas with the most fanatical and lawless portion of northern society." Antislavery men called the southerners "pukes," described by the *New York Tribune* as a "border ruffian of the lowest type," poorly dressed, unrefined. [81]

Debates over homestead legislation, designed to give land on the public domain to landless citizens, illuminate the destruction of languages of rural

80. Barnes, *Antislavery Impulse*; Genovese, *World Slaveholders Made*, part 2; Green, "Duff Green, Militant Journalist," 258 (quote).

81. Rawley, *Race and Politics*; Oates, *To Purge This Land with Blood*, part 2; Potter, *Impending Crisis*, chap. 9; Fellman, "Rehearsal for the Civil War," 287–308 (second quote, 292); Paskoff and Wilson, eds., *Cause of South*, 193 (Committee of the Law and Order Party, "The Voice of Kansas — Let the South Respond," [1856], first quote).

class, based on national political parties. Southern Democrats no longer supported free land and settler democracy. Too many northern antislavery settlers would take advantage of free land, leaving white southerners in
minorities in the West. In contrast, former Whigs, now members of the new
Republican party, rallied to the cause of free land for settlers. Free land would
encourage the free labor system they supported, creating thousands of small
capitalist farms.[82]

When Homestead legislation passed Congress in 1860, Democratic President James Buchanan, who had been a strong supporter of preemption and
settlers' rights during the late 1830s, vetoed the bill, complaining that it gave
away land and would be unfair to those who had previously purchased land.
Unlike current law, which protected "the equal rights of all, whether they be
rich or poor," this one created a special privileged class and would "open one
vast field of speculation." Buchanan's rhetoric, despite its democratic imagery, resembled more the older Whig class language than that of Jacksonian
Democrats.[83]

Daniel Hundley's 1860 portrait of southern society reflected growing regional differences in rural class language. Notwithstanding his insistence
that "middle class planters" and the "Southern Yeomen" resembled northern middle class farmers, slaveownership sharply distinguished them from
northern farmers. Yeomen who own slaves "always work side by side with
their own human chattels"; those without slaves strive for ownership, but
remain "almost unanimously pro-slavery in sentiment," fearing competition from free blacks. Though cultural attitudes and class language may have
united rural folk in North and South in the 1830s, northern farmers now
espoused free labor, expressing horror at the ownership of human beings,
practiced or defended by southerners like Hundley.[84]

Meanwhile, a northern language of rural class came to reflect the growth
of capitalist agriculture. In 1859 Abraham Lincoln, speaking to the Wisconsin Agricultural Society, took time from agitating against slavery in the territories to support the small capitalist farmer. Lincoln rejected Physiocratic
ideas about the primacy of agriculture, ignored ideas about natural rights to
land, and reinterpreted the labor theory of value to fit a capitalist age. He
repudiated the "'*mud-sill*' theory" that "nobody labors, unless somebody
else, owning capital, somehow, by the use of capital, induces him to do it"
but presumed that "labor is prior to, and independent of capital," that every-

82. R. M. Robbins, *Our Landed Heritage*, chap. 11; Genovese, *Political Economy of
Slavery*, 35, 162, 243–74.
83. Goodrich, ed., *Government and Economy*, 173–80, reprints the veto message
(quotes on 178, 180).
84. Hundley, *Social Relations in Our Southern States*, 82, 201, 193, 219.

one has an opportunity to acquire capital through labor. Most men "are neither *hirers* nor *hired,*" but work with their families, "for themselves, on their farms, in their houses and in their shops, taking the whole product to themselves, and asking no favors of capital on the one hand, nor hirelings nor slaves on the other."

Lincoln meshed systematic individualism with support for the reforms farm journals had long espoused. Men gained success by their own initiative, their own labor. "The prudent, penniless beginner . . . labors for wages awhile, saves a surplus," and buys "tools or land . . . ; then labors on his own account . . . and at length hires another new beginner to help him." Such a man hardly needed the free use of land as a natural right. Rather, he created his own capital through education, intensive cultivation of small quantities of land, and the use of agricultural machinery. As much as these ideas appealed to improving farmers who attended agricultural fairs, they gave little comfort to traditional pioneers, who moved west to provide land for growing families and sought merely a comfortable sufficiency.[85]

Languages of class, like the class relations in which they are embedded, have a history. Invented in the Revolutionary era, the contested rural class languages we have discussed structured rural social relations, helping to define conflicts between speculators and settlers, farmers and capitalists. But the rapid diffusion of capitalism in the North, along with the growth of southern slavery, outmoded Whig and Democratic theories of rural class. After the Civil War, when farmers involved in the Grange and Farmers' Alliances reinvented the producer ideology of earlier Democrats, they faced monopoly capitalists. To sustain any small-producer security required collective action unimaginable among yeomen or farmers before the Civil War. Ultimately unable to sustain their agenda within a major party, they joined oppositional movements, outside the mainstream of capitalist America.[86]

85. Basler, ed., *Collected Works of Lincoln*, 3:471–82 (quotes on 477–79). For northern free labor ideology, see E. Foner, *Free Soil, Free Labor, Free Men*, chaps. 1–2.

86. For differing viewpoints on the class language of the Alliance, see Goodwyn, *Democratic Promise*, esp. chaps. 3–7; B. Palmer, *Man over Money*, chaps. 1–9; Pollack, *Just Polity*.

Capitalism and the
American Revolution

Chapter 4

Was the American Revolution a Bourgeois Revolution?

IN 1795 MARY HEWSON, who had arrived in Philadelphia from England a decade earlier, wrote her son, then studying in England, about politics. Tutored by Benjamin Franklin as a child when he stayed in her mother's house, she had learned political philosophy well. "You did not expect politics from me I dare say," she wrote, understanding the proper place of women. Her letter shows a strong sense of class prerogative. Decrying both "universal liberty" and "perfect equality" as unattainable, she insists that "when people boast that in their nation all men are free and equal they think only of their own class." Everywhere "some men are set above the people, whether by hereditary succession or election is of little importance while they are in power." All rulers show the same "air of superiority," but in a republic, like the United States, such airs "are more provoking than it would be from one whose station was always above yours. Setting aside . . . slavery," she concluded, "perhaps the government of this country is as good as any, but I question whether the people are happier under it than under any other."[1]

Hewson's letter exposes contradictions inherent in the American Revolution. She challenged popular sovereignty, an idea that legitimated the American republic, but her antislavery sentiments implied equality. She dared to be unfeminine, stating strong political views, but longed for a more hierarchical government. Such examples of the contradictory results of the Revolution could be multiplied, and they defy easy explanation. Influenced by the Revolution's principle of equality, Virginia planters freed thousands of slaves, but at the same time hundreds of other planters signed proslavery petitions, seeking to protect ownership of their human property. The people-out-of-doors demanded their right to determine public policy, but their rul-

1. Hewson to Thomas Hewson, 18 Feb. 1795, Hewson Family Papers, reel 103, American Philosophical Society, Philadelphia. I am indebted to Susan Branson for this reference; her dissertation, "Politics and Gender," greatly illuminates our knowledge of elite women's political interests.

ers insisted, that since elections guaranteed popular sovereignty, all crowd actions be put down as against the people.[2]

These examples suggest, as J. Franklin Jameson argued in 1926, that the Revolution was a momentous social movement that altered "the relations of social classes to each other . . . in the direction of levelling democracy." Jameson painted vivid images of democratic revolution: the reduction of slavery, western settlement, abolition of primogeniture and entail, expansion of the franchise, disestablishment of state churches. Revolutionary historians in the 1950s and 1960s usually dismissed Jameson's work as exaggerated. A democratic revolution that denied full citizenship to all white men, let alone women and blacks, hardly deserves the label democratic. Notwithstanding his critics, Jameson's vision of a social revolution remains powerful and historians have recently returned to it.[3]

This recent scholarship suggests the possibility of a new synthesis broad enough to include the different Revolutions made by different classes of Americans. Such a synthesis should connect structural changes in the colonial economy to the coming of the Revolution; it should explain the process of change through the war, the creation of new governments, and the structural transformation the Revolution encouraged. To focus debate on the social consequences of the Revolution, this essay argues that it was a "bourgeois revolution" that set into motion capitalist development *and* conflicts over capitalist transformation.

At first glance it hardly seems appropriate to label the American Revolution "bourgeois."[4] The idea evokes violent and sudden transformation, the struggle of well-organized classes against one another. Driven by the need of capitalists to expand, a bourgeois revolution occurs after feudalism has decayed, when a new capitalist class rises to challenge and destroy an entrenched feudal aristocracy.[5] This version of bourgeois revolution neither

2. Albert, "Protean Institution," chaps. 4–7; Schmidt and Wilhelm, "Early Proslavery Petitions in Virginia," 133–46; G. S. Wood, *Creation of American Republic*, 403–13.

3. Jameson, *American Revolution Considered as a Social Movement.* Tolles, "American Revolution Considered as a Social Movement: A Re-Evaluation," 1–12; R. E. Brown, *Middle Class Democracy*, chaps. 14–15, critique Jameson. Morris, "'We the People,'" 1–19; G. S. Wood, "Interests and Disinterestedness," 73–77; and essays in A. F. Young, ed., *Beyond the American Revolution*, resurrect Jameson's vision of transformation.

4. In a capitalist society, the bourgeoisie, who own the means of production, live off profits (industrial capitalists), rents, or interest (bankers).

5. For the Revolution as a bourgeois revolt, see Hacker, *Triumph of American Capitalism*, chaps. 12–14; Aptheker, *American Revolution*, chap. 1. Lynd, *Class Conflict, Slavery, and United States Constitution*, 12–14, and Morris, "Class Struggle and the American Revolution," 3–29, are compatible with the idea.

resembles the idea Marx devised nor reflects the ways Marxist historians have modified and enriched the theory.

The origin of bourgeois revolutions, Karl Marx and Frederick Engels argued, can be traced to preexisting class struggles among feudal lords, peasants, and bourgeois burghers. As the bourgeoisie grew in strength, it demanded political power from the ruling feudal aristocracy. These struggles culminated in "three great, decisive battles," the Calvinist Reformation, the English Revolution of the 1640s, and the French Revolution. In each revolt the bourgeoisie won control of the state from feudal lords and overthrew vestiges of feudalism.[6]

Great ambiguity lies at the center of Marx's theory of bourgeois revolution. The term refers to both a long era of social transformation and political events, over a few years, capable of launching or sustaining such a transformation. Understanding the problem, Marxist historians have turned from evoking the bourgeois intent of revolutionaries to highlighting the consequences of revolution. Eric Hobsbawm, writing about the French Revolution, assumes "that in great revolutions . . . the unintended consequences are almost certainly more important than the intended ones." One must understand, Barrington Moore argues, that "those who provide the mass support for a revolution, those who lead it, and those who ultimately profit from it are very different sets of people." Christopher Hill, in a brilliant essay on the English Revolution of 1640, argues that "the phrase in Marxist usage does *not* mean a Revolution made by or consciously willed by the bourgeoisie." Bourgeois revolution "was caused by the breakdown of the old society," the development of capitalist agriculture, for instance, within a still feudal legal framework. He goes on to show how varied and contradictory the goals of revolutionaries were, how radicals attacked any attempt to impose capitalism. Notwithstanding the revolutionaries' goals, the "*outcome*" of the Revolution, Hill argues, "was the establishment of conditions far more favorable to the development of capitalism than those which prevailed before 1640." Popular democracy was defeated, private property enshrined in legal doctrine, remaining peasants dispossessed, the English bourgeoisie sustained in power. Bourgeois revolutions end, Eric Hobsbawm concludes, in the creation of a liberal state, usually by constitutional means, that protects private property.[7]

---

6. Marx and Engels fullest statements about bourgeois revolutions come in polemical rather than theoretical works. Marx and Engels, *Manifesto of the Communist Party*, 36–38 (quotes); K. Marx, *Eighteenth Brumaire*, 97–100; Engels, *Socialism*, 388–93, 400–402.

7. Hobsbawm, "Revolution in the Theory of Karl Marx," 557–70, "Revolution," 20–30, and "The Making of a 'Bourgeois Revolution,'" 7–9 (quote). C. Hill, "A Bour-

Bourgeois revolutions and the growth of capitalism are intricately linked in Marxist theory. The struggle to establish capitalism took centuries to complete and at any point could have been reversed. Separate strands of capitalism (like banks) could coexist and even be subsumed in noncapitalist social formations. Bourgeois revolutions changed all this. Revolutionaries linked individual liberty to property and the states they created guaranteed private property and the hegemony of the market, thereby making capitalist development irreversible.[8]

The Marxist concept of bourgeois revolution turns attention from causes to consequences, often unintended, of the American Revolution. This chapter will explore the contours of an American bourgeois Revolution. We will examine the impact of the Revolution on economic change and the class conflicts they spawned; consider the intricate interplay among colonial policy, revolution, Constitution making, and capitalist development; analyze the individualistic presumptions behind revolutionary ideology; and finally turn to the class conflicts of the Revolutionary era, suggesting ways common people shaped revolutionary ideology to their own, often anticapitalist ends.

The evidence presented below hardly proves that the American Revolution should be counted as a bourgeois revolution. Other labels — democratic revolution, liberal revolution, even anticapitalist revolution — also fit some of the evidence.[9] But examining the Revolution as a bourgeois revolution does illuminate some of the contradictions of American social development with which we began. My purpose is not to close an argument but to open one, to incite historians to debate, develop, and test alternative models of the impact of the Revolution on economic development and social change.

The Revolution and the Diffusion of Capitalist Economic Relations

Although the origins of American capitalism can be traced to the earliest period of settlement, the Revolution and the adoption of the Constitution

---

geois Revolution?" 109–39, quotes 110–11; B. Moore, *Social Origins of Dictatorship and Democracy*, chap. 7 (quote 417); Countryman and Deans, "Independence and Revolution in the Americas," 144–71. For critiques, see Tibebu, "Feudalism, Absolutism, and Bourgeois Revolution," 97–102, and Duchesne, "French Revolution as a Bourgeois Revolution," 297–304.

8. A fully articulated argument about capitalism and the bourgeoisie within the Atlantic world can be found in Fox-Genovese and Genovese, *Fruits of Merchant Capital*, prologue, chaps. 7–8, 10–11, and for the American case, see F. McDonald, "Constitution and Hamiltonian Capitalism," chap. 3, esp. 50. The debate over rural capitalism is discussed in chap. 2 above.

9. For these alternative visions, see Jameson, *American Revolution Considered as a Social Movement*; Appleby, *Capitalism and a New Social Order*; Merrill, "Anticapitalist Origins of the United States," 465–97.

were key events in the diffusion of capitalism throughout America. Seeking to invest accumulated capital, English capitalists had financed colonial settlement. The mercantilist system they created constrained colonial economic development, even when colonists evaded its provisions. The colonial relationship was one of dependence: colonial merchants dealt more often with London merchants than with each other; colonial economic policies had to be ratified in London; and English authorities might prohibit the printing of paper money or collect unpopular taxes. London merchants controlled the trade that was crucial to colonial growth, mandating the export of staples directly to England and sending inexpensive imported manufactured goods in return. Despite the potential for capitalist development in the colonies, the colonial relationship precluded the full emergence of capitalism.[10]

Colonial opportunities also constrained capitalist development. Even though nearly all families participated in the market on occasion, colonial migrants had often moved to escape wage labor and dispossession common in England. Many whites came as indentured laborers, but opportunities for independent landownership were high. Northern landowning farmers achieved communal self-sufficiency in food, avoided wage labor, and remained mostly outside a money economy. But they sent small surpluses to market, using the money they earned to pay taxes, buy consumer goods, and sustain local exchange. Southern staple producers participated vigorously in markets, sustaining a large class of merchant capitalists, but the slave society they created was the opposite of the system of free labor, freely contracted, at the heart of capitalist economic relations.[11]

Subsequently, late colonial economic development involved northern colonists more intensively in international commodity markets than ever before. When warfare and poor crops reduced European grain supplies, Pennsylvania and Shenandoah Valley farmers seized opportunities to export grain there. As the wheat trade grew, a wealthy indigenous merchant class emerged. The home market grew as well. Although towns like New York and Philadelphia were tiny, they had grown sufficiently large to create demand for butter, cheese, vegetables, and fruit from the surrounding countryside, thereby encouraging a new form of market-surplus farming.[12]

Tenancy and wage labor grew from these structural economic changes. As population rose and land supplies diminished in settled areas during the 1760s and 1770s, short-term tenancy grew in regions like the Hudson River

10. McCusker and Menard, *Economy of British America*, chaps. 2, 4, 16, and Lee and Passell, *New Economic View of American History*, chap. 2, summarize a vast literature.

11. K. Marx, *Capital*, 1: chap. 33; chap. 2 above.

12. McCusker and Menard, *Economy of British America*, chaps. 9, 11, 13.

Valley, where tenancy was already common, and in places tied to growing urban markets like southeastern Pennsylvania. Just as the rise of cottagers in the Delaware valley documents the beginnings of extensive agricultural wage labor, the growth of mercantile dockwork and journeyman labor (which developed as urban slave imports and indentured servitude declined) shows the growth of urban wage labor.[13]

Such growth of merchant capital, tenancy, and wage labor did not necessitate the development of capitalism. The "sole function" of merchant capital, common in feudal societies, "is to mediate the exchange of commodities" among a network of merchants. Production remains in the hands of independent producers. Although merchant capitalists can throw up pockets of wage labor (operating putting-out systems, for instance), generating new relations of production, commerce remained the foremost function of their capital. In contrast, in capitalist economies, "commercial capital rather appears simply as capital in a *particular* function." Other capitalists live on interest (bankers) or expropriate surplus value from wage workers (shop owners, industrialists).[14]

A slow, imperceptible transformation of merchant capitalists — who had blended into the surrounding society, serving farmers and artisans — into a class of capitalists probably began in the late colonial era. In Philadelphia, for instance, Quakers saw the glaring contradiction between slavery and freedom and insisted in the 1770s that their members free their slaves. Such men, often merchants, then turned to wage labor, replacing traditional hierarchies with a cash nexus. These few isolated capitalists, however, hardly constituted a capitalist class.[15]

One must not exaggerate these changes. Northern merchants, except those in the largest towns, were embedded in the mutual obligations of the local exchange system, granted long-term "book debt," and were limited by communal norms in charging high rates of implicit interest. At least two-thirds of colonial white men owned their own farms or shops. Not only did

13. Simler, "Tenancy in Colonial Pennsylvania," 542–69; Countryman, *People in Revolution,* 13–25; Soderlund, *Quakers and Slavery*; B. G. Smith, *Lower Sort,* chap. 3; Kulikoff, "Progress of Inequality," 375–414; Nash, *Race, Class, and Politics,* chap. 4. For a dissenting view, see Grubb, "Immigrant Servant Labor," 253–56.

14. K. Marx, *Capital,* 3: chap. 20 (quotes on 442, 444); Fox-Genovese and Genovese, *Fruits of Merchant Capital,* prologue; Dobb, *Studies in the Development of Capitalism,* chaps. 3–4.

15. For the transformation of merchant capital into capital, see Fox-Genovese and Genovese, *Fruits of Merchant Capital,* chaps. 1, 7. Soderlund, *Quakers and Slavery,* chaps. 4–6; Nash and Soderlund, *Freedom by Degrees,* chaps. 1–2; and Doerflinger, *A Vigorous Spirit of Enterprise,* chaps. 2, 7–8, illustrate the beginnings of this transformation, without using the language; Countryman, "Uses of Capital in Revolutionary America," 3–28, illuminates the contradictions and ambiguities inherent in the process.

slaves and servants perform a substantial part of manual labor in every colony, but most northern blacks remained in bondage and laborers were still concentrated in mercantile pursuits. Colonial gentlemen hardly saw themselves as capitalists, but demanded deference from their social inferiors. As tenancy increased, some landlords attempted to mask capitalist ground rent in traditional, almost feudal language.[16]

The Revolution accelerated this incipient capitalism, throwing up in its wake a new class of financial and industrial capitalists. The diffusion of commodity markets continued apace, encouraged by the new states and a federal Constitution that mandated a continental common market and protected private property. Taking the egalitarian promises of the Revolution seriously, masters manumitted slaves and reduced reliance on indentured labor, thereby accelerating the growth of free wage labor. Although such developments indicated the direction of change, the Revolution itself did not make capitalism dominant but set into motion substantial resistance from yeoman farmers and urban craftsmen.[17]

Merchants were key actors in this transformation. Conservative men, they desired nothing more than to continue to invest money in old ways — in land companies, exporting agricultural goods, importing consumer goods. Their conservative behavior belied their belief in an expansive, continental America that grew out of their heavy land speculation. When English policy turned against them in the 1760s and 1770s, temporarily ending their dreams of expansion and wealth, they led a colonial war for independence, with momentous consequences for capitalist development.[18]

The Revolution removed legal constraints on colonial industry that England had imposed to provide a market for her manufactured goods. Massive state investments in internal improvements, so common by the early nineteenth century, were inconceivable as long as colonials attached themselves more to London than to neighboring colonies. The Revolutionary victory cleared legal hurdles to the land settlement, home manufacturing, and industrialization. Moreover, warfare (the Revolution and later wars in Europe) cut off textiles imports, especially encouraging home manufacture of cloth, a new putting-out industry, and eventually textile mills. Neither warfare nor

16. Nobles, "Rise of Merchants," 5–12; Berthoff and Murrin, "Feudalism, Communalism and Yeoman Freeholder," 256–88; Galenson, *White Servitude*, chap. 7; Greene and Harrington, eds., *American Population before Federal Census of 1790*, 104–5, 110–11, 119–20; Berlin, *Slaves without Masters*, 46–47; Smith, *Lower Sort*, chap. 3, 213–23; Nash and Soderlund, *Freedom by Degrees*, chaps. 1–2; Murrin, "Myths of Colonial Democracy," 53–69; Kulikoff, *Tobacco and Slaves*, chap. 7.

17. Though using very different terms, this argument is compatible with Cochran, "Business Revolution," 1449–66, esp. 1455–61.

18. Schlesinger, *Colonial Merchants and the American Revolution*; Egnal, *A Mighty Empire*; Countryman, "Uses of Capital in Revolutionary America," 3–28.

the removal of legal constraints immediately triggered industrialization, but they did make manufacturing easier once economic resources were in place.[19]

Once the break with England had freed capital to develop, conflicts between would-be capitalists and indebted farmers escalated. Although all property holders, including small farmers, wanted to enjoy secure property, conflicts surrounded its use, "between those whose property was a means of livelihood and those whose property was a means of accumulation." Nationalists in the 1780s longed for a strong government that could sustain a national debt and a sound currency. At the Philadelphia Constitutional Convention, the ruling classes — merchants, lawyers, great planters — tried to end the instability that these conflicts brought by planning a new government. Few delegates, except Alexander Hamilton, sought to create a government that would encourage capital formation. But most delegates (especially northern merchants) did seek to establish a national government that would protect creditors from depreciated paper money and merchants and artisans from internal tariffs while protecting infant industries from foreign competition and improving the transportation system.[20]

Whatever the motivations of the founders, the document they produced created a federal state system, clearing the way for the growth of a strong capitalist economy. Article 1, sections 9 and 10 are the key clauses. In section 9, the founders prohibited internal duties between the states, ending trade barriers common in the 1780s. Section 10 resolved creditor-debtor conflicts of the 1780s in favor of creditors, forbidding states from coining money, printing paper money, and passing laws that impaired contract obligations. Through these clauses, the Constitution facilitated commerce and triggered an explosion of banking, and the state governments it created financed internal improvements, accelerating capital formation. Such activities were essential elements in the making of both the capitalist and proletarian classes. Notwithstanding the protection these clauses afforded to property, the Constitution hardly resolved the issue of capitalist development, but set the terms of political conflict over corporations, contracts, and developmental uses of property.[21]

19. McCusker and Menard, *Economy of British America*, chaps. 13, 15; Henretta, "War for Independence and American Economic Development," 45–87.

20. F. McDonald, "Constitution and Hamiltonian Capitalism," 49–71; J. R. Nelson, *Liberty and Property*, chap. 1 (quote on 13); Ferguson, "Nationalists of 1781–1783," 241–61; Parenti, "Constitution as an Elitist Document," 41–47; Walton and Shepherd, *Economic Rise of Early America*, 186–89, 210–11; McGuire, "Constitution Making," 482–522; McGuire and Ohsfeldt, "Economic Model of Voting Behavior at the Constitutional Convention," 79–112. Unlike Beard, *Economic Interpretation*, chap. 5, the argument here concerns the uses of property and capital and not the kind of capital owned.

21. F. McDonald, "Constitution and Hamiltonian Capitalism," 57–71; Horwitz, *Transformation of American Law*, chaps. 1–4.

By eliminating trade barriers and imposing federal mediation in economic disputes between states, the Constitution created a national common market. Such regulation did not immediately lead to an explosion of interregional trade. Even in the 1850s, most farmers and artisans still traded with neighbors or sent their goods to other places within the region. Goods, however, *could* move freely. Once access to the Mississippi River had been secured, frontier farmers in the Ohio valley floated crops to New Orleans, where they entered interregional or international trade. As soon as the Erie Canal (and other canals) opened in the 1820s and 1830s, a vigorous two-way trade of grain and manufactured goods developed between the West and the East. The common market encouraged the formation of a national class of merchants, making them into a cohesive political group capable of influencing state and national economic policy.[22]

With a national common market secured, the need to bind the country together with internal improvements became pressing. Federalists and Jeffersonians alike knew that the state had a role in building roads and canals but disagreed on who—the federal government, the states, or private businessmen—should build, finance, and operate them. Jefferson approved the development of a national road system but had great reservations about the constitutionality of federal financing. The federal government, immobilized by constitutional divisions and local contests for federal money, did not finance construction of internal improvements. But states chartered and financed roads and canals; after 1815 when major canal building began, states promised nearly three-quarters of the capital, through stock subscriptions and direct or guaranteed loans.[23]

Government-sponsored or -financed internal improvements, combined with private initiatives, cut the time and cost of communication and commerce. Between 1790 and 1820, mail was delivered over an ever-growing network of post roads; the cost of interurban travel declined by half; and the importance of domestic trade grew. The construction of canals during the 1820s and 1830s accelerated this process, binding the country ever closer together. The development of this economic infrastructure provided markets for the credit and commodities produced by the growing class of financial and early industrial capitalists.[24]

Private banks developed as substitutes for paper money states had printed. There were no organized private incorporated banks in pre-

22. North, *Economic Growth of the United States*; Lindstrom, *Economic Development in the Philadelphia Region*.
23. Goodrich, *Government Promotion of American Canals and Railroads*, chaps. 2–4; J. L. Larson, ' "Bind the Republic Together,' " 363–87; Harrison, "*Sic et Non:* Jefferson and Internal Improvements," 335–50; Segal, "Cycles of Canal Construction," 183–89, 208–15; Cranmer, "Canal Investment, 1815–1860," 553–60.
24. See Pred's impressive *Urban Growth and the Circulation of Information*.

Revolutionary America. Despite English prohibitions, colonies often emitted paper money (sometimes using the value of land as collateral). These land banks had functioned in an egalitarian way, sustaining small producers on their land by providing mortgages to them, rather than serving as a vehicle for capitalist development. The Pennsylvania land bank, for instance, distributed paper money between 1724 and 1756 by granting mortgages to holders of real estate. No one could receive more than £100, and two-thirds of the recipients were yeomen who farmed fifty to two hundred acres. They received average loans of £65 to expand farm operations, buy livestock, or purchase land for sons. Similarly, small farmers constituted the overwhelming majority of subscribers in frontier Worcester County to the Massachusetts Land Bank in 1739. Artisans and a scattering of inland merchants subscribed to the Land Bank in Boston.[25]

Bankers, who played a key role in nineteenth-century economic development, owed their influence and even their existence to the Revolution. The hyperinflation of the Revolutionary era soured creditors on state-printed paper money. As a result, three banks formed in port towns in the 1780s. Fearing the loss of the value of loans repaid in depreciated paper money, and the negative impact of differing state monetary policies on interstate commerce, delegates to the Constitutional Convention forbid states to emit paper money. Farmers, artisans, and merchants still needed far more money than the small supplies of specie could provide. The federal government did not print money, but until state emissions were retired, some paper money remained in circulation. Eventually the Bank of the United States and new state-chartered banks printed bank notes that could be used for currency and provided loans to merchants and capitalists bent on development. By 1798 there were 22 chartered banks in the United States, almost all in northern cities. Economic expansion and warfare in the years when Republicans ruled encouraged an explosion of bank formation: the number of chartered state banks grew from 29 in 1800 to 89 in 1811 and reached 208 in 1815.[26]

Banks served capitalists but ignored farmers who had been aided by colonial land banks. In 1786 John Witherspoon attacked Philadelphia's Bank of North America, claiming that "banking companies give credit only so as to be serviceable to merchants, and those immediately connected with them, but do not extend it to husbandmen, or those who improve the soil, by tak-

---

25. K. Marx, *Capital*, 3: chap. 36; Schweitzer, *Custom and Contract*, chaps. 4–5; Brooke, *Heart of the Commonwealth*, 55–65; Remer, "Old Lights and New Money," 570–71.

26. Schweitzer, "Currency and the Constitution," 311–22; Cochran, *Frontiers of Change*, 20–21, 28–35; Nettels, *Emergence of a National Economy*, 75–88, 295–301; U.S. Bureau of Census, *Historical Statistics of the United States*, 2:1018.

ing mortgages for a considerable time."[27] Other Antifederalists agreed, seeing banks as benefiting only the wealthy. Studies of banking sustain these fears; merchants and retailers held four-fifths of the active accounts in the Bank of North America. Bankers, often former merchants or merchant-farmers, became key figures in capitalist development. They helped finance early textile mills and canals; frequently lent money to merchants and manufacturers; but less often granted mortgages to farmers. They sometimes favored their own directors, further limiting their utility to farmers and mechanics. The only advantage most men received from banks was use of bank notes that circulated as currency.[28]

Notwithstanding small budgets, tiny bureaucracies, and great hostility among some policymakers to capitalism, the constitutional system that divided power between a national government and strong states provided potent encouragement for capitalism. State and federal governments together regulated markets, allowing capital to grow: they financed internal improvements, encouraged banking and interregional trade, protected inventions through patent registration, sustained colonization of Indian lands, and rewrote the common law to protect developmental uses of property.[29] These state functions, inconceivable when the colonies were still tied to the British mercantile system, grew mightily in the new nation, helping to create a capitalist society in its wake.

The changes transformed productive relations, impelling the decline of traditional systems of unfree and craft labor and the growth of classes of wage laborers and capitalists. During the mid-eighteenth century, workers could be divided into five groups: farm families; farm hands; master craftsmen, journeymen, and apprentices; indentured servants; and slaves. A traditional hierarchy permeated the workplace: yeomen ran patriarchal households, making all economic decisions; farm hands and journeymen received a traditional, set wage; apprentices and journeymen hoped to become master craftsmen, once they had mastered their trade; servants and especially slaves understood (and often resisted) the power of their masters.

27. Schweitzer, "Currency and the Constitution," 317; Riesman, "Money, Credit, and Federalist Political Economy," 128–61; Klubes, "First Federal Congress and the First National Bank," 22–24.
28. Doerflinger, *Vigorous Spirit of Enterprise*, 296–310; Davis and Payne, "From Benevolence to Business," 386–406; H. R. Stevens, "Bank Enterprisers in a Western Town," 139–56; Olmstead, "New York Mutual Savings Bank Portfolio Management," 815–34, and "Investment Constraints and New York Mutual Savings Bank," 811–40; D. R. Adams, "Bank of Stephen Girard," 841–68; Beveridge, "Local Lending Practice," 393–403; Lamoreaux, "Banks, Kinship, and Economic Development," 647–68.
29. For the small size of government, see J. S. Young, *Washington Community*, chap. 1; for patents, see Sokoloff, "Inventive Activity in Early Industrial America," 813–50.

Relations between social classes depended upon a worker's place in a social hierarchy, not upon a market nexus. Struggles occurred when subservient classes saw traditional rights—the appropriate journeyman's wage, the slave's Sunday holiday—denied by the master.[30]

This class system began to dissolve under the impact of the Revolution. A new urban capitalist class, encouraged by the political economy of the new nation, began to form in the 1780s and 1790s. Drawn from wealthier merchants, land speculators, lawyers, machine makers, master craftsmen, and gentleman farmers, these bankers and early manufacturers (millers, builders, textile mill owners) knew one another, sometimes banding together in societies to encourage manufacturing. Immigrants, especially textile manufacturers and machine makers, melded into this class, borrowing from bankers and merchants. The manufacturers formed small family partnerships or (in New England) devised industrial corporations. By their activities, they almost imperceptibly turned themselves into capitalists. The class differed from colonial merchants: it was more national, practiced more innovative financing, searched for more efficient production techniques, and employed more wage labor.[31]

At the same time as a capitalist class was emerging, a proletariat grew rapidly in the Northeast, especially in the region's cities. Long before large factories opened, urban workers suffered a debasement of their skills, the atrophy of the apprenticeship system, and the creation of sweatshops. Because they worked on low profit margins, early manufacturers tried to organize the workplace rationally, dividing labor more minutely and paying market rather than traditional wages, if they were lower. Despite repeated resistance from working men and women, they usually succeeded in imposing their will. Similar developments occurred in the rural hinterlands of the cities. Requiring seasonal labor for planting and harvest but few hired hands, commercial farmers paid workers high daily wages but released them when the harvest was complete. Agricultural laborers unable to find winter work subsisted in rural poorhouses, increasingly built in the generation after the Revolution.[32]

30. For contrasting surveys of colonial labor systems, see Rediker, "Good Hands, Stout Hearts, and Fast Feet," 123–44, and Dunn, "Servants and Slaves," 157–94.

31. There has been little systematic work on the pre–1830 development of the American capitalist class, but see Doerflinger, *A Vigorous Spirit of Enterprise*, chaps. 2, 7–8; East, *Business Enterprise in the Revolutionary Era*, chaps. 13–14; Countryman, "Uses of Capital in Revolutionary America," 3–28; Krooss, "Financial Institutions," 115–20; Jeremy, *Transatlantic Industrial Revolution*, chaps. 12–15, 83–84, 148–59; Scranton, *Proprietary Capitalism*, chaps. 1–4; Shelton, *Mills of Manayunk*, 1–11, 27–34; Nobles, "Rise of Merchants," 12–19.

32. Wilentz, *Chants Democratic*; Stansell, *City of Women*; Clemens and Simler, "Rural Labor and the Farm Household," 106–43; Rothenberg, "Emergence of Free La-

The emancipation of northern slaves was a key part of the process of proletarianization. Whig revolutionaries feared being reduced by repressive British legislation to the abject dependence of African slaves. Yet real chattel slavery existed everywhere, exposing the Whigs to charges of deceitfulness. Even though southerners condemned British attempts to free slaves of rebel masters and slave attempts to gain their freedom in a war for liberty, northern legislators and judges, responding to this contradiction of slavery and freedom, the implicit promise of the Declaration of Independence, and pressure from patriotic slaves, emancipated their slaves in the decades after the Revolution. By the end of the Revolution, the New England states (where slavery was least entrenched) had emancipated their slaves and Pennsylvania (where far more lived) had passed a gradual emancipation bill, freeing newly born slaves when they reached adulthood. By 1800 only one of every fourteen blacks in New England and one of every ten in Pennsylvania were still enslaved. Emancipation proceeded more slowly in New York and New Jersey: gradual emancipation laws were passed between 1799 and 1804, but in 1820 nearly two-fifths of New Jersey's black people and a quarter of those in New York were still in bondage.[33]

Rural freed people, unwelcome in the countryside, often moved to Philadelphia or New York. Lacking urban skills and facing discrimination, at first most of them lived in white households (usually of merchants, professionals, or master craftsmen), and nearly all worked for wages, forming a substantial part of the new urban proletariat, replacing both slaves and indentured servants. Eventually, they formed independent households. While most continued to be manual laborers, some gained craft skills and joined the ranks of journeymen, ultimately suffering the same debasement of skills as white mechanics.[34]

The growth of northern capitalism was linked to the Revolution. Granted, some developments—like the growth of wage labor—had already begun; others—like canal construction—reached a peak a half century after the war ended. None were consciously willed by any group, nor did capitalist

---

bor Markets," 537–66; Cray, *Paupers and Poor Relief,* chap. 5; Earle and Hoffman, "Foundation of the Modern Economy," 1055–85.

33. For southern fears and realities see Olwell, "'Domestick Enemies,'" 21–48; Quarles, *Negro in the American Revolution,* chap. 2. The standard work is Zilversmit, *First Emancipation,* but see also Grimsted, "Anglo-American Racism," 394–444, and Nash and Soderlund, *Freedom by Degrees,* chaps. 3–5, which sees substantial resistance even to gradual emancipation in Pennsylvania. Okoye, "Chattel Slavery as the Nightmare of the American Revolutionaries," 3–28, denies the antislavery tendencies of Revolutionaries while documenting their fears of enslavement.

34. Nash, *Race, Class, and Politics,* chap. 11, and *Forging Freedom;* White, *Somewhat More Independent,* chaps. 2, 6; Salinger, *To Serve Well and Faithfully,* chap. 7, epilogue.

or proletarian class consciousness develop speedily. But all grew out of structural changes that independence and the constitutional system of nation and states permitted. Before the Revolution, for instance, only radical groups like Quakers manumitted slaves, but the contagion of freedom the war provoked ended northern slavery. The end of northern slavery, in turn, led to the growth of urban free labor, a long-term economic process. Similarly, the beginnings of American banking were triggered by the Revolution, but the building of canals occurred as a result of independent economic policies, in part predicated upon bank loans.

Capitalist development was both incomplete and highly selective. The Northeast and Middle Atlantic states led the way, emancipating their slaves, organizing banks, building canals, opening factories. Only there did the transformation of merchants into capitalists, and journeymen and ex-slaves into proletarians, proceed very far. The South was the main exception to the growth of capitalism. Notwithstanding thousands of manumissions and the growth of a class of free Blacks in the upper South, slavery grew explosively in the new nation. The few southern capitalists and workers remained embedded in an anticapitalist slave society. Southern delegates at the Constitutional Convention demanded, and received, protection for slavery, not only in the fugitive slave clause but in apportionment of taxes and congressional representatives. Yet the slave South was part of a nation where northern capital increasingly predominated in the economy and slaveowners had to accommodate to it. As the contradictions between expanding northern capitalism and vibrant southern slavery gradually became apparent, southerners rose to defend their threatened way of life, slowly severing the slave South from the free labor North.[35]

Revolutionary Ideology and Possessive Individualism

The bourgeoisie justified their revolution, according to Engels, by referring to "equality based on Nature and the inalienable rights of man." They made private property into "one of the essential rights of man" and turned equality into "bourgeois equality before the law." For yeomen, peasants, and artisans equality became "the freedom to sell their small property, crushed under the overmastering competition of the large capitalists and landlords." So too ideals of equality, grounded in systematic individualism, informed American revolutionary ideology. This ideology legitimated not only private

35. Berlin, *Slaves without Masters*, chaps. 1–4; Finkleman, "Slavery and the Constitutional Convention," 188–225; Lynd, *Class Conflict, Slavery, and the Constitution*, chap. 8; Genovese; *World Slaveholders Made*, part 2.

property but political action by smallholding citizens to protect their interests, thereby structuring political conflict for a century or more.[36]

Systematic individualism rejects any attempt to group people on the basis of hierarchy or corporate membership, whether of community or class, identifying each citizen as "proprietor of his own person and capacities," free "from dependence upon the wills of others." However, the individual does not live in an unattached autarky but combines with other individuals by freely made contracts. Within the state, the individual is the unit of sovereignty, the measure of citizenship. Only those free men, defined as individuals, can legitimately participate in politics and thus protect their property; groups, classes, and interests as such are not represented. In such a society, conflict over which individuals might be citizens, and therefore have full political rights, was inevitable. Notwithstanding the wide range of views Americans held in the new nation about family and community, often antagonistic to systematic individualism, all subscribed to it in the political realm.[37]

Bourgeois individualism breaks down the contradiction of community and individual common in hierarchical, noncapitalist economies. Since each individual has equal legal rights, each can join with others to form a voluntary community, choosing to abide by its strictures. Those who make voluntary covenants lose neither their individuality nor their freedom but at least theoretically can choose to withdraw at any time. Established churches thereby become voluntary denominations; industrialists reconstitute paternal authority over youthful workers in textile mills; citizens join communitarian societies.[38]

Both capitalism and the English Revolutions of 1640 and 1688 were grounded in individualist presumptions. Although English immigrants brought individualism to the colonies, the complexity of cultural transmission belies any simple diffusion of the idea. Ideals of individual conscience

36. Engels, *Socialism*, 388–93, 400–402; the best analyses of the uses of individualism by subservient groups is Fox-Genovese, *Feminism without Illusions*.

37. Fox-Genovese, *Feminism without Illusions*, 7–8, 38, 42–43, 58–60, 62, 121–30; C. B. MacPherson, *Political Theory of Possessive Individualism*, esp. 3 (quote); Appleby, *Economic Thought and Ideology*. Curry and Goodhart, "Individualism in Trans-National Context," 2–9, lists eleven discrete definitions of the term. See Masur, "'Age of the First Person,'" 189–208, and Shalope, "Individualism in the Early Republic," 66–86, for assertions of the hegemony of individualism in the political realm.

38. Zuckerman, "Fabrication of Identity," 183–214, brilliantly evokes the contradiction between individual identity (not systematic individualism) and community in noncapitalist societies; the classic account on voluntarism in capitalist society is Tocqueville, *Democracy in America*, 2:104–18, but see Arieli, *Individualism and Nationalism*, 83–84.

and of forced community coexisted in early New England; freedom and bondage appeared everywhere, without raising moral issues. Studded with ambiguities, individualism in the eighteenth-century colonies competed with and was embedded in contradictory political suppositions, such as classical republicanism (sometimes democratic, more often anticommercial) and evangelicalism (individualistic and collectivist at the same time). One could hold classical republican, liberal, Calvinist, and evangelical views at the same time and see no contradiction among them.[39]

On the eve of the Revolution, individualism was still embedded in religious and ideological systems antithetical to it. Calvinism mandated that each individual seek personal salvation. But New England Puritans considered individuals neither superior nor prior to society, and identified individuation with barbarism. Puritan ideas of "ordered liberty" imposed communal constraints on behavior and gave freedom only to those who practiced the true faith. New England emigrants, however, also brought radical ideas with them, and their descendants remembered them, placing memories of Oliver Cromwell into a context at once evangelical and egalitarian. Virginia gentlemen justified their rule on the traditional grounds of status, family, and wealth, not on their achievements in the marketplace. They devised an ideology that guaranteed individual rights to propertied men but at the same time justified their absolute rule over slaves. Individualism attained greater importance among groups like middle-colony Quakers, with their distrust of clergy, "modern" childrearing techniques, and insistence upon the infusion of spirit as the basis for religion, but even here it never gained political hegemony.[40]

When the Revolution began, gentlemen attacked Parliament for refusing to fulfill its obligations to protect colonists' rights as Englishmen. But as revolutionary ideology developed, political words took on new meanings.

39. C. B. MacPherson, *Possessive Individualism*; Appleby, *Economic Thought and Ideology*; C. Hill, *World Turned Upside Down*, chaps. 4, 6–7, 10; Higonnet, *Sister Republics*, chap. 1; Calhoon, "Religion and Individualism," 44–65. Banning, "Jeffersonian Ideology Revisited," 3–19; Appleby, "Republicanism in Old and New Contexts," 20–34; and Kramnick, *Republicanism and Bourgeois Radicalism*, chap. 8, debate the relative importance of classical republicanism and liberalism. Kloppenberg, "Virtues of Liberalism," 9–33, synthesizes strands of political philosophy on a new basis, compatible with the one here.

40. For Puritans, see Zuckerman, "Fabrication of Identity," 183–214; E. Johnson, "Individualism and Puritan Imagination," 230–37; Calhoon, "Religion and Individualism," 46–51; Lockridge, *New England Town*. The diffusion of English radicalism and individualism is discussed in A. F. Young, "English Plebeian Culture," chap. 11; Appleby, "Radical *Double-Entendre*," 275–83; Fischer, *Albion's Seed*, 199–205, 410–18, 595–603, 777–82, argues that colonists brought over conflicting ideas of liberty from their British regions of origin; the term *ordered liberty* is his. For Quakers see Levy, *Quakers and the American Family*, chaps. 3–4, 7.

Hardly an explicit part of revolutionary ideology, individualism was embedded in the words—*inalienable rights, popular sovereignty, liberty, democracy, republicanism*—revolutionaries used. To protect their class, gentlemen made property into an inalienable natural right of individual citizens. Liberty became a natural right, attributed to individuals, not to communities or classes. For the most radical revolutionaries, democracy turned from the consensual democracy of some New England town meetings to the individual voter's right to elect officeholders and instruct them on public policy.[41]

Gentlemen had no desire to extend rights to poor white men excluded from politics, not to mention the white women and slaves who constituted a majority of adults in the colonies. But the individualist presumptions of their ideology transformed social rights inherent in traditional natural law into private rights potentially available to all adults. Rejecting all communal authority not sustained by popular demand, common folk embraced these ideas of popular sovereignty as a political weapon. Coming to understand their rights unmediated by churches or rulers, they avidly read Paine's *Common Sense* and Jefferson's Declaration of Independence. They understood the language in these documents as grants of individual civil and political rights. The Revolutionary ruling classes refused to draw such conclusions from that language. Beginning in the 1780s and 1790s, decades of political conflict ensued.[42]

Thomas Paine's *Common Sense*, the most widely circulated pamphlet in Revolutionary America, used language so biblical, direct, and unadorned that even barely literate Americans could understand it. Its popularity was immediate: as many as 150,000 copies were sold in 1776 alone, enough to reach two-fifths of all the white households in the colonies, and thousands of other unlettered Americans—women, poor whites, even slaves—heard it read or overheard conversations about it. Paine justified his plea in *Common Sense* for the immediate independence of the colonies from England with a primer on eighteenth-century political theory, one tinged with possessive individualism. All kings, he insisted, lacked legitimacy because they had not gained the assent of the people, as individuals, in their rule. Law, not a monarch, was king in America. Americans owed nothing to England but had a "natural right" to form a free government. A new society, based upon indi-

---

41. G. S. Wood, *Creation of American Republic,* is the key work, but for natural rights language, see Lynd, *Intellectual Origins of American Radicalism,* chaps. 1–2; D. T. Rogers, *Contested Truths,* chap. 2; Countryman, "'To Secure the Blessings of Liberty'"; and—with reservations about his insistence on the nonrevolutionary character of the American Revolution—Habermas, *Theory and Practice,* chap. 3.

42. DePauw, "Land of the Unfree," 355–68; Appleby, "American Heritage: The Heirs and the Disinherited," 798–813; Masur, "'Age of the First Person Singular,'" 192–97.

vidual rights, beckoned. After all, America had already "been the asylum for the persecuted lovers of civil and religious liberty from every *part* of Europe." Once free of the English king, Americans could devise a democratic republic, with annual elections, representatives responsible to the people, and — by implication — widespread citizenship and the rights of equal treatment.[43]

The Declaration of Independence, with its egalitarian preamble, natural rights language, and contract theory of government, circulated with great rapidity once it was signed. Read before the troops throughout the country and to crowds in every American city and village, its message passed to the smallest child through pomp and ceremony. Thousands of others read it when it was reprinted in Whig newspapers. Connecting political and natural rights, the Declaration spoke to each person as an individual, unconstrained by status. Public reading of the Declaration linked English tyranny for each listener to the momentous events about to happen and to the formation of a new government, of which each of them was a part.[44]

However commonplace the ideas of the Declaration of Independence, they were new to unlettered colonials. Commoners — farmers, mechanics, soldiers — took the political rights demanded by Paine and the Declaration seriously. While public reading of the Declaration was rare in the 1770s and 1780s, ministers, political leaders, and constitution makers referred to natural rights of citizens frequently. During the 1790s, the natural rights language of the Declaration became embedded in partisan politics. Jeffersonian Republicans began to praise the Declaration as sustaining "the rights of human nature, political equality, and a government founded on the authority of the people," the rights of mechanics and the poor to gain equal access to justice, property, and citizenship as individuals. Federalists, in contrast, damned the Declaration for its "seductive doctrines of 'Liberty and Equality.'"[45]

The Declaration contained a radical message, one that potentially liberated dependent groups. Granted, the Declaration did not imply economic leveling and was read to limit political rights to those with property, exclud-

43. Paine, *Common Sense*, 7–9 (quotes on 84, 98); E. Foner, *Tom Paine and Revolutionary America*, chap. 3; W. Jordan, "Familial Politics," 294–99, 305–7; Seaman, "Thomas Paine: Ransom, Civil Peace, and the Natural Right to Welfare," 120–42; Kramnick, *Republicanism and Bourgeois Radicalism*, chap. 5; Durey, "Thomas Paine's Apostles," 661–88.

44. Pole, *Pursuit of Equality in American History*, 51–58; Arieli, *Individualism and Nationalism*, 77–87; Lucas, "Stylistic Artistry of the Declaration of Independence," 25–43; Hazelton, *Declaration of Independence*, chaps. 10–11. For a vivid example of reading the Declaration in York, Pennsylvania, see Dann, ed., *Revolution Remembered*, 115–16.

45. Detweiler, "Changing Reputation of the Declaration of Independence," 557–74 (quotes on 559, 569, 570); Newman, *"Principles* and not *Men,"* 38–40; Pencak, "Declaration of Independence," 225–35; D. T. Rogers, *Contested Truths*, 65–71.

ing slaves, women, and children. But, as Federalists saw to their horror, it also led excluded groups to demand fuller individual rights. Such beliefs extended even to the slave societies of Maryland and Virginia, where numerous men (some, but by no means all, Quakers) manumitted slaves in the 1780s and 1790s. And it formed the basis of calls by nineteenth-century farmers, workers, and women for their individual rights of property and citizenship.[46]

The Promise of the Revolution

Revolutionary ideology, with its individualistic presumptions, provided the only way citizens — artisans and farmers, capitalists and planters, blacks and women — could expand their rights in the new nation or defend their collective rights as classes or communities. Any such defense of rights invited conflict over the ambiguities implicit within individualism. Could self-government be restrained by self-control? Who should be counted as a citizen, worthy of political rights? How should property, which political society had to protect, be defined? The answers individuals gave to such questions were grounded in their class interest, but, at the same time, the conflicting answers shaped class conflict for generations.[47]

The Revolution transformed subjects of the king into citizens of a republic, linking civil rights (open access to justice, equality under the law, universal property rights) to political rights. Every new state insisted that each free man individually swear an oath of allegiance to the revolutionary government. The oath implied volitional allegiance, the right of all men (but not women) to choose to ally themselves with the state, accepting the benefits of citizenship along with the responsibility to obey the just dictates of the majority's law. However limited such rights consciousness may have been in the 1770s and 1780s, it provided an opening for poor whites and eventually women and blacks to demand the same individual rights as the Revolution granted to propertied men.[48]

Not all men welcomed expansion of individual rights. Some Federalists

46. J. P. Greene, *All Men Are Created Equal,* suggests that the Declaration did not imply radical political change; Pencak, "Declaration of Independence," 225–35, insists that it did. For examples, see Handlin and Handlin, eds., *Popular Sources of Political Authority,* 253–58; Albert, "Protean Institution," 272; P. Foner, ed., *We the Other People,* 47–83.

47. D. T. Rogers, *Contested Truths,* prologue, chap. 2; Kramnick, *Republicanism and Bourgeois Radicalism,* chap. 8; Horne "Bourgeois Virtue," 317–40; J. Matthews, "Race, Sex, and the Dimensions of Liberty," 275–92, esp. 280; Masur, "'Age of the First Person Singular,'" 193–208.

48. Kettner, *Development of American Citizenship,* chaps. 6–7, 9–10; Steinfeld, "Property and Suffrage," 335–76; T. H. Marshall, *Class, Citizenship, and Social Development,* chap. 4.

and New England clergymen reaffirmed the hierarchical class language of the colonial period to justify subservience of women, slaves, and poor white men. The state, they insisted, had an obligation to sustain these principles, affirming the authority of the natural aristocracy of educated and wealthy men. Federalists, especially those of an older generation, imagined that Jefferson's victory presaged the breakdown of social order, the leveling of social distinctions. In response, some horrified conservative clergy in New England built new defenses of slavery, racial inequality, and hierarchy in the household and state. Even before the Federalist party collapsed, corporatist ideology disappeared, as Federalists began to realize that individualism might be a positive good, if it was appropriately restrained by self-denial, self-control, and self-improvement. Only after 1830, when southerners finally realized that individualism and capitalism were intertwined, that democracy and slavery were contradictory, did they begin to build a more corporate, hierarchical ideology.[49]

Ideologies grounded in individualism can support a range of policies, from tariffs to free trade, from an aristocracy of talents to democratic control over capital. Ideas of *democratic* individuality, reflected in political debate and works of great literature, provided room for communalism, state action, and a critique of competitive capitalism. The grounds of ideological struggles — the desirability of economic development, the protection of rights of journeymen to control their labor or farmers to graze livestock in unenclosed fields — show how conflicts over capitalism structured the contested meanings of political language.[50]

Some Jeffersonian Republicans and Federalists wrote within a liberal calculus that directly linked private interest and public virtue. With Adam Smith, they saw commerce as self-correcting and wealth-producing, if left to the free workings of the market. Such an ideology of "bourgeois selfishness" suggests a strong commitment to private property rights over the collective rights of the state. Individualism in these cases did serve to justify the classical liberal ideas of free trade, unfettered development, and contractual labor

49. Kerber, *Federalists in Dissent*, chap. 6; Fischer, *Revolution of American Conservatism*, chap. 1; Masur, "'Age of the First Person Singular,'" 191–205; Shalhope, "Individualism in the Early Republic," 44–65. Tise, *Proslavery*, chaps. 2–3, 7–8, gives New England proslavery advocates more credit than they deserve; see Genovese, "Tise's *Proslavery*," 670–83.

50. Appleby, *Capitalism and a New Social Order*, captures one element in Republican ideology but exaggerates its strength. The complex uses of individualism to sustain collective rights *and* liberal capitalism can be traced in Wilentz, *Chants Democratic*; D. T. Rogers, *Contested Truths*, chap. 3; Ashworth, *Agrarians and Aristocrats*; Hahn, *Roots of Southern Populism*. For the democratic, but conflicted, literary uses of individualism, see Gilmore, *American Romanticism and Marketplace*, chap. 1; Kateb, "Walt Whitman and Culture Democracy," 545–71.

relations that legitimated capitalism. Justifications of the free market increased over the nineteenth century, but as late as the eve of the Civil War jostled with other more communal and democratic uses of individualistic presumptions.[51]

Protection of property rights stood at the center of these conflicts. Notwithstanding universal acceptance of private property, with its absolute rights of use and alienation, legal controversies over property dominated private law in the American North from the Revolution to the Civil War. Should owners of land (and the water on it) have rights to enjoy their property or could capitalists develop property, even if their actions reduced the rights of other owners? Judges supported developmental visions of property, permitting capitalists "reasonable" uses of their property against poorer neighbors. This capitalist defense of property rights placed defenders' common rights on the defensive. Communal rights could be justified only as the rights of individuals not "to be excluded from the use or benefit" of property.[52]

Common folk borrowed and shaped revolutionary ideologies, with their individualistic grounding, incorporating them in economic conflicts and struggles for citizenship rights that stretched from the Revolution to the end of the nineteenth century. Different groups read the promise of the Revolution differently. Yeomen sustained their own collective aspirations for a republic of small property holders with appeals to their rights as virtuous citizens. Women on occasion requested political rights, but men, whatever their class, ridiculed that demand, forcing them to build individual identities in the bourgeois home. Black petitions for freedom, couched in the language of equality, competed with white slaveholder demands for the protection of slave property. These visions clashed with ideas of a free market, the division of labor, and the pursuit of profit that capitalists embraced. Demands made by free blacks and white women, and the opposition they created, document the point.[53]

Even before Independence was declared, northern slaves began demanding freedom, running away, pressuring masters to grant them freedom, and petitioning for emancipation. Massachusetts slaves, "detained in a state of Slavery in the Bowels of a free & Christian Country," petitioned the Massachusetts General Court in 1777 for immediate freedom for adults and

51. Appleby, *Capitalism and a New Social Order*, makes the case for liberal Jeffersonian Republicanism; Kramnick, *Republicanism and Bourgeois Radicalism*, chap. 8, suggests that both Federalists and Republicans used liberal language on occasion. Horne defines "bourgeois selfishness" in "Bourgeois Virtue," 320.

52. C. B. MacPherson, "Capitalism and the Changing Concept of Property," 105–24 (quote on 107); Horwitz, *Transformation of American Law*, chaps. 2–4.

53. See chap. 5 below; for women, see Kerber, *Women of the Republic*; for free Blacks, see Nash, *Forging Freedom*, chap. 5.

emancipation of children at age twenty-one. They "apprehend that they have in common with all other men a Natural and Unaliable Right to that freedom which" God "hath Bestowed equalley on all menkind." Torn away from their homes by violence, living as good Christians, they had repeatedly petitioned for the freedom they deserved. Only when they were free would "the inconsistancey of acting themselves the part which they condem and oppose in others" end.[54]

Appeals by blacks to guarantee civil and political rights, based upon their natural rights as individuals, availed little beyond the partial freedom northern emancipation brought. However much policymakers believed slavery to be an evil, they understood that slave property, especially in the South, had to be protected. To ignore the contradiction between equality and slavery seemed prudent. The clause of the 1787 Northwest Ordinance outlawing slavery north of the Ohio River passed at the last minute, without debate, but other sections of the law protected slavery and kept slaves already in the territory in bondage. Without mentioning slavery, the Constitutional Convention wound up protecting the institution in numerous ways, making it impossible for the national government to disrupt slave property.[55]

Slaves freed by gradual emancipation acts in the North had little more than their freedom and sometimes not even that. If some masters negotiated with their slaves, permitting them to buy freedom before they had to be emancipated, others held onto their slaves until required to free them. Not only were slaves in most states held in bondage until reaching adulthood, thereby paying for their own emancipation, but masters could still sell them to the South before manumission was final. Once freed, they became part of the growing rural and urban proletariat. Philadelphia's elite whites, sympathetic to the plight of poor freed slaves, refused to help finance churches blacks themselves organized, preferring to keep them subservient. Hostility toward blacks in that city, and elsewhere in the North, increased after 1800, and most northerners, hoping that blacks would not live among them, denied them civil and political rights.[56]

54. D. B. Davis, "Emancipation Rhetoric, Natural Rights, and Revolutionary New England," 248–63; Quarles, "Revolutionary War as Black Declaration of Independence," 283–301; Nash and Soderlund, *Freedom by Degrees*, 74–85, 139–41; Aptheker, ed., *Documentary History of the Negro People*, 1: chaps. 1–2 (Massachusetts petition on 9–10).

55. The classic examination of racial attitudes and the limits of antislavery is W. Jordan, *White over Black*, chaps. 7–10, but see also Grimstead, "Anglo-American Racism," 394–444; Finkleman, "Slavery and the Northwest Ordinance," 343–71, "Evading the Ordinance," 21–52, and "Slavery and the Constitutional Convention," 188–225; Lynd, *Class Conflict*, chaps. 7–8.

56. White, "'We Dwell in Safety and Pursue Our Honest Callings,'" 446–47; Fogel and Engerman, "Philanthropy at Bargain Prices," 377–82, 391–93; Nash, *Forging Freedom*, chap. 6; Nash and Soderlund, *Freedom by Degrees*, chap. 6. For antebellum dis-

Southerners, some of whom had manumitted slaves, soon turned uniformly hostile. After a brief flurry of manumissions in the 1780s and 1790s, they limited the rights of masters to free slaves. Virginians who signed proslavery petitions in 1784 and 1785 insisted that slaves were property, incapable of enjoying the rights of free citizens. In order to protect property, Lunenberg County petitioners wrote, we fought with England, creating "a Constitution . . . grounded on a full and clear Declaration of such rights as naturally pertain to Men born free." Among those individual rights of citizens was the right to hold property, including slaves. But the legislature threatened to consider general emancipation, which would "wreste from us . . . the most valuable and indispensible part of our Property, our Slaves."[57]

Southern hostility to black freedom left slaves who took promises of revolutionary democracy, bourgeois individualism, and evangelical egalitarianism seriously with little recourse but escape or open rebellion. Escape from slavery to free black communities in southern towns or the North probably increased. Few slaves organized to gain their freedom, knowing how unlikely success would be. But encouraged by successful revolutions in America, France, and especially Haiti, a few acculturated slaves conspired to gain their own freedom and to overthrow the system, fomenting rebellion in Virginia in 1800, North Carolina in 1802, and Louisiana in 1795 and 1811.[58]

Unlike slaves, white women were already free, in the sense of self-ownership, so crucial to bourgeois liberty. But under the common law, dependence upon husbands severely constrained any individualistic interpretation of female self-ownership. Despite continued familial dependency, women gained some leverage during the Revolution. Daughters and wives of propertied men served with distinction in the Revolutionary cause, sewing homespun, boycotting tea, joining men in crowd actions, exhorting public support for the war, taking care of farms and businesses when husbands were away at war, and lending money to the new government. Thousands of wives of poor soldiers followed the troops, serving as nurse, cook, seamstress, or water carrier for artillery.[59]

crimination against blacks in the North, see Litwack, *North of Slavery*, esp. chaps. 3–5, and L. P. Curry, *Free Black in Urban America*, chaps. 2, 5–6.

57. Jackson, "'American Slavery, American Freedom,'" 81–93; Albert, "Protean Institution," chap. 7; Schmidt and Wilhelm, eds., "Proslavery Petitions," 133–46 (quotes on 140–41); Robson, "'An Important Question Answered,'" 644–52; Tise, *Proslavery*, chap. 2.

58. Genovese, *From Rebellion to Revolution*, chap. 3; Aptheker, *American Negro Slave Revolts*, 3–4 and chaps. 9–10; Mullin, *Flight and Rebellion*, chaps. 4–5; J. H. Dorman, "Persistent Specter," 389–404.

59. Salmon, *Women and the Law of Property in Early America*; Kerber, *Women of the Republic*, esp. chaps. 2–3, 7–8; M. B. Norton, *Liberty's Daughters*, chaps. 6–9; A. F. Young, "Women of Boston," 193–207; Ulrich, "'Daughters of Liberty,'" 211–43, esp.

The Revolution opened up contradictions between the citizenship of free people and the dependent status of women in a hierarchical family. If women were free individuals, they should have the same rights to choose allegiance to the state as free men and the same control over their own property. Yet Revolutionary states generally refused to recognize their property rights. Citizenship was tied to political independence, which, in turn, was linked to military service, supposedly outside women's proper role.[60]

Middling women saw the contradictions of individualism and their dependent status with great clarity. As wives and daughters of free men, they sought some political and property rights (if rarely the franchise) already granted to their husbands and fathers. Some of them had signed the Continental Association of 1767 or the Solemn League and Covenant of 1768, promising to boycott English goods. They, too, read *Common Sense* and the Declaration of Independence. Just like men, they petitioned the Continental Congress, beseeching repayment for requisitioned goods or a widow's pension. After the war they formed voluntary societies, began female academies, read Wollstonecraft's *Vindication of the Rights of Women*, and discussed politics among themselves and with husbands, sometimes venturing public opinions on political issues.[61]

Politically assertive white women saw rights in terms of equity and fairness. Abigail Adams, for one, feared the tyranny of giving "unlimited power." Connecting legal equality to individual rights, she insisted that women "will not hold ourselves bound by any Laws in which we have no voice, or Representation" but would rather "foment a Rebelion." The 1786 petition to Congress of Rachel Wells, a middling woman impoverished by the war, for repayment of New Jersey war bonds shows that such views spread beyond upper class women. As a patriot, Wells insisted, she deserved to share in the country's bounty. "I have Don as much to Carrey on the Warr as maney that Sett Now at ye healm of government," she claimed, lending money that "bought ye Sogers food & Clothing & Let Them have Blankets."[62]

Notwithstanding the moderation of female desires—the rights to be

211–20; Kerber, "'History Can Do It No Justice,'" 10–25; Chalouo, "Women in the American Revolution," 73–90; DePauw, "Women in Combat," 209–26.

60. Gunderson, "Independence, Citizenship, and the American Revolution," 59–77; Kerber, "'History Can Do It No Justice,'" 20–36, and *Women of the Republic*, chaps. 3–4.

61. Branson, "Politics and Gender"; Kerber, *Women of the Republic*, esp. chaps. 2–3, 7–8, and "Can a Woman Be an Individual?" 171–76; M. B. Norton, *Liberty's Daughters*, chaps. 6–9; A. F. Young, "Women of Boston," 209–18.

62. Butterfield et al., eds., *Book of Abigail and John*, 120–21 (Abigail Adams to John Adams, Mar. 31, 1776); Wells petition quoted in Kerber, "'I Have Don . . . Much to Carrey on the Warr,'" 231.

heard and to gain control over their own property—men, no matter what their class, denied women equal legal rights as individuals. Even Paine and Jefferson viewed women as outside the social contract and the individual rights it implied. Every state, except New Jersey, refused women the right to vote. Federalist women voters in New Jersey, Jeffersonians agreed, corrupted elections, providing unfair advantage to Federalists, and New Jersey soon removed women from voting rolls. John Adams's response to Abigail suggests fear of sharing power with the dispossessed, of the end of proper subservience of dependents within family and republic. He pointed, half in jest, to universal demands for rights: "We have been told that our Struggle has loosened the bonds of Government everywhere," he wrote. "Children and Apprentices were disobedient," and "Indians slighted their Guardians and Negroes grew more insolent to their Masters." But now women "were grown discontented," equally threatening public order. Adams, for one, would not "repeal our Masculine systems," would not subject the country "to the despotism of the Peticoat."[63]

In the face of such hostility, and their own reluctance to demand full rights as citizens, women of the Revolutionary generation had few options open to them. By and large, politically aware women acted as individuals, petitioning for redress or seeking to influence the political decisions of husbands or other men in the privacy of their homes. For more than a generation, middle class white women stood back from political participation, failing to organize politically, in sharp contrast to white yeomen or even free black men.[64]

Forced from the public arena, middle class women manipulated the republican need for virtuous male citizens to their advantage. Republican theorists made the virtuous wife and mother, companion to the male citizen and educator of his sons, the protector of public morality, the guarantor of her husband's virtue. Accepting neither the implications of inferiority nor the strict separation of public and private inherent in an ideology of separate spheres, middling women tried to build autonomous lives in their own "sphere" of home and child nurture, demanding equality with husbands in the family and the right to control their own fertility.[65]

63. Kerber, "'I Have Don . . . Much to Carrey on the Warr,'" 227; Butterfield et al., eds., *Book of Abigail and John,* 122–23 (John Adams to Abigail Adams, Apr. 14, 1776); Dowd, "Declarations of Dependence," 53–58; DePauw, "American Revolution," 206–8; Gunderson, "Independence, Citizenship, and the American Revolution," 65–66.
64. Kerber, "'I Have Don . . . Much to Carrey on the Warr,'" 227–58.
65. Kerber brilliantly analyzes the literature on domesticity in "Separate Spheres, Female Worlds," 9–39, but see also Kerber, *Women of the Republic,* chap. 9; Bloch, "American Feminine Ideals in Transition," 101–26, and "Gendered Meanings of Virtue," 37–57; Lewis, "The Republican Wife," 689–721; Cott, *Bonds of Womanhood.*

The debate between John and Abigail Adams illuminates the contradictions of possessive individualism in the Revolutionary era. A consistent respect for individuals would open the state to the unruly or dependent, but anything less seemed to forfeit the universal promise of rights revolutionaries fought to attain. Far from unifying classes, consensus over individualism in the political realm only served to deepen conflicts. Many-sided struggles for citizenship rights, supposedly guaranteed by the Revolution, continued for generations. Every group, without quite realizing it, tried to deny other groups full rights of individual citizenship, thereby precluding them from full humanity in societies defined by contract rather than by traditional hierarchical relations. Access to a language of individualism and citizenship, however, hardly predetermined the outcome of class struggles. In these century-long conflicts, those with wealth, property, and standing—propertied farmers and capitalists, wives of propertied men, the few blacks who escaped poverty—could more readily persuade the citizenry that they should be full members of the body politic.

A Bourgeois Beginning

The American Revolution can be dubbed a bourgeois revolution because its dominant ideology meshed with bourgeois ideals, and the contingencies of war and state formation accelerated capitalist development. But the Revolution did not lead to a final or even partial victory for the bourgeoisie. Northern development of a full market society, with growing classes of capitalists and proletarians, proceeded apace through the antebellum decades. But slavery became even more fully embedded in the South. Slaveholders created an anticapitalist niche for themselves in the capitalist world economy. Contradictions between slavery and free labor, between individualism and the growing corporatism of proslavery writers and their supporters, ultimately led to the Civil War. It would take a bloody civil war, innumerable class, racial, and gender struggles, before corporate capitalists gained full political and economic power.[66]

The Civil War unleashed class conflict, social tensions, and dissension. Pitting anticapitalist planters against early industrial capitalists, the war reawakened violent confrontation between regional ruling classes and the dispossessed. Poorer southern whites often refused to support the Confederacy; white workers resented fighting for capitalists; slaves voted for freedom with

66. Compare Genovese, *Political Economy of Slavery*, introduction, chaps. 1, 7–10, epilogue, and Genovese, *World Slaveholders Made*, new introduction and part 2 (South as prebourgeois) with Oakes, *Ruling Race*, introduction, chaps. 2–5, epilogue (South as a market society).

their feet, making emancipation inevitable once the Union gained the upper hand.[67]

The Civil War settlement completed the American bourgeois revolution, but it was controlled to a far greater degree by capitalists, both North and South, than the American Revolution. Notwithstanding intense struggle by blacks to gain political rights, the legal equality that was a hallmark of the post-Revolutionary era dissipated. Freed slaves temporarily gained voting rights, but rising white hostility and northern impatience with the politics of racial equality slowly eliminated black suffrage and with it the political rights of poor whites. Despite free black's desires for land, growing southern capitalism (in the guise of sharecropping or urban wage labor) ensured that blacks and poorer whites in the cotton South would become dependent upon markets controlled by northern capitalists and their southern allies.[68]

The broader significance of the American Revolution, seen as a bourgeois revolution, is illuminated by comparison with Ontario, where capitalism developed without a bourgeois revolution. At first glance, Ontario greatly resembled the American Northwest. Both frontier areas were settled by small landholders, and in both tensions between speculators and settlers were great. Ontario's wheat economy, with its eventual transition to commercial agriculture, was comparable to that of New York state.[69]

Such similarities mask great differences between the two nations. Upper Canada resembled the eighteenth-century colonies more than the United States. Ruled from London or by appointed commissioners, Canadians enjoyed little representative government. Significant minorities of its people were British emigrants or loyalist refugees, who had immigrated just after the Revolution, bringing with them a hierarchical vision rapidly disappearing in the United States. Not surprisingly, neither liberalism nor individualism gained an ideological foothold; few Canadians argued for a universal franchise, and voting was limited to those with property.[70]

Lacking either a strong state to encourage capitalism or a class commit-

67. J. M. McPherson, *Battle Cry of Freedom*, chaps. 1, 20; Escott and Crow, "Social Order and Violent Disorder," 373–402.

68. For the Civil War as a bourgeois revolution, see Beard and Beard, *Rise of American Civilization*, chap. 17; B. Moore, *Social Origins of Dictatorship and Democracy*, chap. 3; Lynd, *Class Conflict*, 14–15. E. Foner, *Reconstruction*, brilliantly synthesizes Reconstruction literature, but see also Fields, "Advent of Capitalist Agriculture," 73–94; Kousser, *Shaping of Southern Politics*.

69. L. F. Gates, *Land Policies of Upper Canada*; Gagan, *Hopeful Travellers*, esp. chaps. 2–3; McCallum *Unequal Beginnings*, chaps. 2, 4–5; Cohen, *Women's Work*.

70. Curtis, "Representation and State Formation in the Canadas, 1790–1850," 59–87; Hansen and Brebner, *Mingling of the Canadian and American Peoples*, chap. 1; Craig, *Upper Canada*, chap. 1; C. Moore, "Disposition to Settle," 306–25; D. W. L. Earle, ed., *Family Compact*; Mills, *Idea of Loyalty in Upper Canada*, chaps. 1–2.

ted to it, economic development in early nineteenth-century Upper Canada lagged behind adjacent parts of the United States settled at the same time. The area remained a colony, dependent upon trade of its wheat staple. Wealthy men concentrated on land speculation, not on manufacturing or banking. They hired few wage laborers, except journeymen carpenters or grist and grain mill workers, and faced little of the labor radicalism so common in the United States.[71]

However much the rulers may have wished to sustain a deferential smallholder society, continued migration from the United States led to great internal tensions. After 1790 most American settlers migrated for land, rather than out of a commitment to the crown, and they wished to see more republican institutions in their adapted country. Americans and their descendants, and a few Irish and Britons from a reforming England, revolted in 1837. This rebellion, perhaps an incipient democratic revolution, failed, for it lacked both consistent leadership and radical action from below so characteristic of successful bourgeois revolutions.[72]

By the 1860s capitalist development in Canada began to catch up with the United States. A capitalist ruling class slowly replaced the family compact; urban proletarianization proceeded apace. The abortive rebellion of 1837 perhaps illuminated tensions similar to those of the colonies but it failed to trigger capitalist transformation. This hardly challenges the importance of bourgeois revolutions. Canada's bourgeois revolution occurred in the United States: American capital financed part of Canadian development; American immigrants — imbued with individualism and notions of economic development — spread across the Canadian countryside.[73]

Where does the Revolution fit within these long struggles over capitalism and bourgeois individualism in the United States? It was an essential first step, a sweeping away of remaining constraints on capitalist development, a crucial victory of the ideology of systematic individualism over the idea of collective rights of communities beyond the discrete rights of each citizen. More than any other event it created the American bourgeoisie. That such radical change was not fully achieved by the Revolution is hardly surprising. But the bourgeois beginning of the Revolution presaged the ultimate victory of capitalism.

71. M. G. Cohen, *Women's Work*, chaps. 2–4; Curtis, "Representation and State Formation," 83; Ryerson, *Unequal Union*, chap. 4.

72. Hansen and Brebner, *Mingling of Canadian and American Peoples*, chaps. 4–5; Landon, *Western Ontario and the American Frontier*, chaps. 2, 10–11; Stuart, *United States Expansionism and British North America*, chaps. 5–6; Ryerson, *Unequal Union*, chaps. 5–6; Read, *Rising in Western Upper Canada, 1837–8*.

73. Ryerson, *Unequal Union*, chaps. 9, 11–13; Katz, Doucet, and Stern, *Social Organization of Early Capitalism*; B. D. Palmer, "Social Formation and Class Formation in North America," 229–309.

Chapter 5

The Revolution and the Making of the American Yeoman Classes

IN JULY 1775, FEARING slave rebellions in time of civil unrest, Virginia's revolutionary assembly, composed of wealthy slaveholders, exempted over-seers of four or more adult slaves from militia musters and army drafts. They particularly sought to protect slave property from the interference of Governor John Dunmore, the royal governor of Virginia, who had offered to free any slave who would fight the rebels. The exemption raised a firestorm of dissent from yeoman planters (men who owned few or no slaves). Hundreds of angry men petitioned the assembly. For instance, 225 petitioners from Lunenburg County, a frontier county south of the James River, complained that the law led "many persons" to "become Overseers that Otherways wou'd not . . . to Secure themselves from Fighting in defense of their Country as well as their Own Property." The law was unjust to poor freeholders, as men who owned land were called. When they were drafted, as they must be because so many overseers were exempted, they would leave their families without support, forcing them to go "up & down the County abeging or [stay] at home aSlaving, and at the same time quite unable to help them to the Necessaries of life, while the Overseers are aliving in ease & Affluence at the Expense of their Employers."[1]

These Virginia yeomen, who constituted three-fifths of the white household heads in the colony, knew that the land they owned was their only claim to political participation, their only security against impoverishment. They sold tobacco to merchants, but grew most food needed to feed their families and traded with neighbors for what they did not make. Willing to accept advances from merchants until their crops were sold, they avoided incurring large debts that might lead to loss of their land. As long as gentlemen had protected their property, most Virginia yeomen had acquiesced in the rule of wealthy gentlemen. These men, the gentry, about a tenth of the population, members of a few interrelated families who owned many slaves

1. Van Schreven et al., eds., *Revolutionary Virginia*, 6:474–77. I have placed this incident in broader perspective in chap. 6.

and thousands of acres of land and dominated both local and provincial government, comprised the colony's ruling class.[2]

The petitioners saw the exemption of overseers as an attempt to deprive them of their property, the basis of their familial authority. Coming from Southside Virginia, where yeomen had adopted an evangelical religion that put them in opposition to gentry-dominated Anglican culture, they challenged any political attack from gentlemen. They linked household and state: like all married men, they were obligated to support their families and wanted state policy to advance that goal. Exemption from militia musters and military service for overseers not only threatened yeomen with loss of land but was inequitable, creating a leisured class, safe from the dangers of war. Clearly, if yeomen were to support the Revolution and its gentry leaders, the exemption had to be ended. Listening to petitions like this one, the legislature abandoned the law in May 1776, just seven months after Dunmore's offer of freedom to slaves.

Such petitions and their success raise important questions about the loyalty of yeomen to the Revolutionary cause. Building on recent work on the Revolution in rural America and on rural revolts, this chapter explores the Revolution common rural folk made.[3] Focusing on farmers who supported the Revolution, it will try to disentangle the social basis of patriotism. Historians who have studied this issue sometimes assume that gentlemen made farmers politically aware, persuading them to support the Revolution the gentry wanted.[4] The success of Lunenburg petition suggests otherwise. Petitioners were patriots but rejected gentry control. Through actions like theirs, patriots in every region sought democratic participation as landholders, without any tinge of what they considered to be aristocratic domination.[5] They insisted that they be respected as citizens of the republic, thereby giving new meaning to political declarations from gentlemen and merchants and often appropriating the rhetoric of Whig patriots to their own ends. Forced by wartime military needs, gentlemen acquiesced frequently to yeoman demands. When gentlemen sought to reassert hegemony in the 1780s,

2. Kulikoff, *Tobacco and Slaves*, chaps. 3, 4, and 7. Chap. 2 above relates the history of other colonial yeoman classes; for other gentry classes, see Kornblith and Murrin, "Making and Unmaking of the American Ruling Class."

3. R. L. Bushman, "Massachusetts Farmers and the Revolution," 77–124, is the seminal examination of rural ideology. For rural revolts, see Countryman, "'Out of the Bounds of the Law,'" 39–69; R. M. Brown, "Back Country Rebellions and the Homestead Ethic," 73–99; Slaughter, "Crowds in Eighteenth-Century America," 12–26; A. Taylor, "Backcountry Conclusion to the Revolution"; Szatmary, *Shays' Rebellion*; Slaughter, *Whiskey Rebellion*.

4. R. D. Brown, *Revolutionary Politics in Massachusetts*, is an example of this kind of argument.

5. Bogin, "Petitioning and New Moral Economy of Post-Revolutionary America," 391–425, provides a framework for understanding petitioning.

yeomen tried to salvage the democratic republic they believed their blood had created by electing legislators who would do their bidding, joining Shays's Rebellion, or fighting ratification of the Constitution. Although gentlemen, merchants, and lawyers suppressed rural uprisings and used the Constitution to reestablish a representative republican government they might control, they still had to search for votes. Yeomen had long believed that their independence made them virtuous and productive citizens. To gain votes, gentlemen, especially Jeffersonian Republicans, placed this yeoman self-image at the center of their message.

We have no vision to help us understand these dramatic political events. To explain them, we must place the Revolution yeomen made into the context of the history of class relations and capitalist development in rural America. As we have seen, the Revolution was a key event in the formation of classes of yeomen and capitalist farmers, especially in the North. Northern yeomen, whose independence would be destroyed in a capitalist economy, resisted capitalist entrepreneurs, using Revolutionary ideology to legitimate their place in political and economic life.[6]

The success of farmers in legitimating yeoman democracy was predicated upon individualism, the idea that they, like all men, possessed rights as individuals, rights they felt protected their property and the cooperative communities they formed. Individualism, however, was a cornerstone of capitalist ideology, one that reduced each person to an individual attached to community only by freely made contracts. Seeking intensive rural development, capitalists found allies among commercial farmers, who had become comfortable with full market embeddedness even before the Revolution. As we shall see, commercial farmers grew in number after the war, and the capitalist development their behavior encouraged provoked disputes between yeomen and capitalists, both urban and rural.[7]

Our analysis examines three themes. First, we will show how yeomen shaped an ideology in the decades before the Revolution. Then, we will turn to the problem of rural loyalty to the patriot cause from the 1760s to the 1780s. And third, we will examine the ways yeomen helped shape Revolutionary institutions as well as explore the economic consequences of the Revolution in the countryside.

The Emergence of a Yeoman Ideology

The ownership of land, the means of agricultural production, created the class identity of the yeomanry. J. Hector St. John Crèvecoeur, a French immigrant who became a gentleman-farmer in the Hudson valley of New York, ably expressed this sentiment. Writing in the guise of a simple American

6. See chaps. 1–2 for exposition of these themes.
7. For individualism, see chap. 4; for capitalist agriculture, see chap. 2.

farmer of the 1770s, he explained the value of land. "What should we American farmers be without the distinct possession of the soil? It feeds, it clothes us; from it we draw . . . our best meat, our richest drink." But land meant more than prosperity; it created the "only philosophy of the American farmer." A man's labor, not mere purchase, improved the soil, sustained a man's ownership of land and gave him a political identity. "This formerly rude soil has been converted by my father into a pleasant farm," he added, "and in return, it has established all our rights; on it is founded our rank, our freedom, our power as citizens."[8]

Notwithstanding their attachment to land, eighteenth-century yeomen often had little consciousness of themselves as a class. That would require an ideology to justify their place in the social order. The origins of a yeoman class ideology can be traced to justifications of their rights to land made when gentlemen threatened the security of their land tenure. When the threat was imminent, yeomen petitioned legislatures, rioted, and even went to war. Even in the heat of conflict, class language was often subsumed in communal, ethnic, or religious rhetoric, with yeomen seeking no greater political end than a redress of grievances. But after each conflict, yeoman folk memory of gentry oppression and the need for secure land tenure strengthened. To legitimate their rights to land, yeomen embraced a labor theory of value. Land, they insisted, was made valuable only by labor that improved it, and therefore farmers who worked the land should own it, even if speculators were the legal owners. Owing his livelihood to no one, a landholder became an independent man, eligible to vote. Yeoman statements in conflicts in Massachusetts, New York, and the Carolinas suggest the widespread diffusion by 1770 of this class ideology.[9]

In Massachusetts, agrarian fear of dispossession began early. In 1687 when Governor Edmund Andros suggested that local land titles might be in doubt, Samuel Sewall reported that farmers were "very averse from complying with anything that may alter the Tenure of their lands." Yeoman fears of threats to secure land tenure persisted, especially in debate during the 1740s and 1750s over the expansion of paper currency. Farmers who wanted paper money viewed creditors opposed to it as conspirators seeking to reduce them to dependence: "We must sell our lands to pay them; then go and work upon their Farms; or Starve, or go to Sea as their Slaves, or go to—Jail." Although few Massachusetts farmers in the late colonial era lost land because of debt,

8. Crèvecoeur, *Letters from an American Farmer*, 54. Notwithstanding paeans to American classlessness and blindness to American poverty and diversity, his portrayal of land and yeoman identity rings true. See Echeverria, *Mirage in the West*, 147–55.

9. Contrast R. M. Brown, "Back Country Rebellions," 73–99, and A. Taylor, "Backcountry Conclusion to the American Revolution," with Kim, *Landlord and Tenant*, chaps. 4–6.

they understood how vulnerable their land might become if tyranny returned.[10]

In New York, yeomen, mostly from New England, vigorously defended their land rights during the Hudson River land riots of 1766. When land in New England was fully cultivated, settlers poured into New York, where great landlords owned the best land. In order to gain freeholds or at least avoid short-term tenancy, the New Englanders resorted to violence. Their grievances were clear from their petitions and trial records. As some tenants put it in a 1764 petition, they had worked the land "for near 30 years past and had manured and cultivated" it thinking it was theirs, but now landlords "would not lease the land" to them for "3 lives or twenty years" but "would oblige them to buy their farms paying money down for it or else remove immediately." When Dutchess County landlords ejected some settlers and put new tenants on the land, the former tenants, under William Prendergast, formed a militia and returned the old residents to their homes or tried to get new tenants to pay them for their improvements. Testimony at Prendergast's trial for treason suggests that the rioters had a fully articulated ideology. Prendergast led the rebellion "on accot. of Largeness of rents and Shortness of Leases" and because he "pitied poor people who were turned out of possession." He and his supporters sought a settlement "to compel their Landlords to alter their Rents." They "*had made him a desperate Man.*" After all, "it was hard that they were not allowed to have any *property.*" Because "there was no Law for poor Men," he urged his followers to "pay their honest Debts but not their Rents until Settlemt. with their landlords." Prendergast himself had never paid rent, withholding payment "for the good of the Country."[11]

In the Carolinas, participants in the Regulator movements expressed vigorously yeoman concerns about land security. During the late 1760s and early 1770s, North Carolina Regulators, western men of poor to middling status opposed to high taxes and autocratic gentry rule by eastern creditors and their local allies, briefly went to war. Calling themselves "farmers," "planters," and "poor industrious peasants," they contrasted themselves with rich and powerful men, who expropriated the fruits of their labor. Anson County Regulators made three demands in a 1769 legislative petition: more equitable taxation, less venal local government, and fairer land distribution. "The poor Inhabitants," they wrote, "are much oppress'd by reasons of disproportionate Taxes," and of their inability to pay taxes with produce,

10. R. L. Bushman, "Massachusetts Farmers and the Revolution," 104–7 (Sewall quote on 105), 111–20, and *King and People*, 199–201 (201 second quote).

11. For differing versions of the riots, see Lynd, *Anti-Federalism in Dutchess County, New York*, chap. 2 (first quote on 48); Kim, *Landlord and Tenant*, chap. 8; and Mark and Handlin, "Land Cases in Colonial New York, 1765–1767," 165–94 (quotes on 172, 175, 177, 181, 191).

as planters in eastern North Carolina did. The monopoly on the best unimproved lands enjoyed by friends of the governor and Council, moreover, increased that burden, for "great numbers of poor people" had to "toil in the cultivation of bad Lands whereon they hardly can subsist" while great men let their land stand idle.[12]

In South Carolina, when provincial authorities refused to organize local government in the backcountry and bring bandits to justice in the late 1760s, Regulators rebelled, justifying their action as a defense of their labor, land, and rights. "We are *Free-Men* — British Subjects — Not Born Slaves — We contribute our Proportion in all Public Taxations" yet, they claimed, we enjoy few rights. Secure property was the key to all rights: "Property is of no Value, except it be secure" and theirs was very insecure, with their cattle stolen, horses "carried off," and personal property "plunder'd." Without local courts, with bandits running loose, "No improvements are attempted — No New Plans can take Place . . . And (shameful to say) our Lands (some of the finest in *America*) lye useless and uncleared being rendered of small Value from the many licentious Persons intermixed among Us, whom We cannot drive off without Force or Violence." Therefore, they were "obliged to defend our Families, by *our own Strength*: As *Legal Methods* are beyond our Reach."[13]

The yeoman response to the American Revolution should be seen in the context of the development of a yeoman class ideology. By the mid-eighteenth century, yeomen had their own agenda — sustaining familial autonomy (and male authority over the family), landownership, a modest freeholder egalitarianism. Northern merchants and wealthy southern planters may have started the revolt against England, but they needed widespread support to succeed. How rural Americans would respond to their demands — whether they became patriots or joined the disaffected — depended upon prior relations between the two classes and how well revolutionary governments responded to the wishes of yeomen for a more egalitarian social order of men of property. How the yeomen made *their* Revolution, then, is a significant issue for historical inquiry.[14]

Yeomen and the Making of the Revolution

The Revolution in the countryside was rent with contradictions. As the conflict with England deepened in the 1760s and 1770s, Whig gentlemen at-

12. Kay, "North Carolina Regulation," 72–123 (quotes on 74–75); petition reprinted in J. P. Greene, ed., *Colonies to Nation*, 105–7. For other views of the North Carolina regulation, see Ekrich, "North Carolina Regulators," 199–256; Kay," North Carolina Regulation"; and Whittenberg, "Planters, Merchants, and Lawyers," 215–38.
13. Remonstrance reprinted in J. P. Greene, ed., *Colony to Nation*, 99–105 (quotes 100, 102); R. M. Brown, *South Carolina Regulators*, is the key work.
14. Hoffman, "'Disaffected' in Revolutionary South," 273–318, and Young, "Afterword," 451–54.

tempted to mobilize poorer freeholders. Many yeomen interpreted these calls to action through the lenses of their own democratic agenda, thereby pushing revolutionary politics toward greater participation of male property holders, and encouraging white women and blacks to demand greater political rights. The Revolution for yeomen was a cumulative process that started slowly in the Stamp Act crisis, accelerated in the crises of 1774–76, and reached political maturity during the war. By the late 1770s yeoman political participation rose to levels never before achieved. If some yeomen tried to democratize the Revolution, others opposed the revolutionaries because they feared that Whig gentlemen would dispossess them of their lands as they had attempted to do earlier in the century.

At first, yeomen listened to the Whig political program with some disinterest; after all, the Stamp Act of 1765, with its tax on legal and commercial papers, deeds, wills, newspapers, almanacs, land warrants and surveys, affected urban folk — merchants, lawyers, even artisans — more often than yeomen. In towns, the tax would be a daily nuisance; in the countryside, it would be an infrequent and irregular one when a man appeared at court, procured land, bought an almanac, or died. Moreover, the rhetoric of Whig leaders during this crisis harkened back more to the country ideology of the eighteenth century than the democracy of radicals in the English Revolution. Corruption had led Parliament to reduce colonial rights, and luxuries imported by English merchants threatened to undermine colonial virtue. Their stress on the virtue of the people (defined narrowly), the public interest, and communal consensus and their attack on conspicuous consumption may have been an attempt to unify their own class (the only people wallowing in luxury) while passively incorporating poorer folk.

Such appeals worked in the towns where most of the Stamp Act riots occurred, but they generated little response in the countryside. Here and there yeomen participated in crowd actions. In Virginia's Northern Neck, about fifty yeomen (a tiny part of that class) joined an equal number of gentlemen (nearly the entire class) and marched on Leedstown to prevent a merchant from distributing stamps; inhabitants of two western Massachusetts towns rioted to prevent imprisonment for debt by courts lacking stamped papers that would permit them to sell land to pay their own debts.[15]

Rural folk interpreted arguments of the Whig Sons of Liberty about the

---

15. E. S. Morgan, ed., *Prologue to Revolution*, 35–43, prints a copy of the act. For the absence of rioting in rural Massachusetts, see Nobles, *Divisions throughout the Whole*, 157–58; R. L. Bushman, "Massachusetts Farmers and the Revolution," 79–81. The examples are found in Kulikoff, *Tobacco and Slaves*, 306; Hoerder, *Crowd Action in Revolutionary Massachusetts*, 132–38. Kornblith and Murrin, "Making and Unmaking of the American Ruling Class," explain the response of gentlemen.

Stamp Act in the light of their beliefs about land and labor. John Adams, who rode the legal circuit in Massachusetts and understood the countryside well, put rural economic concerns in the instructions on the Stamp Act he wrote for his hometown of Braintree to its representatives; more than forty other towns adopted his language. The Stamp tax was "a burthensome tax because the duties are so numerous and so high . . . that it would be totally impossible for the people to subsist under it," and considering the "scarcity of money, we have reason to think the execution of that act for a short . . . time would drain the country of its cash, strip multitudes of their property and reduce them to absolute beggary." The Stamp tax, he concluded, was inherently unfair because "the public money of this country is the toil and labor of the people." Yeomen opposed the Stamp Act in ways consistent with these ideals. The New York land rioters called themselves Sons of Liberty. Rioters in Scarborough, Maine, linked merchant Richard King, who had "destroyed the poor and taken away Peoples Estates," with English ministers who drafted the Stamp Act, all the while calling themselves "Suns of liburty." [16]

Whig leaders came to understand that to gain the support of white property holders they had to appeal to the lived experience of yeomen, to their fears of losing their land. In 1774 and 1775 gentlemen and merchants throughout the colonies organized mass meetings to gain the support of ordinary folk. In Virginia, patriot leaders like Patrick Henry spoke with an evangelical fervor many of their auditors shared. New England Whigs insisted that English ministers were corrupt men, who in Samuel Adams's words, threatened to "take away your Barn and my house." This aristocracy, John Adams wrote, was bent on "reducing the country to lordships" by taxing land and property, making virtuous yeomen into tenants and servile laborers, much like English landlords. In June 1774, in a letter to rural towns, the Boston Committee of Correspondence directly appealed to this fear. What "if a favorite of a perverse Governor should pretend title to our lands?" they asked. "Of what value are our lands or estates to us if such an odious government should be established among us? Can we look with pleasure . . . on the fields cultivated by our own industry?" [17]

New England yeomen made their own radical initiatives, refusing to lis-

16. Peek, ed., *Political Writings of John Adams*, 22–25; R. D. Brown, *Revolutionary Politics in Massachusetts*, 24–26; Mark and Handlin, "Land Cases," 183; Hoerder, *Crowd Action*, 134–35.

17. R. D. Brown, *Revolutionary Politics in Massachusetts*, and Isaac, *Transformation of Virginia*, chaps. 11–12, detail popular mobilization. For the ideological appeal to yeomen, see R. L. Bushman, *King and People*, 190–210 (quotes 202–3, 198), and "Massachusetts Farmers and the Revolution," 77–124; G. S. Wood, *Creation of American Republic*, chaps. 2–3, 8–9; the letter from the Boston Committee can be found in Force, comp., *American Archives*, 4th ser. 1:397–98.

ten to the moderate counsel of their betters. Seeing a relation between taxes imposed by Parliament and the security of their land, they expanded upon the Whig message. Between the passage of the Intolerable Acts in 1774 and the outbreak of war in April 1775, they sometimes took over the revolutionary movement, protecting their property and pushing the colonies closer to independence. The Intolerable Acts that closed the port of Boston and curtailed the Massachusetts government and the Quebec Act that tolerated Catholics aroused more New England yeomen into political action. More than ever, Anne Hulton, sister of a customs commissioner, reported "the common people" feared that taxes would dispossess them of their land, with custom's commissioners having "an *unlimited* power given them to tax even their lands . . . in order to raise a Revenue for supporting . . . Bishops that are coming over." They attended illegal town meetings and insisted that courts be closed or democratically appointed their own judges, both to defy the British and to help poor rural debtors. Dramatic evidence of the response of rural people took place in late 1774, when General Gage supposedly captured patriot arms stored in Charlestown. As many as fifty thousand Massachusetts, Connecticut, and New Hampshire men marched toward Boston. Ezra Stiles, an eye witness, reported that "all along were armed Men rushing forward . . . , at every house Women and Children making Cartridges, Running Bullets, . . . crying and bemoaning and at the same time animating their Husbands and Sons to fight for their Liberties."[18]

Freeholders in New York who were fearful that the colonial or English government might evict them from their land vigorously supported independence, in contrast to some tenants. In late 1774 citizens of Newtown, on Long Island, linked their attack on the Intolerable Acts to land. They insisted that the acts "absolutely tended to deprive" them of their "most inestimable rights and privileges," their property rights, adding that "man ought to have the disposition of his property either by himself or his representatives." In May 1775 the Green Mountain Boys of Vermont captured Fort Ticonderoga, continuing their warfare against New York landlords. They tied support for independence with separation from New York, arguing that the landlords had deprived them "by frawd viollance and oppression" of "thire property and in particular thire Landed interest."[19]

One can find hints of radical action by yeomen in other colonies. In 1775, Virginia gentlemen sometimes lost control over revolutionary com-

18. Alfred Young research (Hulton quote, 1768); R. L. Bushman, "Massachusetts Farmers and the Revolution," 80–81 (quote); Hoerder, *Crowd Action*, 276–97, 301–4; Patterson, *Political Parties in Revolutionary Massachusetts*, chap. 4.

19. Kross, *Evolution of an American Town*, 199–201; Countryman, *People in Revolution*, chap. 5 (quote on 156).

mittees to small planters. In Pennsylvania, Delaware valley and backcountry farmers united with Philadelphia artisans and journeymen to support the democratic Pennsylvania constitution of 1776, a document that enraged conservatives by rejecting the mixed government of England and all the colonies. In Maryland several militia companies in rural Anne Arundel County drafted a radical constitution in June 1776; one month later 855 men — about two-fifths of the county's white men — demanded universal white manhood suffrage.[20]

Between 1776 and 1781 the yeomanry made a revolution for themselves, one that disrupted and might have transformed relations of power and production. Because they fed the soldiers of the fledgling nation and they and their sons defended their states against the English foe, they deserved a more democratic polity. The 200,000 men who served in militia and army — many of them poor — expected decent pay, respect, the franchise, and sufficient land after the war to remain yeomen or pull themselves up from the ranks of the dispossessed. "The strength of the country," Abraham Yates of New York (an Antifederalist supporter of the yeomanry) remembered, "lays in the yeomanry thereof, who . . . had been upon hard militia duty, in which a man worth no more than ten pounds had to do equal duty with a gentleman of 10,000 pounds . . . ; if the rich intended to avail themselves of the yeomanry . . . to fight for their riches, it would require to shew them . . . that they intended no partiality." As Yates's language suggests, yeomen radicalized Revolutionary rhetoric about slavery and freedom, taxation and representation, tyranny and popular sovereignty. For them "the sovereignty of the people" suggested a democracy of property holders in which their views would be paramount, not merely a legal relation between voter and representative. The people would make policy through assemblies, but if these bodies ignored them, yeomen could resort to other means to assert their will.[21]

Neither gentlemen nor yeomen could prevent the radicalism of the Revolution from spreading to farm women. Much as yeomen, farm women had actively participated in fomenting revolt, supporting nonimportation by spinning American fabrics and boycotting tea, urging husbands and sons to support the war. Listening carefully to male rhetoric in the 1760s and early 1770s, middling farm women took advantage of Revolutionary ferment,

20. Kulikoff, *Tobacco and Slaves*, 306–8, and "Tobacco and Slaves," 429; Skaggs, *Roots of Maryland Democracy*, 183–86, 220–26; Gough, "Notes on Pennsylvania Revolutionaries of 1776," 89–103; Thayer, *Pennsylvania Politics and the Growth of Democracy*, chap. 13, esp. 179, 182–89.

21. A. F. Young, *Democratic Republicans of New York*, 18 (Yates quote). For Revolutionary War service, see Shy, "Legacy of the American Revolutionary War," 43–60, esp. 45–46; Royster, *Revolutionary People at War*, chap. 1, appendix; and chap. 6 below.

slowly becoming more conscious of themselves as potential citizens, implicitly rejecting yeomen efforts to limit democratization to themselves.[22]

Politicized by the war, farm women tried to act as good citizens, circulating petitions, testifying against Tories, managing farms, making cloth and clothes, tending to the domestic needs of the Continental Army, and giving goods and money to the Revolutionary cause. Women linked their activity both to their status as virtuous housewives and to the war against English bondage. Ideas of independence and individualism espoused by revolutionary leaders seemed to offer them greater autonomy at home or at least greater respect than they received in patriarchal farm households. Yeomen opposed such aspirations for they attacked the patriarchal base of *yeoman* citizenship.[23]

The success of the appeal of revolutionaries depended upon *prior* relations between yeomen and gentlemen. Where Whig gentlemen had protected the property of yeomen and sustained their control over wives and children, yeomen often joined the patriot cause, paying taxes to the new governments and enlisting in militia or army. In these places yeomen expected democratic social change. Such patriotism was most common in New England, most of New Jersey, eastern Pennsylvania, the Chesapeake region, and the eastern parts of the Carolinas. The long tradition of town meetings and local autonomy in New England gave ordinary citizens a voice (even if subordinate) in politics and linked the destiny of gentleman and yeoman. Local control of resources such as water and pasture lands constrained the behavior of wealthy men. In the Chesapeake colonies, where yeomen acquiesced in gentry rule in return for protection of their land and slaves, yeomen often borrowed money from gentlemen to purchase slaves.

In contrast, wherever yeomen (or would-be yeomen among tenants) saw Whig gentlemen as enemies, they joined the British. Partisan warfare between Whigs and Tories broke out in the Hudson River Valley, in Vermont, and in the Carolina backcountry, where landlords or wealthy planters had ignored the demands of yeomen. Such violence led many farm families to run for cover, away from both patriots and loyalists. Others, like residents of Livingston Manor in New York, joined the British hoping that the British would distribute land to them. And where loyalist gentlemen or landlords had maintained good relations with farmers — along Virginia's Eastern Shore — rural folk stayed loyal.[24]

22. Kerber, *Women of the Republic*, chap. 2; M. B. Norton, *Liberty's Daughters*, chap. 6.

23. Kerber, *Women of the Republic*, chaps. 3–4; M. B. Norton, *Liberty's Daughters*, chaps. 6–7; chap. 4 above.

24. W. Brown, "American Farmer during the Revolution," 327–38; Countryman, "Consolidating Power in Revolutionary America," 645–77; Kulikoff, *Tobacco and*

Yeomen and the Shaping of Revolutionary Institutions

In patriot regions yeomen extracted a steep price from gentlemen for their support, insisting upon a direct role in making public policy. Of course, they could not establish direct democracy, deciding political action as a group. Yet they achieved remarkable success. They attended mass meetings; they sent some of their number to the new state assemblies; they voted for representatives to conventions to draft state constitutions; they signed a multitude of petitions on public issues. And they sometimes achieved substantial success in vetoing or creating laws.

In the late 1770s and 1780s, written constitutions were new and untried vehicles to restrain government. As popular pressure on legislatures grew, states replaced constitutions written by legislatures in 1776–77 with those composed by special conventions where delegates sometimes received instructions from constituents. Reacting to demands for popular democracy, writers of the later constitutions (1777–86) in Massachusetts, New York, Vermont, and New Hampshire included more frequent and direct instances of consent of the people as a whole or as legislators. The constitution writers in New York and Massachusetts rejected democracy, but they understood that to maintain political control, they had to bend to accommodate the democratic desires of the yeoman and mechanic majority.[25]

Massachusetts, alone among states, sent its new constitutions to the people for ratification at town meetings. Practicing their right of consent, the citizens of Massachusetts, mostly farmers and craftsmen, rejected the first proposed constitution in 1778. In town after town, they voted against the document, usually reaching a consensus. Underneath the legal language of small-town returns, the concerns of yeomen for local autonomy, security, and freeholder democracy shone brightly. Inhabitants of various towns raised demands for emancipation of slaves; a universal male franchise (or at least one that included all men of property); election of militia officers and justices of the peace; laws favoring debtors; local control over the militia; limited powers for the governor; and a bill of rights.[26]

Listening to these farmers, the town leaders who wrote attacks on the proposed constitution espoused egalitarian ideals and an implicit labor theory of value. Men in the western Massachusetts town of Lenox insisted

---

Slaves, 300–313; Hoffman, "'Disaffected' in Revolutionary South," 273–318; Hast, *Loyalism in Revolutionary Virginia*; A. F. Young, "Afterword," 451–54.

25. Main, *Sovereign States*, chap. 5; G. S. Wood, *Creation of American Republic*, chaps. 4–5, 8–9; Lutz, *Popular Consent and Popular Control*, 38–52, chap. 6.

26. Handlin and Handlin, eds., *Popular Sources of Political Authority*, 21–23, 190–323.

that since "All Men were born equally free and independent," they had rights of "enjoying and defending Life and Liberty and acquiring, possessing and protecting Property." By excluding free Negroes and those too poor to pay taxes from the polls, the 1778 constitution made "Honest Poverty a Crime," depriving "a large Number of the true and faithfull Subjects of the State who perhaps fought and bled in their Countrys Cause" of their rights. "For how can a Man be said to [be] free and independent, enjoying and defending Life and Liberty and protecting property, when he has not a voice allowed him in" electing legislators who "can make laws to bind him." Not surprisingly, these men also decried the way the courts reduced men to subservience, complaining that the law "obligated a poor Debtor to go through a course of Law and pay the extravigant Costs, when he was willing to confess Judgment and submit to justice, which is an oppressive and Tyrannical Law and beneficial to none but Attornies."[27]

Freeholders had frequently petitioned colonial assemblies for redress of local grievances—location of the courthouse, contested local elections, creation of new counties. But the Revolution empowered ordinary men to launch petition campaigns on broader political issues. A deluge of petitions aiming at a more democratic society, for instance, reached the Virginia Assembly between 1776 and 1782. Most of these petitions still concerned local issues, but yeoman planters now demanded action on a multitude of issues: disestablishing the Anglican Church, reducing high prices speculators charged for land, paying debts in kind or paper money rather than specie, repealing unjust poll and commodity taxes, equalizing land taxes, and confirming titles of land farmed by squatters. These campaigns often generated opposition; the Assembly, for instance, received petitions asking that taxes be raised to restore the credit of the state or that the established church be kept. Residents of Orange County alone sent remonstrances to the legislature on the inequities of the land tax, the necessity of home manufactures, the operation of the militia, and freedom of religion. On average a tenth of the county's white men signed each petition.[28]

In almost every state, yeomen circulated similar petitions, creating through their diversity a new moral economy, centered around a demand for political and economic equality. They defined equality in everyday terms of ready access to unimproved land, relief from the burdens of debt, and taxes proportionate to ability to pay. Petitioners, for instance, wished to pay

27. Ibid., 253–58. The Lenox response is more radical than those from commercial towns.

28. Bogin, "Petitioning and the New Moral Economy," 391–425; Bailey, *Popular Influence upon Public Policy*; Church, comp., *Virginia Legislative Petitions*; and Kulikoff, *Tobacco and Slaves*, 309–10 (Orange County) and 423–24.

debts and taxes in paper money because they had little specie. Poll taxes forced everyone to pay at the same rate, despite differences in wealth; land taxes usually taxed the improved land of yeomen at a higher rate than the large unimproved holdings of speculators. The state, petitioners concluded, had an obligation to ensure the land tenure of poorer freeholders by issuing paper money or taxing the wealthy proportionately more heavily. They believed state action necessary because a republic could survive only if a majority of its citizens were independent farmers capable of making political choices without servile dependence upon patron, creditor, or employer.[29]

Not only did the formation of new governments encourage local attempts at instructing legislators through petitions, but voters elected more farmers of middling wealth to state legislatures, hoping men like themselves would be receptive to their views. From the 1760s to the 1780s the number of men of moderate wealth elected to lower houses in New Hampshire, New York, and New Jersey increased from a sixth to more than three-fifths, and the proportion of farmers rose from a quarter to over a half. Even in the South, which changed less, the percentage of farmers (excluding gentlemen) more than doubled, from an eighth to over a quarter. The election of farmers gave yeomen hope that their petitions (like those we have described) would be heard and the instructions they contained be made into policy. Given the divisions of opinion on most issues, petitioners gained approval with remarkable regularity.[30]

One might expect to find few successful petitions in Virginia, with its great planter ruling class. Even there, yeomen sometimes persuaded their supposed betters. We have seen how petitioning led to repeal of the law exempting overseers from service in county militias. Other examples can be found. When citizens of Kentucky County complained in October 1779 that the four hundred acres granted them for defending the county was insufficient, the assembly gave them more land. In 1780 petitioners from Amelia County, who desired both dissolution of church vestries and the right of Dissenting ministers to perform marriages, succeeded in getting several bills introduced and passed. And in 1780 citizens of Amherst County gained an extension of time to pay their taxes. When the legislature failed to grant relief—as was often the case on the issue of the religious establishment—a committee aired the issue, leaving hope for eventual favorable action.[31]

---

29. This paragraph leans heavily upon Bogin's important work "Petitioning and the New Moral Economy," 402–25.

30. For instructions, see G. S. Wood, *Creation of American Republic*, 188–96; for lower houses, see Main, "Government by the People," 391–407.

31. Church, comp., *Virginia Legislative Petitions*, 303, 356, 363; and for the campaign over the church establishment, see Buckley, *Church and State in Revolutionary Virginia*.

In state after state, the success of the yeomanry in influencing public policy during the war years led yeomen to believe that they, the majority of voters, could actually rule. In every state legislature, yeomen and their allies made up a significant minority that supported the minimal government expenditures, low taxes, credit relief, and emissions of paper money that yeomen wanted. But merchants, great planters, and small capitalists who still ruled the states opposed the yeomanry and often prevailed. When yeomen failed to gain relief in the 1780s, they turned to organizing conventions of the people or to the traditional remedy of crowd action. Shays's Rebellion of 1782–86 is a case in point. Debtor farmers in western Massachusetts tried, but failed to gain legislative relief and local control of courts and judges. Nor did a decade of endemic riots against tax collectors or auctions for property seized for debt resolve the issue. In 1786, fearing debtors prison and the loss of their lands, they closed the courts, preventing the operation of credit laws. Similar debtor agitation occurred in Maryland, South Carolina, New Jersey, Virginia, and Pennsylvania. All these agrarian upheavals were suppressed.[32]

The people-out-of-doors had often participated in crowd actions in pre-Revolutionary times, seeking a redress of grievances or a return to traditional rights. In contrast, rebels of the Revolutionary era challenged the ruling classes, demanding a democracy in which small property holders as citizens would determine public policy. The gentry ruling class and their allies observed this growth of democracy with horror and set about reimposing discipline upon an unruly agrarian population. Classical republican texts suggested their cause was virtuous and worthy of consensual support. Instead the mob had insisted upon instructing their betters, the natural aristocracy, in the business of government; had destroyed the economy; had elected venal men to state legislators (who then passed class legislation favoring debtors); and in Massachusetts had revolted against constituted republican authority. Fear of the mob, and its rejection of the "natural" aristocracy of men of talent, unified ruling classes, whether or not they eventually supported the Constitution.[33]

The intolerance of men of means toward popular democracy can be seen in their frenzied reaction to rural uprisings in the 1780s. Sometimes an extension of government, more often an example of class tensions, gentlemen had accepted but attempted to control riots in the 1760s. But since

32. Main, *Political Parties before the Constitution*, chaps. 12 and 13 discusses yeoman politics. See Szatmary, *Shays' Rebellion*, for rural uprisings in the 1780s, chap. 7; V. B. Hall, *Politics without Parties*, chaps. 6 and 7; Brooke, "To the Quiet of the People," 425–62; A. Taylor, "Backcountry Conclusion to the American Revolution"; Lee, "Maryland's 'Dangerous Insurrection,'" 329–44.

33. Main, *Political Parties*, esp. chaps. 12–13; G. S. Wood, *Creation of American Republic*, chap. 10; Cornell, "Aristocracy Assailed," 1149, 1157, 1168–69.

American states were now republics whose people were sovereign, any crowd action constituted rebellion against the people. Governments used military force to end crowd actions, like Shays's Rebellion. Once they had ended dissension, political leaders turned to incorporating local men of wealth and middling farmers who had supported yeomen into the political system.[34]

Yeomen and the American Constitution

Tiring of what they saw as democratic chaos, wealthy Whig leaders organized the Constitutional Convention in order to create a republic that constrained popular legislative behavior and the people out-of-doors. New England newspapers, for instance, increasingly insisted in 1786 and 1787 that only a stronger central government could suppress rebellion and resolve the tax and debt problems that induced deluded Massachusetts farmers to revolt. James Madison reflected these concerns in early 1787. The Confederation had failed to "guaranty to the states of their Constitutions & Laws against internal violence," increasing the odds that a minority of voters would unite with "those whose poverty excludes them from a right of suffrage, and who . . . will be more likely to join the standard of sedition than that of the established government." State legislatures, influenced by debtors, were equally pernicious, reducing the rights of creditors. "Paper money, instalments of debts, occlusion of Courts, making property a legal tender," Madison wrote, "affect the Creditor State, in the same manner they do its own citizens who are relatively creditors toward other citizens."[35]

Most delegates to the Philadelphia Convention sought a stronger national government, with the power to tax, regulate commerce, suppress internal conflict, and encourage economic development. They uniformly opposed agrarian legislation that might redistribute wealth, thereby leveling property. Not surprisingly, the document they produced reflected the interests of the commercial classes — merchants, great planters, lawyers, master craftsmen, commercial farmers. Nevertheless, the convention had to pay attention to the agenda of the people-out-of-doors, if for no other reason than to get it ratified. Although some sympathized with Alexander Hamilton's plan to establish a nation-state with a president for life and an veto over the states, they understood that the people would absolutely reject it. In this

34. For changes in gentry reactions to the people-out-of-doors after the Revolution, see G. S. Wood, *Creation of American Republic*, 319–28, 411–13; A. Taylor, "Backcountry Conclusion to the American Revolution."

35. Meyers, ed., *Mind of the Founder*, 57–65 (Madison, "Vices of the Political System of the United States"; quotes 58–59); G. S. Wood, *Creation of American Republic*, 409–13; R. R. Parker, "Shays' Rebellion," 95–113. For the views of the rulers, see Kornblith and Murrin, "Making and Unmaking of the American Ruling Class."

spirit, they rejected attempts to establish national qualifications for voting or officeholding that would have disenfranchised many urban mechanics and poorer rural folk.[36]

If the Constitution had been put to a national plebiscite of property holders, it probably would have been rejected. Most yeoman farmers living in the large states opposed it. Following the views of rural property holders, ratifying conventions in the populous states of Massachusetts and New York initially opposed the Constitution, and the final vote in these states and Virginia was very close. But rural opinion on the Constitution was split. Commercial farmers, especially those living near cities, joined urban artisans in supporting the Constitution because it created stable and larger markets for their goods and eliminated trade barriers among states.[37]

Although few essays by yeoman farmers survive from the ratification period, some writers reflected their concerns about the Constitution. Yeomen believed that a few men of wealth and prominence would dominate the new federal government and oppress common freeholders. The old concerns about land security resurfaced. In the language of the eighteenth century, yeomen feared "aristocracy," even if it turned out to be an aristocracy of talents, of educated men. Not only would these "aristocrats" ignore the legitimate demands of the yeomanry, they would support creditors and land speculators and raise unfair taxes. Yeomen unable to pay taxes or debts could lose their land and with it their class identity and their ability to support their families. Only a popular and democratic government, one with yeomen and mechanics in positions of authority, could avoid the abyss of aristocratic tyranny.[38]

The mood of the controversy led commentators to adopt the language of class. "Address of the Lowborn," an Antifederalist satire by "John Humble" published in a Philadelphia newspaper, captures yeoman anger. Denying the greater virtue of the six hundred "wellborn" men over "three millions of *lowborn* American slaves," the writer insists that "yet our feeling, through the medium of the plow, the hoe, and the grubbing axe is as acute as any nobleman's in the world." The Constitution, he thinks, has replicated the aristoc-

36. For ideological and economic divisions among the delegates to the Constitutional Convention, see F. McDonald, *Novus Ordo Seclorum*, chap. 6; for the impact of the people-out-of-doors on the Constitution, see A. F. Young, "Conservatives, Constitution, and 'Spirit of Accommodation,'" 130–38. Kornblith and Murrin, "Making and Unmaking of the American Ruling Class," quote Madison on agrarian legislation.

37. Soltow, *Wealth and Income in the United States in 1798*, chap. 10; Main, *Antifederalists*, 285–88.

38. Cornell, "Aristocracy Assailed," 1157–68, documents plebeian Antifederalism. For an example see "Speeches by Melancton Smith," in Storing, ed., *Complete Anti-Federalist*, 6:158–59.

racy of England, replacing *"kings, lords,* and *commons"* with *"President, Senate,* and *Representatives,"* the only government the wellborn believe "can save this our country from inevitable destruction." Only passive obedience will please the wellborn. When they send their standing army, "composed of the purgings of the jails of Great Britain, Ireland, and Germany" to gather taxes, "should any of those soldiers when employed . . . collecting the *taxes,* strike off the arm . . . of one of our fellow *slaves,* we will conceive our case remarkably fortunate if he leaves the other arm on."[39]

Yeomen demanded political respect from wealthy men because of their control of productive land, their large numbers, and their virtue. As Melancton Smith (a yeoman's son who became a successful merchant and a leader of the Antifederalist party) argued at the New York Convention, "those in middling circumstances . . . are inclined by habit and company with whom they associate, to set bounds to their passions and appetites . . . hence the substantial yeomanry of the country are more temperate, of better morals and less ambition than the great." For these reasons, "a representative body, composed principally of the respectable yeomanry is the best possible security to liberty."[40]

Farmers often differed in the conventions. At the Massachusetts ratifying convention, two farmers debated the Constitution, one insisting that it took property, the other that it cured the anarchy of Shays's Rebellion. Amos Singletary, a farmer from Worcester County, repeated Antifederalist fears of tyranny and aristocracy. Like Great Britain in 1775, the Constitution "claimed a right to tax us and bind us in all cases whatever," thereby taking "all we have—all our property" by taxing land. "They . . . get all the power and all the money into their own hand, and then they will swallow up all us little folks, like the great *Leviathan* . . . ; yes, just as the whale swallowed up *Jonah.*" Jonathan Smith's response supporting the Constitution is revealing. "I am a plain man," he begins, "and get my living by the plough. I am not used to speak in public, but I beg your leave to say a few words to my brother ploughjoggers." Then he explains the "effects of anarchy, that you may see the reasons I wish for good government," arguing that men took up arms to defend their property. When he "saw this Constitution, I found that it was a cure for these disorders. . . . I got a copy of it, and read it over and over," trying to understand it, looking for "checks and balances of power" and finding "them all here." Just as a small farmer would want his neighbor's support, even if a wealthy "man of learning," when his "title was disputed,"

39. M. Jensen, ed., *Documentary History of Ratification of Constitution,* 2:205–6 (*Independent Gazetteer,* Philadelphia, 29 Oct. 1787).

40. Storing, ed., *Complete Anti-Federalist,* 6:158–59; A. F. Young, ed., *Debate over the Constitution,* 23.

farmers should politically support wealthy men for "these lawyers, these moneyed men, these men of learning, are all embarked in the same cause with us . . . ; and shall we throw the Constitution overboard because it does not please us all."[41]

Notwithstanding the opposition of the yeomanry, the Constitution was ratified by the "people." If the Constitution had a popular mandate, then any challenge to constitutional federal government could be construed as an attack on the "people." Plebeian Antifederalists, however, often refused to accept the authority of the new government, as calls for new constitutional conventions and continued upheavals through the 1790s and early 1800s attest. Violence permeated backcountry regions: opponents of the Constitution rioted in Carlisle, Pennsylvania; secession movements disrupted western Virginia and North Carolina; antitax violence against the whiskey and federal direct taxes broke out in Pennsylvania, New York, and the Carolinas; squatters in Maine prevented survey of their lands by the speculator owner.[42]

Rioters expressed their concerns about land, taxes, and democracy through violent confrontations with the fiscal representatives of the new federal government, as the Fries Rebellion against the 1798 direct tax attests. The tax, passed after the Whiskey Rebellion, when Federalists realized that excise taxes on whiskey were a poor way to raise revenue, assessed dwellings, land, and slaves. Republicans attacked it because "the farmer" had to "pay impost for every foot of land" while a capitalist pays "nothing for certificates he purchased at a tenth part of their public value." Trying to defuse criticism, Federalists insisted that "poorer classes of the community would be almost wholly exempt from the tax." When put into operation, the tax was astonishingly progressive. Two-thirds of the revenue was to be raised from the tax on dwellings, and most of that gentlemen paid on their elegant homes. Frontiersmen paid just twenty cents on their log cabins, a level so low as to suggest that assessors may have deliberately underestimated their wealth.[43]

However fair the tax may have been, middling German farmers in eastern Pennsylvania rebelled against it in many ways, from petitions and public meetings to tax resistance and intimidation of assessors. When troops led by John Fries freed several tax protesters from federal custody, he was captured, tried for treason, sentenced to hang, but reprieved by President Adams. The

41. Elliot, ed., *Debates on Adoption of the Federal Constitution*, 2:101–4. I am indebted to Alfred Young for this reference.

42. Slaughter, *Whiskey Rebellion*; Cornell, "Aristocracy Assailed," 1148–72; A. Taylor, *Liberty Men and Great Proprietors*, chap. 4; Crow, "Whiskey Rebellion in North Carolina," 1–28; chap. 3 above (for direct tax).

43. Soltow, "America's First Progressive Tax," 53–58 (see 54 for quotes from James Callender and from Annals of Congress); P. Levine, "Fries Rebellion," 242–43; Beard, *Economic Origins of Jeffersonian Democracy*, 214–16.

protesters, Jeffersonian Republicans who supported the French Revolution (some wore "french cockades in their hats" to protest meetings), linked the law to the Stamp Act and called assessors and supporters of the act "Stamplers" and "Tory rascals," threatening to force one assessor "to go to the liberty pole and dance around it." At their meetings they made "a great noise; huzzaing for liberty, and democracy, damning the tories." They or their fathers had "fought for liberty" during the Revolution and they "would fight for it again." The "house tax," along with the Alien and Sedition Acts, proved that "the government is laying one thing after another, and if we do not oppose it, they will . . . make slaves of us." Listening to farmers like these Germans, Republicans ended the direct tax in 1802.[44]

Rural democratic movements that depended upon the people-out-of-doors lost legitimacy and faced, like the Pennsylvania Whiskey and Fries tax rebels, the iron hand of federal power. To influence government, they had to work through electoral politics. Once yeomen were willing to accept the dictates of majority rule, no matter how remote the majority, they could legitimately gain a place in politics. Even though the national government was dominated by men of wealth from the outset, as Antifederalists had feared, yeomen insisted on their right to gain a hearing. They participated in republican politics, electing and attempting to influence their representatives. Party politics became an arena for complex class negotiations between yeomen and rulers, negotiations often mediated by ethnicity, region, religion, and occupation.[45]

The Revolution was a crucial event for the American yeomanry. In pushing for greater freeholder democracy, they had become more conscious of themselves as a political class distinct from gentlemen and merchants. They placed their desire for secure land on state and national political agendas. But other classes — merchants, gentlemen, commercial farmers — were more powerful, as the suppression of rural rioters documents.

The Legacy of the Revolution

As we have seen, the Revolution brought the problems of yeomen and commercial farmers alike to the forefront of politics. Because politicians of all persuasions sought farm votes, they universally acknowledged the connection of the plow to liberty. But was agrarian virtue the vision of the yeoman

44. P. Levine, "Fries Rebellion," 241–58, misses the ideological context of the rebellion documented in Carpenter, stenographer, *Two Trials of John Fries*, 38, 40, 49, 58, 68, 75–77, 81, 105–6.
45. Formisano, "Deferential-Participant Politics," 473–87, sees more deference than suggested here.

for familial autonomy, patriarchal households, and local exchange or the vision of the commercial farmer for market participation, commercial development, and improving agriculture? Historians have just begun to uncover the extent and character—ideological and social—of conflicts between yeoman and capitalist. We do know, however, that profound ideological differences developed after the Revolution. In the Northeast, capitalist transformation threatened to engulf the yeomanry but in the West, where the Revolution had opened up millions of "virgin" acres, the yeomanry had room to reinvent their class and struggle with their capitalist adversaries— land speculators, creditors, improving commercial farmers—over such issues as land policy, agricultural credit, and the desirability of specialized, commercial agriculture.

In chronic uprisings we have detailed, yeomen discovered that they still had to protect their lands from rapacious creditors and landlords. Striving to feed themselves and sell small surpluses, they avoided the entangling debts that often accompanied market dependence, thereby retaining the independence needed to make virtuous political decisions. If they sought rapid settlement of unimproved lands, they opposed intensive development that might force them or their sons from farm to workshop. But creditors tied them so firmly to commodity markets that loss of their land was possible; textile mill operators recruited their children, reducing farm labor and increasing the need for farmers to hire wage labor; commercial farmers perfected new capital-intensive techniques, making older strategies of communal self-sufficiency in food difficult.[46]

The struggle of yeomen to maintain the independence that sustained their households sharpened their class language. Yeomen insisted that they were the most productive class in the country, whose surpluses accounted for much of the nation's exports. They deserved the fruits of their own labor, and since land gained value only through labor, they demanded the ownership of land they used and the right to control their family's labor on it. These ideas set yeomen against anyone, capitalist or creditor, who threatened to take their land from them, sell it at the highest price the market would bear, or disrupt the labor of the family enterprise.[47]

These yeoman ideals influenced political leaders who created a powerful ideology, often called "Jeffersonian agrarianism," but better dubbed "agrar-

46. Chap. 2 above and chap. 7 below; A. Taylor, "Backcountry Conclusion to the American Revolution"; Vickers, "Competency and Competition," 3–29.
47. Merrill and Wilentz, "Money and Justice"; Bogin, "Petitioning and the New Moral Economy," 391–425 but esp. 404–7, 422–25, and Morison, ed., "Manning's *Key to Libberty*," 215–19.

VENERATE THE PLOUGH

Fig. 3. Medal of the Philadelphia Society for the Promotion of
Agriculture, 1786.

ian realism."[48] Agrarian realists like Thomas Jefferson contended that the
best possible society was one dominated by small, independent producers.
Only widespread distribution of land could prevent usurpation of power and
destruction of the republic by wealthy merchants, lawyers, and gentlemen.
Jefferson even drafted legislation that would have given all free men in Virginia seventy-five acres of improved land upon marriage. These ideas faithfully reflected yeoman views. But the "agrarian realists" linked small-scale
farming to agricultural improvement in ways that implied greater market
embeddedness than yeomen seeking a vent for small surpluses desired. Unlike yeomen, they were committed to rapid economic development and ex-

48. Merrill, "Political Economy of Agrarian America," chap. 5, coined the term
agrarian realism in a brilliant evocation of John Adams, Thomas Jefferson, and Adam
Smith. See also R. K. Matthews, *Radical Politics of Thomas Jefferson*, chaps. 2–3.

panding foreign markets for staples. Landowners, they insisted, improved their property more rapidly than did tenants forced to pay steep rents. Since freeholders reaped all profits of their toil, they sought more productive ways to increase their output and raise exports.

However much they agreed with yeomen on the virtue of farming, northeastern commercial farmers devised a very different ideology, one based on their growing reliance on the market and desire for the intensive development of the country. The Revolution was a watershed for them. In the war high inflation had reduced the value of their "book" debts, impelling them to invest in commercial paper, once inflation had diminished. When the growth of cities created more integrated regional markets, they eagerly expanded their output and more and more of their neighbors joined their ranks.[49]

The early history of the Philadelphia Society for Promoting Agriculture illuminates the improving spirit that animated commercial farmers. Founded in 1785 by merchants, doctors, and gentlemen farmers (including Benjamin Rush, Robert Morris, and James Wilson), nearly all of its early members opposed Pennsylvania's democratic constitution of 1776 and vigorously supported ratification of the federal Constitution. They gave their first prize, a gold medal inscribed with the words "Venerate the Plough," to a member, George Morgan, a gentleman farmer from Princeton. The medal (fig. 3) shows a farmer plowing his fields with an allegorical female figure of liberty at his side. Yeomen would surely have applauded such imagery. The "agrarianism" of the Philadelphia Society, however, varied dramatically from that of yeomen. The medal showed a neat barn and farmhouse and beneath that the *Columbian Magazine* reprinted Morgan's plan for an efficient barnyard, "for affording the best shelter for cattle and procuring the greatest quantity of manure" necessary to improve output for the market which won the society's award.[50]

Commercial agriculture, with its emphasis upon individual productivity, gave farm wives an ideological opening for political participation, however circumscribed. If productivity and individual virtue should be each farmer's goal, then women's contributions should be recognized as equal to their husbands'. Although Whig leaders encouraged the Daughters of Liberty to emulate patriotism of the Sons of Liberty, they suppressed every attempt women made to claim rights as citizens. Lacking any possibility of

49. Chap. 2; Rothenberg, "Market and Massachusetts Farmers," 283–314; Clemens and Simler, "Rural Labor and Farm Household," 106–43; and Doerflinger, "Farmers and Dry Goods," 166–95, present alternative viewpoints.

50. Baatz, *"Venerate the Plough,"* chap. 1, 109–11; G. Morgan, "An Essay, exhibiting a plan for a FARM-YARD," 76–82.

gaining a public political role, wealthier rural women either kept their political opinions within their homes or diverted politics inward upon the household. With support from male Whigs, they turned themselves into republican mothers, with the political duty of training the next generation of republican men and women. The ideology of republican motherhood, which required that women be educated in politics and morality, spread through much of the countryside, but rural women interpreted it to sustain not only child nurture but rational management of farm kitchens and female market participation.[51]

If capitalist farmers seemed ready to prevent yeoman farming in the Northeast, the western frontier, won from the British and confiscated from the Indians, provided a safety valve for yeomen searching for secure land. Hundreds of thousands of whites migrated to frontier areas during the early decades of the new nation. In order to attain relative autonomy, migrating yeomen needed cheap frontier land and control over their family's labor. Men who felt most adamant about their traditional familial role left older areas overrun by commercial farms, on which women demanded equality within marriage, and migrated to rawer western frontiers.[52]

The goal of western yeomen to own land led to a century of political conflict. The question of the distribution of frontier land set land speculator and yeoman against each other. If men should have the fruits of their labor, then free land for farmers was the best policy. Free land might limit capitalist land markets; fostering petty capital accumulation might sustain the familial independence of yeomen but reduce the profits of speculators. Men of wealth sought a capitalist land system. They feared the "savagery" they thought inevitable if men were permitted to squat on unimproved land without paying for it. Insisting that location and the fertility of land, not the labor put into it, created value, they wanted state and federal governments to sell land at market prices.[53]

The American Revolution transformed class relations between yeomen and rulers. Long before the Revolution farmers, influenced by the wide availability of land in the colonies, had devised economic strategies that placed them between full self-sufficiency and the market, creating households that could be called "independent." In many colonies gentlemen attempted to

---

51. For details, see chap. 3. Kerber, *Women of the Republic*, chaps. 4, 9; Branson, "Politics and Gender"; Bloch, "American Feminine Ideals in Transition," 101–26; J. M. Jensen, *Loosening the Bonds*, chaps. 5–7.

52. Chap. 7; A. F. Young, *Democratic Republicans*, 258–61; McClelland and Zeckhauser, *Demographic Dimensions of the New Nation*, 138–39; Faragher, *Women and Men on the Overland Trail*, chaps. 2, 6.

53. Chap. 3; Onuf, *Statehood and Union*; P. W. Gates, *History of Public Land Law Development*, chaps. 4, 7–11.

gain greater control over yeoman property. Responding to these gentry actions, yeomen had devised a class ideology to sustain their rights to land.

The American Revolution both disrupted older rural class relations and created a democratic class of small property holders. Not content with passively voting for gentlemen, yeomen insisted upon democratic decision making. The labor theory of value that had sustained their property rights justified the democratic political dominance of their class in states and the nation. Small landowning property holders, as the most independent and virtuous of classes, they believed, had a right to rule. In the ferment of the 1770s and 1780s, they sometimes succeeded, electing farmers to legislatures. These men on occasion made laws emmiting paper money whose inflationary impact would allow farmers to pay their debts in depreciated currency. More often, gentlemen and early capitalists dominated the legislatures, and rural folk turned to the venerable tactics of the people-out-of-doors, closing courts, chasing tax collectors away, denying the legitimacy of faraway authorities. States and the federal government refused to abide such behavior, and widespread violence disrupted the American countryside from the 1770s to the early 1800s. Only after 1800 did yeomen pull back from crowd actions and willingly become part of the republican body politic.

The defeat of yeoman popular democracy, however, was only the first stage in the century-long struggle of yeomen to maintain their communal and patriarchal social order. On every frontier, yeomen reinvented their class, remade a world of patriarchal family government, food-producing farms, local exchange, and local self-sufficiency. But capitalist farmers and bourgeois women came to every northern frontier, igniting conflicts between yeomen and capitalists. Struggles between southern planters and yeomen were different and tended to ensure the continued viability of yeoman society. Still, the direction of change is clear. The yeoman classes, precariously poised between community and market, ultimately succumbed to a capitalist system of bourgeois farmers and farm laborers. Only the radical legacy of the Revolution sustained yeoman democracy for so long, nurturing the yeomanry in its conflict with capitalists.

Chapter 6

The Political Economy of Military Service in Revolutionary Virginia

IN 1781 EIGHTEEN-YEAR-OLD Ellis Adkisson of Bedford County, Virginia (on the western edge of the Southside piedmont frontier), served a six-month term as a substitute for Caleb Compton, who "had previously been drafted for a three month tour and had failed to go." Once draft-dodger Compton was captured, he was required to serve an additional three-month term as a mobilized militiaman. He "was under guard at the time Adkisson agreed to go in his place." This raw recruit marched toward Richmond, but when he reached the town, "news of Cornwallis' surrender had just been received." He spent his time guarding loyalists until he was discharged in March 1782. Similarly, Bartlett Belcher of Patrick County, also on the Southside frontier, had volunteered in the spring of 1780, at the youthful age of sixteen, for three months to fight Indians. Though he was as untrained as Adkisson, he marched westward for a month, but "was then permitted to take the place of his father who had been drafted for three months and left the army without permission, in consequence of which he was returned to serve six months." Wounded twice as his father's substitute and taken ill, Belcher was finally sent home. In spring 1781, after he recovered, "he volunteered to go against Cornwallis to intercept his march through Virginia." He was discharged after several months and was drafted in the summer of 1781 for another short term, but missed the Yorktown campaign.[1]

Historians have interpreted stories similar to these from varying perspectives. Military historians have insisted that short terms of service, desertion, the ready acceptance of substitutes, and the dominance of untrained soldiers in both the Continental Army and among mobilized militiamen failed to create a military force capable of defeating British troops. More recently, historians have focused upon social description of Continental soldiers and upon the development of republican ideology among them. A large proportion of young men fought in the war, but immigrants and poor

---

1. A more technical version of this essay, with a methological appendix, appeared as Kulikoff, "Political Economy." For quotes see J. F. Dorman, *Virginia Revolutionary Pension Applications*, 1:29, 5:26–27.

men among them who enlisted in the Continental Army served far longer terms than the militiamen, who tended to be sons of freeholders. Although some men joined the army because their poverty provided them with few other choices, others served because they believed in the republican principles of Whig leaders or sought democratic change. Even militiamen wanted to support the Whig cause, and an honest volunteer like Barlett Belcher could be found for every deserter like Caleb Compton.[2]

The military incompetence of militia units (and often the Continental Army), the dominance of poor men in the army, and the patriotic service of a majority of young Americans are all well documented. Public officials apparently failed to mold enthusiastic young men into a viable fighting force. An examination of military procurement policies in Virginia during the Revolutionary War suggests that public enthusiasm for the Whig cause and military failure may have been related. The principles of equity and voluntarism that underlay Virginia's procurement policies ensured that most white men served as soldiers. The way these principles were applied, however, prevented Virginia's authorities from mobilizing an effective army to fight the British invasion of the state.

Ideas of voluntarism and equity presumed that each white man was an individual, separate from other individuals, capable of freely contracting to serve in militia or army. The operation of procurement in Virginia illuminates contradictions embedded in an individualistic system. If all are free to make contracts, then a market system in enlistments, including the purchase of substitutes, can develop. These markets ensure inequality, for they encourage greater sacrifice from those too poor to avoid service while permitting those of wealth to choose how, and when, they will serve.

Principles and Practice of Military Procurement in Virginia

Gentlemen ruled pre-Revolutionary Virginia. The Assembly made economic policy, passing laws regulating the economy and setting taxes. Nonetheless, justices of the peace and sheriffs — who implemented regulations the assembly passed, administered county government, and tried civil and criminal cases — maintained substantial local autonomy. These wealthy gentlemen, who constituted Virginia's ruling class, enjoyed easy political

2. E. W. Carp, "Early American Military History," 259–84, summarizes the colonial background; Martin and Lender, *A Respectable Army*, 210–22, surveys the social history of the war; essays in Hoffman and Albert, eds., *Arms and Independence*, integrate social history with traditional military history. The best social histories of American warfare between 1754 and 1783 (besides these works) include Shy, *People Numerous and Armed*; F. Anderson, *People's Army*; Royster, *Revolutionary People at War*; Selesky, *War and Society in Colonial Connecticut*; Rosswurm, *Arms, Country, and Class*; Higginbotham, *War and Society in Revolutionary America*; Higginbotham, ed., *Reconsiderations on the Revolutionary War*.

and economic control over less wealthy men. Although small planters could choose between gentlemen standing for elections to the assembly and expected their representatives and justices to protect their landed and slave property and guarantee their autonomy in their own homes, they played no role in making policy.[3] The war fought to protect the new nation complicated the relation between gentlemen and small planters. Military service disrupted family life and threatened the property of planters. In return for their loyalty in the war effort, planters insisted upon helping form and execute military procurement policies.

The start of war in 1775 forced legislators who made Virginia political policy to provide for both national and local defense in ways consistent with their principles and acceptable to potential soldiers. The Continental Congress, which tried to meet chronic shortages of men by requiring each state to send an annual quota to the Continental Army, exacted a heavy toll on Virginia, demanding 38,850 men between 1777 and 1781, two-fifths of the white men in the state. Every Virginia company of Continental soldiers that left Virginia reduced local security. County and state leaders faced four major problems of local defense: English depredations along the broad rivers of the state, Indian and English hostility on the western frontier, loyalist attempts to disrupt good order, and the possible rebellion and desertion of slaves from their plantations.[4]

Virginia policymakers could have chosen among the three kinds of military organization common in the eighteenth century: a standing army manned by draftees and mercenaries, similar to that kept by England during wartime; a *levée-en-masse*, like French armies of the 1790s, which required every young white man be in a constant state of readiness and kept most of them under arms; the pre-Revolutionary militia system, which obligated every white man to muster periodically and to be mobilized during crises. Gentlemen adapted the militia system because it fit most closely their republican principles. They sought voluntary enlistments from an informed citizenry and, at the same time, wanted military service to be equitably distributed among citizens. To conscript men to serve in a standing army led to despotism and, in Thomas Jefferson's words was, "the last of all oppressions," one colonists recognized as such "even under monarchical government." George Mason exemplified republican military principles in a 1775 speech before the Fairfax Independent Company of volunteers. The Independent Company, he insisted, was "essentially different from a common

3. Sydnor, *Gentlemen Freeholders*; J. P. Greene, "Society, Ideology, and Politics," 14–76; Isaac, *The Transformation of Virginia*, chaps. 7–8, 11; and Kulikoff, *Tobacco and Slaves*, chap. 7.

4. Knox, "Troops Furnished by the Several States," Class V, 1:14–19; Cometti, "Depredations in Virginia," 135–51; McBride, "Virginia War Effort, 1775–1783," 6–17; Mullin, *Flight and Rebellion*, 124–36; Frey, *Water from the Rock*, 67–69, chap. 5.

collection of mercenary soldiers. It was formed upon the liberal sentiments of public good, for the great and useful purposes of defending our country, and preserving the inestimable rights we inherit from our ancestors." Since all authority depended upon a compact between people and government, no permanent officers could be tolerated. Whenever an army "is not, by some certain mode of rotation, dissolved into and blended with that mass from which it was taken, inevitable destruction to the state follows." Rotation in office, moreover, was equitable. "In a company thus constituted, no young man will think himself degraded by doing duty in the ranks, which he may in his turn command, or has commanded." A mass mobilization, however equitable, was hardly voluntary, and was not considered a viable alternative until the British invaded the state late in the war. Small planters supported these principles because they permitted them to maintain personal independence and protect their property.[5]

The principles of voluntarism and equity in military service, though compatible as long as men volunteered in great numbers, were soon rent with contradictions. During the *rage militaire* of 1775 and 1776, more than enough men volunteered to fill Continental quotas and man state units committed to Virginia's defense. Since all able-bodied men between sixteen and sixty belonged to a militia unit and could be mobilized in an emergency, the military system was both voluntary and relatively equitable. But once the *rage militaire* had passed, many fewer men volunteered, and Virginia frequently resorted to drafts to fill quotas for the Continental Army. Virginia's policymakers used draft laws to induce men to volunteer, either by prepaying their salaries through bounties or by permitting men who were drafted to buy substitutes. Since all men in the militia risked exposure to the draft, the system remained somewhat equitable. These compromises, however, transformed the meaning of voluntarism: Whigs considered bounties to be bribes, and the men who "volunteered" tended to be recently arrived immigrants or sons of poor men.[6]

The decision by Virginia's gentlemen to adapt the militia system to wartime needs greatly complicated both making and implementing military procurement policy. The Virginia legislature passed, and the governor executed, laws regulating militia mobilization and drafts for Continental and

5. Boyd et al., eds., *Jefferson Papers*, 2:18–19 (Jefferson to John Adams, 16 May 1777); Rutland, ed., *Mason Papers*, 1:229–32 ("Remarks on Annual Elections for the Fairfax Independent Company"). The best analysis of the American debate over a standing army is found in Cress, *Citizens in Arms*, chap. 4. F. Anderson, *A People's Army*, chap. 6, is the best examination of ordinary soldiers' beliefs (of Massachusetts men in the Seven Years' War).

6. McBride, "Virginia War Effort," is the best detailed examination; Van Atta, "Conscription in Revolutionary Virginia," 263–81, documents social origins of draftees.

state service. In an emergency, the governor, with advice from his Council, could act alone to get men to the battlefield. Local officials, small planters, and generals constrained the legislature and governor. Small planters insisted that gentlemen live up to their principles and enlist men in an equitable fashion; on occasion, they forced changes in laws and frequently influenced the execution of drafts. Justices of the peace, the county lieutenant (the governor's deputy in the county responsible for the procurement of men and goods), and militia officers jealously guarded their local authority over the militia; they all paid attention to public opinion, ran drafts in ways local planters thought equitable, and refused to draft men unwilling to serve. Finally, during the invasion of Virginia, the governor delegated authority to impress men from the militia into active duty to generals in the field.

The increased power of small planters to influence policy deserves emphasis. Once they began their revolution, gentlemen could no longer rely upon the king's authority to legitimate their power, and republican rhetoric of popular sovereignty increased the need for gentlemen to gain the assent of the populace before embarking upon any controversial policy. The gentry class, in fact, could rely only upon its prestige to command the assent of small planters in government policy. Gentlemen, then, had to make policies that would maintain the loyalty of all planters. Small planters went beyond the desires of gentry leaders and demanded a role in making policy, not just the right to assent to it. An examination of procurement policies in Virginia—including how the pool of men at risk to serve was determined, how men were mobilized to fight, and what provisions were made for personal emergencies of enlistees—illustrates the impact of ordinary men upon the war effort.

Virginia authorities placed only militiamen at risk to be drafted into the Continental Army or state units or to be mobilized in case of invasion. The fewer the number of men who could obtain exemptions from militia musters, the larger the pool eligible for drafts. Unsurprisingly, small planters wanted to make militia membership obligatory for men between sixteen and fifty. Almost all exemptions from militia musters and drafts common in the 1760s and 1770s—including those for doctors, slave overseers, millers, tobacco inspectors, faculty and students at the College of William and Mary, and boat pilots—were withdrawn for the war. Despite controversy, the legislature refused to exempt members of the civilian quartermaster corps who procured military supplies for militia and army. Only men with physical disabilities, ministers, and Quakers and Mennonites consistently avoided militia duty during the war.[7]

Universal risk of young men to military service, however, could reduce the security of slave plantations. Large slaveholding gentlemen feared slave

7. Alexander, "Exemption from Military Service," 163–71; McBride, "Virginia War Effort," 29–30, 43–44, 69–84.

runaways and rebellion during wartime so much that they exempted overseers of four or more adult slaves from militia musters and army drafts in
July 1775. In November 1775 John Dunmore, the last royal governor of Virginia, offered freedom to any slave who would fight the rebels; in response,
Virginia's Revolutionary Assembly maintained the exemption but required
that overseers keep arms and patrol slave quarters when so ordered by militia
officers.[8]

The exemption of overseers raised such severe criticism of its inequitable effects that it was abandoned in May 1776, just seven months after
Dunmore's proclamation. Hundreds of planters from five counties in piedmont Virginia railed against that exemption in petitions to the fifth Virginia
Convention. All the petitions made similar points. Thirty-nine "Freeholders
and Sundry Inhabitants" of Mecklenburg County complained that the law
exempting overseers "from bearing arms in the Militia & . . . being Drafted"
led "many persons" to "become Overseers that Otherways would not . . . to
Screen themselves from Fighting in defense of their Country as well as their
own Property." Poor men among the petitioners considered the exemption
"to be extreamly hard & in no ways equatable or Just." When drafted, they
would have to leave their families without support and force them to go "up
& down the County abeging, or [stay] at home starving." The overseers were
mostly youths of prime age to serve, and their exclusion would substantially
reduce the pool of eligible men. The petitioners from Amelia County even
claimed that there were 250 overseers in the county; if that number was ac-
curate, it included a fifth of the white men in Amelia.[9]

Most of the signers of these petitions were poor to middling planters
who owned few slaves. In Lunenburg County, a poor part of the Southside,
for instance, at least a quarter of those who signed a petition denouncing the
exemption of overseers owned no slaves and over two-thirds of the rest
worked with only one to five slaves. In wealthy Amelia County, where two-
thirds of the householders owned slaves, most petitioners were small slaveholders. Although just a fifth of the signers owned no slaves, about half of
the petitioners owned between one and ten slaves of all ages, too few to take
advantage of the law. Richer men, including eleven justices in Lunenburg
and eight in Amelia, rounded out the petitions. Despite benefits justices and
large slaveholders gained from the exemption of overseers from militia duty,
some of them came to understand the inequity of the practice and therefore
joined poorer neighbors in petitioning to end it.[10]

8. Mullin, *Flight and Rebellion*, 130–36; Hening, *Statutes at Large*, 9:28, 89, 140.

9. Van Schreeven and Tarter, eds., *Revolutionary Virginia*, 6:474–77; 7:47–48, 87–
88, 114–15 (quote), 236–39 (Amelia petition). There were 1,215 white male adults in
Amelia in 1782 (Martinac, "'Unsettled Disposition,'" 10).

10. Van Schreeven and Tarter eds., *Revolutionary Virginia*, 6:474–77 and 7:236–39,
linked to 1783 Lunenburg tax list (Bell, ed., *Sunlight on the Southside*, 387–417), 1768

Once overseers were placed on militia rolls, and therefore eligible for drafts, gentlemen pursued two strategies to maintain order in their slave quarters. They began monthly patrols by four men chosen from militia companies "to visit all negro quarters, and other places suspected of entertaining unlawful assemblies of slaves, servants, or other disorderly persons." In addition, great planters purchased substitutes for their own overseers if they were drafted. For instance, when Col. John Thronton commanded the Culpeper County militia regiment, and his overseer Ambrose Atkins was drafted, Thronton asked him "to procure a substitute as it was inconvenient and improper for both to leave home at the same time." [11]

The influence of small planters and local officials can be inferred from the methods legislators used to raise men from the militia for the Continental Army. They experimented with three devices: inducing men to volunteer, random draft lotteries, and self-selection by militia class. All three sought to maintain the appearance of equity and voluntarism. They forgave taxes and paid bounties to volunteers and removed their names from draft lists. Local officials most commonly permitted men to choose draftees among themselves. After justices, militia leaders, or the county lieutenant had divided the militia into a number of classes equal to their quota of men, each class chose one man for the draft, offering him any inducement they wished. This method allowed men to avoid entering the service if they had money to pay the market price of enlistment, and it permitted local officials to keep the peace in their communities. If a class refused to select anyone, justices either chose a man "who in their opinion can be spared" or held a draft lottery to determine who would go. [12]

Legislators hoped that unmarried men would volunteer "to fill the places of those who had families and would otherwise be compelled to serve" and thereby save their counties the expense of supporting wives and children left behind. They devised two methods to ensure the predominance of young men among enlistees: draft lotteries of bachelors, and the payment of substitutes by draftees. Married men were considered such poor risks by legislators that they were excluded from a 1777 draft designed to replenish Virginia's Continental forces. Each never-married man was required to participate in a draft lottery. This experiment was quite successful, but it was

---

and 1782 Amelia tax lists (Virginia State Library, Richmond [VSL]; U.S. Bureau of Census, *Heads of Families*, 11–13). For a detailed breakdown, see Kulikoff, "Political Economy." Names of justices of the peace, 1764–82, are found in Beeman, *Evolution of the Southside Backcountry*, 234–36; *Justices of the Peace of Colonial Virginia*, 63, 69. See Martinac, "'Unsettled Disposition,'" 39, for Amelia slaveholding.

11. Hening, *Statutes at Large*, 9:278; J. F. Dorman, *Virginia Pension Applications*, 3:42–43.

12. McBride, "Virginia War Effort," chap. 3; Hening, *Statutes at Large*, 9:89–90, 274–77, 291, 338–43, 588–92, 10:18–21, 32–34, 257–62, 326–37, 391–93, 417–21; J. F. Dorman, *Virginia Pension Applications*, 2:44–45.

never repeated because it unfairly placed the full burden of the war — both army service and financial losses — on the backs of young men.[13]

Through most of the war, Virginia officials raised an army of young men by permitting militiamen to choose among themselves or procure a substitute. Any draftee who wished to avoid service could buy a substitute and receive credit for the time his employee served. Both of these strategies spread the cost of warfare over the male population. Young men who served as substitutes or who were chosen by their militia companies received both the state bounty and extra payments by their class; older family men avoided service but either added to the booty given to the classes' substitutes or paid for their own replacements.[14]

Gentlemen and substantial yeomen procured substitutes in great numbers, especially late in the war. At least a sixth of Virginia soldiers were substitutes, and a few of them served numerous short terms for other men. Substitutes were young men; over a third of all substitutes first enlisted as adolescents, sometimes as young as fourteen or fifteen. They were substantially poorer than the men they replaced, having rarely formed households, and may have accepted military service to establish personal independence.[15]

Substitutes not only spread the cost of warfare throughout the adult population, but replaced older men in militia or army, permitting fathers to support their families at home. Over a third of substitutes replaced fathers, brothers, or other kin in army or militia. Several examples suggest how family heads allocated war service within their families. In 1781 David Bartee, then sixteen, twice took his father's place, serving about half that year. Similarly, Shadrack Barns, age fourteen, served two months in 1778 "as a substitute for his father Francis Barns who had been selected by the division of the militia to which he belonged." Young Barns apparently enjoyed the experience, for he continued to take other men's places for a year, until November 1779, when "he again substituted himself for his father . . . for three months." The service of Bartee and Barns allowed their fathers, men in their forties, to provide for their families. Other family allocations were also common. In 1781 Stephen Bailey, age seventeen, served four months "as a substitute for his brother Simon Bailey who had just completed a term of service for three years when he was drafted in a company."[16]

13. McBride, "Virginia War Effort," 98–101; Hening, *Statutes at Large*, 9:337–49.

14. McBride, "Virginia War Effort," 60, 96, 113–14, 169–72.

15. Age data calculated from a sample of 62 soldiers with known kinds of service from pensions in J. F. Dorman, *Virginia Pension Applications*, vols. 1–6; Kulikoff, "Political Economy," describes these data. See Van Atta, "Conscription in Revolutionary Virginia," 275–83, for similar age data and for data on wealth of draftees and substitutes.

16. J. F. Dorman, *Virginia Pension Applications*, shows that 18 of 49 men who substituted for a known individual served for kindred (9 for fathers, 3 for brothers, 6 for

As long as young men readily accepted bounties and payments to join the militia and army, the system of substitution allocated military service equitably, except for exposing poor men with limited options to greater risk of injury or death. But in 1780 and 1781, when hyperinflation and the English invasion of Virginia reduced the number of men willing to be substitutes, poor planters could no longer afford them. In March 1781, 132 men from Orange County, most of whom were nonslaveholders or owned just a couple of slaves, complained that a recent call to draft men by class was unfair, even though they had "Liberty to hire a man for three years or during the War." They had failed to hire a substitute and wanted to serve three-month militia terms rather than provide a man for eighteenth months, as the law required, "not only as seperation for that length of Time from our dear families would so depress our spirits as to Cool our Zeal . . . but also our families (which is Very dear unto us) losing our Care of two Crops [and] must in all human probability come to misery and ruin." These men had a point. Although two-thirds of the wealthiest quarter of men drafted in Culpeper County in 1781 procured substitutes, less than two-fifths of drafted nonslaveholders could afford to buy one.[17]

Although this system encouraged voluntarism, democratic or random choice of draftees, and the market allocation of military service through the purchase of substitutes, it sometimes seemed inequitable to draftees. Nineteen of the forty-seven men chosen in Fauquier County in the "bachelor" draft of 1778 refused to enlist because "the Law was partial." Perhaps a tenth of the men drafted for Continental service in 1778 failed to rendezvous with their units, and about one out of seven evaded the draft in 1780. Once they entered military service, a majority of soldiers and militiamen stayed under arms. About a tenth of Virginians mobilized to fight in 1780 deserted before reaching the Continental Army. The Continental Army itself suffered a much higher rate of desertion: one in five deserted throughout the war, with peaks in 1778 (the Valley Forge winter) when a third left without permission, and in 1781 when a quarter deserted.[18]

---

other kin). Cases cited may be found ibid., 5:94–95, 13; 4:33. A lower percentage (9/ 41 or 22%) served for kin in Culpeper in 1781 (Van Atta, "Conscription in Revolutionary Virginia," 277–78).

17. Van Atta, "Conscription in Revolutionary Virginia," 271–73; W. H. B. Thomas, *Patriots of the Upcountry*, 125–27. I identified 68 of 132 petitioners in a 1782 tax list printed in U.S. Bureau of Census, *Heads of Family*, 39–40, counting duplicate names as half, and found 23.5 men with 0 slaves, 15 men with 1–3 slaves of all ages, 18 men with 4–9 slaves, and 11.5 men with 10+ slaves.

18. McBride, "Virginia War Effort," 100–101, 104–5, 111–15; Goldenberg, Nelson, and Fletcher, "Revolutionary Ranks," 185, 189; Edmundson, "Desertion in the Army during the Revolutionary War," chap. 8, esp. 242.

Soldiers deserted for a variety of reasons, both honorable and disreputable. Most men who evaded the draft apparently stayed at home, running their households or helping their parents. More landowners than agricultural laborers deserted. These men apparently feared their families would become destitute if they stayed in the army; these fears, and perhaps the rate of desertion rose during spring planting and fall harvests of corn, wheat, and tobacco. Other deserters, including sick and injured men sent home on furloughs who failed to return, believed that they had served their full terms. Men in the field sometimes left their units after defending their country. Two militia companies from Bedford County, for instance, deserted in 1781 "after six weeks service, claiming a Discharge at the end of that Time" because the county lieutenant had promised that "they should not be compelled to serve more than six weeks." Poor food, inadequate clothing, and a lack of weapons induced others to desert. Some men evaded the draft, or deserted, for other reasons: they repeatedly volunteered to collect multiple bounties, ran away from the field of battle, or refused to defend their republican liberties.[19]

Virginia legislators only moderately penalized draft evasion and even desertion because they knew that the military system was neither entirely equitable nor completely voluntary. Draft evaders were sent to join their units; deserters were supposed to serve an additional six or eight months under arms, in addition to their current term. Until nearly the end of the war, moreover, deserters captured by a militia class could be forced to serve as their draftee. Those who harbored deserters risked fines or imprisonment, but parents and spouses — those most likely to hide deserters — escaped punishment.[20]

Local authorities, mindful of home emergencies and inequities in the execution of draft laws, enforced even these mild laws against deserters with discretion. The lieutenant of Hanover County permitted men he felt drafted unfairly to live peaceably, and there were too few officers in Greenville County to institute a court martial to try deserters. The court martial of Augusta County was active but lenient: it fined less than a third of the fifty-nine men brought before it between 1776 and 1778 for "failure to rendezvous"; it tried just eleven of the eighty-seven men charged with desertion in 1778 and 1779, and acquitted six of them; and in 1781, only about a third of the seventy-four men charged with desertion were required to serve an extra six months. Extenuating circumstances may explain most decisions of county

19. Goldenberg, Nelson, and Fletcher, "Revolutionary Ranks," 185, 189; Alexander, "Deserters from the Virginia Forces," 137–46, and "Desertion and Its Punishment," 383–97; McBride, "Virginia War Effort," 246–60 (249–50 for Bedford).

20. Alexander, "Desertion and Its Punishment," 383–97; McBride, "Virginia War Effort," 246–47.

officials favorable to deserters. For instance, in 1778 after some untrained Virginia militiamen had fled British troops in South Carolina, and lost their clothing and equipment, their officers illegally permitted them to return home. Although they were charged with desertion, few of them had to serve extra time. Faced with such meager enforcement of anti-desertion laws, military authorities were reduced to complaining to Governor Jefferson about the "open toleration" and even "protection which is afforded to deserters."[21]

Although many men deserted to support their families, most poor soldiers left young wives and aged parents to cope with farms in their absence. State authorities recognized the needs of families of soldiers. In 1778 the Virginia Council distributed salt and wool and cotton cards to families of soldiers. The legislature required county courts to provide aid for "the wives, children, and aged parents of all poor soldiers who cannot by their own industry support themselves during their absence from home in the publick service" and paid pensions to widows of men killed in action. The generosity of justices varied. While justices in Charlotte and Pittsylvania counties apparently supported a handful of the poorest wives of soldiers, Caroline County court paid allotments to about one family in twenty during the war. Two-thirds of the recipients were wives and widows; the rest were old men who had been supported by their sons.[22]

Wartime public policy in Virginia, in summary, was designed to ensure both voluntarism and equity in military service. Local officials responded to pressure from planters and their sons by implementing laws and executive orders in ways that granted these men great independence. Inducements to voluntary enlistment, democratically organized drafts, and the development of the substitute system all provided flexibility and substantial freedom for freeholders and their sons. But it was an imperfect system that often forced youths and poorer men to fight more often than their elders and betters; country gentlemen understood these inequities and tolerated draft evasion and desertion in the name of equity and freedom.

Patterns of Wartime Service

Only an examination of the war records of Virginia's soldiers can document how successfully state authorities implemented principles of equity and voluntarism. We need to know the proportion of the white men of Virginia who served in the army or mobilized militia and to examine the age at which men

21. McBride, "Virginia War Effort," 59–62, 153–56, 250–57.
22. McIlwaine, ed., *Journals of Council of State*, 2:23, 34; Hening, *Statutes at Large*, 9:279, 344–45, 588; 10:212, 225–26, 262; W. S. Morton, comp., "Charlotte County, Va.," 85–86; Clement, *History of Pittsylvania County*, 176–77; T. E. Campbell, *Colonial Caroline*, 376–78.

first enlisted, the branch of service they entered, and the number of months they served. Such an analysis can distinguish between volunteer soldiers (probably mostly poor) and drafted militiamen (a cross-section of the population). Retrospective lists of men who served, contemporary muster rolls, and a sample of Revolutionary War pension records provide data for this kind of analysis.[23]

A remarkably high proportion of the white male population of Virginia served during the Revolutionary War. Around half of white men over sixteen saw active duty either in the army or in a militia unit activated for state defense or national service. But the Revolution was a young man's war. Around four-fifths of youths between the ages of sixteen and twenty-five in 1775 or who turned eighteen during the war enlisted, but men above thirty rarely entered military service.[24]

An entire generation of white men, born in Virginia between 1750 and 1765, participated in the war effort. Half of these men first enlisted as teenagers, and another third entered military service by age twenty-five (table 1). Men in the Tidewater tended to marry in their mid-twenties, while Piedmont men probably wed by age twenty-two. Most enlistees, therefore, were unmarried youths, some of whom volunteered to gain independence from their families for the first time. Unmarried soldiers apparently postponed marriage until they thought their service was complete or until the war ended. These youthful soldiers served their terms almost exclusively with men their own age. Despite reenlistments and sometimes lengthy terms of service, two-fifths of Virginia soldiers found on two muster rolls were still teenagers, and two-thirds of the rest were under twenty-six.[25]

Married Virginians enlisted much less frequently. Just one-sixth of Virginia's soldiers entered the military in their mid-twenties, thirties, or forties. Some of these men may have still been unmarried, and most of the rest prob-

23. Data analyzed in this section are from two pension rolls (Chesterfield Supplement, and Revolutionary War Records, collected by Kenneth Sokoloff and Georgia Villaflor) and from the 537-case sample from J. F. Dorman, *Virginia Pension Applications*. My findings are consistent with Goldenberg, Nelson, and Fletcher, "Revolutionary Ranks," 182–89; Sellers, "Common Soldier in the American Revolution," 151–61; Van Atta, "Conscription in Revolutionary Virginia," 267–81.

24. I estimated the number of men in arms from a random sample in Gwathmey, ed., *Historical Register of Virginians*. I calculated the population at risk to serve from data in Brumbaugh, ed., *Maryland Records*, 1:1–88, and from age at first service in the pension sample. Using 1781 as a benchmark year, I assumed that all men 19–30 were at risk with 35% of those 16, 55% of those 17, 76% of those 18, 66% of those 31–35, 50% of men age 34–44 and 10% of men age 45–54.

25. For age at marriage of white men in Prince George's County, Maryland, see Kulikoff, "Tobacco and Slaves," 436–38. Men born in that county in the 1750s and 1760s married at an average age of 27.3, about 1.5 years older than surrounding cohorts.

Table 1.
Age structure of the population under arms

Age group[a]	Percentage of men			
	In general population	At age of entry	Age of men under arms Va. born	foreign born
11–16	12	20	8	*[b]
17–19	10	31	35	9
20–22	11	19	24	17
23–25	11	14	12	21
26–29	15	9	8	18
30–34	11	5	6	15
35–39	10	1	3	8
40+	19	1	4	14
Number	1174	451	1353	332

Sources: For general population, ages of men found in the Prince George's County, Maryland, 1776 census, in Brumbaugh, ed., *Maryland Records,* 1:1–88; for age at entry, pension sample in J. F. Dorman, *Virginia Revolutionary Pension Applications,* vols. 1–6; for age of men under arms, see Chesterfield Supplement; Revolutionary War Records, vol. 1.

[a]In the general population, only those 15–16 were counted under 11–16, and the 40+ group included those 40–51. Eleven was the youngest age of entry found in the pensions, but the youngest Virginia-born soldier on the muster rolls was 13. The oldest age of entry was 49 but the oldest native soldier was 59 and the oldest immigrant was 60.

[b]Represents less than .5%.

ably left a young wife and only one or two children at home. Men between thirty and fifty, who had growing families of small children to support, almost never enlisted. While about two-fifths of men between fifteen and fifty were age thirty or older, just 7 percent of soldiers first enlisted after their thirtieth birthday and less than a seventh of the men under arms late in the war were over thirty (table 1).

Local authorities drafted immigrants or induced them to enlist without regard to age because they less often relied upon them for political support. Nearly a fifth of Virginia's mobilized soldiers were foreigners, most of them probably Scots-Irish immigrants in the early 1770s who had moved from Pennsylvania to the back reaches of the Northern Neck or to the Valley of Virginia. These newcomers, mostly poor men without land or good prospects, enlisted in large numbers throughout the war. Moreover, a higher proportion of immigrants than native sons served as substitutes. The largest group of immigrant soldiers entered military service in their early twenties, soon after they arrived in Virginia. Nonetheless, proportionately far more immigrants than natives served in their thirties and forties; in fact, nearly two-fifths of the men over thirty on active duty were immigrants.[26]

Young men from nearly every section of Virginia participated equally in the patriot war effort. Revolutionary leaders maintained firm control over the Northern Neck (between the Potomac and Rappahannock rivers), the Tidewater between the Rappahannock and James rivers, and all of the piedmont, and local authorities from all these areas sent large numbers of men to fight. (Men from the Southside were fighting in South Carolina much of the time the muster rolls were taken in Virginia). Local officials on the Eastern Shore and in the area surrounding Norfolk, however, tended to support the crown, and these counties sent fewer than half of their fair share of men to join the Revolutionary army and militia (table 2).[27]

Militiamen chose and local officials enlisted remarkably similar kinds of men throughout Virginia. Procurement officials sought toenlist youths for the first time in their late teens and kept them under arms for almost two years at various times during the war. Men in every section except Tidewater enlisted at an average (mean) age of about twenty-one, and there were similar distributions of age at first enlistment in each region.[28]

The great length of the Revolution severely taxed human resources in Virginia, and the principles of equity and voluntarism that gentlemen pursued in running the war compounded the problem. Early in the war local officials could call upon a large population of young men who had not yet been mobilized and expect them to serve an equitable term under arms. Nearly half of Virginia's soldiers probably first enlisted during 1776 or 1777, the first two full years of the war. Since so many men had not served, gentlemen excused young men from further risk of service once they had been under arms for about a year and a half, and soldiers apparently came to believe that further service was unfair (see table 5). As a result, there were many fewer men available to replace these early enlistees once they returned home; only men unfit for service and boys too young to join early in the war had avoided mobilization by early 1778. The smaller population at risk, combined with American demoralization after the winter at Valley Forge, further reduced the number of new men under arms. Just a tenth of Virginians who

26. Chesterfield Supplement and Revolutionary War Records, I, VSL; Kulikoff, *Tobacco and Slaves*, 142; Mitchell, *Commercialism and Frontier*, 16–18, 34–36, 40–44, 55–56, 104–7, 113–15; Van Atta, "Conscription in Revolutionary Virginia," 280–82.

27. Hast, *Loyalism in Revolutionary Virginia*, chaps. 5–8.

28. Similarities in distributions are suggested by the similar standard deviations of age at first enlistment in each of the regions: 4.8–5.8 years in all regions but Tidewater (4.2 years).

Table 2.
Regional distribution of Virginia soldiers

Region[a]	Percentage of men		
	In population	On muster rolls	In pensions
Loyalist Tidewater	9.9	7.3	3.1
Rest of Tidewater	12.6	12.3	8.6
Northern Neck	14.6	22.6	17.0
Central piedmont	21.5	32.0	31.3
Southside	20.6	10.3	18.0
Shenandoah Valley	12.9	7.4	16.2
West Virginia	7.9	8.2	5.7
Number	58,169	1576	511

Sources: "State of the Inspector's Accounts"; Chesterfield Supplement; Revolutionary War Records, vol 1; J. F. Dorman, *Virginia Revolutionary Pension Applications,* vols. 1–6.

   [a]Loyalist Virginia includes the Eastern Shore and counties surrounding Norfolk; rest of Tidewater includes all other counties on the James, York, and Rappahannock rivers to the heads of navigation; Northern Neck includes counties on the Potomac River; Central piedmont, counties above the heads of navigation between the James and Rappahannock rivers; Southside, piedmont counties south of the James; the Shenandoah Valley, counties between the Blue Ridge and Allegheny Mountains; and West Virginia, counties currently in that state.

served during the war first joined in 1778. Even the need for men for the southern campaigns and the invasions of Virginia in 1779, 1780, and 1781 turned up few new men. Only two-fifths of Virginia's soldiers first enlisted during those years (table 3).

   Procurement practices varied markedly over the course of the war. In 1776, when few men had been mobilized, youths began their first term at an average age of twenty-two. As men in their twenties completed their terms, militia classes enlisted younger and younger men, and by 1778 youths first enlisted, on average, when they were nineteen. When the southern campaigns and the invasion of Virginia led officials to draft older, possibly less fit, men to join army or militia, the average age of first enlistment rose to the level attained early in the war (table 3).

   Since the war continued long after most eligible men had been mobilized, officials were forced to enlist veterans. Men who first joined the Continental Army or state units early in the war served more than two years — less than half the time between their enlistment and the end of the war — before the war concluded. Men young or lucky enough to hold off

Table 3.
Participation in the war effort in Virginia, 1775–1782

Year of first enlistment	Percentage of enlistees	Average number months served	Average age at enlistment
1775	5	30.2	21.9
1776	24	26.5	21.8
1777	22	27.4	20.5
1778	10	21.7	18.9
1779	14	16.8	19.6
1780	13	12.8	21.7
1781	12	13.2	21.1
1782	1	9.8	23.2
Number	432	—	—

Source: J. F. Dorman, *Virginia Revolutionary Pension Applications,* vols. 1–6.

enlisting until later in the war served, in total, less than half as long. The average length of service, in fact, began to decline in 1778, three years before the end of the war; by 1780 and 1781, new enlistees naturally served only about a year under arms (table 3).

Although every white youth was at risk to serve by age twenty or twenty-one, he could choose, within limits, the terms of his enlistment. He might decide to "volunteer" to join the Continental Army or the Virginia State Line, and accept governmental bounties and other inducements from his militia class in payment for giving up his freedom for either three years (early in the war) or eighteen months (in 1780 or 1781). As many as half the men who enlisted in Virginia served solely in the army, and on average, they were under arms for twenty-seven months. A man who wanted to avoid lengthy service could wait to be drafted by his militia class for a few months under arms. At least a third of the enlistees served just in the militia; they were drafted several times and served about a year (table 4).

Virginia legislators were reluctant to coerce men to join the army for long terms, but provided inducements (as we have seen) to encourage men to volunteer. So many youths accepted bounties and payments from militia classes that only a fifth of all men under arms refused to "volunteer," and these reluctant draftees served, on average, a total of only eleven months. Most draftees also volunteered or served as substitutes, but they usually volunteered for mobilized militia duty and served an average of only fifteen months. Men who "volunteered" for the army served on average terms of twenty-seven months, about twice as long as draftees (table 5).

Table 4.
Participation in the war effort in Virginia by branch of service

Branch of service	Percentage of enlistees[a]	Average number months served	Average age at 1st enlistment
Militia	32	12.6	20.9
Army	56	27.1	21.2
Army & militia	9	23.0	19.8
Navy & other	3	38.4	18.9
Number	482	470	409

Source: J. F. Dorman, *Virginia Revolutionary Pension Applications,* vols. 1–6.
[a]Since pension laws required men to prove six months service to receive a stipend, the pension applications undercount the proportion of militiamen and exaggerate the proportion of men in the Continental Army.

Table 5.
Participation in Virginia's war effort by form of enlistment

Form of enlistment	Percentage of enlistees	Average number months served	Average age at 1st enlistment
Draftees	21	10.6	21.3
Volunteers	48	27.4	21.3
Substitutes	4	13.6	17.8
Draft + volunteer	14	14.6	20.9
Draft + substitute	4	15.2	19.7
Volunteer + substitute	4	14.6	21.7
All three forms	3	14.6	19.1
Number	428	416	373

Source: J. F. Dorman, ed., *Virginia Revolutionary Pension Applications,* vols. 1–6; all known cases of the 537-man sample are included in the table.

Although gentlemen pursued policies meant to be both equitable and voluntary, the results were neither completely equitable nor entirely voluntary. Gentlemen permitted the marketplace to determine the length of time men spent under arms. Sons of men who owned slaves or land or both, a majority of the white youths of the region, set the terms of their participation in the war effort, volunteering for patriotic reasons or paying substitutes when mobilization proved inconvenient. These men, along with gentry youths who did not wish to become officers, left most of the fighting to the poor and immigrants, men with few opportunities outside of the military, who were induced to volunteer for long terms in the army.[29]

Notwithstanding these inequities, Virginia's policymakers achieved a substantial degree of equity, within the constraints of a hierarchical, slave society. Service during the Seven Years' War had been far less equitable. Native-born property holders and their sons refused to serve, no matter what inducements were offered. About half the soldiers were immigrants, usually poorer laborers or craftsmen, a far higher proportion than in the general population. Many had probably been indentured servants, now free; most of the rest were probably sons of smaller landowners or tenants, unlikely to get land, and induced to serve by the promise of western land.[30]

It is difficult, however, to determine precisely how equitable and voluntary military procurement was in Revolutionary Virginia because there were so many independent influences on the time a man would spend under arms. Volunteers *and* men who first enlisted early in the war served long terms; draftees *and* men who first enlisted late in the war served short terms; Continental soldiers served longer than mobilized militiamen. Age at entry, year of birth, branch of service, and form of enlistment all could have had an impact upon the number of months a man stayed under arms. Only an analysis that independently accesses each of these variables can help disentangle this puzzle (table 6).

Virginia officials and probably militia members expected all young white men to participate in the war for roughly the same number of months. The year a man of appropriate age was born had no influence on the number of months he served; a youth born in 1765 served about the same length of time, all other things being equal, as his older brother born in 1750. More-over, the age at which a man joined did not matter; a youth who was first mobilized when he was seventeen served no longer than his cousin who first enlisted at age twenty-two. This unvarying pattern of service resulted from both the unwillingness of men to serve terms longer than their neighbors and the refusal of local officials to force men who had already served fair terms to enlist again.

Nonetheless, there were substantial variations in the number of months served by young men. The year of first enlistment, branch of service (militia or army), form of enlistment (volunteer or draftee), and region of enlistment together explain over one-third of the variation in the number of months

29. Kulikoff, *Tobacco and Slaves*, 132–38, 152–57, gives data on slaveholding. For the overrepresentation of poor Virginians in the Continental Army see Van Atta, "Conscription in Revolutionary Virginia," 267–81; for other states, see Papenfuse and Stiverson, "General Smallwood's Recruits," 117–32, and Lender, "Social Structure of the New Jersey Brigade," 27–44.

30. Ferling, "Soldiers for Virginia," 307–28.

Table 6.

Determinants of mean number of months served by Virginia enlistees[a]

Type of enlistee	Mean number of months by year of enlistment		
	1775–1776	1777–1779	1780–1782
Draftee or substitute	19.3	13.9	10.7
Only volunteers	32.1	23.2	17.8
Volunteer militiaman	22.1	16.0	12.3
Draftee or substitute militia	13.3	9.6	7.4

Source: J. F. Dorman, ed., *Virginia Revolutionary Pension Applications,* vols. 1–6. See Kulikoff, "Political Economy of Military Service," Appendix for computational details.

[a]Mean length of service was predicted by an ordinary least squares multiple regression equation. The table computed estimated months of service for enlistees from every region of the state except Southside (the only regional variable that was statistically significant), where men served, on average, 10.3% shorter terms. The table accesses the independent impact of year of entry, branch of service, and form of enlistment on logged number of months served (the dependent variable).

Virginians served under arms. Much of the rest of the variance could probably be explained by the wealth and social class of youths and their fathers if those data were available.

This analysis strongly suggests that local officials and militia members considered total service of a year to eighteen months to be the maximum equitable term a young man could be forced to endure. A youth first drafted in 1775 or 1776 (and therefore at risk for seven or eight years) spent nineteen months under arms; a man drafted during the middle of the war served fourteen months. This definition of equity was apparently formulated by the middle of the war, when militia companies stopped drafting veterans who had already served terms of sufficient length. By 1780, when the British invaded Virginia, a substantial portion of the militia had already put in their time and could not be called on again without challenging this definition of equitable service.

Local officials induced a sufficient number of men to volunteer to limit draftees to a maximum total term of nineteen months. Men who volunteered (and received bounties and other payments for their effort) served an average of ten months longer than draftees. Patriotic youths who volunteered for the Continental Army during 1775 and 1776 often enlisted several times during the war and spent, on average, nearly three years under arms. This difference between volunteers and draftees held up for the entire war. Volunteers who first enlisted in 1780 and 1781 served eighteen months, through the Yorktown campaign. In contrast, men drafted from militia units in 1780 or 1781 served only seven months, often missing important engagements in the Virginia campaign.

Militiamen and local gentlemen rotated enlistments. Every soldier had the right to spend time at home after he completed a term. Soon, however, the veteran risked exposure to new drafts. The earlier in the war one first enlisted, the more times one risked being drafted for additional short terms or faced requests for army "volunteers." Men who first entered army or militia units during 1775 and 1776 served five months longer than men who first enlisted between 1777 and 1779 and endured service nine months longer than those who were first mobilized in 1780 or 1781.

Patriotic Virginia youths understood they had to help defend their state and new country but insisted that the burdens of service be distributed equitably among all young men. Gentlemen who administered military procurement pursued policies of equity and voluntarism by trying to enlist men in a manner consistent with both republican ideology and the desires of planters. When these policies conflicted with each other, officials usually permitted the marketplace to determine who would become a soldier and how long he would fight the British. The military units created by these policies were almost by definition temporary, manned by ill-trained citizen-soldiers or poor volunteers, and likely to disintegrate when the terms of a substantial portion of their members came due.

The Militia and the Invasion of Virginia

This militia-based, voluntary, and market system of military manpower procurement worked well early in the war but failed when the British invaded Virginia in force in late 1780. Between 1776 and 1779, Virginia provided most of the men the Continental Congress demanded, usually by holding drafts. They mobilized other militiamen to police slaves and loyalists, to guard prisoners of war, patrol the state's rivers, and serve in state-operated forts. These successes carried within them the seeds of failure in 1780 and 1781. The militia was not trained to fight regular army units and came to expect short terms of service and liberal leave policies. Governor Jefferson and other officials had to adapt the defense of the state against the British to these expectations. The ill-trained troops sent to fight the invasion for short terms were, not surprisingly, defeated whenever they faced the British and were saved only by Continental and French troops and by the French navy.[31]

Between 1776 and 1779, Virginians flocked to the Continental Army and

31. McBride, "Virginia War Effort," chaps. 4–6; Selby, *Revolution in Virginia,* chaps. 14–15.

fought in every important battle. In 1776 and 1777 between six and eight thousand Virginians — about a seventh of the white men in Virginia between the ages of fifteen and thirty — fought with the army. Even in 1778, Virginia sent 5,500 men, and there were still 4,500 Virginians in the army in 1779. War weariness set in and Virginia officials could replace neither the men whose terms had expired nor those captured when Charleston fell to the British. In 1780 the army could count on only four thousand Virginians, nearly two-fifths of them untrained militiamen. Only 1,200 Virginians remained in the Continental Line by 1781, and Governor Jefferson succeeded in mobilizing just 2,900 additional unprepared militiamen to help repel the invasion of the state.[32]

Virginia state units and mobilized militia helped maintain Virginia's security. These men functioned as a local police force, searching slave quarters for runaways and malcontents, intimidating loyalists, searching rivers for British invaders. Whenever invasion seemed imminent, county officials mobilized local militia units to meet the danger. Militiamen performed these tasks well. Few slaves ran away unless large numbers of British came to their neighborhood. Militiamen tightened their watch when rumors of invasion reached them, devising complicated signals to warn the populace. The county militia were called out and planters were warned to evacuate their plantations when small British contingents landed. Virginia loyalists were forced to pledge support to the new government, were exiled, or watched carefully if they stayed in Virginia. Loyalists failed to mount the kind of guerrilla warfare that kept backcountry Carolina in chaos. Nevertheless, the militia could not prevent loyalist domination of the Eastern Shore and the area around Norfolk, stop resistance on the western frontier, or fully protect frontiersmen from the Indians.[33]

The militia provided logistical and support services for the army. They aided the quartermaster corps in requisitioning and delivering supplies to army units, thereby freeing more seasoned troops to fight. Guarding prisoners of war — loyalists, Quaker resisters, English and German troops — was the most important support service provided by the militia. The problem of guarding prisoners increased greatly in late 1778 when four thousand men captured at the battle of Saratoga arrived in Albemarle County. The Council called out the militia of six counties surrounding Albemarle to guard the

32. Knox, "Troops Furnished by the Several States," Class V, 1:14–19, including Knox's estimates of short-term militiamen, reduced to full-time equivalents. These numbers are probably inflated (not all the men served full years) but represent the trend adequately.

33. McBride, "Virginia War Effort," chaps. 1, 5; Hast, *Loyalism in Revolutionary Virginia*; McIlwaine, ed., *Journals of Council of State*, 2:43, 86; McIlwaine, ed., *Official Letters Governors of Virginia*, 1:65–66, 182, 184.

troops, alerted county lieutenants to watch for prison insurrections, and recruited volunteer companies to replace the militiamen. This unpleasant duty, and poor camp conditions, almost led to mutinies, and the situation worsened when the British invaded Virginia, for these troops had to move prisoners across the mountains.[34]

Early in the war, when a British invasion seemed far away, Virginia militiamen developed a benign image of their role as citizen-soldiers. Most Virginians probably realized by early 1778 that soldiers in the Continental Army risked death from disease and injuries, but mobilized militiamen expected to serve only a few months away from their families. Virginia officials sometimes responded favorably to militia complaints, thus solidifying their expectations. In November 1776 a battalion stationed at Portsmouth asked to be relieved because of illness, difficult service some of them had faced in North Carolina, and "the great length of time they have been on Duty and consequently absent from their families." The Council considered their request just and tried to find ways to permit their release. A year later the Council ordered the release of Brunswick and Southampton county militiamen on duty at Portsmouth, even though they were "of Opinion, that they had not been long enough in Service to Expect to be relieved." The insistence of citizen-soldiers that their tours be brief became a political issue in Caroline County when Col. James Upshaw supposedly refused to support the desire of his men for a discharge "to return home to se and take care of their wives and Children," treating "it lightly, saying he wanted to come home too, to se his Mares and Colts, but they must all stay to do their duty; thus comparing, they say, *His Mares and Colts to their wives and Children.*" Until the rumor was disproved, Upshaw lost most of his support for election to a legislative seat.[35]

By early 1780, even before the British invaded Virginia, the state's military establishment had reached a point of crisis. The terms of many Virginia Continentals were running out and hyperinflation and war weariness made it difficult to enlist replacements. In December 1779 George Washington reported that over half of the enlistments of the three thousand Virginia soldiers on active duty with the Continental Army expired by the end of 1780. Since these men expected their enlistment contracts to be honored, Washington could not extend their terms unilaterally. Over half of the remaining Virginians under arms were in South Carolina, where they were either cap-

34. Sanchez-Saavedra, comp., *Guide to Virginia Military Organizations,* 116–23; Chase, "'Years of Hardship and Revelations,'" 9–53; McIlwaine, ed., *Journals of Council of State,* 2:9, 15, 225, 247–48, 254; Boyd et al., eds., *Papers of Jefferson,* 2:31–32, 3:423–24, 4:98–99 (Jefferson to Samuel Huntington, 7 Nov. 1780).

35. McIlwaine, ed, *Official Letters of Governors of Virginia,* 1:62–64, and *Journal of Council of State,* 2:31, 94; Mays, ed., *Letters and Papers of Edmund Pendleton,* 1:228, 236 (Pendleton to William Woodford, 11 Oct. and 8 Nov. 1777).

tured when Charleston fell or ran away under fire at the Battle of Camden; most of the others guarded prisoners in Albemarle or were on duty at Fort Pitt.[36] Local officials replaced these men with great difficulty. There were draft riots in Loudoun County (in 1778) and in Lancaster County (in 1780), areas previously strongly Whig. Most of the young men had already served appropriate terms, and only married men over thirty, who had been spared war service, were left. As a result, few new men enlisted for Continental duty, and only two thousand Virginians were left in Continental or state service by January 1781. Enlistees deserted with greater frequency than early in the war. Finally, local officials had requisitioned arms from inhabitants so often, and the state armories were so inefficient, that many men left for battle without weapons.[37]

The invasion of Virginia in late 1780 compounded these problems. The British forces did not seek to occupy Virginia (except some loyalist strongholds as bases), but instead practiced guerrilla warfare. Through the first half of 1781, they attacked communities all over the James River basin, and ventured into the Northern Neck, destroying munitions, burning market crops, stealing cattle and horses, destroying plantations of local gentlemen, and setting slaves free wherever they marched. Such a strategy would have been difficult for any eighteenth-century army to fight, given the poor roads of that time.[38]

Governor Jefferson fought the invasion with vigor, but he could overcome neither the insistence of gentlemen for autonomy in local affairs nor the principles of equity and voluntarism that continued to underlie manpower procurement policies. The most efficient way to fight the British would have been to have mobilized the most proficient militia units and kept them under arms for the duration of the invasion. Even if these men could not have defeated seasoned British troops, they might have kept them engaged until munitions could be moved. But that plan would have been

36. Boyd et al., eds., *Papers of Jefferson*, 3: pages following 254, 364–65, 472. These reports show in May 1780 3,393 troops with armies outside the state (1,547 enlisted for the war, tours for 1,131 expired between December 1779 and the end of May 1780, 445 expired between June and December 1780, 133 left sometime in 1780, 74 expired in 1781), at least 1,455 men in South Carolina, 671 on guard duty or at Fort Pitt, 406 men in miscellaneous units. In January 1781 there were 1,392 prisoners at Charleston. See F. Anderson, *People's Army*, chap. 6, for contractual principles.

37. McBride, "Virginia War Effort," 147–56; McIlwaine, ed., *Journals of Council of State*, 2:86, 93–94, 180–81, 254; Boyd et al., eds., *Papers of Jefferson*, 3:432–33, 593–97 (Jefferson to Washington, 11 June and 3 Sept. 1780), 4:97–98 (Richard Elliot to Jefferson, 7 Nov. 1780), 4:18 (George Mason to Jefferson, 6 Oct. 1780), 4:470–72, "Statement of Arms and Men in Service."

38. Cometti, "Depredations in Virginia," 142–51; C. Ward, *War of the Revolution*, chap. 82; McBride, "Virginia War Effort," chap. 6, analyze the invasion.

coercive and inequitable, taking a few men away from their families while leaving other men free. Governor Jefferson instead placed all white men under arms, mobilizing a quarter or more of the militia for two-month terms, and then replacing them with other militia. When the British invaded a neighborhood, the governor immediately called out the entire militia of the counties surrounding the site of the fighting.[39]

This *levée-en-masse* created a logistical nightmare. Men spent as much time moving from their homes and back again as they did under arms. They often marched without weapons, hoping to use the arms of men whose terms had expired, but they often found none at camp. After the British reached an area, it took several days to mobilize local militia or move men from distant camps. When the British invaded near Williamsburg in April 1781, Governor Jefferson ordered nine lieutenants from nearby counties to "assemble every man of your County able to bear Arms," but no troops had arrived two days later. "The Enemy's Fleet commands our Rivers," George Mason wrote his son in June 1781, "and puts it in their Power to remove their Troops from place to place, when and where they please without Opposition; so that we no sooner collect a Force sufficient to counteract them in one part of the Country, but they shift to another, ravaging, plundering, and destroying everything before them. Our Militia turn out with great Spirit," he added, "but they are badly armed and appointed."[40]

Jefferson and his successor, Thomas Nelson, were caught between the contradictory demands of military officers and of local officials and the planters they represented. Generals intensely disliked short enlistments and wanted to command well-trained, well-armed troops for the duration of the invasion. On occasion they sent unarmed and untrained men home, hoping they would be replaced by better people.[41] Local officials wanted to maintain security within their counties and were loath to send men beyond county boundaries. Planters and their sons refused to serve long terms because that meant impoverishing their families. To keep their local power base, gentlemen often supported demands of planters for relief from drafts and constant mobilization.

39. Boyd et al., eds., *Papers of Jefferson*, 4:61–63 ("Steps to Be Taken to Repel Leslie's Army"), 4:351–53 (Jefferson to Friedrich Steuben, 13 Jan. 1781), 4:646–47 (Jefferson to county lieutenants, 18 Feb. 1781), 5:310–11 ("Recapitulation of Tours of Duty Performed by the Virginia Militia," [March, 1781]).

40. Boyd et al., eds., *Papers of Jefferson*, 5:496–97 (Jefferson to certain county lieutenants of Henrico and certain other counties, 19 Apr. 1781), 5:520–21 (Jefferson to James Innes, 21 Apr. 1781); Rutland, ed., *Papers of George Mason*, 2:692–93 (Mason to George Mason, Jr., 3 June 1781).

41. For the reactions of commanders, see H. M. Ward, *Duty, Honor or Country*, chaps. 8–10; Boyd et al., eds., *Papers of Jefferson*, 4:345–46 (Steuben to Jefferson, 12 Jan. 1781), 615–16 (Nathanael Greene to Jefferson, 15 Feb. 1781).

There were two elements in the procurement system Jefferson and his advisors devised to meet the invasion. The governor repeatedly called out a quarter or more of the militias of the piedmont counties of Southside and Central Virginia, areas close to the center of the fighting. Too many young men had left these counties to hold an equitable draft for Continental soldiers. Under pressure from piedmont county lieutenants, Jefferson suspended their draft until the entire militia had returned. The governor used militiamen from Tidewater (near the fighting) and the Northern Neck (distant from the war) far less frequently, but kept these men in reserve for emergencies and continued to hold drafts for the army.[42]

The lieutenants of piedmont counties had great difficulty meeting these demands for men. The problem was demographic: Jefferson was asking for so many men that a full response would have included many men over thirty and married men, a full two-fifths of the militia, who had been spared military duty. Since family men procured substitutes or resisted enlistment, not wanting to leave their families destitute, county officials repeatedly enlisted the same young men. Almost as soon as they returned home from a tour of duty, they faced a new draft for another short tour. Young men apparently disliked this revolving door. Although men could not be drafted for two months after the completion of a tour, the time between the expiration of their term and their return home — sometimes more than two months — was counted toward that exclusion.[43]

County lieutenants understood the reluctance of many militiamen to be mobilized and sent many fewer men than requested. They sent young boys or invalids, knowing they would be immediately returned; they claimed that most married men were unfit; or they underreported the true number of militiamen. Two examples suggest the intensity of the problem. New Kent County, located in Tidewater north of the James on the York River, supposedly had 418 militiamen. The county lieutenant, however, could muster only 350 privates in March 1781 and just 268 were effective; 75 men were

42. See letters from Jefferson in Boyd et al., eds., *Papers of Jefferson*, 4:297 (to Thomas Nelson, 2 Jan. 1781); 4:351–53, 668–70, 5:366, 500–01 (to Steuben, 19 Jan., 20 Feb., 6 and 19 Apr. 1781); 4:400–402 (to county lieutenants, 19 Jan. 1781); 4:33–37 (to Speaker of the House of Delegates, 1 Mar. 1781); 5:179–81, 644–47 (to Lafayette, 19 Mar. and 14 May 1781); 5:291–92 (to Nathanael Greene, 30 Mar. 1781). See also 5:310–11, 29 ("Recapitulation of Tours" [Mar. 1781] and "Return of Militia by Counties").

43. An age census of Prince George's County, Maryland, in 1776 shows that 42.5% of white men between 16 and 50 were over 30 (Brumbaugh, *Maryland Records*, 1:1–81). See Boyd et al., eds., *Papers of Jefferson*, 5:22–23 (Leroy Peachey to Jefferson, 23 Mar. 1781) for an early attempt at draft insurance. For revolving door enlistments, see ibid., 441–42 (William Call to Jefferson, 14 Apr. 1781), and W. P. Palmer, ed., *Calendar of Virginia State Papers*, 2:353–54 (Robert Lawson to Thomas Nelson, 26 July 1781).

"Adjudged unfit for duty" and the others were Quakers. Men in New Kent had been called out in October 1780, and his failure to send "down the full number required from us does not arise from any disaffection," but from his men "having been so much on Duty (tho Necessarily) all this winter." Procurement of men was even more difficult in the Southside. In April 1781 Charlotte County's lieutenant reported 565 militiamen, 342 of whom were on active duty and another 70 eligible for an exemption from a tour of duty for volunteering previously. With only 153 men remaining, he could not meet a militia draft of 156 men, and added that his militiamen insisted that Charlotte had "more men in duty than any of the Neighboring Counties, and frequently Complain, alledging they Can't Cultivate their plantations for even a prospect for bread." Moreover, "the young and single men have nearly all turned out Voluntarily, and [are] in duty; those to be Ordered will be Composed Chiefly of Married Men."[44]

Jefferson and Nelson knew that counties would not send their full complement of men, and called up larger numbers of men than were needed. Deficiencies were high. Less than two-thirds of the 2,506 militiamen called by Jefferson in September 1780 reported for duty. There was little improvement after the invasion began. Around three-quarters of the men called in January 1781 had arrived by February. As a result, generals had fewer men than they needed. When General Steuben complained about shortfalls from New Kent County in March 1781, Jefferson angrily explained to him the limits of executive power. *"We can only be answerable for the orders we give, and not for their execution. If they are disobeyed from obstinacy of spirit or want of coercion in the laws it is not our fault."*[45]

Despite these shortfalls, most young men from piedmont Virginia were mobilized during 1781. Since nearly all guns in private hands had been requisitioned, planters were nearly defenseless when bands of British guerrillas

---

44. Boyd et al., eds., *Papers of Jefferson*, 5:197 (William Davies to Jefferson, 21 Mar. 1781, young boys and invalids); 5:310–11 ("Recapitulation of Tours," Mar. 1781); 5:154–55 (William Clayton to Jefferson, 16 Mar. 1781, New Kent); 5:344–45, 370–72 (Thomas Read to Jefferson, 4 Apr. [quote] and 7 Apr. 1781 (Jefferson to Read 7 Apr. 1781 [Charlotte]). For other Southside counties, see 5:212–13, 402–3, 6:3, 76 (James Callaway to Jefferson, 23 Mar., 11 Apr., 21 May, and 4 June 1781); 6:67–68 (Robert Wooding to Jefferson, 1 June 1781); W. P. Palmer, ed., *Calendar of Virginia State Papers*, 2:232–34, 245 (Wooding to William Davies, 21 July 1781; N. Hobson to William Davies, 24 July 1781).

45. Boyd et al., eds., *Papers of Jefferson*, 5:179–81 (Jefferson to Lafayette, 19 Mar. 1781); 3:599–601 ("Estimate of Militia Strength," ca. 4 Sept. 1780), and "Recapitulation of Tours," [Mar. 1781], compared with 5:311–12, 29 ("Return of Militia by Counties," 28 Feb. 1781); 5:119–20 (Jefferson to Steuben, 10 Mar. 1781); 5:644–45 (Jefferson to Lafayette 14 May 1781). Culpeper County, far from the fighting, was an exception; see Van Atta, "Conscription in Revolutionary Virginia," 267–69.

invaded. Planters hid the few guns they still owned. By July 1781, for instance, the few gunowners in Halifax County had hidden "them and Say
they will do it for their own Defence against Insurrections of Slaves or Tories." These few weapons could not repel an invasion. In July 1781 Banastre
Tartleton's irregulars invaded Southside, destroying everything in their path.
Residents feared his threatened return because there was no army camp
nearby and "not one man in twenty . . . has a gun &c in this County (they
having [been] . . . Impressed into the Countries' service and not returned)."
Later that summer, several hundred citizens of Amelia County petitioned
Governor Nelson to arm the county's militia "to repel . . . ravaging Parties of
the Enemy." Amelia families had been "Plundred and robbed of their Slaves,
Horses, [and] Cloaths" by small bands of men, "armed only with swords and
Pistols."[46]

Not surprisingly, militiamen were loath to leave their neighborhoods
but would enthusiastically defend their families and communities. Jefferson
understood this reluctance, writing General Greene that "it is much more
practicable to carry on a war with Militia within our own Country than out
of it." For that reason, Jefferson refused Greene's March 1781 request to send
all the militia stationed at Portsmouth out of state with him but instead tried
to raise 1,500 more militiamen. Virginia officials found it almost impossible
to enlist these men; a month after the call went out, there were "many Counties very deficient in sending the quota call'd for — some of them send none
at all." Not only did men resist enlisting for a tour in the Carolinas, but "the
Extreme Busy Season of the Year, among the Common People, Exceeds their
Conception of the Necessity of Turning out, Especially as the enemy is not
immediately Pressing upon them." When the British invaded a neighborhood, militiamen turned out with alacrity. Charlotte County had reluctantly
sent men to General Greene, but when the British reached nearby Peters-
burg, county militia officers offered to send a hundred militiamen "notwithstanding the whole of the Militia have just returned from a tour of Duty." As
long as companies stayed in Virginia, near the homes of enlistees, militiamen remained in camp ready to fight, and despite disease and lack of weapons, "they showed a noble undaunted Spirit," ready "to go down and oppose
the Enemy at all Events."[47]

46. W. P. Palmer, ed., *Calendar of Virginia State Papers*, 2:232–33, 240–42, 684
(Wooding to Davies, 21 July 1781; David Garland to Nelson, 23 July 1781; Inhabitants
of Amelia to Nelson, [summer] 1781).
47. Boyd et al., eds., *Papers of Jefferson*, 5, 275–77, 312–13, 291 (Jefferson to Nathanael Greene, 1 Apr. and 30 Mar. 1781); 5:372 (Jefferson to Thomas Read, 7 Apr.
1781); 5:583 (Robert Lawson to Jefferson, 1 May 1781); 6:3 (James Callaway to Jefferson, 21 May 1781); 5:571–72 (Thomas Read to Jefferson, 28 Apr. 1781); W. P. Palmer,
ed., *Calendar of Virginia State Papers*, 2:287–88, 299–301 (Josiah Parker to William Davies, 3 Aug. 1781; John Page to Nelson, 7 Aug. 1781).

Planting and harvesting crops further complicated troop procurement. Men under arms feared that their families would suffer if they did not plant corn. Planting corn retarded enlistments and led men under arms to seek to leave the service. As Col. James Slaughter wrote Jefferson in early April 1781, his men considered "the present season . . . the only one for makeing the necessary preparations for raiseing a Crop of Corn for the support of their famelies." Since "many of them are obliged to labour," Slaughter hoped that their terms would be brief. Although Jefferson understood the plight of the families of poorer soldiers, he considered the war effort more important, it being "vain to plant and sow and leave the Enemy unopposed to reap." He hoped that neighbors would help plant corn on farms of mobilized men. But so many men were away that the social welfare system, designed to aid a few people, was overwhelmed. In Culpeper County, for example, a local official tried "to get the Crops of Corn planted of those now on duty but we have such a number of poor distress'd Famlys in this County that I fear we shall not be able to Accomplish it."[48]

The Virginia Militia and the Revolution

The 1781 defense of Virginia by the militia was a military disaster that bred political success. Usually unopposed, the British wandered the countryside at will, destroying military stores and crops and forcing citizens to sign paroles forbidding support of the patriots. These depredations probably unified support for the Whig government, making "Whigs of Tories."[49] Only Continental troops under Lafayette and the French navy defeated the British. Small planters remained patriots despite military defeat because the Whig gentlemen who ruled Virginia managed to earn their loyalty. By executing draft laws and mobilization orders equitably and championing local resistance to unfair manpower demands, they helped local planters sustain their families and their own independence.

This political success challenged the republican ideals of equity, independence, and voluntarism it was meant to sustain. Sons of small planters and gentlemen could voluntarily choose when to enter military service. The market system, however, replaced republican ideals for poorer whites. They sold their labor power to wealthier neighbors for a wage consisting of bounties and, in return, bore disproportionate risks of disease, injury, and death.

48. Boyd et al., eds., *Papers of Jefferson*, 5:441–42 (William Call to Jefferson, 14 Apr. 1781); 5:407–8 (Slaughter to Jefferson, 11 Apr. 1781); 4:464–65 (Jefferson to James Callaway, 16 Apr. 1781); 5:587–88 (James Barbour to Jefferson).

49. McIlwaine, ed., *Official Letters Governors of Virginia*, 3:13–14 (Nelson to George Washington, 27 July 1781).

In a slave society, where race and class were so closely bound, such class distinctions among whites invited conflict.

The triumph of the militia during the Revolution was one step in the triumph of localism in Virginia and of federalism in the new nation during the late eighteenth century. Antifederalism was strong in Virginia, and even after the ratification of the Constitution and the creation of new statewide courts, appointed justices of the peace kept firm control over the administrative and judicial functions of local government. At the same time, vigorous debate about the military failures of the militia during the war led to the slow development of a professional army. By the time of the Civil War, concepts closer to a coercive *levée-en-masse* had replaced the older virtues of equity and voluntarism in military service.[50]

The contradictory republican goals of equity and voluntarism, however, permeated political debate as late as the Civil War era. At first, both Union and Confederate armies relied upon volunteers, and the popularity of the war meant that armies attracted enough volunteers to appear equitable. But by 1862 enthusiasm waned in both North and South, thereby requiring institution of the draft, if for no other purpose than to encourage voluntary enlistment. Given the increasing unwillingness of young men to serve, both governments permitted the purchase of substitutes or (in the North) allowed men to pay $350 to avoid serving. Men who wished to avoid service often paid fees, found substitutes, or gained exemptions. Such a market system raised charges that the war was a "rich man's war but a poor man's fight," and incited desertion, draft evasion, and riots. However inequitable the system, a third of Northern young white men, half of Northern free black men, and three-fifths of Southern young white men served in Union or Confederate armies. Immigrants, the wealthy, married men, property holders, and perhaps Northern Democrats opposed to the war may have evaded service or bought substitutes more often than poorer young men, but no class — even the wealthy — completely evaded enlistment.[51]

The Revolution's democratic ideology of popular sovereignty raised for the first time questions of equity and voluntarism in military service. From the Revolution through the Persian Gulf war, Americans have disliked the draft but insisted upon voluntary enlistments and an equal risk of injury or death among social classes. The paradox is inescapable: if fair conscription remains involuntary, a volunteer army is still inequitable.

50. Kulikoff, *Tobacco and Slaves*, chap. 7 and Afterword; Cress, *Citizens in Arms*, chaps. 6–10.

51. McPherson, *Battle Cry of Freedom*, 306–7, 312–23, 429–33, 492–94, 600–615; Levine, "Draft Evasion in the North," 816–34; Quarles, *Negro in the Civil War*, chap. 9; Rorabaugh, "Who Fought for the North?" 695–701; Vinovskis, "Have Social Historians Lost the Civil War?" 39–50; Kemp, "Community and War," 31–77.

Rural Migration and
Capitalist Transformation

Chapter 7

Free Migration and Cultural Diffusion in Early America, 1600–1860

Since the end of the nineteenth century, historians have struggled to connect migration and social development in North America. In the 1890s Frederick Jackson Turner argued that movement to the "free" lands of North American frontiers turned Europeans into Americans, creating a democratic, egalitarian, and individualistic society, profoundly different from the communal order they left behind. After generations of criticism, the impact of the frontier environment has receded into the background.[1] Instead, cultural ideas about migration predominate. This work points to the persistence and subtle change of older cultures under new circumstances. David Fischer, for one, traces the persistence of British "folkways," defined as "the normative structure of values, customs, and meanings" in the colonies. The twenty-four folkways Fischer describes are remarkably diverse, ranging from speech and naming patterns to systems of wealth, rank, and power. All, he argues, originated in contrasting regional cultures of Britain. Given the relatively homogeneous regional origins of settlers in each colony, migrants readily adapted old cultural practices.[2]

As used in migration literature, both environment and culture tend to be separated from the daily relations of production in which people worked. Both models, moreover, tend to ignore the impact of class, race, and ethnic relations in sustaining migration and in the making of American cultures. To understand the relationship between migration and culture, a framework is needed that integrates environment and culture. Only by returning to pro-

---

1. Turner, *Frontier in American History*. Among studies Turner inspired are Hofstadter and Lipset, eds., *Turner and Sociology of Frontier*; L. K. Mathews, *Expansion of New England*; Malin, *History and Ecology*; W. P. Webb, *Great Plains*; Curti, *Making Frontier Community*. Hofstadter, *Progressive Historians*, chaps. 2–3; and Cronon, "Revisiting the Vanishing Frontier," 157–70, summarize scholarly debate.

2. Allen, *In English Ways*; Wyatt-Brown, *Southern Honor*; McWhiney, *Cracker Culture*; Fischer, *Albion's Seed*. For responses to Fischer's book see Silverman, "Roots Revisited," 254–68, and Greene et al., "*Albion's Seed*: A Symposium," 224–308.

ductive relations can we show how rural migrants used culture to shape the environment and, in turn, how the environment shaped the culture.

Growing out of recent ecological concerns, a new environmental history leads in this direction, showing how the spread of capitalism can transform the environment. Carolyn Merchant contends that capitalism, with its emphasis on market production, agricultural mechanization, and industrialized forests, fed an ecological revolution in nineteenth-century New England. By the early twentieth century, Donald Worster argues, American farmers were imbued with a capitalist ethos. Not only did they believe that "nature must be seen as capital," as a marketable commodity, but contended that men had "an obligation to use this capital for constant self-advancement." Such exploitation raised productivity and encouraged migration to new areas, but disrupted fragile ecosystems, repeatedly triggering natural calamities like grasshopper plagues and fierce dust storms. At such times migration ceased and settlers rapidly departed.[3]

We need to go beyond the emphasis of ecological historians upon capitalist ideology to show how capitalism transformed migration patterns. As capitalism spread, permanent migration (versus seasonal movement or short-distance circulation) from rural to urban areas and to colonies dramatically increased, as peasants lost land and laborers vied for jobs. During the early development of capitalism, greater opportunities appeared in rural areas, especially in nations with internal frontiers. Migrants, however, not only sought opportunities but sometimes wished to create ideal societies, reflecting religious belief or an egalitarianism they believed capitalists had destroyed.

Migration over long distances required the active participation of capitalists. To profit from trading agricultural staples for manufactured goods, merchant capital financed colonial migration, paying the passage of those who sought opportunities in new lands or building canals or railroads to open land for settlement. Peripheral regions settled in this manner were slowly incorporated into the world capitalist system. The European or urban demand for staples structured the timing of migration to rural areas, influencing movement even to arid regions, with environments hostile to cultivation. As staple production grew, the labor needs of capitalist farmers rose, thereby creating a class of migrant laborers.[4]

3. Worster, "The Vulnerable Earth," 3–20, esp. 10–18, and "Transformations of the Earth," 1097–1106; Cronon, *Changes in the Land*; Merchant, *Ecological Revolutions*, chaps. 5–8; Worster, *Dust Bowl*, 6 (italics in original); Atkins, *Harvest of Grief*, esp. chap. 3. Cronon, "Modes of Prophecy," 1124–31, critiques the use of capitalism by environmental historians.

4. These speculations are informed by Osborne and Rogerson, "Conceptualizing the Frontier Settlement Process," 1–3; B. Thomas, *Migration and Economic Growth*,

This essay relates free migration in the United States to the spread of capitalism, stressing emigration from Europe and internal migration in rural America before 1860. Our examination of migration and capitalism raises questions about rural class relations. Forms of production (tenancies, freehold farms, slave plantations) determine household needs for labor and the level of economic opportunity, thereby encouraging persistence or migration. Since decisions to migrate are made within a household economy, age and gender relations within the household must be understood.[5] The problem is further complicated by economic, social, and cultural change in areas migrants leave. Without understanding how families responded to these changes, one cannot explain either immobility (are opportunities high *or* are families satisfied with current social relations?) or migration (do families seek opportunities *or* given the need for sufficiency, do they wish to replicate a disappearing social order?).

English Capitalism, English Migration, and Colonial Immigration

Successful transatlantic emigration in the early modern era required far more than willing emigrants and potential opportunities in a new land. Merchants had to recruit immigrants and finance their ocean voyage, thereby foregoing immediate returns for potential profit once immigrants became productive; the state had to allow its people to migrate, understanding that the trade between colony and mother country would more than compensate for lost taxes.[6] Such behavior was more characteristic in capitalist societies than countries still embedded in feudal relations of production.

Transatlantic emigration from England, where capitalism was most advanced, varied fundamentally from Spanish and French emigration. The English migration rate was much higher, and far more foreign nationals came to English colonies than to those of other European powers. About half a million Britains and Germans immigrated to the mainland English colonies between 1630 and 1780. In contrast, between 650,000 and 750,000 Europeans, nearly all Spaniards, reached all of Spain's colonies between 1492

---

chap. 3; Zelinsky, "Hypothesis of Mobility Transition," 219–45, esp. 230–40; Standing, "Migration and Modes of Exploitation," 192–201.

5. See intro. and chaps. 1–2 above. My framework is compatible with the findings, but not the theory, of migration research summarized by Greenwood, "Research in Internal Migration," 397–433. For kinship and migration, see J. S. MacDonald and L. A. MacDonald, "Chain Migration," 82–97; Litwak, "Geographic Mobility and Extended Family Cohesion," 385–94. Fox-Genovese, "Antebellum Southern Households," 215–83, connects class relations and household structures.

6. For a similar argument, see Moogk, "Reluctant Exiles," 464–65.

and 1700, perhaps one-third of them emigrating to Mexico, the most common destination. About 30,000 immigrants came to New France, almost all French, but over two-thirds of them returned to France. In other words, about 3,300 European immigrants reached the mainland English colonies annually, while only 3,400 came to all of Spain's colonies, and merely 200 arrived in Quebec (of whom just 65 stayed).[7]

Explanation of these differences should begin with the varying rates of proletarianization in Europe. In England rapid population increase and enclosures in the seventeenth century sustained a growing working class, available for migration. However exploited by landlords or the state, French and Spanish peasants still controlled their land. Spanish colonial migrants came from places where small pockets of capitalist development had occurred, like the hinterlands around Seville, where enclosure had been common. The poor who lived in more feudal areas moved within the countryside or to a nearby town, but feared leaving their families and inheritances for an unknown New World.[8]

The rise of a capitalist class in England, interested in trade and colonization, sustained more vigorous emigration than was found elsewhere in Europe, where only pockets of capitalism yet existed. The Spanish rarely supported migration, fearing that peasant emigration would depopulate the countryside. Even though their regulations had only limited success, most migrants were either younger sons of the nobility out to make their fortunes or their servants. The French crown intermittently funded migration to Quebec but impeded completely free movement. Since promotional literature was not published in France, and peasants—no matter how poor—wished to stay home, merchants infrequently financed migration.[9]

In contrast, the English published numerous promotional pamphlets encouraging movement, often arguing that the poor should be sent to the open environment of the colonies. Notwithstanding occasional fears of depopulation, England chartered joint-stock companies to support initial colonization, and later put no impediments in front of merchants who financed

7. Morner, "Spanish Migration to the New World," 737–82, esp. 738, 750–53, 759, 767; Borah, "The Mixing of Population," 707–22, esp. 707–8; Boyd-Bowman, "Patterns of Spanish Emigration," 580–604; Moogk, "Reluctant Exiles," 463–64, 497–505; Boleda, "Les Migrations au Canada," 34–35.

8. Brenner, "Agrarian Class Structure," 46–62; Lachmann, *Manor to Market*, 16–18, 105–10; 138–41; Wordie, "Chronology of English Enclosure," 483–505; Moogk, "Reluctant Exiles," 468–73, 482–87; Vassberg, *Land and Society in Golden Age Castile*, chaps. 2, 4–6.

9. Morner, "Spanish Migration to the New World," 750–59; Borah, "Mixing of Population," 712–15; Moogk, "Reluctant Exiles," 467, 470–82, 490–505; Altman, "Emigrants and Society," 170–90.

migration. Parliament itself funded the early settlement of Georgia, sending over two thousand poor people to that colony. A private market in servants soon developed. Merchants hired recruiting agents to fill their ships with passengers, both free and indentured. Given this encouragement, high levels of migration were soon achieved and potential migrants, even those who had to indenture themselves, understood relative opportunities in various colonies.[10]

An understanding of immigration to the mainland colonies requires analysis of the premigration experiences of emigrants. Internal migration was increasingly common in early modern England, fed by the dispossession of peasants, growth of wage labor, and urban development. The English migration system was related to family labor but became increasingly responsive to a capitalist labor market. If most migrants moved short distances in the countryside, searching for land or work, others moved from the countryside to nearby villages, from villages to towns, and from towns to London. Colonial migration was often the last step in this migration system.[11]

The growth of wage labor played a key role in English migration. By the mid-seventeenth century two-fifths of rural England's population worked for wages. Thrown off the land by enclosures or unable to procure land in the face of population growth and the unwillingness of landlords to rent small parcels to them, cottagers and laborers provided workers for growing rural industries. Cottagers, both men and women, had to supplement their meager subsistence with by-employments, spinning and weaving in rural putting-out industries, harvesting crops, working in mines and forests.[12]

Unable to find work, adolescents left home for other villages or towns, serving as apprentices or servants in husbandry. Agricultural jobs for adults were hardly permanent; rapid turnover forced families to move often. Seasonal migrants moved across the countryside, harvesting grain or performing specialized labor. Cottagers often worked in the neighborhood but most apparently moved about a good deal. Unable to accumulate sufficient capital

---

10. Menard, "British Migration," 106–9; Shammas, "English Commercial Development," 151–74, esp. 163–64; Galenson, *White Servitude*, 97–99, 212–17; Craven, "Early Settlements," 10–43; E. S. Morgan, *American Slavery, American Freedom*, 21–22, 30-33, 65–70; Meinig, *Shaping of America*, 1:28–35, 49–52; Taylor, "Colonizing Georgia," 119–27; Bailyn, *Peopling British North America*, 9–10, and *Voyagers to the West*, chap. 2; Gemery, "Emigration from British Isles," 179–231, and "European Emigration to North America, 1700–1820," 283–342.

11. Clark and Souden, Introduction, 11–48, summarizes recent literature; for a somewhat different view, see R. Thompson, "Early Modern Migration," 65–69.

12. A. Clark, *Working Life of Women*, esp. chaps. 3–4; Shammas, "World Women Knew," 99–115; Everitt, "Farm Labourers," 396–442, 454–65; A. H. Smith, "Labourers in Late Sixteenth-Century England," 11–52, 367–94.

to become husbandmen, families squatted on the fens or migrated to towns to find work.[13]

An examination of servants in husbandry illuminates the relationship of the English labor market to migration. Servants in husbandry, unmarried youths hired by farmers on annual contracts, were an essential component in the household economy of rural England. Although masters paid servants they hired a stipend, they treated them as household members, not as wage laborers. Masters housed, fed, and clothed servants, and in return put them to work in their homes, dairies, pastures, and fields. Since the state delegated the same authority over servants to masters as to parents over children, servant rebellion over discipline was common. Servants provided essential labor for farmers whose children were too young to work or had left home and at the same time permitted poor families to reduce the number of people they had to support.[14]

At least three-fifths of rural English youths worked as servants in husbandry during the seventeenth and eighteenth centuries. Most of them were the children of laborers and cottagers, but even children of husbandmen served. Nearly all boys became servants, starting in their mid-teens. They served six or more years under different masters and married in their mid-twenties, soon after they left service. Fewer girls entered service; they began their terms in their late teens and left by their mid-twenties to marry. Servants moved but a few miles from home, choosing masters who lived nearby. Although servants saved most of their wages, their accumulated savings rarely permitted them to procure a tenancy and most—like their parents—became laborers or cottagers.

Opportunities for youths to become servants varied with population growth and commodity prices. Rising population glutted the servant market and reduced real wages, encouraging farmers to hire daily wage laborers rather than servants. High prices for wheat, relative to livestock, led farmers to limit their herds (which required constant labor) and increase grain output (which required seasonal labor at harvest). While low population density and high beef prices in the mid-sixteenth century suggest substantial opportunity, the system declined rapidly from the late sixteenth to the mid-seventeenth century, when high rates of population growth combined with

13. Clark and Souden, Introduction, 28–35; A. H. Smith, "Labourers in Late Sixteenth-Century England," 16–21; Kussmaul, *Servants in Husbandry*, chap. 4; Patten, "Patterns of Migration," 111–29; Millward, "Emergence of Wage Labor in Early Modern England," 21–39.

14. Kussmaul, *Servants in Husbandry*, provides the best analysis and is the source for this and succeeding paragraphs, but see also A. H. Smith, "Labourers in Late Sixteenth-Century England," 14–18, 33–36.

high grain prices to reduce demand for servants but to increase demand for wage labor at planting and harvest.

The miseries of early capitalism — enclosure, growth of wage labor, declining wages, the depressed cloth trade, diminished opportunities to become servants — led to increasing transiency in the late sixteenth and early seventeenth centuries. Called "masterless men" by contemporaries, these "vagabonds" were underemployed but able-bodied itinerant migrants capable of obtaining only casual wage labor. Counted among vagabonds were runaway apprentices, servants searching for new masters, journeymen looking for work, seasonal wage laborers, sailors and soldiers returning home, deserted wives, unmarried pregnant women, abandoned children, Gypsies, Irish, and unlicensed beggars. If most were unmarried and young, as many as half were older than thirty. Upland areas and towns, toward which most transients moved, could provide them with neither jobs nor a secure home.[15]

If movement began in the countryside, it often ended in cities, especially in London, whose population more than doubled during the seventeenth century. One-sixth of the mid-seventeenth-century English probably lived in London sometime in their lives. Seventeenth-century English cities attracted workers from a vast rural hinterland; migrants to Bristol came from an area within 60 miles of town and London migrants traveled as much as 125 miles to reach the city. Skilled workers and vagrants alike gravitated toward cities, hoping for greater opportunities. Urban growth displaced more rural folk: landlords seeking to take advantage of the London food market improved their farms, displacing peasants, who ultimately wound up in London, adding their numbers to the urban poor.[16]

Immigration to British North America

English and European migration to mainland British North America grew out of the conjuncture of internal movement at home and the expansion of English merchant capital. The mainland attracted men and less commonly women who had left their villages, searched for employment in nearby towns, or migrated to cities. After working in the city for several years, dissatisfied servants or newly unemployed youths (almost all male) indentured themselves for service in the American colonies. Colonial opportunities, combined with meager opportunities for full-time employment at home,

15. Beier, "Poverty and Progress in Early Modern England," 201–39, and *Masterless Men*, chaps. 1–6, 207–26; Slack, "Vagrants and Vagrancy," 361–79.

16. Findlay and Shearer, "Population Growth and Suburban Expansion," 37- 53; Wrigley, "Simple Model of London's Importance," 44–70, esp. 50–51, 55–58; Patten, "Patterns of Migration," 111–29.

propelled some of these migrants across the Atlantic, usually as servants whose passage English merchants financed.[17]

Servant migration to the English North American colonies illuminates the relation between migration and merchant capital. Labor markets in Britain and the colonies, the behavior of shippers, recruitment by large-scale land speculators, and prior migration all structured the destinations of servants. A market for servants quickly developed; colonial agents combed the countryside in search of potential migrants. Emigration to the Chesapeake colonies in the seventeenth century, for instance, rose when English real wages declined and tobacco prices in the region were high; emigration declined when English wages rose and tobacco prices dropped.[18]

English emigration to North America began in the early seventeenth century when merchants, seeking profits from New World staples, sent thousands of servants to the sugar and tobacco colonies. Rapid population growth, high prices, and low wages led emigrants to risk a dangerous ocean voyage and a nasty disease environment for a chance for wealth. Like servants in husbandry, immigrants tended to be young men. These first English emigrants landed in New England in the 1630s and 1640s and in the Chesapeake colonies between 1630 and 1680. Immigration averaged twenty thousand a decade in the 1630s and 1640s, twenty-five thousand a decade between 1650 and 1690. But by the late seventeenth century the number of new workers entering the English labor force had declined, raising real wages and reducing the pace of emigration. This decline coincided with diminished opportunities in the Chesapeake colonies, where as many as two-fifths of British immigrants had gone. English emigration therefore plummeted to just ten thousand a decade in the 1690s and 1700s.[19]

When immigration began to recover in the 1710s, the origin of immigrants had shifted dramatically. Few English emigrated, but they were replaced by Scots, Ulster Irish Protestants, and Germans. Decennial European immigration averaged forty-five thousand in the 1710s and 1720s and thirty-three thousand in the 1730s and 1740s, but sixty-one thousand came in the 1750s and 1760s and seventy-four thousand between 1770 and 1775. At least a third of European immigrants who came to mainland colonies before 1775 landed after 1750. Although German migration diminished after the onset of war in 1754, the number of British immigrants (including a resurgence of

17. Bailyn, *Peopling British North America*, 20–43.
18. Menard, "British Migration," 116–19; Souden, "'Rogues, Whores and Vagabonds,'" 23–41; Horn, "Servant Emigration to the Chesapeake in the Seventeenth Century," 51–95; Wareing, "Migration to London and Transatlantic Emigration," 356–78.
19. Galenson, *White Servitude*, 216–17; Gemery, "Emigration from British Isles," 215–16.

English migration and great increases from Scotland and Ulster) skyrocketed in the 1760s and early 1770s.[20]

Deteriorating conditions in Britain and the spread of capitalism to areas previously on the periphery, combined with expectations of great opportunities in the colonies, led to this increase. Renewed English population growth reduced real wages and opportunities for servants in husbandry; at the same time, crop failures raised the price of bread for laborers. Rack-renting policies of capitalist landlords in Scotland and Ulster encouraged thousands to sell out and emigrate before they lost their land. German colonial immigration was a small part of a larger movement, mostly to eastern Europe. Although many of the migrants were serfs who had to pay manumission fees to emigrate, population pressure on land, combined with enclosures and the growth of rural industry and agricultural labor, led peasants to migrate.[21]

A dual migration system fed movement to North America in the 1770s. One group of emigrants, mostly from London and its hinterland, consisted of young, unmarried craftsmen who came as indentured servants. The other group, from Yorkshire and Scotland, fled the threat of land expropriation, moved in family groups, and had sufficient income to procure colonial land. Once they arrived, mid-eighteenth-century English indentured servants were sold in large colonial towns or to southern planters. Urban residents purchased contracts from unmarried German redemptioners as well. In contrast, Scots, Irish, and German immigrants made their homes in frontier areas recently conquered from Indians in New York, Pennsylvania, and the southern backcountry from Maryland to Georgia. Settlers could procure and develop these recently abandoned lands with minimal capital.[22]

Since perhaps two-thirds of English-speaking emigrants to North America came as indentured servants, an understanding of the servant trade illuminates the process of immigration. Indentured servitude maintained the *form* of service in husbandry but transformed the social relations that underlay it, destroying the constraints that bound masters of servants in husbandry in England. While servants in husbandry worked a year at a time,

20. Galenson, *White Servitude*, 212–17; Gemery, "Emigration from British Isles," 215, and "European Emigration," 286, 303, 311; Kulikoff, "Migration and Cultural Diffusion," 168.

21. Bailyn, *Voyagers to the West*, 43–49; Wrigley and Schofield, *Population History of England*, 219–28, 402–12; Dickson, *Ulster Emigration to Colonial America*, 60–81; Fogelman, "Review Essay," 322–23, and "Immigration, German Immigration and Eighteenth-Century America," 37–53.

22. Bailyn, *Voyagers to the West*, chaps. 5, 11–16; Galenson, *White Servitude*, 212–37; Gemery, "European Emigration," 286–87, 311; Wokeck, "Flow and the Composition of German Immigration," 249–78; Mitchell, *Commercialism and Frontier*, 34–45; Grubb, "Immigrant Servant Labor," 249–75.

indentured servants over the age of twenty-one signed on for four years to repay their ocean passage. Indentured servants could not choose their masters but had to accept whoever purchased their contracts and had to accept his authority. Masters could buy and sell servants at will during their terms. Indentured servants were not paid a wage but received freedom dues at the end of their term. The longer terms and frequent sales they suffered suggest that they were less likely than servants in husbandry to be treated as family members.[23]

The ages, occupations, gender, and class of servants the colonies attracted suggest the reasons they migrated. Seventeenth-century colonies, except in New England, attracted mostly young single men, the same group who worked as servants in husbandry.[24] About three-quarters of the servants were males and two-thirds were between fifteen and twenty-four years of age. Seventeenth-century indentured servants represented a cross-section of the younger middling and poorer sorts of England, including the unskilled, agricultural laborers, husbandmen and yeomen, and craftsmen. These men came to the colonies expecting to improve their economic condition by setting up their own farms once their terms expired. Those who could aspire to land in England stayed at home.[25]

Youths who came to the American colonies as indentured servants negotiated with the merchant who paid their transportation costs. Since transit costs were identical for all emigrants, differences in the number of years they had to serve suggest variations in colonial demand for labor. Adolescents, on average, served over five years. Potential servants with skills, literate servants, and older youths — who had gained strength or agricultural skills — negotiated shorter terms. And the few girls who emigrated as servants to colonies short of women could demand a premium of a year and a half off their terms.[26]

The destinations of indentured servants varied with the colonial demand for white labor. During the mid-seventeenth century, servants migrated mostly to West India sugar plantations and to Chesapeake tobacco farms. But after African slaves replaced white servants in the labor force of

23. This analysis summarizes Galenson, *White Servitude*, but see A. E. Smith, *Colonists in Bondage*, as well.

24. Menard, "British Migration," 119–20; V. D. Anderson, "Migrants and Motives," 346–55.

25. Compare M. Campbell ("Social Origins of Early Americans," 63–89, "Rebuttal," 526–40, and "Reply," 277–86), who argued that indentured servants came mostly from the middling classes, with Galenson's ("'Middling People' or 'Common Sort'?" 499–524, and "Social Origins of Early Americans," 264–77) contention that many were laborers. Galenson's inferences fit the status of servants in husbandry better than Campbell's.

26. Galenson, *White Servitude*, chap. 7.

staple colonies and had proved their skills, demand for white labor plummeted. This process was completed in the West Indies by the 1670s, in South Carolina soon after 1700, and in the Chesapeake by the 1720s. Since most English emigrants were servants bound for staple colonies, the decline of English emigration can be explained in part by diminished colonial demand for all but skilled servants. By the mid-eighteenth century, nearly half the servant migrants were craftsmen, a third were unskilled youths, and the rest were divided between farmers and laborers.[27]

English conditions in the 1770s reignited servant immigration. Coming to London for the reputedly high wages found there, craftsmen had great difficulty landing employment. Hardly London's most debased proletarians, they usually had craft skills. Over two-thirds of men who left London as indentured servants between 1773–75 were craftsmen, mostly journeymen who had suffered extended periods of casual employment. Recruited by middlemen, they migrated to the colonies expecting to improve their economic condition once their terms had expired. Since colonial planters, merchants, and craftsmen sought *skilled* servants, most of them landed in Maryland, Pennsylvania, and Virginia, where labor demand was high. Servants with the skills that colonists needed—building tradesmen and ironworkers, for example—were sold quickly but those with less desired skills were often carried by colonial jobbers from port towns through the back country to find a farmer to buy their indentures.[28]

The redemptioneer labor system, increasingly common in the colonies after 1750, resembled, but was not identical to, indentured servitude. Both were methods of paying for passage by working as servants for a term of years. Under the indenture system, merchants bartered space and provisions for the right to sell the migrant's labor upon arrival. The shipper risked not recovering his costs, but in turn, the servant neither could choose his master nor negotiate the terms of the contract. In contrast, shippers loaned redemptioners the cost of passage. The migrant, who assumed the risk, had to sell himself (and perhaps his family) to repay the shipper. This system provided the migrant greater choice of masters and terms of service and permitted immigrant families to stay together. Nearly all German servants, substantial peasants who had sufficient property to pay manumission fines and finance movement through Europe, came as redemptioners; more surprisingly, about two-fifths of the English servants who arrived in Philadelphia between 1771 and 1773 were redemptioners as well.[29]

27. Galenson, *White Servitude*, chap. 4; Menard, "Servants to Slave," 355–90, and "Africanization of Lowcountry Labor Force," 81–108.

28. Bailyn, *Voyagers to the West*, chaps. 5–9.

29. Grubb, "Redemptioner Immigration to Pennsylvania," 407–18, esp. 409–11, and "Immigrant Servant Labor," 255–61.

Although only about a third of colonial immigrants financed their own passage, free emigration was crucial to colonial society. Given the expenses of passage and of making a new household, free immigrants had to have substantial means and access to credit. Most settlers of New England came as free immigrants; arriving as families, they could begin to create new societies as soon as they landed. Even in the Chesapeake, where the vast majority of migrants were indentured servants, a few free immigrants arrived, especially in the mid-seventeenth century. These yeomen, craftsmen, and merchants soon constituted the first families of the region, and played a major role in crafting an indigenous culture.[30]

Scot and Yorkshire migrant families of the 1770s provide a case study of free immigration. Over half of them migrated in family groups, including many children and adults over thirty. Divided between artisan families from the Scottish lowlands (mostly textile workers) and farm families from the Scottish highlands and Yorkshire, most emigrants paid their passage. The farmers among them had sold their livestock, crops, and household goods when improving landlords raised their rents so rapidly that they feared displacement from the land. They wanted land of their own, far from venal landlords. Textile workers left because they feared poverty, and most other artisans came to America hoping to get land or higher wages. Even families that emigrated to escape poverty or high rents, however, usually expected to improve their condition in the colonies. Farmers and artisans listened avidly to land speculators who offered passage to America or organized communal migration societies. Since most good land in the older colonies had long been cultivated, they moved to the peripheries, Nova Scotia, northern New York, and North Carolina, where abundant land lay fallow. Once they arrived, some quickly found land, struggled in primitive conditions, but eventually created profitable farms.[31]

European Emigration and Cultural Invention before the Revolution

The impact of the culture emigrants brought with them upon social relations and culture in the colonies they conquered was complex. The received culture and the colonial environment clashed, forcing reinvention of cultural norms. The economy, class relations, religious beliefs, and politics of European countries sending emigrants to British North America could change

30. Menard, "British Migration," 119–21; Cressy, *Coming Over*, chaps. 2, 4; V. D. Anderson, "Migrants and Motives," 339–83; Archer, "New England Mosaic," 487–88.
31. Bailyn, *Voyagers to the West*, chaps. 5, 11, 14, 16.

radically at the same time as Indian wars, vast land supplies, mixed colonial populations (Indian, English, Scottish, German, African), and the peculiarities of the colonial economy challenged the goals of European emigrants.

How, then, are we to understand cultural continuities between English regions (or Germany or Scotland) and American colonies? Economic differences between England and its colonies belie any simple direct cultural transmission from mother country or region. Capitalism had transformed Britain, raising the proportion of laborers and artisans in the population. Most English and Scottish emigrants were either artisans or laborers. Indentured servants were mostly young laborers or craftsmen; only a third had been in agriculture. Similarly, just a third of emigrants to New England had agricultural occupations, while over half were artisans. Even fewer eighteenth-century emigrants came from farming backgrounds: merely 15 percent of English emigrants and one-fifth of the Scots, 1773–76, worked in agriculture; over half the English and two-fifths of the Scots were craftsmen, with those in textiles predominating. Even among household heads, only half were in agriculture. Immigrants left capitalist Britain not because they desired to replicate that system of social relations; rather, they sometimes sought to escape, to create a small producer society. The vast majority of colonists became farmers; the textile industry, so important in England and Scotland, was small in the colonies. These farmers created freehold or slave societies profoundly different from capitalist Britain.[32]

Only a dynamic model that sets changing productive relations in sending and receiving areas side by side can fully explain the culture of new communities. The process begins before migration, continues with emigration, and concludes with adjustment or transformation in both old and new areas. Colonists invented new traditions, consciously adapting older cultural forms in new situations, building upon the culture they left behind. The creation of new traditions in the colonies was both public (distributing land, writing charters) and private (naming children). Community development, with its invention of new traditions, takes place following initial occupation; once set, such traditions change slowly as emigrants come into contact with Indians or other settlers. At the same time, the older area suffers disruption, as those who are left must adjust to relative depopulation.[33]

Notwithstanding great diversity among migrants, communities invented cohesive cultures throughout the colonies. Migration to the colonies tended to be highly selective. During the seventeenth century, East Anglians

32. Fischer, *Albion's Seed*, 152–55, 228; Galenson, *White Servitude*, chap. 3; Horn, "Servant Emigration," 56–60; Bailyn, *Voyagers to the West*, 147–86.

33. Hobsbawm, Introduction: "Inventing Traditions," 1–8; Ostergren, *Community Transplanted*, 25–27; Conzen, "Mainstreams and Side Channels," 6–7, 11–15.

concentrated in New England while those from the southeastern part of the country moved to the Chesapeake. The Middle Colonies were more polyglot than other regions, yet even here the Quaker core tended to emigrate from the North Midlands or London. Germans, Scots, and Scots-Irish settled Pennsylvania and the eighteenth-century southern backcountry, where proportionately fewer descendants of English settlers lived. The localized ethnic cultures such groups created, with their unique public institutions and familial customs, depended upon these concentrated patterns of migration and settlement.[34]

By 1790 as many as two-fifths of the people would have needed to move to ensure equal numbers of ethnic groups in each state. About three-fifths of the white population in 1790 were of English origins, located especially in New England, where over four of every five residents were English. Half of the whites elsewhere could trace their origins to England, but concentrations of Dutch lived in New York, and between a quarter and a third of the people in the Carolinas, Georgia, and Kentucky were Scots, Scots-Irish, or Irish. Pennsylvania was polyglot: two-fifths were German, one-quarter English, one-third North British. Such aggregate data do not tell the whole story, for ethnic groups concentrated within states. Pennsylvania Germans, for instance, lived mostly in the east central part of state, where they constituted nearly two-thirds of the populace; Scots-Irish, Irish, and Scots migrated to the western portions of the state; English and Welsh lived near Philadelphia and in the far west. Similar concentrations could be found in New Jersey and New York counties.[35]

Despite these ethnic concentrations, cultural contact among Europeans did help shape colonial cultures. Everyone had to accommodate to English common law and the capitalist market system.[36] English farmers settled near German or Scottish communities, and internal migration was so common that further contact and a degree of acculturation were inevitable. Some Ger-

34. Fischer, *Albion's Seed*, 31–36, 236–46, 438–45, 605–21; Conzen, "Mainstreams and Side Channels," 6–20, for the idea of the "localization" of immigrant cultures.

35. Fogelman, "Immigration, German Immigration, and Eighteenth-Century America," 18–26; Purvis, "European Ancestry of United States Population," 85–101, esp. 98, which raises English totals from that in F. McDonald and E. S. McDonald, "Ethnic Origins of the American People," 179–99, esp. 195–99. Such data, based upon counts of surnames, only suggests general trends (see Akenson, "Why Accepted Estimates of Ethnicity Are Unacceptable," 102–18, 125–29; Purvis, "Commentary," 119–25). For individual states see Purvis, "Ethnic Settlement in Pennsylvania," 107–22, "European Origins of New Jersey's Population," 15–31, and "National Origin of New Yorkers," 133–53.

36. This modifies Fischer, *Albion's Seed*, but see also Roeber, "Origin and Transfer of German-American Concepts of Property," 115–18, 156–60, for a very different view that sees both accommodation and resistance.

mans, for instance, engaged in land speculation, produced for the market, and farmed in ways similar to those of their English neighbors.[37] Such contact set limits on cultural innovation but hardly precluded the creation of ethnic class cultures.

Indians had less impact upon the creation of Eurocolonial cultures than the intercourse among Europeans. Intermarriage and the formation of biracial communities were uncommon; colonists looked with horror at white captives who chose to remain in Indian communities. Indians taught the first colonists cultivation techniques (burn-and-slash agriculture, corn and tobacco husbandry), preparation of Indian foods, and ways of forest warfare. But colonists embedded Indian techniques they learned in a market system alien to Indian cultures: Indians burned underbrush to find game, whites to create pastures for domesticated animals that chased game away. Unsurprisingly, confrontation, conquest, and Indian dependency characterized contacts between whites and Indians.[38]

To delineate the ways colonists invented new traditions, one needs to examine specific cultures and the social relations of which they were a part, paying attention to both origins and destinations. New England migration suggests how great cultural transfer might be. Most settlers from East Anglia, the West Country, and Wiltshire were pulled from England by population pressure on land, poor harvests, and the decline of the cloth trade; religious conflict encouraged Puritan preachers to lead emigrants from Yorkshire, East Anglia, and the West Country. Migrants experienced economic distress in religious terms, seeking success in a Godly country. Given these underlying reasons for movement, individuals, however, often moved to New England to join kindred or, after being actively recruited, to overcome personal setbacks or family disruptions.[39]

The family nature of emigration permitted some settlers to reinvent the cultures they left behind with remarkable fidelity, as a case study of Rawley, Hingham, Newberry, Watertown, and Ipswich, Massachusetts, shows. Most of the settlers who emigrated to these towns came from a single village or contiguous villages. The land system (mix of open or enclosed fields), eco-

37. Wolf, *Urban Village*, 6–14, and chap. 4; Lemon, *Best Poor Man's Country*, esp. 13–22, 43–48, 73–87; Lemon, "Agricultural Practices of National Groups," 467–96.

38. Meinig, *Shaping of America*, 1:65–72, 205–13; Axtell, "White Indians of Colonial America," 55–88, and *European and Indian*, chap. 10; Merrell, *Indians' New World*, chap. 5; Herndon, "Indian Agriculture," 284–86; Cronon, *Changes in the Land*, chaps. 4, 7; Nash, *Red, White, and Black*, chap. 12.

39. These are contested points; for the debate about motivations, see Cressy, *Coming Over*, chap. 3; Allen, *In English Ways*, chap. 6, and "Matrix of Motivation," 408–18; V. D. Anderson, "Migrants and Motives," 339–83, and "Religion, the Common Thread," 418–24; Salerno, "Social Background of Emigration to America," 32–52; Fischer, *Albion's Seed*, 18–31.

nomic activities (mix of grazing, farming, and crafts), wealth distribution, and local government in the English places of origin and the villages they founded in Massachusetts resembled one another. Variations in local social structure that these transfers created persisted through the seventeenth century, but by the late seventeenth century, when provincial government reduced local autonomy at the same time as Indian warfare forced greater unity, greater social homogeneity developed.[40]

The field system documents cultural continuity. Yorkshire settlers of Rawley had lived in open-field communities where an individual's land was scattered in small strips in several fields totaling only a few acres. In Rawley they set up open fields, distributing on average just twenty-three acres per family. For several generations, open fields persisted because farmers rarely consolidated their holdings. In contrast, the East Anglia settlers of Watertown and Ipswich came from villages where farm families had enclosed their land. Although the towns grazed livestock communally, they established no open fields but distributed land in compact parcels, averaging ninety acres per family. Once land was distributed, there was a vigorous land market in both towns.

That commerce played a role in cultural change is suggested by Ipswich. East Anglia settlers of Ipswich recreated the borough government found in the towns they had inhabited. Wealth and political power were more concentrated and there were more artisans and merchants in Ipswich then in the other towns. Officeholders, like those of English boroughs, made economic policy and the town meeting merely elected officers. These patterns were not a simple case of cultural transfer. Ipswich was a commercial center, located far enough from Boston to command its own hinterland, and its peculiarities may owe as much to its location and urban development as to the origin of its citizens.

These towns hardly represent eastern New England—neither Boston nor a fishing town is among them—and they do not encompass the Connecticut River Valley. Tensions over religion and economic development were common, as the witchcraft craze (which pitted commercial and near-subsistence parts of Salem against each other) attests. Early Springfield shows that commercial activities of a single patron could shape productive relations. William Pynchon, an East Anglian entrepreneur, founded Springfield in 1636. By 1641 most of the original settlers had left; Pynchon replaced them with indentured servants—usually artisans—he brought from London or Boston and then used himself or resold. After Pynchon returned to England, his son

40. This paragraph and the next two are based upon Allen, *In English Ways*; for an alternative view that stresses how New England communalism differed from what settlers left behind, see V. D. Anderson, *New England's Generation*, chap. 3.

John took over. He continued to import servants and rented land to freed servants and other migrants.[41]

The two Pynchons built a system of patronage and clientage that incorporated a majority of the population of Springfield. The relations of the Pynchons with their clients were unequal but often reciprocal. The wealthiest men in town, they loaned money to most town families. Through their service to the colony and town, the Pynchons soon owned the best land in town. Freed servants and free immigrants who wished to stay in town usually worked as day laborers or leased land from the Pynchons. More than half the town's adults worked for Pynchon one month or more each year as agricultural laborers, skilled craftsmen, or female domestic servants. They were *not* servants in husbandry; only female house servants labored for a year, and most were day laborers or signed three-month contracts. Some ex-servants became tenants of the Pynchons, signing leases that ran from several years to more than a decade. In return for credit and an outlet for their produce, tenants developed Pynchon land (without retaining rights in the improvements) and paid rent. Residents willing to become the Pynchons's clients had credit extended or even forgiven; those unwilling to accept Pynchon authority had their debts called in and their property confiscated.

Migrants to Springfield came to town searching for economic opportunity. Without the vision of a communal society that motivated some emigrants to eastern Massachusetts, they judged one another by their skills. Residents tolerated deviance, and the town was rent by witchcraft accusations, slander cases, and fornication. Yet a large majority of emigrants and their children stayed, apparently satisfied by local opportunities. The example of Springfield suggests that emigrants may have at best expected to become tenants, a far more secure status than that of a cottager that many might have achieved in England. Improved income, rather than landholding, may have been their goal.

The settlement of Springfield was more representative of European immigrants than the communal villages of eastern Massachusetts. Like most emigrants, Springfield settlers usually arrived as indentured servants; like most communities, Springfield was occupied by families from diverse places. Patrons sponsored migration with some frequency, and the dominance of a community by a single patron could be found in other Massachusetts towns, on the great estates of New York landlords, and in the Chesapeake.[42]

41. Heyrman, *Culture and Community*; Boyer and Nissenbaum, *Salem Possessed*; Demos, *Entertaining Satan*, chaps. 7–9; Karlsen, *Devil in Shape of a Woman*. Material on Springfield in this and succeeding paragraphs summarizes arguments in Innes, *Labor in a New Land*.

42. Innes, *Labor in a New Land*, 173–75; Kim, *Landlord and Tenant in Colonial New York*; L. Morton, *Robert Carter of Nomini Hall*, chap. 1.

Notwithstanding these differences, a New England social order emerged. Freehold land tenure, uncommon in any part of England, dominated each of the towns. Small-producer agriculture and the sale of surpluses predominated throughout New England, and no town duplicated the East Anglia cloth industry. Land and other wealth were less concentrated in New England than in other colonies, and relative equality was sustained by partible inheritance practices brought from East Anglia. Elected town government differentiated all New England settlements from those in other colonies.[43]

Lowland Scottish emigration to New Jersey from the 1680s to the 1770s contrasts greatly to that found in New England. Since New Jersey, like the other middle colonies, was settled by people from a variety of different cultures, Scottish migrants could not set up new societies isolated from alien groups. One can understand the culture they devised in New Jersey only by examining the changing economy in lowland Scotland and comparing it with the development of Scottish communities in New Jersey.[44]

Most lowland Scots, who lived in settlements of two to fifteen households called touns, worked as tenants of a laird or subtenants of the laird's tenants. Tenants, who rarely signed long-term leases, could be evicted at the laird's pleasure. When a laird evicted a tenant, subtenants of the tenant (most of the populace) had to leave. Since tenants and subtenants rarely stayed on the same farm for more than a few years, a collateral kinship system—in which households linked themselves in clanlike structures of fictive kin, women kept their family name upon marriage, and families with property practiced equal partible inheritance—developed instead of the lineal kinship groups common in England.

Internal economic developments differentiated the northeastern and southwestern regions of the lowlands. Since small landowners held little property, wealthy lairds in the northeast held absolute power over tenants. Conservative in their social relations, they adapted English agricultural reforms and joined the Anglican church or Quaker meeting. Lairds used reforms to strengthen their control: instead of turning land over to improving tenants like English landlords, they replaced tenants and subtenants with agricultural laborers. In the southwest borderlands, lairds shared power with numerous small landowners. Laird, small landowner, and tenant were all intensely anti-English and Presbyterian, and lairds infrequently adapted agricultural reforms.

The Quaker great lairds of the northeast sponsored the initial Scottish

43. Fischer, *Albion's Seed*, 13–205, provides numerous examples.
44. This and succeeding paragraphs summarize arguments in Landsman, *Scotland and Its First American Colony*.

occupation of New Jersey in the 1680s. They brought over Scottish indentured servants (families as well as young men) and tenants and set them to work developing their new estates. Although they sought to recreate the reformed estates of the Scottish northeast, they had to compromise to attract settlers and placate New Englanders in their midst. Tenants gained longer terms in New Jersey than in Scotland. Although proprietors refused to sell land to settlers, they granted land and livestock to men who transported themselves after fourteen years of tenancy and gave thirty acres of land to every freed servant at the end of his term. About seven hundred Scots, mostly servants, migrated to New Jersey in the 1680s to take advantage of these terms. Ingrained habits died hard, however, and most former servants who stayed in New Jersey either worked as agricultural laborers for their colonial lairds or rented land from them. When New England settlers, disliking Scottish control and the quitrents they had to pay, rioted against the Scottish landlords, Scottish tenants supported their landlords.[45]

Emigration from Scotland to New Jersey slowed down in the 1690s but picked up again in the mid-eighteenth century. These emigrants were sponsored by merchants from Glasgow and the southwest lowlands who had bought estates in Scotland and greatly improved the terms of their tenants. Once in New Jersey, they created extensive trading networks among themselves and established liberal leasing policies for their tenants. The society these immigrants created varied dramatically from any part of Scotland yet differed from the society of New Jersey residents of New England ancestry. Fathers divided their land among all their sons but expected older sons to find homes elsewhere; sons moved from one cluster of their countrymen to another, making intricate social networks with men of similar status wherever they moved.

A uniform Scottish religion, critical to the formation of the Scottish ethnic group, was born in New Jersey. Scottish Quakers and Anglicans migrated to New Jersey, but their descendants, tiring ofconflicts with New England brethren, joined Presbyterian congregations, especially during revivals, beginning in the 1730s. Unlike Anglo-American revivalists, who demanded an emotional conversion experience, Presbyterian divines insisted that experiential religion be combined with doctrine. Revivalists first successfully converted tenants and servants and then turned to immigrant artisans and merchants. Once they had completed this work, they broke their alliances with Anglo-American revivalists and formed a unified Scottish-dominated Presbyterian Church with Scottish antirevivalists.

Eighteenth-century immigration to the British colonies from southwest-

---

45. Purvis, "Patterns of Agrarian Unrest," 600–627; Landsman, *Scotland and Its First American Colony*, 222–25, describe the riots.

ern Germany, part of a vast outmigration, was caused by population pressure on land in a society where partible inheritance was common. A feudal legal system still predominated, but capitalist enclaves had developed by the seventeenth century, as enclosures, peasant dispossession, and the rise of flax growing and a putting-out industry show. Germans lived in a world without private property. Inheritance practices in southwest Germany were based upon local custom, ducal law, and church law. Despite conflicts among these law codes, peasants understood how to manipulate them to sustain familial and communal norms, to guarantee an appropriate distribution of property at the death of the owner while discouraging individuals from deviating from these practices.[46]

Potential German migrants learned about colonial opportunities from British recruiters and a growing pamphlet and book literature. Once German migrants began to leave for the colonies, however, chain migration quickly developed. Most German members of a Lancaster, Pennsylvania, Lutheran church came from one region in Germany, a quarter from two neighboring villages. Not only did neighbors and kin follow earlier pioneers, but persisting Germans sometimes financed emigration, in return for inheritance rights. Once pioneers had arrived, villagers could finance their voyage as redemptioneers and hope that landsmen would purchase their contracts.[47]

Germans only slowly accommodated to private property. To educate their landsmen, lawyers — educated in English ways — published handbooks and dictionaries explaining English common law. Under the influence of lawyers and clergymen, German settlers in Pennsylvania and Maryland began writing wills, for that was the only way to ensure bequests to local churches and to preserve communal order and such inheritance customs as specifying the provisioning of aging parents. Such customs, however, were difficult to maintain in the South, where German settlers were more isolated.[48]

Germans forged new communal institutions, making themselves into an ethnic group in the mid-eighteenth century. Where they constituted a substantial part of the population, Germans kept to themselves, marrying only within their own group, reading German newspapers, doing business and socializing with their compatriots. The church took on heightened importance: not only did church schools teach children German language and culture, but German families used churches (rather than colonial courts) to resolve questions of inheritance both in Germany and the colonies. Even

46. Roeber, "German-American Concepts of Property," 115–71; Keller, "From Rhineland to the Virginia Frontier," 485–93.
47. Roeber, "German-American Concepts of Property," 152–53.
48. Roeber, "German-American Concepts of Property," 115–19, 145–71.

though the Moravian settlement in North Carolina slowly abandoned the open-field villages of their homeland, they nonetheless created a religious refuge for poor German Moravians, dominated by the church. Germans were so successful that Benjamin Franklin feared being overtaken by them. Yet Germans, at least before 1760, made few moves to participate in provincial politics; those few highly educated men who served as local officials functioned as interpreters of English culture to the German populace, showing them how to retain some vestiges of village custom.[49]

Some Germans adapted well to private property, trading land and raising crops much as their English-speaking neighbors. But even here there were differences, driven by the material culture they brought with them. Germans in Pennsylvania and Virginia grew flax much as they had at home, with women both working in the fields and participating in the processing of flax into linen, activities especially adapted to communal German settlements like those of Mennonites.[50]

Internal Migration in Rural North America, 1600–1800

Seventeenth-century colonies were so peripheral to England that settlers, except large planters, were isolated from English capitalism. Given initial low European populations and Indian resistance, colonists only gradually took up new lands. But as farmers came to expect to own land, they spread across the landscape, each making small farms wherever they went, turning "public property . . . into [their] private property, and [their] individual means of production," thereby opposing "the establishment of capital."[51] In such noncapitalist societies, marriage migration, short moves within a region, and frontier migration can be substantial. Migration from old areas to frontiers grew at accelerating rates from 1607 to 1775, except during periods of depression between 1680 and 1710. Europeans invaded the coastline in the seventeenth century, creating settlements hugging the coast, and their eighteenth-century descendants migrated in great numbers from the Atlantic coastal plain to the piedmont.

After landing on the coast, seventeenth-century colonists fanned out across the countryside, following the courses of rivers and the natural contours of the land, seldom traveling more than a two-day trip from the ocean.

49. Kessel, "'A Mighty Fortress,'" 370–87; Tully, "Englishmen and German," 235–56, esp. 245–56; Becker, "Diversity and Its Significance," 196–221; Thorp, "Assimilation in North Carolina's Moravian Community," 19–42; Roeber, "German-American Concepts of Property," 115–21, 152–71.
50. Lemon, "Agricultural Practices of National Groups," 467–96; Keller, "From Rhineland to the Virginia Frontier," 495–503.
51. K. Marx, *Capital*, 1: chap. 33 (quote on 934).

Constrained by Indian occupation, farm families seldom ventured onto tribal lands until Indians had been defeated. Settlement in isolated areas where Indians maintained numerical dominance could be dangerous, as King Philip's War shows. Driven by settler confiscation of their lands, Indians burned settlements, chasing white families to the relative safety of coastal or Connecticut River settlements. Notwithstanding Indian defeat, and the rapid white repopulation of towns like Deerfield, it took half a century for colonists to resettle all the lands Indians contested.[52]

The majority of immigrants who arrived in New England in the 1630s soon left Boston, moving one or two times with their families to towns near Boston or on the Connecticut River, where they would have a better chance of acquiring land. Although families often persisted for decades, as many as two-thirds of the children of immigrants moved sometime in their lives, at marriage, or to set up an independent farm unit, or to take up mercantile or craft occupations after the death of the husband's father. Most migrants moved to nearby villages, and nearly all lived within thirty miles of their birthplaces. This system was encouraged by state action, which regulated town formation, giving over large parcels of land to the initial settlers when older towns threatened to become overpopulated.[53]

Despite the rapid development of a staple economy, a similar pattern of dispersion could be found in the Chesapeake. Ex-servants, often unable to find land in their former master's county, moved to nearby frontiers, settling along rivers and creeks before moving inland. Notwithstanding this movement and very high mortality, cohesive communities soon appeared. Four-fifths of former servants in Charles County, Maryland, able to gain land, stayed in the community, as did many unable to rise out of the ranks of laborers or tenants. In total, a quarter of surviving immigrants left Charles County and about two-fifths departed from Lancaster County, Virginia. Out-migration from the region increased, as tobacco prices and ex-servant opportunities to find land declined after 1680.[54]

52. Bosworth, "Those Who Moved," 11–16; L. K. Mathews, *Expansion of New England*, 56–63; Melvoin, *New England Outpost*, chaps. 4–5; Crandall, "New England's Second Great Migration," 351–52.

53. Archer, "New England Mosaic," 485–86; L. K. Mathews, *Expansion of New England*, chaps. 2–5; V. D. Anderson, "Migration, Kinship, and Colonial New England Society," 269–87, and *New England's Generation*, 103–24; Cole, "Family, Settlement, and Migration," 171–85; Adams and Kasakoff, "Migration and the Family," 23–43, and "Migration at Marriage," 115–38. For town formation, see P. M. G. Harris, "Social Origins of American Leaders," 235–41.

54. Kelly, "'In Dispers'd Country Plantations,'" 183–205; Mitchell, "American Origins and Regional Institutions," 409–11; Horn, "Moving On in the New World," 176–

The seventeenth-century English mainland colonies were characterized by small producers, even in Chesapeake. Notwithstanding Indian wars that hemmed in European settlement, short-distance internal migration opened new areas for European habitation and may have led to expectations of land ownership. The founding of new colonies — North Carolina, Pennsylvania — encouraged poorer men and their families to move somewhat greater distances to find land and establish themselves as small producers.[55]

Labor migration developed in the seventeenth-century Chesapeake colonies as freed servants tramped the countryside searching for farm or craft labor high-paying enough to permit rental or purchase of land. As opportunities diminished after 1660, tramping probably increased, leading county courts to complain that "vagrant persons . . . remove from place to place . . . to defraud the County of their Levies." Bacon's Rebellion of 1676 was, in part, a response by freedmen and servants to perceived declining opportunities and a desire to conquer Indian lands to make farms for themselves. This nascent labor market dissipated by the early eighteenth century after slaves replaced servants on Chesapeake farms.[56]

During the eighteenth century, internal migration changed in contradictory ways. Levels of persistence in settled areas rose among the grandchildren of the original settlers. Most people moved short distances, either upon marriage or as family members of young adults. In New England, 1750–70, at least two-fifths but as many as three-quarters of marriages were between people from the same town, and nearly all the others were celebrated by residents of contiguous or nearby towns. Migrants born in New England between 1701 and 1740 moved just under forty miles over their lifetimes; soldiers who enlisted in Revolutionary service in Virginia had moved to adjacent counties or stayed in their county of birth. The reasons for this pattern of increasing persistence and short-distance migration are clear. Men waiting for their inheritances stayed close to home until their fathers died. Fathers, if they possessed enough land, settled married sons or sons-in-law on unimproved land near their own or on land they had purchased years

91, 195–200; Walsh, "Staying Put or Getting Out," 89–103; Rutman and Rutman, "'More True and Perfect Lists,'" 67–73.

55. Vickers, "Working the Fields," 49–69; Menard, "Economy and Society," chap. 5, and "From Servant to Freeholder," 37–64.

56. Horn, "Moving On in the New World," 172–73; Walsh, "Staying Put or Getting Out," 172–73, 192–93 (quote); Menard, "Servant to Freeholder," 37–64; Carr and Menard, "Immigration and Opportunity," 206–42; E. S. Morgan, *American Slavery, American Freedom*, chaps. 11–23; S. S. Webb, *1676: End of American Independence*, 41–43, 66–71, 120–25, 144–50.

earlier. Moreover, settlement of the interior proceeded slowly enough that few areas were completely filled in with Euro-Americans. Even after their fathers died, men could therefore still find inexpensive land within several days' journey of their current residence.[57]

Not all migrants achieved landownership; many families, especially near towns like Philadelphia, settled for semipermanent agricultural labor and lived much like English cottagers. Others achieved less stability. Tramping the roads searching for work became more common in settled areas of the North, presaging the development of seasonal agricultural and urban employment. The young transients of coastal Essex County, Massachusetts, often ex-servants, sought agricultural labor at the time of planting and harvest or urban employment in towns near their birthplace. Many rural transients wound up in Boston, working on the docks, in ships, or in workshops. Even after marriage, some could not find permanent employment, and over a third of them had young families with an average of two children. Young couples from old towns often migrated to the frontier, but even there success eluded them. The number of families among transients warned-out in frontier Hampshire County rose from under half to over two-thirds between 1739–43 and 1770–74.[58]

At the same time as labor migration increased in older areas, long-distance migration rose. Colonists and their black slaves colonized the Appalachian piedmont in the thirty years before the Revolution. Long-distance migrants followed a north-south axis, splitting into two regional patterns. Men born in New York and New England tended to move north and northeast, up the Connecticut and Hudson river valleys, settling in northeastern New York, western Massachusetts, and northern New England. Moves of over a hundred miles were far more common in colonies from Pennsylvania south. Migrants in this region moved in a southwest direction, from eastern Pennsylvania and the Susquehanna valley into the piedmont and mountain districts of Maryland, Virginia, and the Carolinas.[59]

Migration was driven by changing local opportunities, increased land prices in older areas, and inexpensive land on frontiers. Rising demand for

57. Adams and Kasakoff, "Migration and the Family," 28–29; Villaflor and Sokoloff, "Migration in Colonial America," 545–48; S. L. Norton, "Marriage Migration in Essex County," 406–18; Kulikoff, *Tobacco and Slaves,* 141–57; Greven, *Four Generations,* 210–14, 273–74.

58. D. L. Jones, "The Strolling Poor," 28–54, and "Poverty and Vagabondage," 243–54; Cray, *Paupers and Poor Relief,* chaps. 2–3, esp. 50–64, 84–99; Nash, *Urban Crucible,* 185–86, 470, and *Race, Class, and Politics,* chap. 7, esp. 181–88; Kulikoff, "Progress of Inequality," 399–404.

59. Villaflor and Sokoloff, "Migration in Colonial America," 539–70; Gragg, *Migration in Early America;* Bosworth, "Those Who Moved," 25–33.

tobacco and a growing population raised land prices in Tidewater counties, impelling poorer planters to move to piedmont areas. In New England, yeoman farmers moved to remake small farms. For instance, as the quantity of unimproved land in Wenham, Massachusetts, declined, partible inheritance diminished among men who left wills, and authorities often refused to divide land of intestates, preferring to grant it to one son but requiring him to pay portions to his siblings. Unfavored sons accumulated little capital but often migrated to northern frontiers or nearby towns, hoping to use their cash inheritance to buy land.[60]

Eighteenth-century frontier migration was embedded within the household economy. Most migrants sought to establish the kind of yeoman economic independence possible within an interdependent market economy. Avoiding urban areas, they moved toward the frontier. Men tended to move long distances in their mid-twenties, after receiving their portions on their marriage and after their fathers died. Since frontier migration entailed both transportation costs and foregone income, only those with some capital could move to the frontier. Poor folk, who rarely persisted, usually moved short distances; those who moved to the frontier squatted on land but were soon forced to move.[61]

Most frontier migrants moved as members of households; the rest were unmarried young men and (less often) women. Since kin groups rarely moved together, except occasional adult siblings or a father and adult son, frontier families could rely upon few kindred for support after arrival at their new homes. Communal chain migration might have been more common. After early migrants had achieved economic success, others from their home villages sometimes joined them. Quakers, who often migrated over long distances from Pennsylvania to Virginia or North Carolina, may have gained communal support for migration from their meetings other frontier migrants lacked, but on occasion other settlers moved in groups, founding colonies of their old communities. Residents of Andover, Massachusetts, for instance, began colonies in Windham County, Connecticut, in the early eighteenth century and moved to a cluster of towns in New Hampshire and western Massachusetts later in the century.[62]

Migration facilitated the redistribution of economic resources in places migrants left, as a study of the Massachusetts farming village of Wenham and the port of Beverly shows. The sons who stayed in Wenham usually pros-

60. Kulikoff, *Tobacco and Slaves*, 141–57; D. L. Jones, *Village and Seaport*, chaps. 4–6; Rutman, "People in Process," 16–37.
61. Adams and Kasakoff, "Wealth and Migration," 363–68.
62. Adams and Kasakoff, "Migration and the Family," 32–33; Gragg, *Migration in Early America*; Greven, *Four Generations*, 156–72, 210–14.

pered; sons who left for frontier areas were partially replaced by migrants seeking their fortunes, but three-quarters of them, unable to establish themselves, soon left. Opportunity was greater in Beverly. As many sons stayed in Beverly as in Wenham, but they achieved less success than Wenham's sons. Nonetheless, far more men came to Beverly, often bringing capital with them to start businesses, and even poor migrants could find mercantile employment. Most inmigrants left Beverly, too, but they included as many middling and wealthy men pulled out by new opportunities as unsuccessful men pushed out by poverty.[63]

Migration and urban employment severed the links that tied marriage to land ownership. In Beverly the growth of urban employment permitted the landless to marry. Since more unmarried men than women left Wenham for the frontier, a surplus of young women appeared, giving men greater choices and permitting them to wed at younger ages. Outmigration of young men had the same effect by reducing some of the pressures on land. Those who stayed either received early inheritances or, knowing that they would inherit land, married and then worked family land.

Internal Migration in an Era of Capitalist Transformation

Progressively tied to commodity and labor markets, nineteenth-century native-born Americans and immigrants alike increasingly migrated in response to capitalist development. If some migrants sought opportunities, others wanted merely to escape the threat of wage labor. As a result, long-distance migration rapidly increased and population turnover in cities and on frontiers skyrocketed. Increased migration sustained new and more integrated labor and commodity markets but permitted some families to continue older ways of life on frontier areas.[64]

Migration choices families made depended upon their class. White wage laborers tramped through the northeastern countryside, migrating to mill villages or cities, where they competed with immigrants and free blacks for seasonal and manual labor. In contrast, farm families with land or access to credit took up land in frontier regions, where they mingled with wage laborers — often immigrants — who broke sod, harvested crops, constructed canals and railroads, and guided flatboats and canalboats to market. White planters and their slaves moved from older parts of the South to rich cotton-growing lands; poorer whites, unable to compete with planters, migrated to inferior lands in upper South and mountain regions.[65]

63. This and the next paragraph summarize D. L. Jones, *Village and Seaport.*
64. Steckel, "Household Migration and Rural Settlement," 199–206; Zelinsky, "Hypothesis Mobility Transition," 219–49.
65. Earle and Hoffman, "Foundation Modern Economy," 1055–94; Simler, "Landless Worker," 63–99; Nash, *Forging Freedom,* 71–79, 144–53; Shepherd, "Restless Amer-

Poorer Americans and immigrants faced constrained migration choices, as their relative concentration in cities suggests. All migrants wanted land and the independence it brought, identifying cities with dependence and exploitation. Only small-town merchants and craftsmen saw cities as beacons of opportunity. German, English, and Irish immigrants moved to frontier regions, making farms with some regularity. But the Irish and, to a lesser extent, Germans and English concentrated more heavily in cities, mill towns, and industrial or frontier villages than native-born white Americans, where they often fell into the worst-paid proletarian jobs.[66]

Notwithstanding dynamic urban growth in the antebellum North, and the great opportunities in cities for capitalists, clerks, or professionals, rural-urban migration remained limited. Most migrants from the countryside were young, unmarried people who left after a few years, often returning to a rural area. Sons of farmers and agricultural laborers who enlisted in the army during the War of 1812 were usually recruited in Boston, Philadelphia, or other cities; New England farm daughters, recruited by factory managers of new textile mills, often stayed only a few years before returning. Only those who found spouses and steady work, like shoe workers of rural origin in Lynn, Massachusetts, tended to stay. In contrast, few farmers moved to cities, even temporarily, and many of them moved back to the countryside. As late as the 1850s over nine-tenths of farm families with children either remained in a rural area or moved between rural places. Even in highly urban New England, two-thirds of the migrants moved between rural areas.[67]

Since they had access to frontier land, farmers avoided cities. Heavy concentrations of Catholic immigrants and fear of falling into a debased working class, moreover, discouraged rural white Protestants from urban

---

icans," 25–45; Wyman, *Immigrants in the Valley*, chap. 4; Tobin, "Lowly Muscular Digger," chap. 3; P. W. Gates, *Illinois Central Railroad*, 89, 94–98; Lightner, "Construction Labor on the Illinois Central," 285–301; Schob, *Hired Hands and Plowboys*; Schafer, *History Agriculture in Wisconsin*, chap. 3; Curti, *Making of American Community*, 61–74, chap. 8; D. N. Doyle, "Irish as Urban Pioneers," 42–43; R. E. Carp, "Limits of Reform," 191–220.

66. Kamphoefner, *Westfalians*, chaps. 3–5, esp. 80–87; D. N. Doyle, "Irish as Urban Pioneers," 41–54; D. H. Doyle, *Social Order Frontier Community*, 92–155, 261, 266–68; Nannini, "Ethnic and Regional Composition LaSalle County," 77–90; Gambone, "Immigrant Presence in Grundy County," 64–75.

67. Lindstrom, "Northeastern Migration," 24–29; Field, "Sectoral Shift in Antebellum Massachusetts," 156–64; Stagg, "Enlisted Men in the U.S. Army," 636–39; Dublin, *Women at Work*, chap. 3; Dublin, "Rural-Urban Migrants," 637–40; Steckel, "Household Migration and Settlement," 192, and "Household Migration, Urban Growth, and Industrialization," 10–20, 26–27. Knights, *Yankee Destinies*, chap. 5, finds a higher persistence rate (56.9%) of rural migrants to Boston, but his data cover a later period (1860–1900).

migration.[68] Landless sons of farmers found jobs in villages, accumulated savings and inheritances, and bought land. Farmers and farm wives often combined craft occupations and agriculture; their sons moved to villages to work as craftsmen. But the exodus from agriculture, even in industrializing New England, was usually temporary; in 1850, seven-tenths of sons of farmers of New England descent living in the North still worked on farms. Two-fifths of the sons of artisans, moreover, returned to farming, especially in the newer sections of New York and the Midwest.[69]

Nineteenth-century northeastern cities attracted highly skilled and educated merchants, craftsmen, and manufacturers acclimated to town life and eager for city opportunities. Migrants to Lynn, for example, tended to be children of farmers of moderate means, whose ability to provide them with farms or the capital to migrate to western frontiers was limited and who had worked in the shoe putting-out industry even before their arrival. Rural craftsmen dominated the migrant stream to Boston. In the mid-nineteenth century, three-fifths of rural migrants to Boston were sons of artisans, merchants, or professionals, three-quarters of whom had lived in nearby towns. Only one-fourth of native-born migrants to Albany had been farmers; another two-fifths came from rural nonfarm environments.[70]

The prospects of rural-urban migrants depended upon the skills they brought with them. Farmers' sons, with few transferable skills, fell to the bottom of Boston's social structure; two-fifths of the migrants from Berks County to a working-class ward in Reading, Pennsylvania, became laborers and merely one of fifteen entered the new tradesman, proprietor, and professional class. In contrast, the skilled laborers and white collar workers who moved to Boston or Buffalo, often from distant places, quickly established themselves, married, formed households, and bought homes.[71]

Immigrants congregated in cities, joining migrants from nearby coun-

68. For these attitudes, see R. Burns, *Success in America*, chap. 3; Horlick, *Country Boys and Merchant Princes*, chap. 2; Billington, *Protestant Crusade*, esp. chaps. 3–5, 9; Knobel, *Paddy and the Republic*, esp. chap. 3 and 183–99; Handlin, *Boston's Immigrants*, chap. 7.

69. Dublin, "Women and Outwork," 51–70; Adams and Kasakoff, "Exodus from Agriculture," 5–16; J. S. Wood, "Elaboration of Settlement System," 338–50.

70. R. L. Bushman, "Family Security from Farm to City," 257–77; Steckel, "Household Migration, Urban Growth, and Industrialization," 10–26; Dublin, "Rural-Urban Migrants," 623–44; Knights, "Characteristics of Rural Migrants," 1–5, and *Yankee Destinies*, chap. 1 (which modifies his earlier work, suggesting that sons of families with farms moved to Boston in numbers consistent with their proportion of the population).

71. Katz, Doucet, and Stern, "Migration and Social Order," 672–77; Davenport, "Migration to Albany," 159–86; Modell, "Peopling of a Working-Class Ward," 75–84; Knights, "Characteristics of Rural Migrants," 1–5, and *Yankee Destinies*, 29–33; Dublin, "Rural-Urban Migrants," 623–44; Glasco, "Migration and Adjustment," 162–71. For a

ties and other cities. Lacking urban skills and facing discrimination, they were disproportionately forced into the lower reaches of the working class. Immigrants especially congregated in northeastern and midwestern cities: in 1850 and 1860, a third of the people in large eastern cities and half the population of major midwestern cities and San Francisco were foreign-born. Even in the slave states at least a quarter of city people were immigrants, and they dominated the southern urban working class. As immigrants continued to come to cities, their children became a substantial part of the populace. The proportion of immigrants and their children in Buffalo rose from three-fifths in 1845 to four-fifths in 1855. Boston received fewer immigrants, but in 1845, when a quarter of the people were foreign-born, a third were of immigrant stock. By 1855, when two-fifths of Bostonians had been born overseas, over half had foreign parents.[72]

Most native-born migrants with capital moved to frontier areas. Settlement of the national domain was connected to the growth of capitalism in older areas and rising national and international demand for American grain and cotton. With increased access to information and the development of integrated commodity and labor markets, long-distance migration became far easier than it had been in the colonial period. The growth of industrial capitalism in England and the American Northeast structured this long-distance migration. Western farmers provided grain to northeastern and English workers and urban residents. Southern migration was partially driven by rising demand for cotton in England and New England, inducing planters to move with their slaves to southwestern plantations.[73]

Pushed by the expansion of capitalism or pulled by new opportunities, white settlers rapidly filled in the millions of acres confiscated from Indians. Both the direction and intensity of interregional migration changed after the Revolution, shifting from a north-south to an east-west axis. While short-distance migration continued, frontier families moved longer distances. Co-

dissenting view, see Parkerson, "How Mobile Were Nineteenth-Century Americans?" 105–6.

72. DeBow, *Statistical View*, 278–79, 399; Still, ed., *Urban America*, 118–19; D. Ward, *Cities and Immigrants*, 57–67; Handlin, *Boston's Immigrants*, chap. 3, 242–46, 250–55; Berlin and Gutman, "Natives and Immigrants," 1175–1200; Glasco, "Migration and Adjustment," 157–63; Katz, Doucet, and Stern, "Migration and Social Order," 674–77; Knights, *Plain People of Boston*, 33–42; Davenport, "Migration to Albany," 161–73; Pierce, *History of Chicago*, 1:415–18; K. N. Conzen, *Immigrant Milwaukee*, 13–18; Ethington, "Structure Urban Political Life," 37, 108. Large cities have 15,000+ people in 1850 and 20,000+ people in 1860; slave-state cities include St. Louis and Baltimore.

73. Steckel, "Household Migration and Rural Settlement," 199–206; North, *Economic Growth of the United States*, chaps. 7, 11.

lonial long-distance migrants usually moved no more than a hundred miles, and often migrated shorter distances, but by the 1840s or 1850s migrants traveled four hundred or more miles over their lifetimes. Southerners, especially planters who moved to the cotton South, tended to move farther than New Englanders, who probably practiced a more land-intensive form of agriculture.[74]

Long-distance migrants covered hundreds of miles in a series of sequential moves, accumulating savings in each place to finance movement further west. Yankee settlers of south central Michigan had often moved from New England or eastern New York to the Rochester, New York, area before going to Michigan. Texas migrants born in Tennessee or Alabama, about half of those to arrive before 1860, moved first to Mississippi, Arkansas, or Louisiana. Nearly three-quarters of migrants to Oregon during the 1840s had settled in Missouri, Illinois, or Iowa before leaving for the West, but many had been born farther east, in Kentucky, Indiana, or Ohio. Irish, English, and German immigrants also moved sequentially once they arrived on the eastern seaboard, residing in New York or Ohio before moving on to such cities as Milwaukee. This pattern of sequential movement continued into the late nineteenth century, as children born in the Old Northwest moved into Iowa, Minnesota, and the Northern Great Plains.[75]

Long-distance migration in the free-labor North and the slave-labor South contrasted greatly. As capitalism diffused through the Northeast, commercial farmers moved west to take advantage of market opportunities, where they competed with, and ultimately chased away, yeoman farmers who had to move to frontiers, far from the contagion of wage labor and complete market dependence. Slavery dominated the southern migration system: planters moved to grow cotton but kept capitalism at bay; yeomen moved to poorer lands, where they remade small producer societies.

As transportation and markets for agricultural goods improved, migration from the Northeast to the Northwest increased rapidly. Between 1800 and 1860, New England suffered a net loss of some 350,000 whites over the age of ten. Most of them moved to western New York or to the northern parts of the Northwest. Migration from New England peaked in the 1810s; the region thereafter maintained population equilibrium through family limi-

---

74. Bosworth, "Those Who Moved," 80–82, 93–94, 107–19; Adams and Kasakoff, "Migration and the Family," 26–29; Schaefer, "Statistical Profile of Frontier and New South Migration," 568–70.

75. Rose, "South Central Michigan Yankees," 35–39; Lathrop, *Migration into East Texas*, 38–46; Bowen, *Willamette Valley*, 28–42; K. N. Conzen, *Immigrant Milwaukee*, 39–41; Bieder, "Kinship as Factor in Migration," 431; Hudson, "Migration to an American Frontier," 247–56

tation and increased industrial employment. Some 2.3 million whites above the age of ten left the mid-Atlantic states east of the Appalachians between 1800 and 1860. The number of outmigrants jumped during every decade but the 1820s, and it nearly doubled each decade after 1830. Migrants usually left for midwest agricultural areas on the frontier or just behind it. Nearly 3.5 million whites over age ten entered the Midwest from the rest of the country between 1800 and 1860, probably including most of the whites who left New England and the mid-Atlantic states.[76]

Capitalist investment in improved transportation structured migration and farm-making in western New York and the Old Northwest in the early nineteenth century. Early settlers, land speculators, and eastern capitalists all sought improved transportation, each pursuing increased farm output. As soon as a canal or railroad was announced, speculators bought up land and advertised to entice farmers. Migration by farm families and development of commercial agriculture immediately followed the completion of canals or railroads. Ohio farmers who lived near canals greatly increased grain production even in the depression years of early 1840s. Dane County, Wisconsin, farmers, located far from Lake Michigan, marketed increasing loads of wheat when railroads developed in the 1850s; similar growth of population and agricultural output occurred along the route of the Illinois Central Railroad. That line not only encouraged settlement to build traffic but urged colonists to buy land the federal government granted it as a construction subsidy. Farmers in these areas, already embedded in commercial agriculture, often practiced improved agricultural techniques, buying mechanical harvesting equipment in the 1850s, for example, to increase output.[77]

More than any other transportation route, the Erie Canal enhanced commercial agriculture, encouraging market specialization in foodstuffs along the route and near the Great Lakes. Agricultural commercialization began almost immediately. By the 1850s a higher proportion of farmers living near the Erie Canal engaged in market agriculture than those in any other part of New York, even the long-settled Hudson River Valley. More-

76. McCleland and Zuckhauser, *Demographic Dimensions of New Nation*, 5–8, 138–43; L. K. Mathews, *Expansion of New England*, 139–249.

77. D. S. Smith, "Malthusian-Frontier Interpretation," 15–23; Cronon, *Nature's Metropolis*, chaps. 2–3; Mahoney, *River Towns in Great West*, chaps. 2, 8; Schriber, *Ohio Canal Era*, chaps. 8–9; Ransom, "Interregional Canals," 12–35; Yuasa, "Commercial Patterns Illinois and Michigan Canal," 9–21; Putnam, *Illinois and Michigan Canal*, chap. 4; Fishlow, *American Railroads*, chaps. 4–5; M. P. Conzen, *Frontier Farming in Urban Shadow*, chap. 6; P. W. Gates, *Illinois Central Railroad*, chaps. 2, 8–12; Brownson, *History of the Illinois Central Railroad*, chap. 5; Atack and Bateman, *To Their Own Soil*, chap. 11; Winkel, *Politics of Community*, 21–28.

over, migrants — especially those from out of state — flocked to the region to take advantage of growing market opportunities.[78]

However much states or railroad companies wanted farmers to migrate, they rarely financed their travel. Transportation costs and forgone income, not to mention farm-making, were often too high for nuclear families to fund on their own. Northern kin groups or communities often migrated together, sometimes paying for their trip or a large plot of land collectively. Such movement reduced migration costs and ensured migrants that familiar community institutions would soon develop. New Englanders established at least twenty-three colonies in Illinois in the 1830s, and others were common in southern Michigan; kin groups and community members traveled together along the Overland Trail and settled together in Oregon. Even when individuals or families migrated alone, they were often soon joined by other kindred or by neighbors or friends. Such chain migration focused settlement: New Yorkers of New England stock settled in Michigan; North Carolina Quakers moved en masse to Indiana; upland South families dominated many southern Ohio, Indiana, and Illinois counties.[79]

The migration of free blacks and runaway slaves to Cass County, Michigan, suggests the importance of chain migration. Most of Cass County's blacks had been born in Virginia or North Carolina. Freed by Quaker masters, many of them came to Cass with newly freed family and friends. Some of these ex-slaves had lived in Ohio or southern Illinois but faced such strong discrimination that they could not set up viable households. Others, knowing that local Quakers would protect them, fled slavery, traveling along the underground railroad until they reached Cass County. Local Quakers probably lent many of them money to set up farms. These black yeomen grew corn and raised hogs, like southern yeomen, but unlike their white neighbors, who concentrated on marketing wheat. Similar small colonies of free blacks could be found in other midwestern communities where southern Quakers settled.[80]

Even though most farm families or kin groups paid for their moves, la-

78. Parkerson, "Migration and Commercial Economy," 20–34 (and embedded tables); Cross, *Burned-Over District*, chap. 4.

79. Atack and Bateman, *To Their Own Soil*, chap. 8; Danhof, *Change in Agriculture*, chaps. 4–5; L. K. Mathews, *Expansion of New England*, chaps. 6–9; Bieder, "Kinship as a Factor in Migration," 429–39; Davenport, "Tracing Rural New York's Out-Migrants," 59–67; Rose, "South Central Michigan Yankees," 32–39, and "Hoosier Origins," 203–32; Bowen, *Willamette Valley*, chaps. 3–4, esp. 24, 33, 40–41; K. J. Carr, "Group Land Acquisition," 5–14; Buley, *Old Northwest*, 2:474–76; D. K. Meyer, "Southern Illinois Migration Fields," 151–60.

80. The most important study is Sawyer, "Surviving Freedom," chaps. 2–3, but see Fields, "Free Negroes in Cass County," 375–83; Steward, "Migration of a Free People," 34–39; Rose, "Distribution of Indiana's Minorities," 248–58.

bor recruiters sent canal and railroad construction workers to the Northwest. As many as several hundred thousand men may have been recruited and brought west to work on railroads alone. Capitalists sometimes complained about high construction wages, and a few of these immigrants and poor native-born Americans did accumulate sufficient savings to procure farms. But most of them made a new western rural proletariat, building internal improvements, harvesting crops or trees, operating canal or river boats, tramping from job to job, from farm to frontier city.[81]

Southern migration patterns varied greatly from those in the North. Slaves, forced to migrate with masters or sold in the interstate slave trade, moved from the old South to the cotton-producing areas of the Southwest. At first white southerners trod similar paths: a million whites over the age of ten left the old South between 1800 and 1840 and close to 300,000 came to the new South. But after 1840, while migration from the old South continued, whites began *leaving* the cotton South as well. About 300,000 whites over ten left the old south in those years, but 400,000 migrated from the new, cotton South. Many of these migrants moved to Texas, but others went to Missouri or the southern parts of the Old Northwest.[82]

These patterns call into question the willingness of nonslaveowners to compete with planters in cotton regions. Far more whites moved from slave *to* free states than from free to slave states, and many whites moved within the South from slave societies to those where few slaves worked. White southerners usually moved in a direct east-west line, from Virginia to Kentucky, southern Ohio, or Missouri or between adjacent states like North Carolina and Tennessee. Because cotton production so thoroughly focused the migration paths of slaves, whites who moved west from the old South often found themselves in virtually free societies.[83]

A comparison of southern farmers and wealthy planters shows how wealth and access to labor structured migration decisions and economic development on agricultural frontiers. Large slaveholders traveled to potential new plantations before deciding to move. They took up the best land, close to water transit; moved a few slaves and part of the family to the new land; began producing market crops almost immediately; and then brought the rest of the family and slaves to their new home. Since they gathered infor-

---

81. Fishlow, *American Railroads*, 410, estimates annual employment building railroads rose from 40,000 in 1840 to over 200,000 in 1855. If twice the number of different men constructed railroads as Fishlow's maximum estimate indicates for a *single* year (448,000), and half of them were transported, then 224,000 were recruited.

82. McCleland and Zeckhauser, *Demographic Dimensions*, 138–43, 159–64; chap. 8 below describes slave migration.

83. McCleland and Zeckhauser, *Demographic Dimensions*, 50–52; Steckel, "Economic Foundations of East-West Migration," 14–17.

mation themselves, shipped goods directly from their plantations, and set their slaves to making plantation implements, they required neither communal nor familial support to move. Most moved as individuals or nuclear family groups. Once they arrived, they set about making cotton, corn, and other crops. When most of the nutrients in the soil had been exhausted, they moved with their slaves to a new frontier.[84]

Unable to travel to find potential farmsites and unwilling to compete with planters, southern plain folk settled upland acres planters avoided. Like northern farmers, they followed recommendations from pioneering kindred and friends and migrated as families or joined groups of kindred or neighbors on the trip westward. Unlike northern migrants, they more often relied upon kindred than community groups. Kentucky settlement provides an example: in 1779, a colony of kindred and neighbors from Berkeley County, Virginia, moved to Strode's Station; in the 1790s and 1800s, poor Catholic tenants from St. Mary's County, Maryland, moved to Washington and Nelson counties; a Baptist congregation from Spotsylvania County, Virginia, moved as a group to Lancaster. Similar clusters of migrants could be found in Missouri in the 1820s and 1830s and in Texas in the 1840s and 1850s.[85]

After they arrived in the upland South or the southern parts of the Midwest, these southern farmers, unlike many northeasterners in the upper Midwest, practiced quasi-subsistence agriculture, establishing local exchange networks, sending small surpluses of meat or grain to market. Most of these areas were so far from canals or railroads that farmers were unable to adopt fully commercial agriculture. In 1860 there were as many miles of railroad track in the Midwest as in all the slave states; most southern railroads, moreover, connected cotton-plantation regions with Atlantic or Gulf ports. Rather than cultivating staples or buying reapers, these migrants built capital by clearing more land each year. Ultimately, they either sold out and moved to a new frontier or gave this improved land to sons. Sons frequently sold inherited acreage, moved to a new frontier, bought large quantities of unimproved land, and began the process again.[86]

84. Weiman, "Slavery, Plantation Settlement, Regional Development"; Wells, "Moving a Plantation to Louisiana," 279–89. Cashin, *Family Venture*, chaps. 1–3, which came to hand too late to use extensively, is generally consistent with these comments, but she argues for more kin involvement than indicated here and sees conflicts between planter sons and fathers and husbands and wives as endemic in the decision to migrate.

85. Weiman, "Slavery, Plantation Settlement, Regional Development"; Otto, "Migration of Southern Plain Folk," 193–98; Wooten, "Westward Migration," 61–71; Eslinger, "Migration and Kinship," 52–66; Spaulding, "Maryland Catholic Diaspora," 163–72; Marks, "Rage for Kentucky," 119–26; Ranck, "'Travelling Church,'" 240–65; O'Brien, "Social Dimensions of Settlement," 210–30; T. Jordan, "Population Origins in Texas," 89–93.

86. Weiman, "Slavery, Plantation Settlement, and Regional Development"; Genovese, *Political Economy of Slavery*, chaps. 7–8; Fox-Genovese, *Within the Plantation*

Notwithstanding the concentration of immigrants in the small southern urban working class, sponsored labor migration occurred far less often in the South than in the North. With fewer canals and railroads, the South needed fewer workers. Southern factories developed slowly, and they employed slaves or local families, rather than migrants. Artisans often did move south from northern cities or Britain, but they financed their own migration. *Skilled* artisans, however, may have commonly tramped southern highways, bringing their skills in blacksmithing or gin building to remote corners of the region where craftsmen were scarce. These men, who started with far more resources than typical canal or railroad workers, accumulated sufficient income from their working travels to open their own shops.[87]

Internal Migration, Class Formation, and American Regional Cultures

Great contradictions permeate the history of internal migration in Antebellum America. Capitalists financed the internal improvements and land settlers required, but migrants often rejected capitalism, hoping to sustain a more communal social formation on the frontier. Men wanted to protect their power within the household, a power threatened in the Northeast by developing industrial capitalism. Such goals were difficult to attain: frontier families moved so often that farm-making took precedence over community formation, and ethnic heterogeneity guaranteed social strife. Northern capitalists and wage laborers arrived in the Northwest with the first farmers, thereby ensuring that a capitalist economy would soon develop. Southern migrants shared anticapitalist goals, but yeomen struggled with planters to ensure white democracy and smallholder control of the areas they numerically dominated. Despite these difficulties, migrants, northern and southern, immigrant and native, managed to reinvent cultures in frontier regions, meshing political individualism with strong communal goals, creating institutions like churches and political parties that both sustained group cohesion and structured social conflict.[88]

The failure of northern rural migrants and southern yeomen to deviate little from an east-west path documents this conservatism. Farmers who moved in an east-west line could replicate familiar farming techniques with-

Household, 66–82; DeBow, *Statistical View*, 189; Pred, *Urban Growth and City Systems*, 40–49; G. R. Taylor, *Transportation Revolution*, 35, 79.

87. Gillespie, "Artisans and Mechanics," 205–20, is the best work, but see also Bateman and Weiss, *Deplorable Scarcity*, 14–20; Randall, *Cotton Mill Movement*, chaps. 3–4; Wallenstein, *From Slave South to New South*, 38–39.

88. Hine, *Community on American Frontier*; Faragher, *Sugar Creek*; Hahn, *Roots of Southern Populism*, chaps. 1–3; D. H. Doyle, "Social Theory and New Communities," 151–65.

out losing productivity because their new homes had the same climate and vegetation they had left behind. Deviation from an east-west path forced migrants to change crop mixes and building patterns because they were sensitive to climatic changes. Planters, who often deviated from a direct east-west path, accustomed themselves and their slaves to a different climate in order to make cotton for international markets.[89]

The rapid turnover of frontier populations increased the difficulties of community formation and cultural development. Between three-fifths and four-fifths of frontier residents moved within a decade of arrival, a level much higher than in the colonies or nineteenth-century settled communities. These low levels of persistence might suggest that migrants stayed in one place too short a time to form institutions. Such a conclusion is misleading. Once frontier conditions had passed, migration declined. Erie County, New York, located at the terminus of the Erie Canal, was colonized during the 1820s. By the 1850s, nearly three-quarters of Erie County residents stayed at least a decade. Even in frontier areas, long-term residents dominated the community. While three-fifths of the people who came to Roseburg, Oregon, in the 1850s left within five years, those in the town for over twenty-six years accounted for three-fifths of the years lived by those resident there in 1860.[90]

Propertied members of rural communities moved far less often than tenants, squatters, or wage workers. The wealthier the farmer, the less often his family moved. These farm families migrated with kindred and called on them in times of economic need. Working to build equity in land, they persisted long enough to begin churches, bequeath land to their children, and establish communal and kinship ties with their neighbors. Landowners in antebellum New York state, for instance, lived an average of 5.5 years longer in a community than tenants or laborers. While as many as nine of ten landless householders on the Iowa frontier in the 1850s and 1860s moved away in less than a decade, two-fifths or more of the landowners stayed that long and at least half of wealthier middle-aged farmers remained in the community a decade or more.[91]

89. Steckel, "Economic Foundations of East-West Migration," 19–33.

90. D. L. Jones, *Village and Seaport*, 104–10; Katz, Doucet, and Stern, "Migration and Social Order of Erie County," 685–92; W. G. Robbins, "Opportunity and Persistence," 279–96; Galenson and Pope, "Economic and Geographic Mobility," 637–42; Winkel, *Politics of Community*, chap. 2.

91. Curti, *Making American Community*, 65–77; Galenson and Pope, "Economic and Geographic Mobility," 642–45; M. P. Conzen, *Frontier Farming in Urban Shadow*, 126–33; W. G. Robbins, "Opportunity and Persistence," 283–90; Bowers, "Crawford Township," 22–25; Cogswell, *Tenure, Nativity, and Age*, chap. 6; Parkerson "Migration and Commercial Economy"; S. E. Gray, "Family, Land, and Credit," 122–27, 334–44, 359.

Migration patterns suggest the emergence of regional cultures. Upland, nonslaveholding southerners predominated in much of Missouri and the southern part of the Old Northwest; New England and New York natives flocked to northern Ohio, Indiana, Illinois, and southern Michigan; Germans concentrated in Wisconsin and northern Illinois. Yet a single cultural strand rarely predominated. Nearly everywhere on the northwestern frontier, for instance, Yankees and southerners, Irish and Germans lived closely together. Only within townships did a single ethnic group often dominate. These ethnic enclaves, located within heterogeneous regions, point to segmented rural class formation—southern yeoman farmers, northern capitalist farmers, Irish workers—and suggest the possibility of conflict within classes but among ethnic groups.[92]

The Old Northwest, located at the crossroads of South and Northeast, which attracted colonists from every part of the country, suggests how segmented cultures that were internally conflicted and divided by class formed. Migration followed transportation routes: the Ohio River system from the South, the National Road from the middle Atlantic states, the Erie Canal from New York and New England. These routes distributed farmers from the Northeast, Middle Atlantic, and upland South in geographic bands from north to south.[93]

Yankee culture in the Midwest was set against itself. Migrants sought to remake northeastern culture, with its small-producer family farms, evangelical Protestantism, and respect for education. But they responded ambiguously to capitalist development. Some male pioneers sought refuge from capitalist wage labor, tenancy, land scarcity, and the ideology of domesticity. Rather than set up individual family farms, New England fathers and adult sons who migrated to Michigan sometimes held and worked land in common, adding to the security of all. The same people, often imbued with the developmental ethos of agricultural improvement, sought to tame the market, making it congruent with communal and patriarchal values. However much they wanted to make petty producer farms, by 1850 capitalist agricul-

---

92. Swierenga, "Settlement of the Old Northwest," 73–106; Cayton and Onuf, *Midwest and Nation*, chaps. 2–3; Rohrbough, "Diversity and Unity," 71–87; and Power, *Planting Corn Belt Culture*, summarize culture formation. For migration see Mathews, *Expansion of New England*, chaps. 6–9; Steckel, "Economic Foundations of East-West Migration," 14–17; Otto, "Migration of Southern Plain Folk," 183–200; D. K. Meyer, "Southern Illinois Migration Fields," 151–60; Nannini, "Ethnic and Regional Composition LaSalle County," 77–90; W. Jordan, "People of Ohio's First County," 1–40. For segmented class formation, see Barrett, "Immigration and Working Class Formation."

93. Rose, "Hoosier Origins," 203–32, and D. K. Meyer, "Southern Illinois Migration Fields," 151–60, are examples of a very large literature.

ture, with its agricultural specialization and bourgeois values, predominated in the colonies of the northeast in the Old Northwest.[94]

Yankees so feared a return to savagery among pioneers that they sent missionaries throughout the Old Northwest. Preachers, booksellers, and female schoolteachers moved through the region, attempting to ingrain their values, starting churches, schools, or libraries. Missionaries and other northeastern migrants made a dynamic bourgeois culture wherever they moved. They brought with them a commitment to the developmental policies of the Federalists and Whigs and emphasized education as a way to ensure success. Usually evangelical Protestants, often from places already burned over with revivals, they quickly built churches and started Sunday schools. A significant minority, imbued with evangelical egalitarianism, supported reforms like temperance or abolition. Even more voted for antislavery Liberty, Free Soil, and Republican parties, especially when persuaded by neighbors of the rightness of the cause.[95]

This bourgeois culture was especially strong in northern Ohio, Indiana, and Illinois, and southern Michigan. Farmers in the eastern counties of the Western Reserve, located near Lake Erie, for instance, specialized in dairying and cheesemaking for the market; voted heavily for the Whig party, endorsing its probanking policies; promoted evangelical religion; built libraries and schools; played host to abolitionist colleges like Oberlin; and gave antislavery parties strong support.[96]

Given the mixed migration to the Northwest, this bourgeois vision vied with semisubsistence cultures. Upland southerners, often descendants of eighteenth-century backcountry settlers, migrated to the Old Northwest to find small farms and escape competition with slaves and planters. Despite their opposition to slavery in the Northwest, they rejected abolition, fearing that free blacks would leave the South, compete with them, and un-

94. Cayton and Onuf, *Midwest and Nation*, chaps. 2–3; S. E. Gray, "Family, Land, and Credit," 4–8, 15, 73–74, 78–82, 99–104, 113–21; Mak, "Intraregional Trade," 489–97.

95. R. L. Rogers, "Destinations Home Missionaries," 4–5, tables 1–2; Kaufman, *Woman Teachers on the Frontier*, 1–51; Pankrantz, "Reading on the Ohio Frontier," 1–23; Power, *Planting Corn Belt Culture*, chap. 1; D. H. Doyle, *Social Order of a Frontier Community*, 23–38; Schlereth, "New England Presence," 125–42; Cardinal, "Antislavery Sentiment," 223–38; Volpe, *Forlorn Hope of Freedom*, esp. chaps. 1–4.

96. French, "Puritan Conservatism and the Frontier," 85–95; S. E. Gray, "Family, Land, and Credit," 28, 48–49, 90–91; Kephart, "Pioneer Michigan Abolitionist," 34–42; Buley, *Old Northwest*, 2:347–69, 616–24; Kaestle, "Public Education in Old Northwest," 63–74; Pritchard, "Burned-Over District Reconsidered," 245–63, and "Disentangling Evangelicalism," 5–14; J. R. Sharp, *Jacksonians versus the Banks*, chaps. 6–8; R. L. Jones, *History Agriculture in Ohio*, chap. 9; E. W. Stevens, "Social Library Membership," 574–94, esp. 579.

dermine their economic security. Wherever they went, they made small producer societies based upon family labor, providing subsistence for their families while sending surplus corn, whiskey, hogs, or cattle to market. Nonetheless, they avoided total dependence upon commodity markets. They set livestock loose on the open range and hunted wild game to supplement their diets. Like yeomen everywhere, they exchanged labor or surplus goods with neighbors to gain what they did not produce.[97]

Upland southerners relied on kindred rather than forming voluntary associations (except churches). Kindred not only migrated together, they may have intermarried often, forming a complex cousinarchy. Moving from place to place, these kin groups became a substitute for any broader community. Husbands insisted upon the subservience of wives, refusing to help limit the size of their families, rejecting any notion of domesticity but presuming that farm women care for home and hearth and work in the fields as well.[98]

European immigrants also created farm communities in the antebellum Midwest, especially in Wisconsin and northern Illinois. Much like eighteenth-century immigrants, they invented their own ethnic cultures, becoming more English or Irish or German in the process. Most English immigrants traveled in family groups and had enough capital to finance their own migration. Only a minority had worked in the agricultural sector, but some middling farmers and many mechanic families migrated to set up farms. Many migrants purchased unimproved frontier land, often after working as laborers to accumulate more capital. Coming from a country where capitalism had long predominated, their relation to markets was nonetheless ambivalent. They sought the independence they believed American yeomen possessed but immediately produced for commodity markets. Notwithstanding their similarities to Yankees, they saw themselves as different and tried to settle among their countrymen.[99]

Germans, in contrast to the English, immigrated to the rural Midwest in large enough numbers to create and perpetuate distinctive cultures. Driven from Germany by destruction of the hand loom industry, poor crops and poverty, or political oppression, Germans — mostly tenants, cottagers, agri-

97. Barnhart, "Southern Contribution to the Old Northwest," 237–48; D. H. Doyle, *Social Order of a Frontier Community*, 51–61; Berwanger, *Frontier against Slavery*, chaps. 1–2; Cartwright, *Autobiography*, 165, 93–94, 111–16; Otto, "Migration of Southern Plain Folk," 183–93; Faragher, *Sugar Creek*, chaps. 5–8, 11.

98. Reid, "Church Membership, Consanguineous Marriage and Migration," 397–414; Faragher, *Sugar Creek*, chaps. 9–12.

99. K. N. Conzen, "Making Their Own America"; Erikson, "Emigration from the British Isles," 357–67, 21–40, and *Invisible Immigrants*, 23–32, 40–78; Van Vugt, "Running from Ruin," 411–28.

cultural laborers, and weavers — often banded together to come to America, sometimes receiving aid from emigrant societies in Germany or America. Once they arrived, they settled with their landsmen. But since communities usually included Germans from all over Central Europe, they had to invent German ethnicity. Resisting the individualism of "grasping" Yankees and the "shiftlessness" of yeoman farmers alike, they defined democracy in terms of communal norms, forming Catholic or Protestant churches and marrying each other almost exclusively. The German Catholics, who flocked to the Sauk valley, Minnesota, in the 1850s and 1860s after a Catholic colony was founded there, persisted on the land for generations, seeking a competency for their families rather than the individualistic goals of neighboring Yankees, who soon left the community.[100]

Emphasis upon regional ethnic cultures obscures complex class conflicts, influenced by the ethnicity and religion, that permeated the Midwest. Men of wealth, no matter their origins, sought incorporation into international commodity markets. Conflicts between yeoman farmers, mostly from the upper South, and more market-oriented capitalist farmers, often of northeastern heritage, may have been common. Conflicts within classes, but between ethnic groups, were common. Irish, German, English, and native-born workers all labored on public works projects, sometimes uniting across groups, sometimes fighting between them. Yankee, German, and upland southern farmers within a community often achieved similar levels of market embeddedness and grew similar crop mixes, but they practiced different family succession strategies. Struggles within ethnic groups may have been as important as those between them. If most northeastern migrants established commercial farms, others wanted merely to send surpluses to market, and a few failed in farming, fell into the working class, and faced the contradiction between their cultural desires and their economic condition. However strong these conflicts, the wealthiest capitalist farmers and their allies had vanquished other groups by the 1850s.[101]

This invention of new cultural constructs took place as well in older regions, like rural New England. Chelsea, Vermont, a farming town of nearly two thousand in 1830, which lost half of its population to migration by 1900, illustrates this process. Chelsea farmers struggled to maintain their

100. K. N. Conzen, "Making Their Own America," 5–22; Johnson, "Location of German Immigrants," 10–41; Kamphoefner, *Westphalians*; Frizzell, "Migration Chains in Illinois," 59–73; Lang, "German Immigrants to Dubois County," 131–49; Rose, "Distribution of Indiana's Minorities," 228–38.

101. Bushman, "Wilson Family in Delaware and Indiana," 27–49; Marshall, *Land Fever*; Atack and Bateman, *To Their Own Soil*, chap. 6, and "Yankee Farming and Settlement," 77–102; Cayton and Onuf, *Midwest and Nation*, 70–92; Tobin, "Lowly Muscular Digger," chap. 7.

farms in the fact of outmigration, changing their agricultural practices and inheritance strategy. In the 1820s, many Chelsea farmers raised sheep to take advantage of increased demand for wool, but when wool prices began to decline, and dairy and beef prices rose in the mid-nineteenth century, farmers continued to specialize in sheep because so many youths had left town that farmers could not command sufficient labor required for milking cows. Because older children left the farm before their parents retired, parents bargained with their youngest son, giving him the farm in return for continuing to work on the farm and supporting his parents once they retired.[102]

Rural Migration and Capitalist Hegemony, 1860–1900

For two and a half centuries, the relationship between capitalism and migration was conflicted and contradictory. Capitalists financed the development of American frontiers yet migrants often resisted the encroachment of capitalism, moving to make new communities based upon petty-producer, small-surplus agriculture. The ability of migrants to manipulate capitalist economic structures to attain noncapitalist ends diminished greatly over the nineteenth century. Capitalism so permeated the countryside after the Civil War that few noncapitalist societies persisted into the twentieth century. Not only did capitalists finance farmer migration and land purchases more often, but they hired a vast rural proletariat of farm laborers, miners, and cowboys.

Railroads provided the impetus to migration in the postbellum era. Construction of railroads preceded white colonization on the Great Plains because farmers, lacking waterways, could not otherwise get goods to market. But the significance of railroads went beyond that. Between 1862 and 1871, railroads received over a hundred million acres from the federal government and millions more from the states. Since railroads owned at least half the lands along their rights-of-way, would-be market farmers on the plains often had to buy from them. The purchase of expensive railroad land, along with the costs of starting a farm, immediately thrust farmers into capitalist commodity markets. Once farmers arrived, railroads became their market lifeline, providing them their only way to sell wheat.[103]

A rural proletariat, divided into many groups, grew rapidly during the last third of the nineteenth century. This growth encompassed the entire rural nation, from the urban Northeast to the cotton South. Labor demands

102. Barron, *Those Who Stayed Behind.*
103. W. P. Webb, *Great Plains,* 273–80; Miner, *West of Wichita,* chaps. 3, 6; P. W. Gates, "Homestead Law," 652–81; Ellis, "Homestead Clause," 47–73, esp. 47–52; Mercer, "Land Grants to American Railroads," 134–51; Williamson, "Midwestern Grain and American Growth," 211–15; Buck, *Granger Movement,* chaps. 4–6; Nordin, *Rich Harvest,* chap. 10; Hicks, *Populist Revolt,* 60–74.

of capitalists—farmers, railroad builders, mine operators, cotton planters, ranchers, lumber mill owners, rural factory owners—structured migration by thousands of freed slaves; Mexican, European, and Asian immigrants; and poorer native-born Euro-Americans. Some capitalists recruited and paid transit costs of migrants; most, however, made their own way. These laborers, often seasonal migrants, harvested cotton or wheat, herded cattle, constructed railroads, cut timber, or made cotton textiles. Moving from job to job or field to field, migrants on occasion struck back at their bosses, demanding an end to perceived inequities.[104]

The growth of a rural proletariat during the late nineteenth century, combined with continued urbanization, led to substantial permanent rural-urban migration for the first time. Although immigrants and their children still dominated most cities in the North, town workers, agricultural laborers, and a few dissatisfied farmers flocked to cities. A few areas in the rural North suffered depopulation. About a tenth of intracounty migrants in Iowa during the 1890s, for instance, reached cities with over 10,000 people, and another quarter went to smaller towns of between 1,000 and 10,000. Pulled by urban opportunities for skilled and unskilled labor that cities and their hinterlands required, migrants were pushed from rural areas by declining agricultural opportunities.[105]

Rural-urban migration was particularly pronounced in the South. New towns and cities grew around the region; for instance, small textile cities developed from mill villages all through the Carolina and Georgia piedmont. Seeking factory jobs or escape from poor economic conditions, thousands of southern white families moved from the hills or mountains to work in the new textile mills. At the same time, former slaves, often unable to rent farms even on a sharecropping basis, left the rural South for the cities, where they could find unskilled jobs and live independently, forming institutions like churches away from the eyes of former masters.[106]

---

104. Kilar, *Michigan's Lumbertowns*; E. Foner, *Reconstruction*, chaps. 3–4; G. Wright, *Old South, New South*, chaps. 3–4; Daniel, *Bitter Harvest*, chaps. 1–3; McWilliams, *Factories in the Field*, chaps. 1–6; Weston, *Real American Cowboy*; Argersinger and Argersinger, "Machine Breakers," 393–410; Mahon, "Wage Labor and Seasonal Migration"; J. D. Hall et al., *Like a Family*, chaps. 1–3, esp. 31–43; Newby, *Plain Folk in the New South*, chap. 3.

105. D. Ward, *Immigrants and Cities*, 65–81; M. P. Conzen, "Local Migration Systems," 351–61; R. Higgs, "Growth of Cities," 369–75; A. F. Weber, *Growth of Cities*, 20–39, 167–69, 188, 241–43, 248–51, 263–66; Fogelson, *Fragmented Metropolis*, chap. 4; Von Ende and Weiss, "Labor Force Changes," 111–15; D. R. Meyer, "Midwest Industrialization," 921–37.

106. J. D. Hall et al., *Like a Family*, chaps. 1–3, esp. 31–43; Miller, "Urban Blacks in the South," 184–204; Rabinowitz, *Race Relations in Urban South*, chap. 2; Ransom and Sutch, *One Kind of Freedom*, 31–39, 61–64.

Older patterns of rural to rural migration and frontier farm-making persisted into the twentieth century. The number of farms in the United States nearly tripled between 1860 and 1900. Yet much had changed. Opportunities for landownership declined, and cash tenancy and sharecropping increased everywhere. Native-born American farmers, either unable to accumulate capital sufficient to stay in business or unwilling to suffer hardships to sustain a farm, often abandoned farming or fell into tenancy. German and Scandinavian immigrants, who dominated much of the upper Midwest, Northern Great Plains, and mountain West, were more successful. Coming from areas in the midst of capitalist transformation, they understood how to accommodate to capitalist commodity markets while sustaining family farms. Willing to defer consumption more than native-born Americans, immigrant families struggled to accumulate sufficient capital to make farms. Once on the land, they devised strategies for intergenerational survival, such as transmitting property to children before death, that allowed ethnic enclaves to persist even when the stream of rural-urban migration became a flood in the twentieth century.[107]

107. U.S. Bureau of Census, *Historical Statistics*, 1:457–59; Shannon, *Farmer's Last Frontier*, 418; K. N. Conzen, "Immigrants in Nineteenth-Century Agricultural History," 303–42, and "Peasant Pioneers," 259–92; Cannon, "Immigrants in American Agriculture," 17–35; Ostergren, *Community Transplanted*; Gjerde, *From Peasants to Farmers*; Chan, *This Bitter-Sweet Soil*.

Chapter 8

Uprooted Peoples:
The Political Economy
of Slave Migration, 1780–1840

In 1817 ANDREW KNIGHT, a poor "mechanic" who lived in Pendleton District, located in the western corner of South Carolina, suffered the loss of his wife, "by which event he was left the sole nurse *of Eight Small Children, one in armes.*" Since he "could not afford from his small savings as a Mechanic to hire a person, Cook, Nurse, Seamstress," he traveled to Virginia "to purchase a Negroe wench slave for these purposes." When he returned to South Carolina, discovering that the legislature had forbidden the import of slaves, he petitioned the assembly to permit him to bring his new slave home because her "aid was so necessary to him in the management of his family of little ones." Sixteen "citizens of Pendleton District" supported his petition.[1]

Knight's story suggests how the interests of slave families and white households often clashed. The black woman Knight brought to South Carolina left her own family behind, but Knight worried only about the welfare of his children. Such conflicts grew from the internal logic of master-slave relations and the expansion of world capitalism. The number of similar conflicts must have grown after the American Revolution when thousands of planters left older regions of the South and others took advantage of the interstate slave trade to sell their surplus chattels.[2]

Southern slave migration was structured by plantation labor demands and the expansion of the textile industry. Although Africans had suffered great loss when forced into slavery, by the time of the Revolution their descendants had made relatively secure families. The end of the Atlantic slave trade combined with the vibrant demand for cotton in England and New

---

1. South Carolina Legislative Petitions, no. 119, 1817.
2. Fox-Genovese and Genovese, *Fruits of Merchant Capital*, chaps. 1–2, 9, 11, and Fox-Genovese, *Within the Plantation Household*, chap. 1, illuminate modern slave societies embedded in a capitalist world and the organization of households that underlie the theoretical position of this essay.

England to create a new interstate slave trade, greatly reducing the familial security of slaves. To meet skyrocketing demand for cotton, planters moved to cotton frontiers, taking some slaves with them and purchasing excess slaves from planters who lived in settled areas.

English Merchant Capital and the Pre-Revolutionary Movements of Slaves

The southern colonies, embedded in world capitalism from the outset of settlement, had developed as modern slave societies. Seeking to export staples — tobacco, rice — in demand in England and Europe, planters from Maryland to Georgia commanded sufficient credit to buy African slaves to tend these crops. English capitalists financed these slave purchases. Notwithstanding the active participation of colonial planters in commodity markets, they developed noncapitalist relations of production, predicated upon slave cultivation of export commodities. The complex household economy and the power masters sometimes relinquished when informally negotiating with slaves whose lives they otherwise controlled, found all over the slave South by the mid-eighteenth century, speak eloquently to the development of noncapitalist relations of production.[3]

The Atlantic slave trade to the Chesapeake and the Carolinas played a major role in creating these noncapitalist societies. Between 1700 and 1775, planters imported close to 200,000 slaves from Africa and (to a much lesser extent) the West Indies. The African slave trade to the Chesapeake grew rapidly during the first four decades of the century, when about 54,000 slaves landed, but declined thereafter. Only 42,000 Africans landed in Chesapeake ports between 1740 and 1775, and by the 1770s fewer came than at the start of the century. The slave trade began more slowly in South Carolina: 32,000 slaves were imported before 1740, more than four-fifths of them after 1725. After Georgia planters forced colonial leaders to adopt slavery, the African slave trade increased. Between 1740 and 1775, about 55,000 Africans landed in South Carolina and Georgia.[4]

Alienated and unhappy, African migrants often ran away or refused to work. Since few women were imported, many of the men could not begin

---

3. McCusker and Menard, *Economy of British America*, esp. chaps. 6, 8, 10, 14; Isaac, *Transformation of Virginia*, part 1; Kulikoff, *Tobacco and Slaves*, chaps. 3–5, 7.

4. Deyle, "'By Far the Most Profitable Trade,'" 107–25; Kulikoff, *Tobacco and Slaves*, 64–67, and "A 'Prolifick' People," 392–96, 417–18; Westbury, "Slaves of Colonial Virginia," 228–37; P. Wood, *Black Majority*, 150–55, 333–41; Higgins, "Geographical Origins Slaves in South Carolina," 34–47; Wax, "'New Negroes Are Always in Demand,'" 198–207; Statom, "Negro Slavery in Eighteenth-Century Georgia," 158–60.

families. Coming from disparate communities, they spoke mutually incomprehensible tongues. Because plantation sizes in the Chesapeake were small, African-born slaves could make communities only by gathering in the woods after dark. Africans slowly accommodated to slavery, and with their American-born children, began building African American slave communities.[5]

By the mid-eighteenth century, as the slave population grew from natural increase and plantation sizes therefore rose, many Creole blacks had secured a stable, if precarious, family life. They had established flourishing communities on the increasingly large quarters of the Chesapeake region and on the vast plantations of coastal South Carolina and Georgia. The growth of evangelical religion in the 1750s, 1760s, and 1770s, whose churches were made by whites and slaves together, gave slaves a claim to spiritual equality with whites and created a new slave institution.[6]

During the mid-eighteenth century, few African-American slaves were forced to move more than twenty miles from their birthplaces. But movement by slaves over short distances was pervasive. Slaveowners gave slaves to each of their children. Men tended to bequeath male slaves to sons (to provide more workers for their plantations) and female slaves to daughters (perhaps expecting them to be used as personal servants). Such inheritance strategies guaranteed the separation of brothers from sisters, and children from parents, sometimes even before they reached adolescence. This system of inheritance and slave sales within counties split families apart, while concentrating slave families within Tidewater Chesapeake and lowcountry neighborhoods. Since family members usually lived within traveling distance, "broad" husbands and other kindred could visit with regularity. The pain of daily family separations, then, was partially mitigated by the cross-plantation slave networks African-Americans created.[7]

White migration to piedmont Virginia and the Carolina backcountry did separate slaves forever from their families. White migrants spread gradually across the South: tobacco and rice planters moved westward from Tidewater and the lowcountry to piedmont and the upcountry while thousands of immigrants landed in Philadelphia and moved southwestward to the val-

5. Kulikoff, *Tobacco and Slaves*, chaps. 8–9; P. Wood, *Black Majority*, chaps. 5, 7–12; Littlefield, *Rice and Slaves*, chaps. 4–5.

6. Kulikoff, *Tobacco and Slaves*, chaps. 8–10; J. B. Lee, "Problem of Slave Community," 333–61; Sobel, *World They Made Together*, esp. chaps. 14–15; P. D. Morgan, "Black Society in the Lowcountry," 83–142.

7. Contrast Kulikoff, *Tobacco and Slaves*, chaps. 8–9, with J. B. Lee, "Problem of Slave Community," 333–61, and "Land and Labor," 331–38; Dunn, "Tale of Two Plantations," 48–51.

leys of Virginia and upcountry Carolina and Georgia. As soon as market agriculture began, wealthier planters moved to the area with their slaves and frontier residents bought Africans from slave traders.[8]

Before the Revolution the internal slave trade remained small, perhaps a twentieth the size of the African slave trade. The trade revolved around local communities, as planters sold surplus slaves or executors or creditors organized estate or insolvency sales. Once African-Americans predominated in the slave population, planters with sufficient capital to choose preferred them to unseasoned Africans. Like the inheritance system, such sales spread slaves across settled neighborhoods. Small groups of slaves, often recently arrived Africans, were sold from areas with many slaves (like Tidewater Virginia or coastal South Carolina) to areas with few slaves, usually to colonies in the North or to the southern frontier.[9]

Slave family and community life remained precarious. Masters held the ultimate power to sell slaves. Even on large units, broad marriages were common and husbands and wives, parents and children were sometimes separated when masters moved to piedmont. Slavery expanded rapidly into piedmont Virginia, disrupting the lives of some 20,000 slaves from 1755 to 1782, mostly youths taken from Tidewater by migrating planters or purchased by men already in piedmont. But piedmont planters bought an equal number of Africans during the same period, thereby reducing the demand for native-born slaves by piedmont tobacco producers. In South Carolina, where heavy imports from Africa continued through the eighteenth century, a substantial majority of slaves working in frontier areas were Africans, thereby making the lives of the growing native-born population somewhat more secure.[10]

The 1790 federal census illuminates this diffusion of slaves. While most slaves lived in tobacco and rice regions in 1790, many slaves lived in farming areas, like the Shenandoah Valley and western North Carolina. Close to three-quarters of the population of the rice coast were enslaved, and nearly half the people in tobacco-growing counties of the Chesapeake were slaves. It mattered little if the county was settled in the seventeenth or eighteenth centuries. Even on tobacco frontiers (places first populated in the 1780s) over a third of the population was enslaved. Farming areas — especially fron-

8. Kulikoff, *Tobacco and Slaves*, chaps. 3–4; Morgan and Nicholls, "Slaves in Piedmont Virginia," 215–27, 238–44.

9. Deyle, "'By Far the Most Profitable Trade,'" 115–19.

10. Kulikoff, *Tobacco and Slaves*, chaps. 8–9; Morgan and Nicholls, "Slaves in Piedmont Virginia," 212–51; P. D. Morgan, "Slave Life in Piedmont Virginia," 436–38, 447–51, and "Black Society in the Lowcountry," 83–141.

tiers — had relatively fewer slaves, but a fifth of the people of farming frontiers was enslaved (fig. 4).[11]

Slave population growth was linked to the crop regime.[12] The number of slaves rose rapidly after initial white habitation, as planters moved in with their slaves or bought Africans. Even on farming frontiers in Georgia or Kentucky, settled in the 1780s, between an eighth and a sixth of the people was enslaved. The adaptation of tobacco or rice led to a rapid increase in the slave population. The percentage of slaves in tobacco counties, including those in piedmont Virginia that began producing large quantities of tobacco only in the 1760s or early 1770s, was about 20 percent higher than in farming regions settled at similar times. Carolina rice production, of course, attracted the densest slave population, over 40 percent higher than in the nearby farming upcountry.

As the tobacco frontier moved westward, the plantation society of the Tidewater Chesapeake spread southwestward. Half the slaves lived in tobacco counties, mostly in places settled in the eighteenth century. Perhaps more surprisingly, nearly a third of all slaves resided in livestock, wheat, and subsistence-production regions like the Shenandoah Valley or backcountry North Carolina. While tobacco and rice planters owned far more slaves, staple production in the pre-Revolutionary era did not prevent diversified farmers from owning a few slaves. They bought a few Africans, carried slaves with them from settled areas, and enjoyed the natural increase of their slave population.[13]

The American Revolution, Industrial Capitalism, and Forced Slave Migration

The era of the American Revolution witnessed major changes in the lives of African-American slaves in the South. Whig understanding of the hypocrisy

11. Computed from 1790 county-level data from the Federal census, Inter-University Consortium, "Historical, Demographic, Economic, and Social Data," with added information on crops grown (Hilliard, *Atlas Antebellum Agriculture*, chaps. 6–7; L. C. Gray, *History of Agriculture*, 2: chaps. 29, 32; "Tobacco Exports, 1782–1799"); and date of county formation (adjusted for divided counties in older areas) found in Everton and Rasmuson, *Handy Book*.

12. This description is based upon an ordinary least squares regression equation, with percentage of slaves as the dependent variable. Crop regime and time together explain two-thirds of the variation in percent slaves: Per $= 23.27$con $+ 20.98$tob $+ 46.14$ric $- 8.74$fro $+ 3.78$set. $R^2 = .678$ where per $=$ percentage of slaves; con $=$ constant; tob $=$ tobacco counties; ric $=$ rice counties; fro $=$ frontier counties settled 1775–90; set $=$ settled counties settled before 1690. Eighteenth-century counties and general farming are the omitted dummy variables (e.g., eighteenth-century farming counties have 23.3% slaves).

13. See n. 11 above for source of data. Kay and Cary, "Demographic Analysis," 72–92, is suggestive of patterns in farming areas.

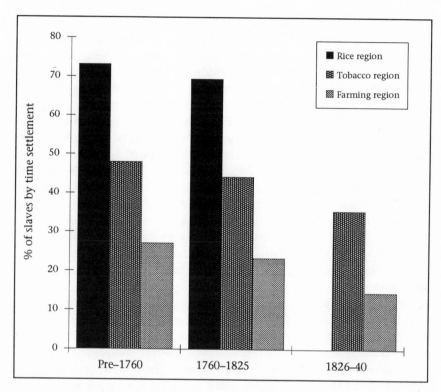

Fig. 4. Percentage of slaves by crop regime and
date of settlement, 1790

of charging England with enslaving them while they kept slaves and continued to buy Africans led to the abolition of the African slave trade, slave emancipation in the North, and thousands of individual manumissions in the
South. But most African-Americans in the South remained enslaved. If the
Revolution temporarily reduced the risk of migration they faced, the expansion of cotton production after 1790 greatly disrupted their lives, tearing
thousands of them from families in interstate migration, both with masters
and in a growing slave trade.

The Revolutionary settlement freed white farmers and planters to evict
Indians from lands west of the Allegheny Mountains, and they poured into
Kentucky, Tennessee, Georgia, Mississippi, and Alabama during the generation following the adoption of the Constitution. The white man's new
opportunities disrupted whatever security slaves had enjoyed before the Revolution. Between 1790 and 1820, slaveowners took nearly a quarter million
of them hundreds of miles from their families and friends to grow tobacco
or cotton on frontier plantations, thereby smashing the fragile security of

the slave community. Even this huge migration failed to meet frontier demand for labor, and at least 100,000 Africans destined for the backcountry
landed at Savannah and Charleston between 1783 and 1807.[14]

The disruption of colonial black life began during the 1770s when both
the patriots and the British vied for the allegiance of slaves. Wherever British
soldiers fought, blacks ran away to join them and escape slavery. About 5,000
Chesapeake slaves from the Eastern Shore and the lower James River reached
British lines, and as many as 19,000 South Carolina and Georgia slaves escaped to the British, the chaotic Carolina backcountry, or Florida. These fugitives, along with others from North Carolina, constituted over 6 percent of
southern slaves. While many of the fleeing slaves died from hunger, disease,
or battle wounds, over 3,000 left with the British at the end of the war and
ultimately reached Nova Scotia. Threatened by large-scale slave desertions
whenever British troops arrived, masters forcibly removed untold numbers
of chattels from battle regions to safe upcountry districts. When the war
ended, planters brought their slaves back to the Tidewater and resumed
farming.[15]

If the war disrupted black life in some respects, it stabilized it in others.
Most slaves lived far from the fighting and had few opportunities to escape,
but, at the same time, war conditions forestalled their relocation and prevented familial separation by limiting their masters' mobility. Many young
white men, who usually predominated among the pioneers, spent the war
years in patriot or loyalist armies. Until the fighting concluded, the movement of planters and their slaves from settled areas to frontiers temporarily
ceased. So too did the importation of slaves. Since the British dominated the
slave trade to North America and patriots refused to trade with them, no

14. Tables 8–9. Most work on slave migration focuses on the antebellum era, but
see P. D. Morgan, "Black Society in the Lowcountry," 84–87; P. S. Brady, "Slave Trade
and Sectionalism," 601–20; LaChance, "Politics of Fear," 162–97; Bancroft, *Slave Trading in the Old South,* chap. 2; Donnan, ed., *Documents Illustrative of Slave Trade,* 4:474–
635; Tadman, *Speculators and Slaves,* 12–21.

15. Quarles, *Negro in the American Revolution,* chap. 9 and 126–27; M. B. Norton,
"'What an Alarming Crisis Is This,'" 223, 233; Dunn, "Black Society in the Chesapeake," 56–58; Frey, *Water from the Rock,* 65–66, 81–89, 97, 117–22, 145–63, 167–69,
210–211 (211 relates inflated contemporary estimates of runaways). For the Chesapeake, see Kulikoff, *Tobacco and Slaves,* 418–19. South Carolina estimates calculated
from 1770 and 1790 censuses; slave imports, 1771–75 and 1782–90; and estimated
deaths of African slaves and natural increase of the rest (E. B. Greene and Harrington,
American Population before the Federal Census of 1790, 175–79; U.S. Bureau of the Census, *Historical Statistics,* 2:1168, 1172–73; P. D. Morgan, "Black Society in the Lowcountry," 88–93). For Georgia, see Wax, "'New Negroes Are Always in Demand,'" 214–
15; Statom, "Negro Slavery in Eighteenth-Century Georgia," 38–41; for Nova Scotia,
see Walker, *Black Loyalists,* chaps. 1–2.

Africans entered the rebellious colonies until 1783, when peace returned to the country.

When the war ended, whites resumed the settlement of backcountry Carolina and Georgia, migrated to Spanish Louisiana, and crossed the Allegheny Mountains into Kentucky and Tennessee. Nearly all the Chesapeake region was thickly populated, and men seeking their fortunes had to leave that region. Groups of Chesapeake migrants, including slaves, migrated to Kentucky, Tennessee, and backcountry Carolina and Georgia during the 1780s and 1790s; other whites living along the Carolina and Georgia coast moved inland to fertile piedmont areas. Some settlers reached Spanish Louisiana, where, after 1785, Protestants were welcomed for the first time.[16]

Planters needed slaves to break the ground and plant marketable crops on their new farms. While Kentucky pioneers could get enough slaves from Virginia and Maryland, Chesapeake blacks were too few to meet the demands of frontier Georgia, South Carolina, and Louisiana planters. Only resumption of the African slave trade could satisfy their needs, and they renewed importations soon after the peace treaty was signed. The African slave trade added nearly 20,000 blacks to South Carolina's population between 1782 and 1790, and slavers also docked at Spanish New Orleans and Natchez after the mid-1780s. In the decade and a half after 1790, this burgeoning African slave trade greatly increased the number of slaveholding planters in the piedmont South Carolina and the Natchez region.[17]

These planters wanted to protect their access to African slaves. At the Philadelphia Constitutional Convention, only the South Carolina and Georgia delegates supported continuation of the foreign slave trade, but in a crucial compromise the new Constitution permitted importations until 1808. Since planters feared that Congress would end the trade as soon as it could, slave traders stepped up the pace of importation. The two decades following adoption of the Constitution witnessed the most massive infusion of African slaves that ever reached the North American mainland. When it became constitutionally possible, Congress ended the trade, and after January 1, 1808, no foreign slaves could legally be imported into the country.[18]

The suppression of the African slave trade by England and the United States in 1807 resulted from a complex transatlantic political movement.

16. See Martinac, "'An Unsettled Disposition,'" chap. 3; Gilmer, *Sketches of the First Settlers of Upper Georgia*; Dinn, "Immigration Policy of Governor Miro in Spanish Louisiana," 156–75, and "Spain's Immigration Policy in Louisiana," 255–76.

17. P. D. Morgan, "Black Society in the Lowcountry," 85–91; McBee, ed., *Natchez Court Records*, 40–53; Klein, *Unification of a Slave State*, 244–57; table 8.

18. P. S. Brady, "Slave Trade and Sectionalism," 601–20; Du Bois, *Suppression of African Slave Trade*, chaps. 5–7.

The American Revolution was vital on *both* sides of the Atlantic. Tearing Africans from their homes and forcing them into slavery seemed to American Revolutionaries and to radical British supporters among artisans the opposite of the liberty they wanted for themselves. American and English Quakers and evangelicals insisted that slavery, and especially the Atlantic trade, sullied the spiritual freedom of both master and African. The strongest support for abolishing the African slave trade came from dynamic capitalist societies, the English Midlands and north, and Pennsylvania. English workingmen and a few industrial capitalists mounted petition campaigns against the trade that led to its prohibition. New Englanders and Pennsylvanians, after abolishing slavery at home, turned to ending the import of Africans to the United States at the earliest possible date.[19]

For a brief moment in the 1780s and 1790s, a minority of upper South planters joined in the fervor, failing to understand how their behavior undermined slavery. Hundreds of Chesapeake planters, influenced by revolutionary ideals of equality and by egalitarian evangelicalism or Quakerism, manumitted thousands of slaves, creating a class of southern free black people. Manumission engendered an immediate response. Small slaveholders in Virginia rallied to defend slavery and attack manumitters; intellectuals resurrected a defense of slavery as an institution.[20]

Notwithstanding their support for slavery, most southerners supported abolition of the African slave trade to the United States. A few, vaguely bothered by slaveholding, thought this would be a step toward better treatment of slaves. Knowing that native-born slaves reproduced at a high rate, southerners expected to get slaves from parents or local slave markets. They believed that ending the African trade would strengthen slavery. Once southern congressmen had protected the coastal trade and granted states the right to dispose of illegally imported Africans, they voted to abolish the African trade. Only those living on southwestern frontiers, where slaves were hard to procure, opposed this position.[21]

The suppression of the Atlantic slave trade by England and the United

19. For a range of viewpoints on the relation of English abolition to American antislavery, see D. B. Davis, *Problem of Slavery in the Age of Revolution*, chaps. 3–6; Anstey, *Atlantic Slave Trade*, part 3; Drescher, "Public Opinion and Destruction of Colonial Slavery," 22–48; Zilversmit, *First Emancipation*; Du Bois, *Suppression of the African Slave Trade*, chaps. 5–7; MacLeod, *Slavery, Race, and the American Revolution*; Fogel, *Without Consent or Contract*, 211–18.

20. Albert, "Protean Institution"; Berlin, *Slaves without Masters*, chaps. 1–2; Schmidt and Wilhelm, eds., "Early Proslavery Petitions in Virginia," 133–46.

21. MacLeod, *Slavery, Race, and the American Revolution*, 35–46 (quote on 39); D. B. Davis, *Problem of Slavery in the Age of Revolution*, 119–36; Du Bois, *Suppression of African Slave Trade*, 94–108; P. S. Brady, "Slave Trade and Sectionalism," 601–20; Chaplin, "Creating a Cotton South," 191; Fogel, *Without Consent or Contract*, 247-49.

States cut off any possibility of American planters buying significant numbers of Africans. Since most Africans had arrived in English ships and since the British navy successfully policed the African coast, normal trade was cut off. Enough smuggling occurred to worry antislavery advocates, but far too few slaves reached the Southwest to satisfy frontier planters. At most, a thousand Africans reached the new South annually between 1811 and 1822 and then ceased, long before the cotton boom, and the insatiable demand for slaves it brought, was over.[22]

The contradictions built into capitalist humanitarianism soon became apparent. The only alternative source of slaves for frontier planters was to be found in the upper South, but relatively few whites from these areas moved southwest and brought slaves to sell. As a result, domestic slave traders began to purchase slaves from Chesapeake planters and sell them to families in the new Southwest. The end of the Atlantic slave trade, then, reduced dramatically the familial and personal security of African-American slaves living in the upper South.[23]

If England and the United States had permitted the African slave trade to continue, a far different outcome might have occurred. Even with the activity of the English navy, 600,000 to 700,000 Africans were sold into slavery (mostly to Brazil and Cuba) per decade between 1811 and 1841 — as high as during peak years of the eighteenth century. A legal slave trade would have increased those numbers. Given the high demand for American cotton in England, cotton producers would have commanded much of the excess and even some of the slaves destined for Brazil. If a hundred thousand Africans had landed each decade between 1810 and 1840, and 60,000 survived until the next census, then roughly a third of the migration of slaves between upper and lower South might have been prevented.[24]

Although a vigorous African slave trade might have reduced the internal slave trade, it would not have eliminated it, no matter how many Africans

22. Eltis, "Nineteenth Century Transatlantic Slave Trade," 133–35; Taylor, "Foreign Slave Trade in Louisiana after 1808," 36–43; Fogel and Engerman, *Time on the Cross*, 1:25. Du Bois, *Suppression of African Slave Trade*, 109–30, suggests higher numbers but presents no numerical estimates. See table 9 for my estimate of the number of Africans smuggled in the 1810s.

23. Bancroft, *Slave Trading*, chap. 2; Phillips, ed., *Plantation and Frontier*, 2:55–56; Calderhead, "Role of the Professional Slave Trader," 197–99; Deyle, "American Independence and Rise of American Slave Trade."

24. For the African slave trade after 1808, see Eltis, *Economic Growth and Ending Transatlantic Slave Trade*, chaps. 6, 11, appendix A. The counterfactual exercise presumed that the net interregional migration figures for 1810–20 are accurately reported in table 9, for 1820–40 in Tadman, *Speculators and Slaves*, 12, 241; that equal numbers of slaves entered each year in a decade; and that arriving slaves followed the mortality schedule found in Kulikoff, "A 'Prolifick' People," 418–22.

landed on our shores. But there would have been less need for an internal slave trade that centered upon cotton frontiers. Mississippi or Alabama planters could have purchased Africans at local markets. Sensing a smaller demand, some internal slave traders would have found other work, perhaps selling Africans rather than Virginians. Thus the horror of initial enslavement of Africans might have continued to prevent the separation of some American-born slave families.

The abolition of the African slave trade, however, coincided with the mechanization of the cotton textile industry. Productivity in the cotton industry rose so rapidly that it sustained exponential increases in the demand for cotton fiber. During the 1780s and 1790s, English cotton manufacturing began its explosive growth. English manufacturers doubled and redoubled their imports of raw cotton: imports almost tripled in the 1780s, rising from 8.7 to 24.7 million pounds, grew by more than two-thirds in the 1790s, and reached 100 million pounds by 1820 and 600 million pounds by 1840. Although American manufacturers used less cotton than British producers, northern textile manufacturing grew rapidly after 1815, with yards of cloth produced rising from about 2 million in 1815 to 142 million by 1830.[25] This demand for cotton influenced the direction and intensity of the forced migration of slaves. Southern planters and farmers rushed to take advantage of the high prices this demand brought, moving to Georgia, Alabama, Tennessee, or Mississippi, where cotton could be grown most easily. They took their slaves with them, but since labor demand outstripped natural increase of their slaves, they soon turned to the interstate slave market to augment their labor forces.

Southern farmers and planters had always produced small quantities of cotton for home consumption, and commercial output rose during the Revolution, when foreign trade was reduced. Growing demand in England (as well as the invention of the cotton gin) invigorated cotton production. Planters in piedmont South Carolina and Georgia and the Natchez region responded speedily to English demand, abandoning tobacco and other crops for cotton. American cotton production grew over 25 percent a year during the 1790s rising from 1.5 to 35 million pounds. This trend continued unabated for more than a generation. Growth slowed during the war-filled years from 1800 to 1819 (5 percent a year), but nonetheless reached 167 million pounds by the end of the period. Thousands of planters moved to Tennessee, Alabama, Mississippi, and Louisiana in the 1820s and 1830s to grow cotton, taking their own or purchased slaves with them. Growth accelerated

25. Bruchey, ed., *Cotton and Growth of the American Economy*, 9, 14–17 (tables 2A, 3A); Deane and Cole, *British Economic Growth*, 182–92; Zevin, "Growth of Cotton Textile Production after 1815," 122–47.

in the 1820s and 1830s (nearly 7 percent annually), the crop increasing to over 800 million pounds by 1840. Planters needed an army of slave migrants to make cotton, for cotton production grew twice as fast between 1820 and 1840 as the slave population.[26]

Cotton planters quickly turned to foreign markets to sell their crop. By the mid–1790s cotton exports grew as rapidly as cotton production; by the 1820s exports grew more rapidly than production. Merchants exported over half the cotton crop by 1800 and that proportion grew to over four-fifths of the crop by the 1830s. Britain was the key market for American cotton. Nearly all American exports went there in the 1790s. Despite conflicts between the two countries, over a third of the crop was destined for Britain in the 1800s and 1810s. Both the proportion of the crop reaching Britain and Britain's share of exports grew after 1820. As the productivity of southern slaves increased, American cotton became cheaper for British manufacturers, who relied increasingly on southern cotton, turning away from other suppliers (thereby reducing production outside the South). The American share of British cotton imports rose from two-fifths in the 1810s and 1820s to over four-fifths by 1840 (table 7).[27]

Links between the world's most advanced capitalist region and its most successful slave economy grew ever stronger. British workers and manufacturers, opposed to slavery and supportive of free wage labor, had suppressed Britain's role in the Atlantic slave trade and forced gradual emancipation upon West Indian planters. But manufacturers bought American slave-made cotton and workers made cloth from it with increasing intensity. These bonds, contradictory as they seemed to those on both sides, even more profoundly influenced the history of slaves in the American South. Rising British demands for American cotton accelerated settlement, and market development of southern soils adaptable to the crop increasingly separated southern whites into slave and nonslave regions, and — given the lack of access to Africans — created and sustained the internal slave trade.

World Capitalism and the Internal Movement of Slaves, 1790–1840

The suppression of the African slave trade, along with the continuing cotton boom, ended the gradual expansion of slavery characteristic of the eight-

26. Bruchey, ed., *Cotton and Growth of the American Economy*, 14–19 (tables 3 A-E); Chaplin, "Creating a Cotton South," 171–200; L. C. Gray, *History of Agriculture*, 2: chaps. 20, 37. Population adjusted for rising cotton labor productivity (about 900 to 1,300 pounds per worker) between 1820 and 1840 (Whartenby, "Productivity in Cotton Production," 54).

27. Bruchey, ed., *Cotton and Growth of the American Economy*, 9, 14–17 (tables 2A, 3A); Whartenby, "Productivity in Cotton Production," 12; Eltis, *Economic Growth and Ending Transatlantic Slave Trade*, 39.

Table 7.
U.S. cotton exports and British cotton imports, 1790–1840

| | \multicolumn{5}{c}{Decade[a]} |
	1790s	1800s	1810s	1820s	1830s
% U.S. crop exported	34.5	59.9	58.9	78.6	83.1
	(27.1)	(25.0)	(22.0)	(13.3)	(4.2)
% U.S. crop exported to	34.1	38.1	37.3	53.0	60.0
Great Britain	(26.8)	(15.9)	(14.1)	(12.5)	(2.9)
% Exports destined for	99.1	66.7	63.4	66.8	72.3
Great Britain	(2.7)	(20.6)	(8.6)	(6.1)	(3.1)
% British imports from	13.6	39.3	38.6	67.0	77.9
US	(11.8)	(17.1)	(12.4)	(8.8)	(5.4)

Source: Bruchey, ed., *Cotton and Growth of the American Economy*, Tables 2A and 3A, 9 on 14–17. The data are mean percentages, with each year counting as a single case. Standard deviations are in parentheses.

[a]Each decade except the 1790s (1790–1800) includes ten years (e.g. 1800s = 1801–1810).

eenth century. After 1808 whites and slaves began to move in different directions. About two-fifths of migrants in a sample of Virginia Revolutionary War pensioners left for Kentucky and the rest migrated to Tennessee or the Old Northwest during the early nineteenth century.[28] After they arrived, they were no longer able to procure slaves, and slave prices rose so high that many must have sold slaves out of necessity in times of economic distress or for quick profits in times of economic expansion. Demand for slaves remained high in newer cotton areas, and since the African supply had been cut off, cotton planters turned to Chesapeake owners to augment their labor force. Black migrants were therefore concentrated in the cotton-producing states.

During the 1790s and 1800s, older patterns of slave movement persisted. Residents of Virginia and Maryland, both white and black, rapidly peopled the new states of Kentucky and Tennessee. Most pioneers were poor whites, but wealthier planters soon moved west and, between 1790 and 1810, forced some 75,000 Chesapeake slaves to relocate with them. Relatively few blacks born in Virginia or Maryland reached states farther to the southwest (table 8). While most migrating whites owned only a slave or two, a few gentlemen, usually the younger sons of the Virginia gentlemen, moved with a large entourage of blacks. Robert Carter Harrison, for instance, migrated from Vir-

28. J. F. Dorman, *Virginia Revolutionary Pension Applications*, vols. 1–6.

Table 8.
Conjectural estimate of net slave migration to and within the United
States, 1790–1810

States receiving slaves	Number of slaves exported from			Number of in-migrants
	Chesapeake states	Africa	West Indies	
Kentucky	54,000	0	0	54,000
North Carolina	6,000	0	0	6,000
South Carolina	4,000	15,000	0	19,000
Georgia	4,000	48,000	0	52,000
Tennessee	25,000	12,000	0	37,000
Mississippi & Louisiana	5,000	18,000	3,000	26,000
Total	98,000	93,000	3,000	194,000

Sources: De Bow, *Statistical View of the United States,* 63, 82; LaChance, "Politics of Fear," 196–97; Ranking, "Tannenbaum Thesis Reconsidered," 21.

Note: For an explanation of method used in compiling this table, see Kulikoff, "Uprooted Peoples," 168–71.

ginia to Fayette County, Kentucky, in 1805 with around a hundred slaves, thus bringing nearly as many chattels as fifty of his poorer neighbors.[29]

Notwithstanding the appearance of a few interregional slave traders in the upper South, a large, organized domestic slave trade from Virginia to Kentucky, Tennessee, and Georgia failed to develop during the 1790s and 1800s. Traders carried a small minority of the slave migrants who crossed the mountains or migrated to piedmont Georgia; nearly all of them moved with their masters, to settle on new farms in the West. The absence of an organized trade slowed the transfer of slaves but did not mitigate the condition of those who moved. Though few professional slave traders bought Virginia slaves for the Kentucky or Tennessee market, slaves sold in Chesapeake markets or inherited by Virginia planters might well wind up in the new regions, far from friends and family.[30]

Georgia, South Carolina, and southwestern planters and farmers pur-

29. Coward, *Kentucky in the New Republic,* 37, 63; Goodstein, "Black History on Nashville Frontier," 101–20; Coleman, *Slavery Times in Kentucky,* 19–21.

30. Deyle, "American Independence and the Rise of Domestic Slave Trade"; Goodstein, "Black History on Nashville Frontier," 403–6; Coleman, *Slavery Times in Kentucky,* 144–47.

chased thousands of enslaved Africans, but they had limited access to Chesapeake markets. Chesapeake planters who wished to sell or transport slaves turned first to Kentucky, where planters and their slaves readily found a home and where slaves were easily sold. Not only did the great distance between the Chesapeake and backcountry Georgia and South Carolina inhibit slave relocation and trade, but South Carolina responded to Gabriel's plot in Virginia in 1800 by prohibiting the domestic slave trade and restricting the free sale of slaves by migrants, further discouraging an influx of Chesapeake slaves. As a result of the lure of Kentucky and the inhospitality of South Carolina, Chesapeake slaveholders sent fewer than 15,000 slaves to South Carolina, Georgia, Mississippi, and Louisiana between 1790 and 1810, and many of these probably accompanied their masters (table 8).

Since the revolt in Saint-Domingue tainted West Indian slaves with the "cancer of revolution," only continuation of the African slave trade would satisfy backcountry planters. While lowcountry legislators in South Carolina suppressed the African slave trade in 1788, ships freely plied their human cargoes at Savannah until 1798, and after intensive pressure from upcountry legislators, South Carolina reopened the African trade in 1804. Meanwhile, American settlers in Louisiana could purchase Africans only fitfully; the slave trade was open (to Spanish ships only) from 1790 to 1795, closed from 1795 to 1800, open (to Spanish and British ships) from late 1800 to 1803, and closed to direct trade after the passage of the Louisiana Ordinance in 1804 by the United States.[31]

Despite these restrictions, roughly 30,000 slaves reached the United States from Africa in the 1790s, and 63,000 more came in the 1800s. During the 1790s most African slavers landed in Savannah and sold them to upcountry planters or local traders. Smaller groups reached backcountry South Carolina, Tennessee, and Louisiana. Almost no African slaves were sold to Chesapeake or Kentucky planters during this period. After 1804 slavers shifted their business from Savannah to Charleston. Before the trade closed, they landed over 39,000 Africans in Charleston, most of whom were purchased by backcountry traders and planters from the expanding frontier region of the South some hundreds of miles inland. South Carolina planters, in contrast, probably purchased fewer than a third of them. Another 24,000 Africans either landed along the Gulf coast or were smuggled into Georgia or South Carolina when the trade there was illegal.[32]

31. LaChance, "Politics of Fear," 195.

32. P. S. Brady, "Slave Trade and Sectionalism," 611–13; Kulikoff, "Uprooted Peoples," 150. About 93,000 slaves came from Africa between 1790 and 1810 (table 8); of these, 39,000 entered Charleston between 1804 and 1808, and another 30,000 ar-

During the 1790s and 1800s, few West Indian slaves reached the United States in spite of the demand for slave labor. The largest group of them, numbering around 3,200, came to New Orleans with their refugee masters in 1809. They had migrated from Saint Domingue to Cuba after the defeat of the French in 1803, and had then been expelled in 1809. While French-speaking citizens of Louisiana welcomed the refugees, English-speaking residents feared both the French culture brought by the whites and the possible rebelliousness of the slaves. The United States government reluctantly permitted them to remain after ascertaining the loyalty of the masters and examining the cost to deport the slaves.[33]

The close of the foreign slave trade to the United States on January 1, 1808, accelerated the domestic slave trade and shifted its terminus. A majority of slaves sold or forced to move with masters in the 1810s went to states southwest of Georgia, cotton frontiers that attracted few white Virginians. Only half as many slaves, proportionately, moved to Kentucky and Tennessee as white Revolutionary War veterans. During the 1810s about 137,000 slaves from the Chesapeake states and North Carolina spread over the frontier South. Kentucky was no longer the most common destination. Nearly six of every ten Chesapeake black migrants left for Mississippi, Alabama, and the territories and states west of the Mississippi; the rest of them went to Kentucky, Tennessee, and Georgia. Most slaves from North Carolina were probably moved to Tennessee (table 9).

Chesapeake slaves reached the West in three ways during the 1810s. A substantial but declining proportion of them came with their masters. These included most slaves who went to Kentucky. But only the wealthiest planters who wished to take advantage of the cotton boom could afford to move the great distance from the Chesapeake to the lower South. One such man was Leonard Covington, a former Maryland congressman and descendant of an old gentry family. In 1808 he moved from Prince George's County, Maryland, to the Mississippi frontier, taking thirty-one of his fifty-seven slaves with him.[34]

Since few Chesapeake planters followed Covington's lead, Chesapeake slaves often moved "down the river" with professional slave traders. Between 1810 and 1819 slave traders carried at least a third of all the forced black

---

33. LaChance, "Politics of Fear," 187–93.

34. Brandon and Drake, eds., *Memoir of Leonard Covington*, 43–64; Sydnor, *Slavery in Mississippi*, 146–50.

Table 9.
Conjectural estimate of net slave migration to and within the United
States, 1810–20

States receiving slaves	Number of slaves exported from			Number of in-migrants
	Chesapeake states	North Carolina	Africa	
Kentucky	24,000	0	0	24,000
Tennessee	10,000	13,000	0	23,000
Georgia	13,000	0	2,000	15,000
Mississippi & Alabama	51,000	0	2,000	53,000
Louisiana, Arkansas, & Missouri	26,000	0	3,000	29,000
Total	124,000	13,000	7,000	144,000

Source: De Bow, *Statistical View of the United States,* 63, 82.
Note: For an explanation of method used in compiling this table, see Kulikoff, "Uprooted Peoples," 168–71.

migrants.[35] While a few had operated in the Chesapeake states before 1808, many of them became active during the 1810s. Taking advantage of this demand, Chesapeake planters sold surplus slaves to traders; between 1809 and 1828, the Virginia Tayloes, for instance, kept only enough women to ensure natural increase and operate the household and sold the surplus. An anonymous traveler in Virginia in 1808 contended that "the Carolina slave dealers get frequent supplies from this state, particularly from the eastern shore." Before 1820 slave traders established offices in most Virginia cities, including Fredericksburg and Alexandria. A regular trade from Kentucky to the lower South also started as slave traders transported Kentucky slaves down the Ohio and Mississippi rivers for sale at Natchez and New Orleans. Traders found a ready market for slaves in cotton states like Louisiana, where even small cotton farmers wanted to buy more laborers. Not everyone depended on professional traders. Wealthy cotton planters sometimes purchased slaves themselves in Virginia or Maryland. Farish Carter of Baldwin County, Georgia, in the cotton-producing backcountry, owned but four slaves in 1816; the next year he possessed fifty, apparently purchased on local mar-

35. If none of the slave migrants to Kentucky and Tennessee found in table 9 were sold and half of those who migrated elsewhere from the Chesapeake were carried by slave traders, then 36% of slave migrants were sold to traders. For higher estimates see Tadman, *Speculators and Slaves,* 25–31, 245–47.

kets. In 1821 Carter journeyed to Virginia, where he bought sixty slaves of all ages to augment his already large work force.[36]

The distribution of slaves in 1840 illuminates how the suppression of the Atlantic slave trade and the growth of the cotton textile industry structured slave migration. During the 1820s and 1830s, from 350,000 to 450,000 slaves were forced to moved from the upper to the lower South. All available slaves were pulled into cotton cultivation, leaving whites in newer tobacco and farming areas with few chattels. Nearly as high a percentage of slaves lived in cotton regions settled in the eighteenth and early nineteenth centuries as in the oldest Chesapeake tobacco counties. The proportion of slaves in tobacco regions (including areas that had shifted to diversified farming) stayed roughly the same between 1790 and 1840. Over a third of the populace in cotton frontier counties, peopled by whites and slaves after 1825, was enslaved. But planters in newer tobacco areas failed to build a slave labor force. Only a quarter of the people in tobacco-producing counties of Kentucky and Missouri were enslaved, many fewer than in Chesapeake counties at a similar stage in their history, and not many more than the number diversified farmers owned (fig. 5).[37]

The expansion of cotton and the growth of slavery were closely linked during the first four decades of the nineteenth century. By 1840 slaves and masters in 300 counties, two-fifths of slave state counties, grew marketable quantities of cotton. Slaves in these places — the "black belt" stretching from South Carolina and Georgia to Alabama, Mississippi, and Louisiana, and pockets in Tennessee, and North Carolina — produced on average 800 pounds of cotton per worker and constituted two-fifths of the populace. In the quarter most productive cotton counties, where workers averaged 2,000 pounds or more, the proportion of slaves reached more than half, proportionately nearly twice as many as other southern counties organized in the early nineteenth century.[38]

36. Dunn, "Tale of Two Plantations," 41, 46–47; Phillips, *Plantation and Frontier*, 2:55–56 (quote); Sydnor, *Slavery in Mississippi*, 146–50; Bancroft, *Slave Trading*, 21–27; Coleman, *Slavery Times in Kentucky*, 144–45; Flanders, *Plantation Slavery in Georgia*, 119–21; Malone, "Searching for the Family," 362–64.

37. Tadman, *Speculators and Slaves*, 12; Fogel and Engerman, *Time on the Cross*, 1:44–47. Data in figures 5–6 computed from 1840 county-level data from the Federal census, Inter-University Consortium, "Historical, Demographic, Economic, and Social Data."

38. See appendix for the findings in this and succeeding paragraphs. Inter-University Consortium, "Historical, Demographic, Economic, and Social Data," for 1840 with the addition of crop production variables from the published census and dates of county formation from Everton and Rasmuson, *Handy Book*. Median cotton production per agricultural worker (where production was 200 pounds or more/ worker and average production rounded to nearest 200 pounds) was 800 pounds (me-

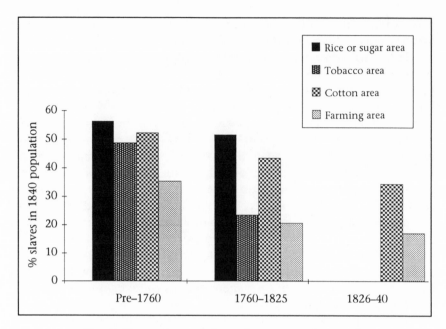

Fig. 5. Percentage of slaves by crop regime and
date of settlement, 1840

Notwithstanding the movement of slaves to the cotton South, slavery
remained important in the tobacco region of the Chesapeake states. Since as
many whites as blacks migrated, about half the population was enslaved in a
typical colonial tobacco county, where workers harvested on average 600 to
800 pounds of the plant.[39] Proportional losses of slaves were under 10 percent even in those Tidewater counties where planters had shifted to grain
cultivation and herding late in the eighteenth century. Masters with surplus
slaves in these farming areas may have sold a few to slave traders but they
hired most excess slaves to neighbors (see appendix).[40]

Tobacco, with fluctuating markets, expanded more slowly than cotton
during the early nineteenth century. In 1840, families in only 137 counties

---

dian) and mean cotton production was 1317 pounds (counting all cases of 4,000
pounds or more as 4,000 pounds). This compares favorably with the range of 1,089 to
1,494 pounds found in Whartenby, "Land and Labor Productivity," 54.

39. Workers could cultivate about 1,000 pounds (L. C. Gray, *History of Agriculture*,
2:776). Median production per agricultural worker in counties where workers grew
200 pounds or more averaged 600 pounds over all tobacco counties.

40. For hiring in a farming community, see Hughes, "Slaves for Hire," 260–86; for
slave sales by masters, see Tadman, *Speculators and Slaves*, chap. 3.

grew substantial quantities of tobacco, and many of these were Chesapeake counties where the crop had been grown before the Revolution. Nonetheless, numerous migrants to Kentucky and scattered groups in Tennessee, Missouri, and Arkansas did cultivate tobacco. These men could have used slaves, much as tobacco-planting pioneers did in the third quarter of the eighteenth century. But Kentucky tobacco growers commanded so little credit that they could rarely buy slaves from internal markets and, in fact, men who brought slaves to Kentucky sometimes sold them to traders or moved to cotton regions themselves.[41]

Slaves reached nineteenth-century farming districts even less often than tobacco areas. At most, one-fifth of the population of wheat counties, where farmers harvested about twenty bushels per hand, was enslaved; in contrast, as many as one-quarter of the inhabitants of nineteenth-century tobacco counties were slaves.[42] And just 15 percent of the population was enslaved in counties where farmers sold small quantities of corn and raised livestock.

Differential migration of slaves and whites in the new nation caused a remarkable redistribution of slaves in the South. Despite the rapid increase of farming counties in slaveholding states, the proportion of slaves living in farming areas declined from about a third to less than a quarter between 1790 and 1840. Not surprisingly, given the slow growth of tobacco cultivation, the proportion of slaves living in tobacco regions (including former tobacco areas of Virginia) declined from about half in 1790 to three-tenths in 1840. Slaves were forced into cotton production. Almost no slaves cultivated cotton in 1790, but by 1840 nearly two-fifths of all southern slaves lived in cotton-producing counties (see fig. 6).

The Process of Forced Migration

The forced migration of slaves into and across the cotton South had enormous human cost: migrants left loved ones at home, departed familiar surroundings, often changed masters, lost privileges they had previously enjoyed, and were forced to live among strangers — both free and enslaved — when they reached their destinations. Migration disrupted the lives of all black participants, but its effects differed depending on the origins of the migrants, their destination, and their mode of transit. African migrants, slaves transported by their masters, blacks sold in the domestic slave trade, and African-American slaves left behind experienced the move south or west

41. Based on the low (about 1 percent) coefficient on dummy for former tobacco counties (appendix). For Kentucky see Bancroft, *Slave Trading in the Old South*, 123–25, 388–92.

42. Only 30 counties fit this group, but the general pattern might have been more widespread.

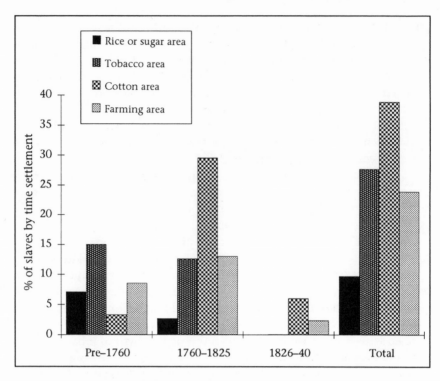

Fig. 6. Percentage of slaves working in various crop regimes, 1840

in diverse ways, and these in turn influenced the rapidity with which blacks could create new slave communities.

Planters in the early cotton South mixed slaves from six sources: their own or their parents' plantations, the Atlantic or interstate slave trades, purchase trips, inheritance, and local sales. Seeking to build productive plantations, planters chose slaves of different ages, sexes, and geographical origins from each of these sources. Although planters understood that slaves surrounded by families would be more contented and productive, they nonetheless defined slave families narrowly as mothers and young children and willingly sold or otherwise separated husbands from wives, children from parents, and brothers from sisters if that would improve the financial security of their own wives and children.[43]

Captured in African wars, driven to the coast, sold to European slave traders, and herded into crowded and unsanitary ships, African survivors of the Middle Passage left their families behind and found themselves sur-

43. Contrast Tadman, *Speculators and Slaves*, 144, 153–57, 217–19, with Genovese, *Roll, Jordan, Roll*, 119–26.

rounded by strangers, both African and European. Though most of their en-slaved shipmates came from a small region, few spoke their language. They sometimes developed friendships with their shipmates of their own sex. Their prospects, once they reached South Carolina or Georgia, were bleak. They might be sold several times, first to a seaport merchant, then to a back-country trader, and finally marched to the interior and sold to a planter hun-gry only for their labor. In such circumstances slave communities developed slowly. Not only were newly arrived Africans separated from their shipmates, but with few African women included among them, transplanted Africans had difficulty establishing families. Slave traders remained as selective as they had been earlier in the century, preferring men and boys to women and girls. On two African slave ships reaching Charleston in 1786 and Savannah in 1797, there were two men for every woman, two adults for every child, and three boys for every girl.[44]

The enslavement in 1788 of Ibrahima, a Muslim prince of the Fulbe, illustrates the adjustments a new African slave had to make. Since he was a military leader captured during war, no sum of money would buy his repatri-ation. His captors sold him to slave traders, who carried him down the Gam-bia River and onto a crowded slave ship. Ibrahima's new masters chained him to a fellow passenger, where he remained for a month and half until the ship landed at Dominica, a new British colony. There fifty-six Africans, in-cluding Ibrahima, were sold to a Philadelphia merchant and transshipped to Spanish New Orleans. Although four months had passed before Ibrahima landed in New Orleans, his new owner placed him in a third ship and took him up the Mississippi River to Natchez, where an American settler pur-chased him. On a frontier Mississippi plantation he began the difficult trans-formation from African to African-American.[45]

The social dislocations faced by slaves sold in the interstate slave trade or carried by masters to the Southwest differed from those of Africans. Creole slaves understood their master's expectations, spoke the same language as other slaves and whites, and sometimes moved with their families. Yet their lives were disrupted as well. No matter how humane a master might be, mi-gration inevitably separated families. Even the largest planter did not own all the significant relations of his slaves, and many husbands and wives lived on the plantations of different owners. A youth sold in the slave trade, even if unmarried, left behind parents, siblings, and other relatives who had lived

---

44. P. S. Brady, "Slave Trade and Sectionalism," 614–17; Donnan, *Documents Illus-trative of Slave Trade,* 4:419–92 (Gambia, to Charleston in 1786, 86 slaves), 633 (Eagle, to Savannah in 1797, 237 slaves); Sydnor, *Slavery in Mississippi,* 141–42. For accultura-tion of Africans, see Kulikoff, *Tobacco and Slaves,* 317–34; Mintz and Price, *Anthropo-logical Approach,* 1–21.

45. Alford, *Prince among Slaves,* chaps. 2–3.

nearby. The proportion of slaves who migrated southwest from Maryland and Virginia, and therefore the number of families torn asunder, grew rapidly after the end of the African slave trade. About one in twelve Chesapeake slaves moved to Kentucky or farther south in the 1790s, and one in ten migrated during the 1800s, but the proportion forced to move doubled during the 1810s, reaching one in five.[46]

The insecurity of Creole slaves increased greatly when the African slave trade ended and the domestic trade accelerated. A black man or woman sold to a slave trader had to endure not only disruption of daily work and communal activities but also separation from family members, forced relocation to an unknown and possibly dangerous place, and the probability of working far harder for a new master on the cotton frontier. Knowing that slaves preferred to remain in familiar surroundings near friends and kin, planters used the threat of sale to control their chattels' behavior. "In Maryland," Charles Ball reported, "it has always been the practice of masters and mistresses, who wished to terrify their slaves to threaten to sell them to South Carolina where it was represented, that their condition would be a hundred fold worse." Ball considered "such a sale of myself as the greatest of evils that could befall me, and had striven to demean myself in such manner to my owners, as to preclude them from all excuse of transporting me to so horrid a place."[47]

All too often planters sold their slaves to traders, vividly reminding both those who were sold and their kin who stayed behind of the precarious circumstances of slave families. Stephen Penbroke, born in Maryland in 1804, understood the fear of being sold, for his "father was sold five times. The last time he was knocked down and seized by three men" before being forcibly carried away. The scene of his father's removal deeply affected the younger Penbroke, and his master, sensing this, played upon the young slave's desire to remain near his family by threatening to send him "further South" if he requested a lighter work load.[48]

The life of Charles Ball encapsulates the experiences of slaves sold from the Chesapeake to the cotton South. Ball, born about 1780 in Calvert County, Maryland, learned early in life that masters did not respect slave family bonds. During the first years of his life, Ball's mother, father, and

46. For kin ties in the Chesapeake, see Kulikoff, *Tobacco and Slaves*, chap. 9; Norton, Gutman, and Berlin, "Afro-American Family," 175–91. Kulikoff, "Uprooted Peoples," 155, computes the proportion of slaves who moved.

47. Ball, *Fifty Years in Chains*. Contemporaries challenged Ball's narrative, first published in 1837, as a fabrication, and it was probably ghost-written, but it has been accepted by John Blassingame, who checked the narrative against original records (see *Slave Testimony*, xxiii-xxvi).

48. Blassingame, *Slave Testimony*, 108–9, 167–69, and 211–13.

grandfather lived apart on plantations operated by different masters. When Ball was about five years old, his mother's master died, and family members living with his mother were sold, each member to a different master. The new arrangement not only further splintered the family, but also prevented his father and mother from seeing each other. Unable to visit his wife, Ball's father became distraught and behaved sullenly toward his owner, who feared he would run away. The master therefore resolved to sell him to a Georgia slave trader. But before the sale was completed, the elder Ball fled to the North, leaving Charles with only his African grandfather for companionship in the old neighborhood.[49]

Before reaching adolescence Ball saw his family disintegrate several times. When he was twelve his master died, and the estate was administered by his father's former owner, a harsh taskmaster who hired Ball out to a shipowner as a cook at a Washington shipyard. During his early twenties, Ball worked at the Washington Navy Yard and then returned to live in Calvert County under two different masters. After returning to Calvert, he married and started a family, but his last Maryland master sold him to a Georgia slave trader, separating him from his family. Ball asked his the slave trader if he "could be allowed to go to see my wife and children, or if this could not be permitted, if they might not have leave to come to see me; but was told that I would be able to get another wife in Georgia."

The Georgia trader took no chances and treated Ball and others he bought harshly. While the nineteen women in the group "were merely tied together with a rope . . . which was tied like a halter around the neck of each," the thirty-two men suffered more severe restraint. "A strong iron collar was closely fitted . . . round each of our necks. . . . In addition to this, we were handcuffed in pairs, with iron staples and bolts, with a short chain, a foot long, uniting the handcuffs and their wearers in pairs." They marched rapidly during the day (ignoring, by the way, the cries of the pregnant women in the group) and slept "promiscuously, men and women, on the floors of such houses as we chanced to stop at."

Ball's sale to a slave trader and separation from his family traumatized him. At first, he "longed to die, and escape from the hands of my tormenters; but the wretched privilege of destroying myself was denied; for I could not shake off my chains, nor move a yard without the consent of my master." He dreamed about his grandfather, wife, and children and longed to see them, but "in a few days the horrible sensation attendant upon my cruel separation from my wife and children, in some measure subsided."

Slaves who migrated with their masters often retained some family ties,

49. Ball's biography, in this and succeeding paragraphs, is based on Ball, *Fifty Years in Chains*, 15–24, 25–38, 41, 68–69.

especially if they were owned by a wealthy planter. Before moving to Mississippi, Leonard Covington wrote to his brother Alexander, who already lived there, to inquire about slave life on the frontier. He wanted to know if "the negroes in the country generally looked as happy and contented as with us, and do they as universally take husbands and wives and as easily rear their young as in Maryland?" Despite his concern, Covington divided his slaves, taking some families with him and leaving others on his Maryland farm. Slave migrants included were five men, four women, and twenty-two children under the age of sixteen. At least one family containing a father, mother, and two children, as well as another two mothers with four children each moved; but a number of the older children left parents in Maryland, and several of the adults may have been married to slaves Covington did not own. Covington apparently wanted youths on his new plantation, for he left behind seven of his nine slaves older than thirty. He consigned the thirty-one migrant slaves, along with about twenty others, to a D. Rawlings, who transported them down the Ohio and Mississippi rivers.[50]

Few slaves willingly consented to leave their families behind. Alexander Covington's slave Sam refused to travel with a group of slaves his master's brother Leonard was shipping to Mississippi. Leonard reported that Sam maintained "a sullen silence on the subject and neither yields consent to accompany my people, or to be sold or exchange." Sam's wife and family probably lived in the neighborhood, and he did not want to leave them. After attempting to persuade Sam that Mississippi slaves were contented, Leonard Covington finally sold Sam locally, purchased another slave in return, and sent that one to his brother.[51]

The internal slave trade and the migration of slaves with masters elided, as is shown in petitions in 1817 to the South Carolina legislature for an exemption to a new law forbidding any slave to enter the state. Petitioners can be divided into three groups. About a third of them, who owned nearly three-fifths of the slaves, sought to move to South Carolina with their slaves and set up farms there. They came, on average, with seventeen slaves, groups large enough to include several families. While this group included some long-distance migrants, many of them moved short distances along the coast or owned adjacent land in two states. Nearly half the petitioners, who owned less than a third of the slaves, wanted to bring in slaves they had

---

50. Brandon and Drake, eds., *Memoir of Leonard Covington*, 43–64, reprints the letters (the passage from Covington's letter is on 51–52); Dunn, "Two 'Privledged' Slaves," 40, found that only 4 of 41 slaves forced by their master William Henry Tayloe to move from his Virginia to his Alabama plantation in 1839 were over age thirty. For a different view of Covington's behavior, see Tadman, *Speculators and Slaves*, 154, 236.

51. Brandon and Drake, eds., *Memoir of Leonard Covington*, 51–54, 57, 59.

Table 10.
Patterns of movement of slaves with their masters into
South Carolina, 1817

Pattern of movement	% Masters	% Slaves	Mean size group
Migration of entire or part of plantation	33	57	17.2
Slaves inherited or part of dowry	45	31	6.6
Slaves purchased by master in upper South	22	13	3.5
Total	100	101	9.7
Number	49	474	

Source: South Carolina Legislative Petitions, 1817.
Note: Not all petitions mentioned number of slaves. I assumed that these masters brought in the mean number of slaves characteristic of the entire group. A total of 421 slaves were actually counted on the petitions.

inherited or received as a marriage portion. These slaves came over great distances, and there were, on average, less than seven slaves in each group. Like slaves sold to traders, most of them had been torn from their communities and even their immediate families. The rest of the petitioners had purchased several slaves out of state and wanted to add them to their labor force (table 10). If the slaves brought into South Carolina were representative migrants, then more than two-fifths of movement with masters resembled the slave trade. Less than two-fifths of slaves forced to move between regions in the late 1810s and early 1820s, then, could have migrated with most members of their immediate families.[52]

Petitioners, who usually moved to South Carolina to join kindred or friends or to improve their economic standing, needed to bring slaves with them to guarantee prosperity after their arrival. James Bilbo of Savannah, for instance, had bought land in the Edgefield District of piedmont South Carolina and was "anxious to remove his family. That to enable him to do so, it was indispensably necessary to obtain . . . permission" to take "house Servants and as many more as will enable him to cultivate a part of the land

52. Based on 36% in interstate trade (see n. 37) and table 9. The way the two elided suggests that attempts to sharply distinguish between the trade and movement with masters might be misleading. While the proportion in the trade is less than Tadman, *Speculators and Slaves*, 241–47, the consequences for slave families are similar.

purchased." He wanted to move about thirty slaves, both "old and young." The petitions of return migrants were particularly revealing. John Clarke had moved in 1816 from the Greenville District of South Carolina (in the northwest corner of the state) to Georgia to seek his fortune, but "found the climate very Injurious to the health of himself and his family which Hath Induced him to return to Greenville District" with his slave family of a woman and her three children. The Wade family, too, disrupted the lives of their slave families twice. Martha Wade was a native of South Carolina, but in "1806 she sittled in the Mississippi territory"; in 1816 her husband "departed this life by which misfortune She is left alone at a great distance from her friends in South Carolina," and "is anxious to return to her native state" with her fifteen slaves.[53]

Petitioners paid little attention to the needs of black families, except when separating black kindred might reduce plantation efficiency. They understood, however, that women and their small children ought to be kept together. John Harris, of York District, who lived near North Carolina, had "through motives of humanity purchased of a Neighbor two Negro Children viz Susan and Linda, age the one six and the other three years; that he now owns and has owned the mother of the Said Children; that he purchased them with the sole intention of making them part of his family." Masters who carried their own slaves to South Carolina kept some black families together, for they never mentioned in their petitions that slaves they brought with them were so unhappy over the move that they ran away. Slaves purchased in the upper South and separated from their families, in contrast, ran away frequently and had to be recaptured in the Chesapeake states and returned to South Carolina.[54]

The petitions often recognized slaves as members of the master's household but only secondarily viewed them as parts of black families. Slaves, they believed, owed obligations to the families of their white masters. Samuel Billue, a lifelong resident of Lancaster District in the north-central part of the state, was a man "of but Moderate circumstances," who had "by his full industry and economy . . . enabled himself to . . . purchase a small Negroe girl [age 11 or 12] for the benefit of himself and family." James Garrison, Sr., who had inherited a male slave from his wife's grandfather in North Carolina, claimed that "it would be inconvenient and disagreeable to sell the said negro out of the family, and would be a loss to the petitioner and his family to be obligated to dispose" of him. Of course, the slave might have preferred to stay among kindred and friends in North Carolina, rather than serve a

53. S.C. Legislative Petitions, nos. 135, 157, 103, 1817.
54. Ibid., nos. 107–8, 1817; statements on runaways are based upon the entire petition sample.

strange family living miles away, but Garrison's white family took precedence.[55]

During the early nineteenth century, most Creole slaves neither suffered
the indignities of the internal slave trade nor were forced to move with their
masters hundreds of miles to new plantations, yet stories such as Ball's were
repeated often enough so that most slaves might reasonably expect to be
separated from their families, and those left behind feared that they might
be next. An adult slave born in Maryland or Virginia in 1800 could expect
many family separations and had a good chance of being sold during his
adult lifetime. If each forced migrant during the 1810s left behind only two
close kindred in the Chesapeake, then almost two-thirds of Virginia and
Maryland blacks were affected by interstate migration in that decade alone.[56]

Almost as soon as the first planters and slaves arrived in an area, African-
American slaves began reproducing. A local market in slaves — probate or distress sales, purchases of individual slaves from planters — appeared soon
thereafter. Since the slaves of mixed ages sold at these sales rarely appealed
to slave traders, nearly all of them wound up in the hands of local buyers.
Estate sales started in tobacco-growing Boone County, Missouri, in the early
1820s, just after the county was organized, and the number of slaves sold at
such sales grew, as a proportion of county slaves, through the 1830s and
1840s. County residents, often heirs of the slaveholder, bought nearly all of
these slaves. Local planters, seeking to build plantations, purchased the rest.
Slaves bought by Lindsey Durham, of Clarke County, in piedmont Georgia,
illuminate this trend. Durham's parents had migrated from Virginia to the
Georgia frontier in the 1780s. After reading medicine with a local physician,
Durham set up a plantation. During the 1820s, he purchased around twenty
slaves from local planters. His choice of slaves — including a number of
young women and several slave families — suggests that Durham desired a
stable, relatively contented, slave labor force. Such local sales, like those in
the eighteenth-century Chesapeake, permitted slaves to reestablish slave
family life and communities with far less disruption than the interstate slave
trade entailed.[57]

Rebuilding Slave Communities

Forced migration of slaves to the New South broke many of the fragile ties of
kinship and friendship that held together black communities in Africa and

55. Ibid., nos. 148, 107–8, 1817.
56. Table 9; Gutman and Sutch, "Slave Family," 110–11.
57. Tadman, *Speculators and Slaves*, 118–21, 136–40, 171–72; McGettigan, "Boone
County Slaves," 193–96; Merritt, "Slave Family and Household," 55–62, 85–98; Burton, *In My Father's House Are Many Mansions*, 174–77.

slave communities in the United States. In the upper South as many as one in five slave marriages may have been broken and one of every three children under age fourteen may have been separated from parents by the interstate slave trade during the antebellum decades. Untold other families were split apart when masters took their slaves south, leaving kindred of slaves on neighboring plantations.[58]

Eventually slaves left behind and slave migrants remade the family networks and familial ideology that bound them together.[59] The age, sexual, and ethnic composition of the migrant population limited the ability of migrating slaves to rebuild communities in new areas. Slave communities and extended kin networks, moreover, could not emerge unless a high proportion of slaves lived on units of twenty or more, where neighborhood blacks could visit kindred, find spouses, or harbor fugitives. Since the demographic makeup of frontier slave populations and the number of slaves who lived on each plantation varied by region and time, the ability of slaves to develop a strong social life differed as well.

Although the internal slave trade and planter migration disrupted families of individual slaves on Chesapeake and North Carolina plantations, the demography of slave sales and transfer with masters often assured that the slave family and kinship groups could be perpetuated. Slave traders purchased adolescents and young adults most heavily, buying many fewer children under seven and older adults.[60] Sales separated some spouses but mostly severed older children from parents and siblings, leaving the rest of their relations behind, permitting these slaves to reconstruct extensive networks of kinship and friendship. They remarried, reared their children, and memorialized departed family members by naming children after them. Within a generation, or even less if the master maintained his credit and did not sell any of his slaves, large plantations of interconnected kindred reemerged. For instance, traders purchased from 3 to 7 percent of slaves per decade from 1810 to 1840 in St. Mary's County, Maryland, a very old tobacco-growing area, and masters carried similar numbers with them, but larger plantations and the slave families on them persisted.[61]

58. Tadman, *Speculators and Slaves*, chap. 6, is the best analysis, but his estimates should be seen as upward bounds.

59. Gutman, *Black Family in Slavery and Freedom*, chap. 4; Cody, "Naming, Kinship, and Estate Dispersal," 192–211, and "There Was No 'Absalom' on the Ball Plantations," 563–96; Tadman, *Speculators and Slaves*, 175–77.

60. Freudenberger and Pritchett, "Domestic Slave Trade," 451–63; Tadman, *Speculators and Slaves*, 28–31, 146–54. Tadman would not accept the interpretation given here.

61. Gutman, *Black Family*, 137–39, and Tadman, *Speculators and Slaves*, 169–78, provide models of the destruction and recreation of kinship networks. For St. Mary's see Marks, "Economics and Society in a Staple System," 153–61.

The 113,000 Chesapeake slaves who migrated to Kentucky and Tennessee, mostly with masters, struggled to recreate the community life they had left behind. Masters probably brought close to a cross-section of slaves with them: almost half the adults were women; there were few children under ten but a surplus of young adults. Since most white migrants owned few slaves, many spouses had lived on different farms and must have been separated by the move west. Once they reached Kentucky or Tennessee and recovered from the shock of involuntary divorce, many remarried, started new families, and rekindled kinship networks. This task was difficult, despite their cultural homogeneity and rough sexual balance. Over seven-tenths of slaves in two Kentucky counties, 1789–92, lived on units of less than ten slaves and almost none on plantations of twenty or more. Slaves faced sales once they arrived, for nonslaveholders frequently bought slaves from planters. In Davidson County, Tennessee, some 700 slaves were sold in the years between 1784 and 1802. Close to two-thirds of them were sold singly and most of the rest were mothers and their young children. Nearly all of those sold were under thirty years old; perhaps half were under sixteen.[62]

African, Chesapeake, and Carolina migrants to the lower South faced greater difficulties in creating new communities during the years after the Revolution. Black settlers formed culturally distinct groups. African and Chesapeake slaves spoke different languages, practiced different customs, and related to slavery in distinctive ways. While Africans fought the system of slavery, Chesapeake slaves (grandchildren and great-grandchildren of Africans) knew from long experience how to gain privileges from within the system. Chesapeake slave men probably found wives more easily than did the African men. Cultural differences and conflicts over scarce women may well have created tensions between the groups.[63]

The international and interstate slave trade shaped the development of African-American families in the lower South. The first black residents of the frontier Southwest were probably Creole slaves brought by their masters, but soon after arrival, whites began to import Africans. Despite the continuing influx of Creoles in the 1790s and 1800s, Africans soon outnumbered them,

62. Kentucky, Dept. of State Archives, "Lincoln Lists, 1789," 209–29, and "Madison Lists, 1792," 116–41 (adjusted for missing slaves), were distributed as follows: 29.6%, units of 1–3 slaves; 41.7%, units of 4–9; 24.6%, units of 10–19; 4.0% units 20 +; Coward, *Kentucky in Early Republic*, 37, 63; Goodstein, "Black History on the Nashville Frontier," 403–5; Fischer, *Albion's Seed*, 751–52; Tadman's data on the composition of slaves taken south by their masters between 1820 and 1860 (*Speculators and Slaves*, 27–30, 234–35, 243–47) underestimate the selectivity by sex and age of migration with planters. See below for a Georgia example.

63. These speculation rely on P. Wood, *Black Majority*; Kulikoff, *Tobacco and Slaves*, chap. 8; and Berlin, "Time, Space, and the Evolution of Afro-American Society," 44–78.

as the geographical origins of slaves sold in Louisiana's Natchez district in the 1780s show. Between 1781 and 1785, when the first American pioneers arrived, only 22 slaves were sold in Natchez — 16 from the United States, 2 from the West Indies, and 4 from Africa. Merchants soon began selling shiploads of Africans at Natchez. Nearly three-quarters of the 157 slaves sold in Natchez between 1786 and 1788 were Africans; only a sixth came from the United States and a tenth from the West Indies. Almost half the Africans were bought singly, and another third were sold in pairs. Males dominated the immigrant group, making marriage difficult for African men. Nearly twice as many males as females were sold; almost two-thirds of the males were between twenty and thirty, prime candidates for marriage. The African slave trade raised the ratio of slave men to slave women: by 1787 there were 161 young adult men for every hundred women and that ratio grew to 168 by 1792. If the sex ratio of the African population was about 200, and the native-born slaves 125, then roughly two-thirds of the adult slaves were African in 1792.[64]

Africans shared some cultural characteristics. Almost half the slaves landed at Charleston between 1804 and 1807 came from the Congo and Angola regions, and nearly three-quarters of them probably belonged to a handful of ethnic groups clustered around the Congo River. These Africans may have spoken similar languages and been familiar with each other's customs. Nearly a quarter of the African immigrants came from the Windward Coast; no more than an eighth of them came from any other region. Given the wide dispersion of Africans throughout the Southwest, however, probably few of them found countrymen living near their homes.[65]

The small size of most pioneer plantations also made it unlikely that countrymen would live together. As cotton demand grew, upland Georgia planters abandoned tobacco for cotton. But they attracted too few slaves to build large units (table 11). Over half the slaves in six upland Georgia counties in the 1790s and 1800s lived on units with fewer than ten slaves; at most, a sixth of them worked with twenty or more other blacks. Some slaves were dispersed on separate quarters, further reducing social interaction. The east Florida frontier in the 1780s had even fewer slaves, and almost all of them lived on units of less than ten slaves.[66]

The Natchez region was an exception. From the outset of white habita-

64. McBee, Natchez Court Records, 1–60; McElligott, "1787 Census of Natchez," 32, and "1792 Census of Natchez," 20. For details of sex ratios and age distributions, see, Kulikoff, "Uprooted Peoples," 162–63.

65. P. D. Morgan, "Black Society in the Lowcountry," 131–33; Donnan, Documents Illustrative of the Slave Trade, 4:474–635.

66. Statom, "Negro Slavery in Eighteenth-Century Georgia," 176–80; Klein, Unification of a Slave State, 246–50; S. R. Parker, "Men without God or King," 149–51.

Table 11.
Distribution of slaves on the southwestern frontier, 1787–1820

Year	Percentage of slaves living on units of				Number of slaves
	1–3 slaves	4–9 slaves	10–19 slaves	20+ slaves	
Georgia*					
1794	19%	37%	32%	12%	5,347
1798/1802	19	33	31	17	3,193
1805/1807	16	38	30	17	15,218
1810/1811	12	30	34	24	20,429
1820/1821	9	24	30	37	24,835
Natchez Area+					
1787	17	27	19	37	603
1792	10	20	26	44	1,945
1805/1810	10	24	24	42	4,723
Other Mississippi#					
1816	17	39	30	14	1,151
Alabama, 1820##					
Black Belt	9	22	28	42	3,778
Tennessee Valley	10	29	33	28	3,654
Coosa Valley	31	30	28	11	958

Sources: Flanders, *Plantation Slavery in Georgia*, 70; Blair, *Tax Digests of Georgia*, 153–89, 292–316; List of Slaves, Richmond County; McElligott, "1787 Census of Natchez," 11–32 and "1792 Census of Natchez," 12–48, 5–35; Morgan, "Census Wilkinson County, 1805," 104–11, and "Census Clairborne and Warren, 1810," 50–63; Capers, "Census Jefferson County, 1810," 33–46; Williams, *Records of Marion County, Mississippi*, 7–8; Williams, ed., *Records of Pike/Walthnall Counties;* Hailes, comp., "Alabama Census Returns, 1820," 339–515. All sources, except as noted, are nominal lists.

*1794: Oglethorpe, Warren, Wilkes; 1798: Richmond; 1800: Oglethorpe; 1802: Wilkes, Hancock; 1805: Oglethorpe, Clark; 1807, Hancock; 1810: Oglethorpe, Clarke; 1811: Wilkes, Hancock; 1820: Oglethorpe, Clarke, Wilkes; 1821, Hancock. All but the 1794 Warren and Wilkes and the 1798 Richmond lists were estimated from categories of slaves by owners.

+The 1787 and 1792 lists include the entire Spanish Natchez District; 1805, Wilkinson; 1810, Clairborne, Jefferson, Warren.

#Marion and Pike Counties.

##Black belt counties are Dallas and Wilcox; Tennessee Valley counties are Limestone and Franklin; Coosa Valley counties are St. Clair and Shelby.

tion in the 1760s, English-speaking large planters, intent on selling staples on international markets, settled rich lands along the Mississippi. A few, who commanded sufficient capital to buy numerous slaves, set slaves to work cultivating tobacco, herding livestock, and finishing forest products. As a result, two-fifths or more of the area's slaves lived on units of twenty slaves or more by the late 1780s. But even after the United States took over the Natchez region in 1795, planters considered the area "the most remote corner of the United States." The 2,000 slaves who lived there in 1792 (two-fifths of the population) were only an eighth of the number found in upcountry Georgia, with its much smaller units. As planters adopted cotton in the late 1790s and early 1800s, slaveowners continued to pour in, and by 1810, less than two decades since large-scale colonization began, half the population of the region was enslaved. The distribution of slaves remained, however, roughly the same, with about two-fifths of the slaves residing on units of twenty or more.[67]

These plantations became polyglot communities of slaves from various African communities and, as women married and bore children, Creole slaves as well. The equal sex ratio of Natchez slave children in 1792 and the 1.6 children per woman there attest to this rapid development of an African-American population in the face of a large-scale slave trade. John Fitzpatrick's slaves illuminate the pattern. Fitzpatrick, a merchant who lived near New Orleans, bought six African slaves from different African nations in the 1770s and 1780s; when he died in 1791, he owned these and five Creole slaves as well, all children of two African women.[68]

African slaves living in the Southwest, like previous African immigrants, refused at first to cooperate with the slave system. Many slaves probably emulated Ibrahima, the African prince forced into slavery in Mississippi. Thomas Foster, a local planter and himself a recent arrival, purchased Ibrahima from a slave trader in 1788. Trouble began soon after they reached Foster's plantation when he attempted to clothe Ibrahima in breeches and cut his hair. Ibrahima's hair style symbolized his position in Africa, and he fought vigorously but unsuccessfully to retain it. That humiliation completed, Foster set him to field labor, a role beneath his former status. When Ibrahima resisted, Foster whipped him, and after several days' punishment,

67. Table 11; Bailyn, *Voyagers to the West*, chap. 13; McElligott, "1787 Natchez Census," 11–32, and "1792 Spanish Census of Natchez," 12–48, 5–35; Rothstein, "'Remotest Corner,'" 92–108 (quote from 1799 petition on 92); Holmes, "A Spanish Province," 166–69; Hamilton, "Mississippi 1817," 271–84.

68. McElligott, "1792 Spanish Census of Natchez," 20; Dayrumple, ed., *Merchant of Manchac*, 425–32.

he ran away. Weeks later, he returned to Foster's plantation, having learned that escape was impossible, and became a "model" field hand.[69]

The numerical dominance of Africans on the frontier disappeared soon after the closing of the African slave trade. While thousands of Africans died before they were immune to the southern disease environment, 100,000 slaves born in the Chesapeake states replaced them on southwestern frontier plantations. A majority of them may have been sold to slave traders or purchased in the upper South by cotton planters and carried south. Most were young and nearly equal numbers of men and women came south with slave traders. In 1820, the sex ratio (number of men per hundred women) of slaves between fourteen and twenty-six, the age group that accounted for nearly half the domestic slave trade, ranged from 96 to 107 in the frontier states of Arkansas, Missouri, Alabama, and Mississippi. However often these forced migrants had been separated from parents, siblings, and spouses, they could remarry and begin new families. While the migrant black population had included only 1.4 children under the age of fourteen for each adult woman, by 1820 there were nearly 2 children for every black woman aged fourteen to forty-five in Missouri and Alabama—a ratio that suggests substantial natural increase—and about 1.5 children under fourteen for each black woman in Arkansas and Mississippi.[70]

Even though African and Chesapeake slaves formed separate subgroups on the cotton frontier in the 1810s, tensions soon diminished and a cohesive African-American community began to form. The enormous influx of Chesapeake-born slaves overwhelmed the surviving Africans, who became a small minority of the adult slave population even in areas they had dominated. In time Africans accommodated to African-American norms and values more easily, for they now spoke English and could form families and join community activities. The development of an African-Christian faith further unified blacks from the Chesapeake, lowcountry Carolina, and Africa living in the cotton South, because that faith encompassed values and ideals they all shared.

African and Creole slaves joined together to make a new black community, based upon kinship and activities in the slave quarters. As the proportion of Africans among adults diminished, adult sex ratios among slaves declined as well, and African men who survived to 1820 probably did find wives and begin families. By 1820, after many Africans had died and some Creole women had come to the frontier, there were five men for every four

69. Alford, *Prince among Slaves*, chap. 3.

70. Tadman, *Speculators and Slaves*, 25–31; the data on 1820 sex ratios and child-woman ratios come from the 1820 federal census.

women under age forty-five—which probably included most of the Africans—in Arkansas, Missouri, Alabama, and Mississippi. Such relatively high ratios of women to men suggest that nearly all slaves could start families.[71]

A Georgia register of slaves entering the state in Richmond County in 1820–21 shows how the process of plantation building structured opportunities of African-American slaves to recreate family networks. During those years, Georgia allowed slaves to enter the state only if they came with masters who intended to settle there with their slaves. The register shows slightly more males than females in every age group, and the surplus was particularly strong among slaves over age forty-five. Migrating planters chose younger slaves to come with them and make new Georgia plantations. Nearly half of slave migrants were under thirteen, mostly children between five and fourteen, and most of the rest were between fourteen and twenty-five. The number of migrants peaked at ages ten to fourteen before starting to decline. Planters brought some of these slaves with them, but once they arrived, they probably purchased additional adolescents or young adults from slave traders across the river in South Carolina. Few older slaves migrated; less than a tenth of all migrants were over forty-five.[72]

Migrating planters took slaves they thought would be productive. Infants and small children would drain their resources; the productivity of women over forty-five had declined and they would bear few additional children. The other slaves would produce a profit almost as soon as they arrived in Georgia. These planters could look forward to exploiting the slaves they took with them for many years. The ten- to fourteen-year-olds, the largest group among the migrants, already produced a profit for their masters, and their skills would improve and their value to the master increase for another twenty years. Masters carried relatively few slaves between ages twenty-five and thirty-four with them, even though slaves of these ages were among the most productive. The kinds of slaves which children received from their parents might explain this decision. When sons migrated to the Southwest, parents may well have given them some of their slaves, but they nonetheless kept their highly skilled slaves at home to maintain output.[73]

As the Georgia frontier economy shifted from tobacco to cotton in the 1790s and 1800s, planters who migrated to Georgia to take advantage of the profits high prices brought purchased more slaves and retained the increase

---

71. 1820 federal census.

72. Richmond County Slave Registration Book. The register lists 945 slaves: 499 male and 446 female (sex ratio = 112), 291 children 0–9 (sex ratio = 122), 346 slaves age 10–19 (sex ratio = 107), 270 adults age 20–44 (sex ratio = 105), 38 slaves over 45 (sex ratio = 138). For slave productivity by age, see Fogel and Engerman, *Time on the Cross*, 1:71–78.

73. Fogel and Engerman, *Time on the Cross*, 1:38–42, 71–78, 149–50.

of slaves they already owned. Needing nearly all their slaves to produce cotton, they sold slaves to interstate traders at only a third the rate of owners in the upper South. As a result, by 1820 over a third of slaves in middle Georgia lived on quarters with twenty or more slaves, plantations that probably housed families of parents and children and perhaps a few other kin. Even on smaller units, most mothers and their small children resided in the same hut. Families and work groups on these quarters were of sufficient size to cook, eat, and celebrate with each other and with slaves from nearby farms after the day's work was complete.[74]

The settlement of Alabama illuminates the link between the expansion of cotton and the ability of African-American slaves to create new communities. Almost as soon as federal authorities confiscated Alabama Indian lands, large planters moved in to take advantage of good soil and high cotton prices. In 1820 more than two of five slaves in the Alabama Black Belt lived on plantations with twenty or more slaves, only five years after the first colonists arrived. The Black Belt, settled after 1818 mostly by Georgians who had moved earlier from piedmont Virginia, included a number of large slaveholders who quickly established cotton plantations. By 1820 over two-fifths of white householders already owned slaves. The growth of slavery occurred with remarkable speed: between 1818 and 1820 the proportion of slaves in Montgomery County rose from one-third to two-fifths. The Tennessee Valley was first settled by nonslaveholders after 1804 and then by a few wealthy Georgians (who owned most of the slaves) after 1809. Less than a third of the householders in 1820 owned slaves, and close to a third of the slaves lived on units with more than twenty slaves, mostly on neighboring plantations. Slaves in both places could begin to form communities soon after arrival (table 11).[75]

Slavery and cotton were intimately connected in the rise of large slave plantations in Alabama's Tennessee Valley. By 1809 planters and slaves in that region sent 10,000 bales of cotton to market and increasing numbers of planters took up the crop. An 1820 census of cotton production in Limestone County illuminates the pattern. Limestone's slaves, living on large units, produced most of the county's crop. Families without slaves infrequently grew cotton and those who did produced very small crops. The more slaves one owned, the more likely one produced marketable quantities of cotton. Units with more than ten slaves constituted only a ninth of the county's

---

74. Table 11; Klein, *Unification of a Slave State*, 246–50.

75. Table 11; Thornton, *Politics and Power in a Slave Society*, 7–10, 22–23; Abernethy, *Formative Period in Alabama*, chaps. 1–4, 7; C. S. Davis, *Cotton Kingdom in Alabama*, chap. 2; W. Smith, "Land Patterns in Ante-Bellum Montgomery County," 196–98.

Table 12.
Cotton production and slavery in Limestone County, Alabama, 1820

Number of slaves	Percentage				Mean lbs. cotton produced per unit[b]	Number of units
	Households	Growing cotton	Cotton growers	Crop produced		
0[a]	61	10	22	4	841	292
1–3	14	36	18	6	1,362	67
4–9	14	50	26	16	2,658	68
10–19	9	76	24	30	5,355	42
20+	3	93	11	44	17,309	14
Totals	101	27	101	100	4,204	482

Sources: Hailes, comp., "Alabama Census Returns, 1820," 416–74. The source lists number of slaves, number of bales of cotton and average weight for county households. It is a flawed document: some items were recorded in the wrong column and production on many units remained unrecorded. I corrected errors and included only pages with two or more farms with cotton indicated (or pages with one farm if the next page had four farms). Adding the other farms would have reduced the proportion of growers in the 0 and 1-3 slave categories more than in the larger slave groups.
[a]Excludes one case of 25,850 pounds with a listed cotton gin.
[b]Includes only those units producing cotton.

households, but nearly all of them grew cotton and they produced three-quarters of the county's crop (table 12).[76]

Cotton production and the slave community grew together in the Southwest. Slave work was structured around the seasonal rhythms of cotton cultivation. On the larger units, where most cotton was grown, planters soon learned to divide slaves into gangs, keeping all their holdings together on the same unit, rather than establishing separate quarters as had tobacco planters. Once they had built their plantations, and migrating slaves were able to remake their families, kindred worked in the fields together, struggling with master or overseer over work rhythms; at night they went home to the slave quarter, where they lived among kindred.[77]

76. Abernethy, *Formative Period in Alabama*, 74; Royall, *Letters from Alabama*, 138–40, 246–47. For the persistence of this system, see G. Wright, *Political Economy Cotton South*, chaps. 2–3.
77. Descriptions of the process of learning and struggle involved with the expansion of cotton production are scarce, but one can find hints in Whartenby, "Land and

In contrast, slaves in frontier regions located too far from market to attract many slaveowners lived on small units. Few households madecotton in the Coosa River Valley counties of St. Clair and Shelby, Alabama, located west of Indian lands. Just one in four household heads owned slaves there in 1820, and only a tenth of all the slaves lived on units with as many as twenty slaves. Equally small units could be found in two Mississippi frontier counties in 1816. Similarly, few masters ventured to bring their slaves to the American colony in the Atacosita District of east Texas while it was under Mexican rule. Not only was the area isolated but Mexicans prohibited slavery. Unsurprisingly, the seventy-six slaves working there in 1826 lived scattered on thirteen plantations, the largest of which had just fifteen slaves.[78]

The great migration of African and African-American slaves to the Southwest coincided with a resurgence of evangelical Protestantism throughout the United States. Slaves, no matter where they were born, shared this religious fervor. By 1820 at least 70,000 slaves belonged to Baptist or Methodist churches, and thousands of others probably participated in revivals. African and Creole slaves together created an African-Christian faith from the West African ethos they shared. Visionary experiences, call-and-shout, and particular views of God and eternity could be found in African religions and in the culture of the most assimilated Chesapeake slaves.[79]

Slave migration was one of the most significant events in the history of black society in the United States. Nearly a third of a million slaves had moved southwestward by 1820, and more than another three-quarters of a million blacks were forced to migrate between 1820 and 1860. As slaves were taken from Africa to the cotton South and from the seaboard states to the interior, different combinations of ethnic backgrounds appeared in the Chesapeake and Kentucky, in coastal Carolina and Georgia, and in the Southwest. Any understanding of African-American societies and cultures should begin with an appreciation of these differential patterns of movement in time and space and an assessment of their impact on the lives of slaves.

Labor Productivity," chaps. 2–4; Fogel and Engerman, *Time on the Cross*, 1:203–6, 236–46; Gutman, *Power and Culture*, 309–18.

78. Table 11; Osburn, "Atacosita Census of 1826," 269–321; R. B. Campbell, *Empire for Slavery*, chap. 1.

79. The best accounts of Afro-Baptist religion can be found in Sobel, *Trabelin' On* (182–83 for black church membership), and *World They Made Together*, chaps. 14–15; Raboteau, *Slave Religion*; D. G. Mathews, *Religion in the Old South*, ch. 5; and Genovese, *Roll, Jordan, Roll*, 159–324.

The Legacy of Capitalism

CAPITALISM, THIS VOLUME has argued, began in the countryside, where the vast majority of Americans resided. But the coming of capitalism led to great conflict, between farmers who welcomed the higher standard of living and bourgeois culture it brought and those who rejected capitalism because it threatened to diminish the economic independence they valued. At times such conflicts over capitalism permeated rural society, involving farmers and yeomen, settlers and speculators, monopoly capitalists and small capitalist farmers.

These struggles lasted centuries, from eighteenth-century antitax crusades through the farm strikes of the 1930s.[1] The chronological boundaries that separate colonial from antebellum history or the antebellum era from the late nineteenth century make analysis of such long-term development difficult. To understand capitalist transformation, we should reach back into early modern England, Europe, and Africa and go forward to the twentieth century. If we fail to examine the entire modern era, we risk misidentifying periods of critical change or labeling as unique processes that occurred repeatedly.[2]

Colonization of American frontiers, the most significant of these repeated social processes, began with the conquest of Indian land. Once the Indians departed, colonists seized the best lands. Some relished participation in commodity markets; others had moved to escape such entanglement. Whatever their goals, white settlers squatted on the land in order to provide for family subsistence. To pay for the land, they made small surpluses to sell on local markets. Those who failed moved on, selling their improvements; few of those who stayed could avoid growing dependence upon the market, no matter what their initial goals. Within a generation, the area was fully populated, and land prices rose so high that poorer folk had to move on to yet newer frontiers. This cycle of conquest, colonization, improvement, and migration could be found in the colonies and was repeated on later frontiers

1. C. C. Taylor, *Farmer Movements*; Saloutos and Hicks, *Twentieth Century Populism*; Saloutos, *Farmer Movements in the South*.
2. Fischer, *Growing Old in America*, and P. M G. Harris, "Social Origins," 159–344, attempt such an analysis, though their frameworks are far different from the one suggested here.

stretching from early national Ohio and Kentucky to the last settlements on the Great Plains in the 1910s.[3]

Households responded innovatively to capitalist development, even when they were powerless to prevent it. The impetus for settlement provided by cotton and grain commodity markets notwithstanding, men sometimes moved to recreate noncapitalist social formations. Others saw the growth of markets as an opportunity to increase production. Middling farm women, horrified by frontier conditions, wanted to remake bourgeois homes, sustained by the individualist ideology capitalist development created, but their husbands sometimes objected, leading to familial tension over the division of labor on the farm.

Despite similarities in ideology and culture, the growth of rural capitalism varied markedly in North and South. Yeomen everywhere sought a competency, the ability to provide much of their family's subsistence. In the free-labor North, nineteenth-century yeomen struggled with speculators and small capitalist farmers, ultimately with little success, to maintain yeoman society. Growing numbers of rural wage laborers, sometimes sons of small landowners, could be found all through the antebellum rural North. But in the slave South planters kept capitalists at bay and yeomen faced fewer pressures to become commercial farmers as long as they acquiesced in the perpetuation of slavery and the rule of planters. Only after the Civil War destroyed slavery did a working class form in the South.

The American Revolution and the Civil War sustained capitalism. We have emphasized the American Revolution, arguing that the origins of yeoman and rural capitalist classes can be traced to the egalitarian impulses that conflict incited. The history of rural America in the nineteenth century would have been far different without it. The Civil War completed the bourgeois revolution begun by the Revolution. The abolition of slavery, accomplished by state decree and slave resistance, paved the way for the rapid growth of large-scale enterprise and wage labor. The spread of a working class, conscious of its place in the economic order, quickly ensued. As monopoly capitalism expanded, it gained some control over the state, which it used to challenge the working class and small producers. Thirty years of conflict between farmers and capitalists over the operation of railroads and the sale of farm commodities resulted, culminating in the Farmer's Alliance and the Populist party.[4]

The long history of rural capitalism has had a great impact upon

3. For a similar model, see Hudson, "Location Theory for Rural Settlement," 365–81, and Warren and O'Brien, "Model of Frontier Settlement," 22–27, esp. 22–28.

4. E. Foner, *Reconstruction*, chaps. 3–4, 8, 10–11; Painter, *Standing at Armageddon*, intro., chaps. 1–3.

twentieth-century America. Notwithstanding the nearly total disappearance of small producer farms, public opinion still supports efforts to "save the family farm" from corporate agriculture. The family farm developed as an ideological construct to distinguish small capitalist units from Communist collective farms and agribusinesses operated with wage labor. If agribusinesses produce nearly all of our food, a majority of American farms are still family-operated, and agriculture is the only major sector of the American economy still partially outside of multinational corporations.[5]

Myths surrounding the superiority of rural life have had great power in urbanizing America. Although only two-fifths of the American populace lived on farms in 1900, middle class rural migrants and even longtime city residents built suburbs to try to recapture rural superiority. Isolated from the urban working class, surrounded by a large yard and trees, the ideal nineteenth-century suburban home permitted the urban middle class to stay close to the city yet imagine they were in the more pure countryside. This positive rural imagery persisted long after the relative isolation of suburbs had ended. When large-scale migration to cities began, urban middle-class reformers were horrified. Seeking to keep farmers in the country, where they belonged, they organized a rural uplift movement to persuade farmers of the virtues of agriculture in an industrial age.[6]

But agriculture had been transformed. The spread of wage labor and farm mechanization threw nearly all rural Americans into dependence on a wage for subsistence or on a government subsidy to continue farming. Expensive machinery, state policy, and world market demands all forced farmers into increasingly specialized production. As market production increased, especially after World War II, household subsistence activities and production of milk, butter, and eggs by farm wives for local sale declined, and farm families were forced to buy their food in grocery stores. At the same time, many farms became unprofitable, and farm women and (to a lesser extent) farm men had to work for a wage to retain their farms.[7]

Conclusions about rural capitalist transformation drawn from this study suggest a number of questions for future research. Although further studies of rural gender and race relations are forthcoming, five other topics have received less attention: communities over long periods of time; the development of rural labor; the relationship between rural and urban areas; the im-

5. Comstock, ed., *Is There a Moral Obligation to Save the Family Farm?*; Volger, *Myth of the Family Farm*; Fink, "Constructing Rural Culture," 46–47; Danbom, "Romantic Agrarianism in Twentieth-Century America," 1–14.

6. Stilgoe, *Borderland*, parts 2–4; C. Clark, *American Home*, chap. 1, esp. 29–33; Donaldson, *Suburban Myth*, chap. 2; Bowers, *Country Life Movement*.

7. Fink, *Open Country Iowa*, esp. chaps. 6–7; Rosenfeld, *Farm Women*, chap. 6.

pact of state policy on rural communities and households; and the ways class languages were encased in rural social life.

Only examination of local communities or regions over centuries can capture the story of capitalist development. Historians have been unwilling to abandon traditional colonial, antebellum, and postbellum periods. Given the great volume of records, the predominance of such studies is hardly surprising. But careful choice of topics, families, or time periods for detailed analysis could overcome this overabundance of sources.[8] For example, study of New England towns from colonial occupation to the mid-nineteenth century would allow us to see how capitalism developed and country villages turned into cities in the first capitalist region. Analysis of midwestern or Great Plains communities from colonization through the 1950s could reveal not only the tensions surrounding capitalist development but the ways rural folk were integrated into urban society. And studies of southern counties from settlement through the 1960s can capture the entire cycle of race and class relations from the establishment of slavery and white yeoman farms through the destruction of legally imposed racial inferiority.

The relationship between countryside and city is an understudied theme in the history of rural capitalism. In noncapitalist economies like the antebellum South, cities — no matter how large — remained subservient to the countryside, serving the economic interests of rural people. But capitalism gradually changed this relationship. The "urbanization of the countryside" included not only rural-urban migration, the growth of urban labor markets, and the economic relation between city and countryside — topics that have received attention — but cultural and political conflicts between farmers and city folk and the spread of urban amenities and values to rural areas. Urban dominance over rural hinterlands grew gradually, becoming especially important with the growth of the railroad, telegraph, automobile, and radio, which directly linked rural people to cities. After this incorporation began, widespread rural-urban migration started. But if rural values came to resemble those of cities, differences persisted into the twentieth century. This array of issues, rarely examined as a whole, ought to be an integral part of regional and community studies.[9]

Through legislation, court decisions, and local execution of law, the state often implemented developmental uses of property. Despite numerous studies of land policy, internal improvements, taxation, development and

8. Warner, *Private City*, and McNall and McNall, *Plains Families*, show how this strategy might work.

9. Hints can be found in Cronon, *Nature's Metropolis*, chaps. 2–4; Gross, "Transcendentalism and Urbanism," 361–81; R. D. Brown, "Emergence Urban Society," 29–51; Stott, "Hinterland Development," 45–71; K. Jellison, "Rural Technological Change"; Larson, "Values and Beliefs," 91–112.

the common law, and the welfare state, the impact of the state on rural folk remains mostly unknown. Even studies of land policy, which examine how settlers acquired land and how many of them managed to retain it, usually fail to trace settlers much after the initial auction of lands. New studies that place state policies within class conflicts in particular communities or that emphasize specific events — railroad construction, woman's suffrage — could illuminate the impact of state policy.[10]

Examination of rural class languages, except in the Populist era, has just begun.[11] Class language provided a way for people to understand their place in society and structured their response to exploitation and state policy. To understand how language and social structure affected one another, one needs to place class languages in the context of the languages of men and women, whites and blacks, Yankees and immigrants. Gendered or racial languages may well have cut through classes, complicating class consciousness. Most studies of class language, including the one presented above, rely on debates in Congress or the states or on writings by wealthy representatives of rural classes. Examination of class language in a local setting can illuminate the relation among languages of class, gender, and race, permitting us to embed political texts in social action and to link individuals using class language to their place in society.

Despite major studies of the postbellum freed blacks and of twentieth-century migrant laborers, analysis of rural proletarianization has barely begun.[12] All too often historians have dismissed nineteenth-century white rural laborers as insignificant because they were mostly youths who could become landowners or because family members performed the nearly all farm work. Such arguments are short-sighted. We should study nineteenth- and twentieth-century agricultural workers as part of a rural proletariat that included industrial outworkers, canal and railroad construction workers, miners, lumbermen, domestics, and factory operatives. As the proportion of farmers declined, the importance of wage workers rose. Even if most *agricultural* laborers were young, only temporarily in wage work, and considered themselves farmers, as long as bosses expropriated part of their efforts as surplus value, they were proletarians.

These diverse topics are intricately linked. An examination of rural women on the Great Plains, for instance, could readily combine them. Such a community study could being with colonization and end with the 1920s or

10. By linking familial relations to state welfare policy in Boston, Gordon, *Heroes of Their Own Lives*, suggests what might be done.

11. B. Palmer, *"Man" over "Money"*; Pollack, *Just Polity*.

12. Ranson and Sutch, *One Kind of Freedom*; Jaynes, *Branches without Roots*; Daniel, *Bitter Harvest*; Majka and Majka, *Farm Workers, Agribusiness and the State*; G. Wright, "American Agriculture and the Labor Market," 182–210.

the 1950s. The relation between market and household and its impact on the gender division of labor on the farm and in the workplace might frame the study. Local implementation of state policy toward women; participation of farm women in the suffrage movement; the growth of wage labor among farm women; the impact of rural industry and migration to cities on women who remained; and the class, religious, or ethnic languages women used to understand their actions could be integrated into the analysis.

It is the final irony that capitalism both made agrarian America and was instrumental in its demise. Capitalists financed rural settlement and commodity markets structured farm decisions, yet farmers struggled for two centuries over capitalist penetration of rural society. Capitalism empowered farmers to buy land and machines, raising their standard of living, but yeomen lost their independence. Farm women gained some autonomy at home, yet enjoyed the debatable freedom of working for wages. Only resources generated by growth of the capitalist economy sustained the rapid colonization of Indian lands, but settlers often courted ecological disaster on fragile environments. The supposedly high wages agricultural workers commanded and the disdain farmers felt toward dependent wage laborers led them to buy farm machinery, and that machinery became so productive that fewer farmers and farm laborers were needed, farm populations plummeted, and rural communities disintegrated. Farmers, the noble majority of our rural mythology, have become a small occupational group, tied to the state and world market as much as any government employee.

Appendix
Bibliography
Index

Appendix: Explaining the Percentage of Slaves in the 1840 Population

USING "Historical, Demographic, Economic, and Social Data" from 1840 (Inter-University Consortium) and crop production data from the 1840 published census, and information on county formation, I ran a series of ordinary least squares regression equations. Percentage of slaves was the dependent variable; crop production and time of settlement were the independent variables. To capture the effects of the intensity of staple production (distinguishing, for instance, between a county with few cotton producers and one with many) I computed "labor productivity" variables, dividing crop production by number of workers. Number of workers was estimated from demographic data in the census, counting men as full hands, slave women as three-quarter hands, and working age children as half hands.

The independent variables included productivity measures. These were used instead of crop dummies to capture the impact of major differences in per worker production. These variables are defined as follows: Cotton = pounds of cotton per agricultural worker/200; Rice = pounds of rice per agricultural worker/100; Sugar Cane = pounds of sugar per agricultural worker/100; Colonial Tobacco = pounds of tobacco per agricultural worker/200 for counties established before 1780; 19th Cent Tobacco = pounds of tobacco per agricultural worker/200 for counties established after 1779; Former Tobacco = dummy for old tobacco counties no longer growing tobacco; Wheat = bushels of wheat per agricultural worker/20; Farming = dummy for counties that never grew tobacco, cotton, rice, or sugar; Year = Years since county formation; Frontier = Dummy for county formed 1827–40; Settled = Dummy for county formed by 1760.

Multiple regressions explaining the percentage of slaves in 1840[a]

	Regression coefficients & T-tests (in parentheses)			
	(1)[b]	(2)[b]	(3)[c]	(4)[c]
Constant	23.39	25.75	24.55	31.968
	(2795.4)*	(2081.0)*	(27.5)*	(29.8)*
Cotton	3.014	3.007	3.260	2.177
	(1491.1)*	(14361.5)*	(17.7)*	(11.2)*
Rice	4.386	4.599	2.947	2.089
	(869.5)*	(911.8)*	(5.6)*	(4.3)*

Multiple regressions (continued)

	Regression coefficients & T-tests (in parentheses)			
	(1)[b]	(2)[b]	(3)[c]	(4)[c]
	.593	.594	.690	.542
Sugar cane	(300.0)*	(298.9)*	(4.6)*	(3.9)*
Colonial	4.863	5.070	4.083	1.851
tobacco	(881.3)*	(917.2)*	(6.9)*	(3.3)**
19th Cent	.312	.355	—[c]	−1.879
tobacco	(51.0)*	(58.062)*		(−3.5)*
Former	8.593	8.575	7.742	−4.955
tobacco	(285.5)*	(275.2)*	(2.6)**	(−1.76)
Wheat	−3.885	−3.720	−3.161	—
	(−747.8)*	(−716.1)*	(−5.9)*	
Farming	—	—	—	−16.752
				(−13.2)*
Year	—	.0554	—	—
		(397.3)*		
Settled	6.373	—	14.233	15.701
	(409.776)*		(8.2)*	(9.8)*
Frontier	−5.568	—	−6.463	−4.413
	(−283.5)*		(−4.4)*	(−3.3)**
F	600538*	645819*	81.7*	101.2*
R²	.435	.424	.482	.559

[a]* = probability of T or F is less than .0000; ** = probability less than .01.
[b] Weighted by total county population.
[c] Unweighted; each county is one observation; 19th tobacco was statistically insignificant in this equation 3.

Bibliography

Abbreviations

AgH	*Agricultural History*
AHR	*American Historical Review*
AQ	*American Quarterly*
JAH	*Journal of American History*
JEH	*Journal of Economic History*
JFamH	*Journal of Family History*
JIH	*Journal of Interdisciplinary History*
JEarR	*Journal of the Early Republic*
RHR	*Radical History Review*
SSH	*Social Science History*
VMHB	*Virginia Magazine of History and Biography*
WMQ	*William and Mary Quarterly*, 3d ser.

Abbott, Richard H. "The Agricultural Press View the Yeoman: 1819–1859." *AgH* 42 (1968): 35–48.

Abernethy, Thomas Perkins. *The Formative Period in Alabama, 1815–1828*. University, Ala., 1965.

Adams, Donald R., Jr. "The Bank of Stephen Girard, 1812–1831." *JEH* 32 (1972): 841–68.

Adams, John W., and Alice Bee Kasakoff. "The Exodus from Agriculture in the American North: The Generational Ladder, 1650–1850." Paper presented at the 1986 annual meeting of the Social Science History Association, St. Louis.

——. "Migration and the Family in Colonial New England: The View from Genealogies." *JFamH* 9 (1984): 24–43.

——. "Migration at Marriage in Colonial New England: A Comparison of Rates Derived from Genealogies with Rates from Vital Records." Pp. 115–38 in Bennett Dyke and Warren T. Morrill, eds., *Genealogical Demography*. New York, 1980.

——. "Wealth and Migration in Massachusetts and Maine: 1771–1798." *JEH* 45 (1985): 363–68.

Agnew, Jean Christophe. "The Threshold of Exchange: Speculations upon the Market." *RHR*, no. 21 (1979): 99–118.

Akenson, Donald H. "Why the Accepted Estimates of the Ethnicity of the American People, 1790, Are Unacceptable." *WMQ* 41 (1984): 102–18, 125–29.

Albert, Peter J. "The Protean Institution: The Geography, Economy, and Ideology of Slavery in Post-Revolutionary Virginia." Ph.D. diss., Maryland, 1976.

Alchian, Armen, and Harold Demetz. "The Property Rights Paradigm." *JEH* 33 (1973): 16–27.

Alexander, Arthur J. "Desertion and Its Punishment in Revolutionary Virginia." *WMQ* 3 (1946): 383–97.

——. "Exemption from Military Service in the Old Dominion during the War of the Revolution." *VMHB* 53 (1945): 163–71.

——. "A Footnote on Deserters from the Virginia Forces during the American Revolution." *VMHB* 55 (1947): 137–46.

Alford, Terry. *Prince among Slaves.* New York, 1977.

Allen, David Grayson. *In English Ways: The Movement of Societies and the Transferal of English Local Law and Customs to Massachusetts Bay in the Seventeenth Century.* Chapel Hill, N.C., 1981.

——. "The Matrix of Motivation." *New England Quarterly* 59 (1986): 408–18.

Altman, Ida. "Emigrants and Society: An Approach to the Background of Colonial Spanish America." *Comparative Studies in Society and History* 30 (1988): 170–90.

American Husbandry. Harry J. Carman, ed. New York, 1939.

Anderson, Fred. *A People's Army: Massachusetts Soldiers and Society in the Seven Years' War.* Chapel Hill, N.C., 1984.

Anderson, Perry. *Arguments within English Marxism.* London, 1980.

Anderson, Virginia DeJohn. "Migrants and Motives: Religion and the Settlement of New England, 1630–1640." *New England Quarterly* 58 (1985): 339–83.

——. "Migration, Kinship, and the Integration of Colonial New England Society: Three Generations of the Danforth Family." Pp. 269–90 in Robert M. Taylor, Jr., ed., *Generations and Change: Genealogical Perspectives in Social History.* Macon, Ga., 1986.

——. *New England's Generation: The Great Migration and the Formation of Society and Culture in the Seventeenth Century.* Cambridge, 1991.

——. "Religion, the Common Thread." *New England Quarterly* 59 (1986): 418–24.

Anstey, Roger. *The Atlantic Slave Trade and British Abolition, 1760–1810.* London, 1975.

Appleby, Joyce. "The American Heritage: The Heirs and the Disinherited." *JAH* 74 (1987): 798–813.

——. *Capitalism and a New Social Order: The Republican Vision of the 1790s.* New York, 1984.

——. "Commercial Farming and the 'Agrarian Myth' in the Early Republic." *JAH* 68 (1981–82): 833–49.

——. *Economic Thought and Ideology in Seventeenth-Century England.* Princeton, 1978.

——. "The Radical *Double-Entendre* in the Right to Self-Government." Pp. 275–83 in Jacob and Jacob, eds., *Origins of Anglo-American Radicalism.*

——. "Republicanism in Old and New Contexts." *WMQ* 43 (1986): 20–34.

Applewhite, Harriet B., and Darline G. Levy, eds. *Women and Politics in the Age of the Democratic Revolution.* Ann Arbor, Mich., 1990.

Aptheker, Herbert. *American Negro Slave Revolts.* 2d ed. New York, 1969.

——. *The American Revolution, 1763–1783.* New York, 1960.

——, ed. *A Documentary History of the Negro People in the United States.* Vol. 1, *From Colonial Times through the Civil War.* New York, 1951.

Archer, Richard. "New England Mosaic: A Demographic Analysis for the Seventeenth Century." *WMQ* 47 (1990): 477–502.

Argersinger, Peter H., and Jo Ann E. Argersinger. "The Machine Breakers: Farm Workers and Social Change in the Rural Midwest of the 1870s." *AgH* 58 (1984): 393–410.

Arieli, Yehoshua. *Individualism and Nationalism in American Ideology.* Baltimore, 1964.

Arrington, Leonard J., Feramorz Y. Fox, and Dean L. May. *Building the City of God: Community and Cooperation among the Mormons.* Salt Lake City, 1976.

Ashworth, John. *"Agrarians" and "Aristocrats": Party Political Ideology in the United States, 1837–1846.* London, 1983.

——. "The Relationship between Capitalism and Humanitarianism." *AHR* 92 (1987): 813–28.

Aston, T. H., and C. H. E. Philpin, eds. *The Brenner Debate: Agrarian Class Structure and Economic Development in Pre-Industrial Europe.* Cambridge, 1985.

Atack, Jeremy. "The Agricultural Ladder Revisited: A New Look at an Old Question with Some Data for 1860." *AgH* 63 (Winter 1989): 1–25.

——. "Tenants and Yeomen in the Nineteenth Century." *AgH* 62 (Summer 1988): 6–32.

Atack, Jeremy, and Fred Bateman. *To Their Own Soil: Agriculture in the Antebellum North.* Ames, Iowa, 1987.

——. "Yankee Farming and Settlement in the Old Northwest: A Comparative Analysis." Pp. 77–102 in Klingaman and Veddar, *Essays on Economy of Old Northwest.*

Atherton, Lewis E. *The Frontier Merchant in Mid-America.* Columbia, Mo., 1971.

Atkins, Annette. *Harvest of Grief: Grasshopper Plagues and Public Assistance in Minnesota, 1873–1878.* St. Paul, 1984.

Austin, Mary. *Early Horizon.* Boston, 1932.

Axtell, James. *The European and the Indian: Essays in the Ethnohistory of Colonial North America.* New York, 1981.

——. "The White Indians of Colonial America." *WMQ* 32 (1975): 55–88.

Baatz, Simon. *"Venerate the Plough": A History of the Philadelphia Society for Promoting Agriculture, 1785–1985.* Philadelphia, 1985.

Bailey, James E. *Popular Influence upon Public Policy: Petitioning in Eighteenth-Century Virginia.* Westport, Conn., 1979.

Bailyn, Bernard. *The Peopling of British North America: An Introduction.* New York, 1986.

——. *Voyagers to the West: A Passage in the Peopling of America on the Eve of the Revolution.* New York, 1986.

Bakhtin, Mikhail M. *The Dialogic Imagination: Four Essays.* Michael Holquist, ed. Austin, Tex., 1981.

Ball, Charles. *Fifty Years in Chains.* Philip S. Foner, ed. New York, 1970.

Bancroft, Frederick. *Slave Trading in the Old South.* Baltimore, 1931.

Banning, Lance. "Jeffersonian Ideology Revisited: Liberal and Classical Ideas in the New American Republic." *WMQ* 43 (1986): 3–19.

Barnes, Gilbert Hobbs. *The Antislavery Impulse, 1830–1844.* William G. McLoughlin, ed. 1933. Reprint. New York, 1964.

Barnhart, John D. "Southern Contributions to the Social Order of the Old Northwest." *North Carolina Historical Review* 17 (1940): 237–48.

Barrett, James R. "Immigration and Working Class Formation in the United States, 1880–1930." Paper presented to the Newberry Library Fellows' Seminar, November, 1990.

Barron, Hal S. *Those Who Stayed Behind: Rural Society in Nineteenth-Century New England*. Cambridge, 1984.

Bash, Wendell H. "Differential Fertility in Madison County, New York, 1865." *Milbank Memorial Fund Quarterly* 33 (1955): 161–86.

Basler, Roy P., Marion Dolores Pratt, and Lloyd A. Dunlap, eds. *The Collected Works of Abraham Lincoln*. 8 vols. New Brunswick, N.J., 1953–55.

Bateman, Fred, and Thomas Weiss. *A Deplorable Scarcity: The Failure of Industrialization in the Slave Economy*. Chapel Hill, N.C., 1981.

Bean, Lee L., Geraldine P. Mineau, and Douglas L. Anderton. *Fertility Change on the American Frontier: Adaptation and Innovation*. Berkeley, Calif., 1990.

Beard, Charles. *An Economic Interpretation of the Constitution of the United States*. New York, 1913.

——. *Economic Origins of Jeffersonian Democracy*. New York, 1949.

Beard, Charles, and Mary R. Beard. *The Rise of American Civilization*. 2 vols. New York, 1930.

Becker, Laura L. "Diversity and Its Significance in an Eighteenth-Century Pennsylvania Town." Pp. 196–221 in Michael Zuckerman, ed., *Friends and Neighbors: Group Life in America's First Plural Society*. Philadelphia, 1982.

Beeman, Richard R. *The Evolution of the Southern Backcountry: A Case Study of Lunenburg County, Virginia, 1746–1832*. Philadelphia, 1984.

Beeman, Richard R., Stephen Botein, and Edward C. Carter II, eds. *Beyond Confederation: Origins of the Constitution and American National Identity*. Chapel Hill, N.C., 1987.

Beeton, Beverly, and G. Thomas Edwards. "Susan B. Anthony's Woman Suffrage Crusade in the American West." *Journal of the West* 21 (April 1982): 5–15.

Beier, A. L. *Masterless Men: The Vagrancy Problem in England, 1560–1640*. London, 1985.

——. "Poverty and Progress in Early Modern England." Pp. 201–39 in Beier, David Cannadine, and James M. Rosenheim, eds., *The First Modern Society: Essays in English History in Honour of Lawrence Stone*. Cambridge, 1989.

Bell, Landon C., ed. *Sunlight on the Southside: Lists of Tithes, Lunenburg County, Virginia, 1748–1783*. Philadelphia, 1931.

Bellingham, Bruce. "Waifs and Strays: Child Abandonment, Foster Care, and Families in Mid-Nineteenth-Century New York." Pp. 123–60 in Peter Mandler, ed., *The Uses of Charity: The Poor on Relief in the Nineteenth-Century Metropolis*. Philadelphia, 1990.

Belsey, Catherine. *Critical Practice*. London, 1980.

Berkhoffer, Robert, Jr. "The Northwest Ordinance and the Principle of Territorial Evolution." Pp. 45–55 in John Porter Bloom, ed., *The American Territorial System*. Athens, Ohio, 1973.

Berlin, Ira. *Slaves without Masters: The Free Negro in the Antebellum South*. New York, 1974.

——. "Time, Space, and the Evolution of Afro-American Society in British Mainland North America." *AHR* 85 (1989): 44–78.

Berlin, Ira, and Herbert G. Gutman. "Natives and Immigrants, Free Men and Slaves:

Urban Workingmen in the Antebellum American South." *AHR* 88 (1983): 1175–1200.

Berlin, Ira, and Ronald Hoffman, eds. *Slavery and Freedom in the Age of the American Revolution.* Charlottesville, Va., 1983.

Bernstein, Michael A., and Sean Wilentz. "Marketing, Commerce, and Capitalism in Rural Massachusetts." *JEH* 44 (1984): 171–73.

Berthoff, Rowland. "Conventional Mentality: Free Blacks, Women, and Business Corporations as Unequal Persons, 1820–1870." *JAH* 76 (1989): 753–84.

——. "Independence and Attachment, Virtue and Interest: From Republican Citizen to Free Enterpriser, 1787–1837." Pp. 99–124 in Richard L. Bushman et al., eds., *Uprooted Americans: Essays to Honor Oscar Handlin.* Boston, 1979.

Berthoff, Rowland, and John M. Murrin. "Feudalism, Communalism, and the Yeoman Freeholder: The American Revolution Considered as a Social Accident." Pp. 256–88 in Stephen G. Kurtz and James H. Hudson, eds., *Essays on the American Revolution.* Chapel Hill, N.C. 1973.

Berwanger, Eugene H. *The Frontier against Slavery: Western Anti-Negro Prejudice and the Slavery Extension Controversy.* Urbana, Ill., 1967.

Beveridge, Andrew A. "Local Lending Practice: Borrowers in a Small Northeastern City, 1832–1915." *JEH* 45 (1985): 393–403.

Bieder, Robert E. "Kinship as a Factor in Migration." *Journal of Marriage and the Family* 35 (1973): 429–39.

Billings, Dwight B., and Kathleen M. Blee. "Family Strategies in a Subsistence Economy: Beech Creek, Kentucky, 1850–1942." *Sociological Perspectives* 33 (1990): 63–88.

Billington, Ray Allen. *The Protestant Crusade, 1800–1860: A Study of the Origins of American Nativism.* New York, 1938.

Blair, Ruth, comp. *Some Early Tax Digests of Georgia.* Atlanta, 1926.

Blassingame, John, ed. *Slave Testimony: Two Centuries of Letters, Speeches, Interviews and Autobiographies.* Baton Rouge, 1977.

Bliss, Willard F. "The Rise of Tenancy in Virginia." *VMHB* 108 (1950): 427–41.

Bloch, Ruth H. "American Feminine Ideals in Transition: The Rise of the Moral Mother, 1785–1815." *Feminist Studies* 4 (June 1978): 101–26.

——. "Battling Infidelity, Heathenism, and Licentiousness: New England Missions and the Post-Revolutionary Frontier, 1792–1805." Pp. 39–60 in Frederick D. Williams, ed., *The Northwest Ordinance: Essays on Its Formulation, Provisions, and Legacy.* East Lansing, Mich., 1989.

——. "The Gendered Meanings of Virtue in Revolutionary America." *Signs* 13 (1987): 37–57.

Blumin, Stuart M. *The Emergence of the Middle Class: Social Experience in the American City, 1760–1900.* Cambridge, 1989.

Bode, Frederick A., and Donald E. Ginter. *Farm Tenancy and the Census in Antebellum Georgia.* Athens, Ga., 1986.

Bogin, Ruth. "Petitioning and the New Moral Economy of Post-Revolutionary America." *WMQ* 45 (1988): 391–425.

Bogue, Allan G. "Farm Tenants in the Nineteenth-Century Middle West." Pp. 103–19 in Peterson, ed., *Farmers, Bureaucrats, and Middlemen.*

——. *From Prairie to Cornbelt: Farming on the Illinois and Iowa Prairies in the Nineteenth Century*. Chicago, 1963.

——. "The Iowa Claims Clubs: Symbol and Substance." *Mississippi Valley Historical Review* 45 (1958): 231–53.

Bohmer, David. "The Causes of Electoral Alignments: Some Considerations on How Electoral Behavior Is Shaped." Pp. 251–76 in Aubrey C. Land, Lois Green Carr, and Edward C. Papenfuse, eds., *Law, Society, and Politics in Early Maryland*. Baltimore, 1977.

Bois, Guy. "Against the Neo-Malthusian Orthodoxy." Pp. 107–18 in Aston and Philpin, eds., *The Brenner Debate*.

Boleda, Mario. "Les Migrations au Canada sous le régime français (1607–1760)." *Cahiers Quebecois de demographie* 13 (1984): 23–28.

Bolton, S. Charles. "Economic Inequality in the Arkansas Territory." *JIH* 14 (1984): 619- 34.

——. "Inequality on the Southern Frontier: Arkansas County in the Arkansas Territory." *Arkansas Historical Quarterly* 41 (1982): 50–66.

Borah, Woodrow. "The Mixing of Population." Pp. 707–22 in Chiappelli, ed., *First Images of America*.

Bosworth, Timothy Woody. "Those Who Moved: Internal Migrants in America before 1840. Ph.D. diss., Wisconsin, 1980.

Bottomore, Tom, et al., eds. *A Dictionary of Marxist Thought*. Cambridge, Mass., 1983.

Bottorff, William K., ed. *The Miscellaneous Works of David Humphreys*. 1804. Gainesville, Fla., 1968.

Bowen, William A. *The Willamette Valley: Migration and Settlement of the Oregon Frontier*. Seattle, 1978.

Bowers, William L. *The Country Life Movement in America, 1900–1920*. Port Washington, N.Y., 1974.

——. "Crawford Township, 1850–1870: A Population Study of a Pioneer Community." *Iowa Journal of History* 58 (1960): 1–30.

Boyd, Julian K., Charles T. Cullen, and John Catanzariti, eds. *The Papers of Thomas Jefferson*. 24 vols. Princeton, 1950-.

Boyd-Bowman, Peter. "Patterns of Spanish Emigration to the Indies until 1600." *Hispanic American Historical Review* 56 (1976): 580–604.

Boyer, Paul, and Stephen Nissenbaum. *Salem Possessed: The Social Order of Witchcraft*. Cambridge, Mass., 1974.

Boylan, Anne M. "Evangelical Womanhood in the Nineteenth Century: The Role of Women in Sunday Schools." *Feminist Studies* 4 (October 1978): 62–80.

Brady, Dorothy S. "Consumption and Style of Life." Pp. 61–89 in Lance E. Davis, Richard A. Easterlin, and William N. Parker, eds., *American Economic Growth: An Economist's History of the United States*. New York, 1972.

Brady, Patrick S. "The Slave Trade and Sectionalism in South Carolina, 1787–1808." *Journal of Southern History* 38 (1972): 601–20.

Brandon, Nellie Wailes, and W. M. Drake, eds. *Memoir of Leonard Covington, by B. L. C. Wailes also Some of General Covington's Letters*. Natchez, Miss., 1928.

Brann, Henry Walter. "Max Weber and the United States." *Southwestern Social Science Quarterly* 25 (1944): 18–30.

Branson, Susan. "Politics and Gender: The Political Consciousness of Philadelphia Women, 1790–1815." Ph.D. diss., Northern Illinois, 1992.

Brenner, Robert. "Agrarian Class Structure and Economic Development in Pre-Industrial Europe." Pp. 10–63 in Aston and Philpin, eds., *The Brenner Debate*.

——. "The Social Basis of Economic Development." Pp. 23–53 in Roemer, ed., *Analytical Marxism*.

Briggs, Peter M. "Timothy Dwight 'Composes' a Landscape for New England." *AQ* 40 (1988): 359–77.

Brooke, John L. *The Heart of the Commonwealth: Society and Political Culture in Worcester County, Massachusetts, 1713–1861*. Cambridge, 1989.

——. "To the Quiet of the People: Revolutionary Settlements and Civil Unrest in Western Massachusetts." *WMQ* 46 (1989): 425–62.

Brown, Richard D. "The Emergence of Urban Society in Rural Massachusetts, 1760–1820." *JAH* 61 (1974): 29–51.

——. *Revolutionary Politics in Massachusetts: The Boston Committees of Correspondence and the Towns, 1772–1774*. Cambridge, Mass., 1970.

Brown, Richard Maxwell. "Back Country Rebellions and the Homestead Ethic in America, 1740–1799." Pp. 73–99 in Brown and Don E. Fehrenbacher, eds., *Tradition, Conflict, and Modernization: Perspectives on the American Revolution*. New York, 1977.

——. *The South Carolina Regulators: The Story of the First American Vigilante Movement*. Cambridge, Mass., 1963.

Brown, Robert E. *Middle Class Democracy and the Revolution in Massachusetts, 1691–1780*. New York, 1955.

Brown, Wallace. "The American Farmer during the Revolution: Rebel or Loyalist?" *AgH* 42 (1968): 327–38.

Brownson, Howard Gray. *History of the Illinois Central Railroad to 1870*. Urbana, Ill., 1915.

Bruchey, Stuart, ed. *Cotton and the Growth of the American Economy, 1790–1860: Sources and Readings*. New York, 1967.

——. *The Roots of American Economic Growth: An Essay in Social Causation*. New York, 1965.

Brumbaugh, Gaius, ed. *Maryland Records, Colonial, Revolutionary, County, and Church from Original Sources*. 2 vols. Baltimore, 1915.

Buck, Solon Justus. *The Granger Movement: A Study of Agricultural Organization and Its Political, Economic, and Social Manifestations, 1870–1880*. Cambridge, Mass., 1913.

Buckley, Thomas E. *Church and State in Revolutionary Virginia*. Charlottesville, Va., 1977.

Buell, Lawrence. "American Pastoral Ideology Reappraised." *American Literary History* 1 (1989): 1–29.

Buley, R. Carlyle. *The Old Northwest: Pioneer Period, 1815–1840*. 2 vols. Bloomington, Ind., 1950.

Burke, Martin Joseph. "The Conundrum of Class: Public Discourse on the Social Order in America." Ph.D. diss., Michigan, 1987.

Burke, Peter. Introduction. Pp. 1–20 in Burke and Roy Porter, eds., *The Social History of Language*. Cambridge, 1987.

Burns, Rex. *Success in America: The Yeoman Dream in the Industrial Revolution.* Amherst, Mass., 1976.

Burns, Sarah. *Pastoral Inventions: Rural Life in Nineteenth-Century American Art and Culture.* Philadelphia, 1989.

Burton, Orville Vernon. *In My Father's House Are Many Mansions: Family and Community in Edgefield, South Carolina.* Chapel Hill, N.C., 1985.

Bushman, Claudia. "The Wilson Family in Delaware and Indiana." *Delaware History* 20 (1982): 27–49.

Bushman, Richard L. "Family Security from Farm to City, 1750–1850." *JFamH* 6 (1981): 238–56.

——. *King and People in Provincial Massachusetts.* Chapel Hill, N.C., 1985.

——. "Massachusetts Farmers and the Revolution." Pp. 77–124 in R. M. Jellison, ed., *Society, Freedom, and Conscience.*

——. "Opening the American Countryside." Pp. 239–56 in Henretta, Kammen, and Katz, eds., *Transformation of Early American History.*

Butterfield, L. H., Marc Friedelaender, and Mary-Jo Klein, eds. *The Book of Abigail and John: Selected Letters of the Adams Family, 1762–1784.* Cambridge, Mass., 1975.

Calderhead, William. "The Role of the Professional Slave Trader in a Slave Economy: Austin Woolfolk, a Case Study." *Civil War History* 23 (1977): 195–211.

Calhoon, Robert M. "Religion and Individualism in Early America." Pp. 44–65 in Curry and Goodheart, eds., *American Chameleon.*

Campbell, Mildred. *The English Yeoman under Elizabeth and the Early Stuarts.* New Haven, 1942.

——. "Rebuttal [to David Galenson]." *WMQ* 35 (1978): 526–40.

——. "Reply [to David Galenson]." *WMQ* 36 (1979): 277–86.

——. "The Social Origins of Some Early Americans." Pp. 63–89 in James Morton Smith, ed., *Seventeenth-Century America: Essays in Colonial History.* New York, 1959.

Campbell, Randolph B. *An Empire for Slavery: The Peculiar Institution in Texas, 1821–1865.* Baton Rouge, 1989.

Campbell, T. E. *Colonial Caroline: A History of Caroline County, Virginia.* Richmond, 1954.

Cannon, Brian Q. "Immigrants in American Agriculture." *AH* 65 (Winter 1991): 17–35.

Capers, Charlotte. "Census of Jefferson County, Mississippi Territority, 1810." *Journal of Mississippi History* 15 (1953): 33–46.

Cardinal, Eric J. "Antislavery Sentiment and Political Transformation in the 1850s: Portage County, Ohio." *Old Northwest* 1 (1975): 225–38.

Carey, Matthew. *Essays on Political Economy; Or the Most Certain Means of Promoting the Wealth, Power, Resources, and Happiness of a Nation. . . .* Philadelphia, 1822.

Carp, E. Wayne. "Early American Military History: A Review of Recent Work." *VMHB* 94 (1986): 259–84.

Carp, Roger E. "The Limits of Reform: Labor and Discipline on the Erie Canal." *JEarR* 10 (1990): 191–220.

Carpenter, Thomas, stenographer. *The Two Trials of John Fries on an Indictment of Trea-*

son; *Together with a Brief Report of the Trials of Several Other Persons, for Treason and Insurrection*. Philadelphia, 1800.

Carr, Kay J. "Group Land Acquisition in an Individual Land System." Paper presented at the 1986 annual meeting of the Social Science History Association, St. Louis.

Carr, Lois Green, and Russell R. Menard. "Immigration and Opportunity: The Freedman in Early Colonial Maryland." Pp. 206–42 in Tate and Ammerman, eds., *Chesapeake in the Seventeenth Century*.

Carr, Lois Green, and Lorena S. Walsh. "Economic Diversification and Labor Organization in the Chesapeake, 1650–1820." Pp. 144–88 in Innes, ed., *Work and Labor in Early America*.

Carr, Lois Green, Philip D. Morgan, and Jean B. Russo, eds. *Colonial Chesapeake Society*. Chapel Hill, N.C., 1988.

Carroll, Edward V., and Sonya Salamon. "Share and Share Alike: Inheritance Patterns in Two Illinois Farm Communities." *JFamH* 2 (1988): 219–32.

Cartwright, Peter. *The Autobiography of Peter Cartwright*. Charles L. Wallis, ed. New York, 1956.

Cashin, Joan E. *A Family Venture: Men and Women on the Southern Frontier*. New York, 1991.

Cayton, Andrew R. L., and Peter S. Onuf. *The Midwest and the Nation: Rethinking the History of an American Region*. Bloomington, Ind., 1990.

Chalouo, George C. "Women in the American Revolution: Vignettes or Profiles." Pp. 73–90 in Deutrich and Purdy, eds., *Clio Was a Woman*.

Chan, Sucheng. *This Bitter-Sweet Soil: The Chinese in California Agriculture, 1860–1910*. Berkeley, Calif., 1986.

Chaplin, Joyce E. "Creating a Cotton South in Georgia and South Carolina, 1760–1815." *Journal of Southern History* 57 (1991): 171–200.

Charlesworth, Andrew, ed. *An Atlas of Rural Protest in Britain, 1548–1908*. Philadelphia, 1983.

Chase, Philander D. "'Years of Hardship and Revelations': The Convention Army at the Albemarle Barracks, 1779–1781." *Magazine of the Albemarle County Historical Society* 61 (1983): 9–53.Chesterfield Supplement. Virginia State Library, Richmond.

Chesterfield Supplement, Virginia State Library, Richmond.

Chiappelli, Fredi, ed. *First Images of America: The Impact of the New World on the Old*. 2 vols. Berkeley, Calif., 1976.

Church, Randolph W., comp. *Virginia Legislative Petitions: Bibliography, Calendar, and Abstracts from Original Sources 6 May 1776–21 June 1782* Richmond, 1984.

Chused, Richard H. "Married Women's Property Law: 1800–1850." *Georgetown Law Journal* 71 (1983): 1359–1425.

Clark, Alice. *Working Life of Women in the Seventeenth Century*. 1919. Reprint with intro. by Miranda Chaytor and Jane Lewis. London, 1982.

Clark, Christopher. "The Household Economy, Market Exchange, and the Rise of Capitalism in the Connecticut Valley, 1800–1860." *Journal of Social History* 13 (1979): 169–89.

——. "Household, Market and Capital: The Process of Economic Change in the Connecticut Valley of Massachusetts, 1800–1860." Ph.D. diss., Harvard, 1982.

——. "The Household Mode of Production—a Comment." *RHR*, no. 18 (1978): 166–71.

——. *The Roots of Rural Capitalism: Western Massachusetts, 1780–1860.* Ithaca, N.Y., 1990.

Clark, Clifford. *The American Home, 1800–1960.* Chapel Hill, N.C., 1986.

Clark, Peter, and David Souden. Introduction. Pp. 11–48 in Clark and Souden, eds., *Migration and Society*.

——, eds. *Migration and Society in Early Modern England.* Totowa, N.J., 1987.

Clemens, Paul G. E., and Lucy Simler. "Rural Labor and the Farm Household in Chester County, Pennsylvania, 1750–1820." Pp. 106–43 in Innes, ed., *Work and Labor in Early America.*

Clement, Maud Carter. *The History of Pittsylvania County, Virginia.* Lynchburg, Va., 1929.

Cmiel, Kenneth. *Democratic Eloquence: The Fight over Popular Speech in Nineteenth-Century America.* New York, 1990.

Coats, A. W. "American Scholarship Comes of Age: The Louisiana Purchase Exposition 1904." *Journal of the History of Ideas* 22 (1961): 404–17.

Cochran, Thomas C. "The Business Revolution." *AHR* 79 (1974): 1449–66.

——. *Frontiers of Change: Early Industrialism in America.* New York, 1981.

Cody, Cheryll Ann. "Naming, Kinship, and Estate Dispersal: Notes on Slave Family Life on a South Carolina Plantation, 1786 to 1833." *WMQ* 39 (1982): 192–211.

——. "There Was No 'Absalom' on the Ball Plantations: Slave Naming Practices in the South Carolina Low Country, 1720–1865." *AHR* 92 (1987): 563–96.

Cogswell, Seddie, Jr. *Tenure, Nativity, and Age as Factors in Iowa Agriculture, 1850–1880.* Ames, Iowa, 1975.

Cohen, G. A. *Karl Marx's Theory of History: A Defence.* Princeton, 1978.

Cohen, Lester H. "Mercy Otis Warren: The Politics of Langauge and the Aesthetics of Self." *AQ* 35 (1983): 481–98.

Cohen, Marjorie Griffin. *Women's Work, Markets, and Economic Development in Nineteenth-Century Ontario.* Toronto, 1988.

Cole, Thomas R. "Family, Settlement, and Migration in Southeastern Massachusetts, 1650–1805: The Case for Regional Analysis." *New England Historical and Genealogical Register* 132 (1978): 171–85.

Coleman, J. Winston, Jr. *Slavery Times in Kentucky.* Chapel Hill, N.C., 1940.

Cometti, Elizabeth. "Depredations in Virginia during the Revolution." Pp. 135–51 in Darrett B. Rutman, ed., *The Old Dominion: Essays for Thomas Perkins Abernethy.* Charlottesville, Va., 1964.

Comstock, Gary, ed. *Is There a Moral Obligation to Save the Family Farm?* Ames, Iowa, 1987.

Congressional Globe. 24th Congress, 2d session; 25th Congress, 2d session.

Conkin, Paul K. *Prophets of Prosperity: America's First Political Economists.* Bloomington, Ind., 1980.

Conzen, Kathleen Neils. *Immigrant Milwaukee, 1836–1860: Accommodation and Community in a Frontier City.* Cambridge, Mass., 1976.

——. "Immigrants in Ninteenth-Century Agricultural History." Pp. 303–42 in Lou Ferleger, ed., *Agriculture and National Development: Views on the Nineteenth Century.* Ames, Iowa, 1990.

——. "Mainstreams and Side Channels: The Localization of Immigrant Cultures." *Journal of American Ethnic History* 11 (1991): 5–20.

——. "Making Their Own America: Assimilation Theory and the German Peasant Pioneer." German Historical Institute Annual Lecture Series, no. 3. New York, 1990.

——. "Peasant Pioneers: Generational Succession among German Farmers in Frontier Minnesota." Pp. 259–92 in Hahn and Prude, eds., *The Countryside in the Age of Capitalist Transformation.*

Conzen, Michael P. *Frontier Farming in an Urban Shadow: The Influence of Madison's Proximity on the Agricultural Development of Blooming Grove, Wisconsin.* Madison, Wis., 1971.

——. "Local Migration Systems in Nineteenth-Century Iowa." *Geographical Review* 64 (1974): 339–61.

Conzen, Michael P., and Melissa J. Morales, eds. *Settling the Upper Illinois Valley: Patterns of Change in the I & M Canal Corridor, 1830–1900.* Chicago, 1989.

Cook, Edward M., Jr. *Fathers of the Towns: Leadership and Community Structure in Eighteenth-Century New England.* Baltimore, 1976.

Cornell, Saul. "Aristocracy Assailed: The Ideology of Backcountry Anti-Federalism." *JAH* 76 (1990): 1148–72.

Cott, Nancy. *The Bonds of Womanhood: "Woman's Sphere" in New England, 1780–1835.* New Haven, 1977.

Countryman, Edward. "Consolidating Power in Revolutionary America: The Case of New York, 1775–1783." *JIH* 6 (1976): 645–77.

——. "'Out of the Bounds of the Law': Northern Land Rioters in the Eighteenth Century." Pp. 39–69 in Young, ed., *American Revolution.*

——. *A People in Revolution: The American Revolution and Political Society in New York, 1760–1790.* Baltimore, 1981.

——. "'To Secure the Blessings of Liberty': Language, the Revolution, and American Capitalism." In Young, ed., *Beyond the American Revolution.*

——. "The Uses Of Capital in Revolutionary America: The Case of the New York Loyalist Merchants." *WMQ* 49 (1992): 3–28.

Countryman, Edward, and Susan Deans. "Independence and Revolution in the Americas: A Project for Comparative Study." *RHR*, no. 27 (1983): 144–71.

Coward, Joan W. *Kentucky in the New Republic: The Process of Constitution Making.* Lexington, Ky., 1979.

Cox, LaWanda F. "The American Agricultural Wage Earner, 1865–1900: The Emergence of a Modern Labor Problem." *AgH* 22 (1948): 95–114.

Craig, Gerald M. *Upper Canada: The Formative Years.* Toronto, 1963.

Craig, Lee A. "The Value of Household Labor in Antebellum Northern Agriculture." *JEH* 51 (1991): 67–82.

Crandall, Ralph J. "New England's Second Great Migration: The First Three Generations of Settlement, 1630–1700." *New England Historical and Genealogical Register* 129 (1975): 347–60.

Cranmer, H. Jerome. "Canal Investment, 1815–1860." Pp. 547–64 in *Trends in the*

American Economy in the Nineteenth Century. Studies in Income and Wealth, vol. 24. Princeton, 1960.

Craven, Frank. "The Early Settlements: A European Investment of Capital and Labor." Pp. 19–43 in Harold F. Williamson, ed., *The Growth of the American Economy*. 2d ed. Englewood Cliffs, N.J., 1951.

Cray, Robert E., Jr. *Paupers and Poor Relief in New York City and Its Rural Environs, 1700–1830*. Philadelphia, 1988.

Cress, Lawrence D. *Citizens in Arms: The Army and the Militia in American Society to the War of 1812*. Chapel Hill, N.C., 1982.

Cressy, David. *Coming Over: Migration and Communication between England and New England in the Seventeenth Century*. Cambridge, 1987.

Crèvecoeur, J. Hector St. John de. *Letters from an American Farmer and Sketches of Eighteenth-Century America*. Albert E. Stone, ed. New York, 1981.

Cronon, William. *Changes in the Land: Indians, Colonists, and the Ecology of New England*. New York, 1983.

———. "Modes of Prophecy and Production: Placing Nature in History." *JAH* 76 (1990): 1122–31.

———. *Nature's Metropolis: Chicago and the Great West*. New York, 1991.

———. "Revisiting the Vanishing Frontier." *Western Historical Quarterly* 18 (1987): 157–76.

Cross, Whitney R. *The Burned-Over District: The Social and Intellectual History of Enthusiastic Religion in Western New York, 1800–1850*. Ithaca, N.Y., 1950.

Crow, Jeffrey J. "Slave Rebelliousness and Social Conflict in North Carolina, 1775 to 1802." *WMQ* 38 (1980): 79–102.

———. "The Whiskey Rebellion in North Carolina." *North Carolina Historical Review* 66 (1989): 1–28.

Curry, Leonard P. *The Free Black in Urban America, 1800–1850*. Chicago, 1981.

Curry, Richard O., and Lawrence B. Goodhart, eds. *American Chameleon: Individualism in Trans-National Context*. Kent, Ohio, 1991.

———. "Individualism in Trans-National Context." Pp. 1–19 in Curry and Goodhart, eds. *American Chameleon*.

Curti, Merle. *The Making of an American Community: A Case Study of Democracy in a Frontier Community*. Stanford, Calif., 1959.

Curtis, Bruce. "Representation and State Formation in the Canadas, 1790–1850." *Studies in Political Economy*, no. 28 (1989): 59–87.

Dalrymple, Margaret Fisher, ed. *The Merchant of Manchac: The Letterbooks of John Fitzpatrick, 1768–1790*. Baton Rouge, 1978.

Danbom, David B. "Romantic Agrarianism in Twentieth-Century America." *AgH* 65 (Fall 1991): 1–14.

Danhof, Clarence H. *Change in Agriculture: The Northern United States, 1820–1870*. Cambridge, Mass., 1969.

Daniel, Cletus E. *Bitter Harvest: A History of California Farm Workers, 1870–1941*. Berkeley, Calif., 1981.

Dann, John C., ed. *The Revolution Remembered: Eyewitness Accounts of the War for Independence*. Chicago, 1977.

Davenport, David Paul. "Migration to Albany, New York, 1850–1855." *SSH* 13 (1989): 159–86.

——. "Tracing Rural New York's Out-Migrants, 1855–1860." *Historical Methods* 17 (1984): 59–67.

David, Paul A. "The Mechanization of Reaping in the Ante-Bellum Midwest." Pp. 3–39 in in Rosovsky, ed., *Industrialization in Two Systems.*

Davidson, Cathy N. *Revolution and the Word: The Rise of the Novel in America.* New York, 1986.

Davis, Charles S. *The Cotton Kingdom in Alabama.* Montgomery, Ala., 1939.

Davis, David Brion. *The Problem of Slavery in the Age of Revolution, 1770–1823.* Ithaca, N.Y., 1975.

Davis, Lance Edwin, and Peter Lester Payne. "From Benevolence to Business: The Story of Two Savings Banks." *Business History Review* 32 (1958): 386–406.

Davis, Thomas J. "Emancipation Rhetoric, Natural Rights, and Revolutionary New England: A Note on Four Black Petitions in Massachusetts, 1773–1777." *New England Quarterly* 62 (1989): 248–63.

Dawson, Michael. "Revamping the Sociology of Class: A Note on So and Hikam's Proposal." *Sociological Perspectives* 33 (1990): 419–22.

Deane, Phyllis, and W. A. Cole. *British Economic Growth, 1688–1959.* Cambridge, 1962.

DeBow, J. D. B. *Statistical View of the United States . . . : Being a Compendium of the Seventh Census. . . .* Washington, D.C. 1854.

Degler, Carl N. *At Odds: Women and Family from the Revolution to the Present.* New York, 1980.

——. "The West as a Solution to Urban Unemployment." *New York History* 36 (1955): 63–84.

Demaree, Arthur Lowther. *The American Agricultural Press, 1819–1860.* New York, 1941.

Demos, John. *Entertaining Satan: Witchcraft and the Culture of Early New England.* New York, 1982.

——. "George Caleb Bingham: The Artist as Social Historian." *AQ* 17 (1965): 218–28.

DePauw, Linda Grant. "Land of the Unfree: Legal Limitations on Liberty in Pre-Revolutionary America." *Maryland Historical Magazine* 68 (1973): 355–68.

——. "Women in Combat: The Revolutionary War Experience." *Armed Forces and Society* 7 (1981): 209–26.

Detweiler, Philip F. "The Changing Reputation of the Declaration of Independence: The First Fifty Years." *WMQ* 19 (1962): 557–74.

Deutrich, Mabel E., and Virginia C. Purdy, eds. *Clio Was a Woman: Studies in the History of American Women.* Washington, D.C., 1980.

Deutsch, Sarah. "Confronting Capitalism: Comparative Perspectives on Capitalism and Gender in Modern America." Paper presented at the conference on "Rural Women and the Transition to Capitalism in Rural America," March–April 1989, DeKalb, Ill.

——. *No Separate Refuge: Culture, Class, and Gender on an Anglo-Hispanic Frontier in the American Southwest, 1880–1940.* New York, 1987.

Deyle, Steven. "American Independence and the Rise of the Slave Trade." Paper presented at the 1989 meeting of the Society for Historians of the Early Republic.

——. "'By Far the Most Profitable Trade': Slave Trading in British Colonial North America." *Slavery and Abolition* 10 (1989): 107–25.

Dickson, R. J. *Ulster Emigration to Colonial America, 1718–1775*. London, 1966.

Dinn, Gilbert C. "The Immigration Policy of Governor Esteban Miro in Spanish Louisiana." *Southwest Historical Quarterly* 73 (1969): 156–75.

——. "Spain's Immigration Policy in Louisiana and the American Penetration, 1792–1803." *Southwest Historical Quarterly* 76 (1973): 255–76.

Ditz, Toby L. *Property and Inheritance: Inheritance in Early Connecticut, 1750–1820*. Princeton, 1986.

Dobb, Maurice. *Studies in the Development of Capitalism*. New York, 1947.

Doerflinger, Thomas M. "Farmers and Dry Goods in the Philadelphia Market Area, 1750–1800." Pp. 166–95 in Hoffman, McCusker, Menard, and Albert, eds., *Economy of Early America*.

——. *A Vigorous Spirit of Enterprise: Merchants and the Economic Development in Revolutionary Philadelphia*. Chapel Hill, N.C., 1986.

Donaldson, Scott. *The Suburban Myth*. New York, 1968.

Donnan, Elizabeth, ed. *Documents Illustrative of the History of the Slave Trade to America*. 4 vols. Washington, D.C., 1930–35.

Dorman, James H. "The Persistent Specter: Slave Rebellion in Territorial Lousisana." *Louisiana History* 18 (1977): 389–404.

Dorman, John F. *Virginia Revolutionary Pension Applications*. 41 vols. Washington, D.C., 1958–90.

Dowd, Gregory Evans. "Declarations of Independence: War and Inequality in Revolutionary New Jersey." *New Jersey History* 103 (1984): 53–58.

Doyle, David Noel. "The Irish as Urban Pioneers, 1850–1870." *Journal of American Ethnic History* 10 (1990–91): 36–59.

Doyle, Don Harrison. *The Social Order of a Frontier Community: Jacksonville, Illinois, 1825–1870*. Urbana, Ill., 1983.

——. "Social Theory and New Communities in Nineteenth-Century America." *Western Historical Quarterly* 8 (1977): 151–65.

Drescher, Seymour. "Public Opinion and the Destruction of Colonial Slavery." Pp. 22–48 in James Walvin, ed., *Slavery and British Society, 1776–1846*. Baton Rouge, 1982.

Dublin, Thomas. "Rural-Urban Migrants in Industrial New England: The Case of Lynn, Massachusetts, in the Mid-Nineteenth Century." *JAH* 73 (1986): 623–44.

——. "Women and Outwork in a Nineteenth-Century New England Town: Fitzwilliam, New Hampshire, 1830–1850." Pp. 51–70 in Hahn and Prude, eds., *The Countryside in the Age of Capitalist Transformation*.

——. *Women at Work: The Transformation of Work and Community in Lowell, Massachusetts, 1826–1860*. New York, 1981.

——, ed. *Farm to Factory: Women's Letters, 1830–1860*. New York, 1981.

DuBois, Ellen Carol. *Feminism and Suffrage: The Emergence of an Independent Women's Movement in America, 1848–1869*. Ithaca, N.Y. 1978.

Du Bois, W. E. B. *The Suppression of the African Slave Trade to the United States*. New York, 1904.

Duchesne, Ricardo. "The French Revolution as a Bourgeois Revolution: A Critique of the Revisionists." *Science and Society* 54 (1990): 288–320.

Dunn, Richard S. "Black Society in the Chesapeake, 1776–1810." Pp. 49–82 in Berlin and Hoffman, eds., *Slavery and Freedom in the Age of the American Revolution*.

——. "Servants and Slaves: The Recruitment and Employment of Labor." Pp. 157–94 in Jack P. Greene and J. R. Pole, eds., *Colonial British America: Essays in the New History of the Early Modern Era.* Baltimore, 1984.

——. "A Tale of Two Plantations: Slave Life at Mesopotamia in Jamaica and Mount Airy in Virginia, 1799 to 1828." *WMQ* 34 (1977): 32–65.

——. "Two 'Privledged' Slaves: Robert McAlpine of Jamaica and Winney Grimshaw of Virginia." Paper presented to the Philadelphia Center for Early American Studies, September 1991.

Durey, Michael. "Thomas Paine's Apostles: Radical Emigrés and the Triumph of Jeffersonian Republicanism." *WMQ* 44 (1987): 661–88.

Eagleton, Terry. "Ideology and Scholarship." Pp. 114–25 in Jerome J. McGann, ed., *Historical Studies and Literary Criticism.* Madison, Wis., 1985.

——. *Literary Theory: An Introduction.* Minneapolis, 1983.

Earle, Carville V. *The Evolution of a Tidewater Settlement System: All Hallow's Parish, Maryland, 1650–1783.* University of Chicago Department of Geography Research Paper, no. 170, 1975.

Earle, Carville V., and Ronald Hoffman. "The Foundation of the Modern Economy: Agriculture and the Costs of Labor in the United States and England, 1800–60." *AHR* 85 (1980): 1055–94.

Earle, David W. L., ed. *The Family Compact: Aristocracy or Oligarcy?* Toronto, 1967.

East, Robert A. *Business Enterprise in the American Revolutionary Era.* New York, 1938.

Easterlin, Richard A. "Population Change and Farm Settlement in the Northern United States." *JEH* 36 (1976): 45–75.

Echeverria, Durand. *Mirage in the West: A History of the French Image of American Society to 1815.* Princeton, 1957.

"Economic Progress." *United States Magazine and Democratic Review* 24 (1849): 97–109.

Edmundson, James H. "Desertion in the American Army during the Revolutionary War." Ph.D. diss., Louisiana, 1971.

Eggleston, Edward. *The Transit of Civilization from England to America in the Seventeenth Century.* 1900. Reprint. Boston, 1959.

Egnal, Marc. *A Mighty Empire: The Origins of the American Revolution.* Ithaca, N.Y., 1988.

Eisinger, Chester E. "The Farmer in the Eighteenth-Century Almanac." *AgH* 29 (1954): 106–12.

——. "The Freehold Concept in Eighteenth-Century American Letters." *WMQ* 4 (1947): 42–59.

——. "The Influence of Natural Rights and Physiocratic Doctrines on American Agrarian Thought during the Revolutionary Period." *AgH* 21 (1947): 13–23.

Ekrich, A. Roger. "The North Carolina Regulators on Liberty and Corruption, 1766–1771." *Perspectives in American History* 11 (1977–78): 199–256.

Eller, Ronald D. *Miners, Millhands, and Mountaineers: Industrialization of the Appalachian South, 1880–1930.* Knoxville, 1982.

Elliot, Jonathan, ed. *The Debates in the Several State Conventions on the Adoption of the Federal Constitution . . . .* 5 vols. New York, 1888.

Ellis, David M. "The Homestead Clause in Railroad Land Grants." Pp. 47–73 in Ellis, ed., *Frontier in American Development.*

——, ed. *The Frontier in American Development: Essays in Honor of Paul Wallace Gates.* Ithaca, N.Y., 1969.

Elster, Jon. *Making Sense of Marx.* Cambridge, 1985.

Eltis, David. *Economic Growth and the Ending of the Transatlantic Slave Trade.* New York, 1987.

——. "The Nineteenth Century Transatlantic Slave Trade: An Annual Time Series of Imports into the Americas Broken Down by Region." *Hispanic American Historical Review* 67 (1987): 109–38.

Engels, Frederick. *Socialism: Utopian and Scientific* (1883, 1892). Pp. 399–434 in *Marx and Engels: Selected Works.*

Engerman, Stanley L., and Robert E. Gallman, eds. *Long-Term Factors in American Economic Growth.* Studies in Income and Wealth, vol. 51. Chicago, 1986.

Erikson, Charlotte J. "Emigration from the British Isles to the U.S.A. in 1841." *Population Studies* 43 (1989): 347–67 and 44 (1990): 21–40.

——. *Invisible Immigrants: The Adaptation of English and Scottish Immigrants in Nineteenth-Century America.* Coral Gables, Fla., 1972.

Escott, Paul D., and Jeffrey J. Crow. "The Social Order and Violent Disorder: An Analysis of North Carolina in the Revolution and Civil War." *North Carolina Historical Review* 52 (1986): 373–402.

Eslinger, Ellen. "Migration and Kinship on the Trans-Appalachian Frontier: Strode's Station, Kentucky." *Filson Club Historical Quarterly* 62 (1988): 52–66.

Ethington, Philip J. "The Structure of Urban Political Life: Political Culture in San Franscisco, 1850–1880." Ph.D. diss., Stanford, 1989.

Evans, George Henry. *The Radical.* Issues for 1841.

Everitt, Alan. "Farm Labourers." Pp. 396–465 in Joan Thirsk, ed., *The Agrarian History of England and Wales,* 4: 1500–1640. Cambridge, 1967.

Everton, George B., Sr., and Gunnar Rasmuson. *The Handy Book for Genealogists.* 3d. ed. Logan, Utah, 1957.

Ewbank, Douglas C. "The Marital Fertility of American Whites before 1920." *Historical Methods* 24 (1991): 141–70.

Faragher, John Mack. "History from the Inside Out: Writing the History of Women in Rural America." *AQ* 33 (1981): 537–57.

——. *Sugar Creek: Life on the Illinois Prairie.* New Haven, 1986.

——. *Women and Men on the Overland Trail.* New Haven, 1979.

Fellman, Michael. "Rehearsal for the Civil War: Antislavery and Proslavery and the Fighting Point in Kansas, 1854–1856." Pp. 287–308 in Lewis Perry and Fellman, eds., *Antislavery Reconsidered: New Perspectives on the Abolitionists.* Baton Rouge, 1979.

Ferguson, James. "The Nationalists of 1781–1783 and the Economic Interpretation of the Constitution." *JAH* 56 (1969): 241–61.

Ferling, John. "Soldiers for Virginia: Who Served in the French and Indian War?" *VMHB* 94 (1986): 307–28.

Field, Alexander James. "Sectoral Shift in Antebellum Massachusetts: A Reconsideration." *Explorations in Economic History* 15 (1978): 146–71.

Fields, Barbara Jeanne. "The Advent of Capitalist Agriculture: The New South in a

Bourgeois World." Pp. 73–94 in Thavolia Glymph, ed., *Essays on the Postbellum Southern Economy*. College Station, Tex., 1985.

Fields, Harold B. "Free Negroes in Cass County before the Civil War." *Michigan History* 44 (1960): 370–83

Findlay, Roger, and Beatrice Shearer. "Population Growth and Suburban Development." Pp. 37–59 in A. L. Beier and Findlay, eds., *London 1500–1700: The Making of a Metropolis*. London, 1986.

Fink, Deborah. "Constructing Rural Culture: Family and Land in Iowa." *Agriculture and Human Values* 4 (Fall 1986): 43–53.

——. *Open Country, Iowa: Rural Women, Tradition and Change*. Albany, N.Y., 1986.

Finkelman, Paul. "Evading the Ordinance: The Persistence of Bondage in Indiana and Illinois." *JEarR* 9 (1989): 21–52.

——. "Slavery and the Constitutional Convention: Making a Covenant with Death." Pp. 188–225 in Beeman, Botein, and Carter, eds., *Beyond Confederation*.

——. "Slavery and the Northwest Ordinance: A Study in Ambiguity." *JEarR* 6 (1986): 343–71.

Fischer, David Hackett. *Albion's Seed: Four British Folkways in America*. New York, 1989.

——. *Growing Old in America: The Bland-Lee Lectures Delivered at Clark University*. Expanded ed. New York, 1978.

——. *The Revolution of American Conservatism: The Federalist Party in the Era of Jeffersonian Democracy*. New York, 1965.

Fishlow, Albert. *American Railroads and the Transformation of the Ante-Bellum Economy*. Cambridge, Mass., 1965.

——. "The Common School Revival: Fact or Fancy?" Pp. 40–67 in Rosovsky, ed., *Industrialization in Two Systems*.

Fitzpatrick, John C., ed. *The Writings of George Washington from the Original Manuscript Sources, 1745–1799*. 39 vols. Washington, 1931–44.

Flanders, Ralph B. *Plantation Slavery in Georgia*. Chapel Hill, N.C., 1933.

Fliess, Kenneth H. "Fertility, Nuptiality, and Family Limitation among the Wends of Serbin, Texas, 1854 to 1920." *JFamH* 13 (1988): 251–63.

Flora, Cornelia Butler, and Jan L. Flora. "Structure of Agriculture and Women's Culture in the Great Plains." *Great Plains Quarterly* 8 (1988): 195–205.

Florey, Francesca A., and Avery M. Guest. "Coming of Age among U.S. Farm Boys in the Late 1800s: Occupational and Residential Choices." *JFamH* 13 (1988): 233–50.

Fogel, Robert William. *Without Consent or Contract: The Rise and Fall of American Slavery*. New York, 1989.

Fogel, Robert Willam, and Stanley L. Engerman. "Philanthropy at Bargain Prices: Notes on the Economics of Gradual Emancipation." *Journal of Legal Studies* 3 (1974): 377–401.

——. *Time on the Cross: The Economies of American Negro Slavery*. 2 vols. New York, 1974.

Fogelman, Aaron. "Immigration, German Immigration, and Eighteenth-Century America." Paper presented at the Philadelphia Center for Early American Studies, October 1989.

——. "Review Essay: Progress and Possibilities in Migration Studies: The Contribu-

tions of Werner Hacker to the Study of Early German Migration to Pennsylvania."
    Pennsylvania History 56 (1989): 318–29.
Fogelson, Robert M. *The Fragmented Metropolis: Los Angeles, 1850–1930.* Cambridge,
    Mass., 1967.
Folbre, Nancy. "The Logic of Patriarchal Capitalism." Paper presented at the confer-
    ence on "Rural Women and the Transition to Capitalism in Rural America,"
    March–April 1989, DeKalb, Illinois.
——. "Of Patriarchy Born: The Political Economy of Fertility Decisions," *Feminist
    Studies* 9 (1983), 261–84.
Foner, Eric. *Free Soil, Free Labor, Free Men: The Ideology of the Republican Party before the
    Civil War.* New York, 1970.
——. *Reconstruction: America's Unfinished Revolution, 1863–1877.* New York, 1988.
——. *Tom Paine and Revolutionary America.* New York, 1976.
Foner, Philip S., ed. *We the Other People: Alternative Declarations of Independence by
    Labor Groups, Farmers, Women's Rights Advocates, Socialists, and Blacks, 1829–1975.*
    Urbana, 1976.
Force, Peter, comp. *American Archives: Consisting of a Collection of Authentick Records,
    State Papers, Debates. . . .* 4th Ser. 9 vols. Washington, D.C., 1837–53.
Ford, Lacy. "Rednecks and Merchants: Economic Development and Social Tensions in
    the South Carolina Upcountry." *JAH* 71 (1984): 294–318.
——. "Republican Ideology in a Slave Society: The Political Economy of John C. Cal-
    houn." *Journal of Southern History* 45 (1988): 405–24.
——. "Yeoman Farmers in the South Carolina Upcountry: Changing Production Pat-
    terns in the Late Antebellum Period." *AgH* 60 (Fall 1986): 17–37.
Formisano, Ronald P. "Deferential-Participant Politics: The Early Republic's Political
    Culture, 1789–1840." *American Political Science Review* 68 (1974): 473–87.
Fox-Genovese, Elizabeth. "Antebellum Southern Households: A New Perspective on a
    Familiar Question." *Review* 7 (1983): 215–53.
——. "Between Individualism and Fragmentation: American Culture and the New Lit-
    erary Studies of Race and Gender." *AQ* 42 (1990): 7–34.
——. *Feminism without Illusions: A Critique of Individualism.* Chapel Hill, N.C., 1991.
——. "Property and Patriarchy in Classical Bourgeois Political Theory." *RHR* 4 (Spring-
    summer 1977): 36–59.
——. *Within the Plantation Household: Black and White Women of the Old South.*
    Chapel Hill, N.C., 1988.
Fox-Genovese, Elizabeth, and Eugene D. Genovese. *Fruits of Merchant Capital: Slavery
    and Bourgeois Property in the Rise and Expansion of Capitalism.* New York, 1983.
Frauendorfer, Sigmund von. "American Farmers and European Peasantry." Pp. 2:160–
    69 in *A Systematic Source Book in Rural Sociology.* Edited by Pitrim A. Sorokin, Carle
    C. Zimmerman, and Charles J. Galpin. 3 vols. Minneapolis, 1931.
"Free Trade." *United States Magazine and Democratic Review* 14 (1844): 291–301.
French, David. "Puritan Conservatism and the Frontier: The Elizur Wright Family on
    the Connecticut Western Reserve." *The Old Northwest* 1 (1975): 85–95.
Freudenberger, Herman, and Jonathan B. Pritchett. "The Domestic United States Slave
    Trade: New Evidence." *JIH* 21 (1991): 447–77.

Frey, Sylvia R. *Water from the Rock: Black Resistance in a Revolutionary Age.* Princeton, 1991.

Friedberger, Mark. *Farm Families and Change in Twentieth-Century America.* Lexington, Ky., 1988.

Friedmann, Harriet. "Household Production and the National Economy: Concepts for the Analysis of Agrarian Formations." *Journal of Peasant Studies* 7 (1980): 158–84.

———. "Simple Commodity Production and Wage Labour in the American Plains." *Journal of Peasant Studies* 6 (1978): 71–100.

———. "World Market, State, and the Family Farm: Social Bases of Household Production in the Era of Wage Labor." *Comparative Studies in Society and History* 20 (1978): 545–86.

Frizzell, Robert W. "Migration Chains in Illinois: The Evidence from German-American Records." *Journal of American Ethnic History* 7 (1987): 59–73.

Fuller, Wayne E. *The Old Country School: The Story of Education in the Middle West.* Chicago, 1982.

Gagan, George. *Hopeful Travellers: Families, Land, and Social Change in Mid-Victorian Peel County, Canada West.* Toronto, 1981.

Galenson, David. "'Middling People' or 'Common Sort'? The Social Origins of Some Early Americans Reexamined." *WMQ* 35 (1978): 499–524.

———. "The Social Origins of Some Early Americans: Rejoinder." *WMQ* 36 (1979): 264–77.

———. *White Servitude in Colonial America: An Economic Analysis.* Cambridge, 1981.

Galenson, David, and Clayne L. Pope. "Economic and Geographic Mobility on the Farming Frontier: Evidence from Appanoose County, Iowa, 1850–1870." *JEH* 49 (1989): 635–56.

Gambone, Michael D. "The Immigrant Presence in Grundy County, 1850–1860: Directions, Developments, and Consolidation." Pp. 61–73 in Conzen and Morales, *Settling the Upper Illinois Valley.*

Gates, Lillian F. *Land Policies of Upper Canada.* Toronto, 1968.

Gates, Paul Wallace. *The Farmer's Age: Agriculture, 1815–1860.* New York, 1960.

———. *History of Public Land Law Development.* Washington, D.C., 1968.

———. "The Homestead Law in an Incongruous Land System." *AHR* 41 (1936): 652–81.

———. *The Illinois Central Railroad and Its Colonization Work.* Cambridge, Mass., 1934.

———. *Landlords and Tenants on the Prairie Frontier: Studies in American Land Policy.* Ithaca, N.Y., 1973.

Gemery, Henry A. "Emigration from the British Isles to the New World, 1630–1700: Inferences from Colonial Populations." *Research in Economic History* 5 (1980): 179–231.

———. "European Emigration to North America, 1700–1820: Numbers and Quasi-Numbers." *Perspectives in American History*, n.s., 1 (1984): 283–342.

Genovese, Eugene D. *From Rebellion to Revolution: Afro-American Slave Revolts in the Making of the New World.* Baton Rogue, 1979.

———. "Larry Tise's *Proslavery*: A Critique and an Appreciation." *Georgia Historical Quarterly* 72 (1988): 670–83.

———. *The Political Economy of Slavery: Studies in the Economy and Society of the Slave South.* 2d ed. Middletown, Conn., 1989.

——. "The Politics of Class Struggle in the History of Society: An Appraisal of the Works of Eric Hobsbawm." Pp. 13–36 in Pat Thane, Geoffrey Crossick, and Roderick Floud, eds., *The Power of the Past: Essays for Eric Hobsbawm.* Cambridge, 1984.

——. *Roll, Jordan, Roll: The World the Slaves Made.* New York, 1974.

——. *The World the Slaveholders Made: Two Essays in Interpretation.* 2d ed. Middletown, Conn., 1988.

Gillespie, Michele. "Artisans and Mechanics in the Political Economy of Georgia, 1790–1860." Ph.D. diss., Princeton, 1990.

Gilmer, George R. *Sketches of Some of the First Settlers of Upper Georgia.* 1835. Reprint. Baltimore, 1980.

Gilmore, Michael T. *American Romanticism and the Marketplace.* Chicago, 1985.

Gjerde, Jon. *From Peasants to Farmers: The Migration from Balestrand, Norway, to the Upper Middle West.* Cambridge, 1985.

Glasco, Laurence. "Migration and Adjustment in the Nineteenth-Century City: Occupation, Property, and Household Structure of Native-born Whites, Buffalo, New York, 1855." Pp. 154–78 in Tamara K. Hareven and Maris A. Vinovskis, eds., *Family and Population in Nineteenth-Century America.* Princeton, 1978.

Goldenberg, Joseph A., Eddie D. Nelson, and Rita Y. Flectcher. "Revolutionary Ranks: An Analysis of the Chesterfield Supplement." *VMHB* 87 (1979): 182–90.

Goldin, Claudia, and Kenneth Sokoloff. "Women, Children, and Industrialization in the Early Republic: Evidence from the Manufacturing Censuses." *JEH* 42 (1982): 741–74.

Goldwin, Robert A., and William A. Schambra, eds. *How Democratic Is the Constitution?* Washington, D.C., 1982.

Goodman, Paul. "Social Basis of New England Politics in Jacksonian America." *JEarR* 6 (1986): 23–58.

Goodrich, Carter. *Government Promotion of American Canals and Railroads, 1800–1890.* New York, 1960.

——, ed. *The Government and the Economy: 1783–1861.* Indianapolis, 1967.

Goodstein, Anita S. "Black History on the Nashville Frontier, 1780–1810." *Tennessee Historical Quarterly* 38 (1979): 401–20.

Goodwyn, Lawrence. *Democratic Promise: The Populist Moment in America.* New York, 1976.

Gordon, Linda. *Heroes of Their Own Lives: The Politics and History of Family Violence, Boston 1880–1960.* New York, 1988.

Gough, Robert. "Notes on the Pennsylvania Revolutionaries of 1776." *Pennsylvania Magazine of History and Biography* 96 (1972): 89–103.

Gragg, Larry Dale. *Migration in Early America: The Virginia Quaker Experience.* Ann Arbor, Mich., 1980.

Grant, Charles S. *Democracy in the Connecticut Frontier Town of Kent.* New York, 1961.

Gray, Lewis Cecil. *History of Agriculture in the Southern United States to 1860.* 2 vols. Washington, D.C., 1933.

Gray, Susan E. "Family, Land, and Credit: Yankee Communities on the Michigan Frontier, 1830–1860." Ph.D. diss., Chicago, 1985.

Greeley, Horace. *Hints toward Reform in Lectures, Addresses, and Other Writings.* New York, 1853.

Green, Fletcher M. "Duff Green, Militant Journalist of the Old School." *AHR* 52 (1947): 247–64.

Greene, Evarts B., and Virginia D. Harrington, eds. *American Population before the Federal Census of 1790*. New York, 1932.

Greene, Jack P. *All Men Are Created Equal: Some Reflections on the Character of the American Revolution*. Oxford, 1976.

——. "Society, Ideology, and Politics: An Analysis of the Political Culture of Mid-Eighteenth-Century Virginia." Pp. 14–76 in R. M. Jellison, ed., *Society, Freedom, and Conscience*.

——, ed. *Colonies to Nation, 1763–1789: A Documentary History of the American Revolution*. New York, 1975.

Greene, Jack P., Virginia DeJohn Anderson, James Horn, Barry Levy, Ned C. Landsman, and David Hackett Fischer. "*Albion's Seed: Four British Folkways in America* — a Symposium." *WMQ* 48 (1991): 224–308.

Greenwood, Michael J. "Research in Internal Migration in the United States: A Survey." *Journal of Economic Literature* 13 (1975): 397–433.

Greer, Allan. *Peasant, Lord, and Merchant: Rural Society in Three Quebec Parishes, 1740–1840*. Toronto, 1985.

Greven, Philip J., Jr. *Four Generations: Population, Land, and Family in Colonial Andover, Masssachusetts*. Ithaca, N.Y., 1970.

Grimsted, David. "Anglo-American Racism and Phillis Wheatley's 'Sable Veil,' 'Length'ned Chain,' and 'Knitted Heart.'" Pp. 338–444 in Hoffman and Albert, eds., *Women in Age of the American Revolution*.

Groseclose, Barbara. "The 'Missouri Artist' as Artist." Pp. 53–91 in Schapiro, ed., *George Caleb Bingham*.

Gross, Robert A. "Culture and Cultivation: Agriculture and Society in Thoreau's Concord." *JAH* 69 (1982): 42–61.

——. "'The Most Estimable Place in All the World': A Debate on Progress in Nineteenth-Century Concord." *Studies in the American Renaissance* (1978): 1–15.

——. "Transcendentalism and Urbanism: Concord, Boston, and the Wider World." *Journal of American Studies* 18 (1984): 361–81.

Grossberg, Michael. *Governing the Hearth: Law and the Family in Nineteenth-Century America*. Chapel Hill, N.C., 1985.

Grubb, Farley. "Immigrant Servant Labor: Their Occupational and Geographic Distribution in the Late Eighteenth-Century Mid-Atlantic." *SSH* 9 (1985): 249–76.

——. "Redemptioner Immigration to Pennsylvania: Evidence on Contract Choice and Profitability." *JEH* 46 (1986): 407–18.

Gunderson, Joan R. "Independence, Citizenship, and the American Revolution." *Signs* 13 (1987): 59–77.

Gunn, L. Ray. *The Decline of Authority: Public Economic Policy and Political Development in New York State, 1800–1860*. Ithaca, N.Y., 1988.

Gutman, Herbert G. *The Black Family in Slavery and Freedom, 1750–1925*. New York, 1976.

——. *Power and Culture: Essays on the American Working Class*. Ira Berlin, ed. New York, 1989.

——. *Work, Culture, and Society in Industrializing America: Essays in American Working Class and Social History*. New York, 1977.

Gutman, Herbert G., and Richard Sutch. "The Slave Family: Protected Agent of Capitalist Masters or Victim of the Slave Trade?" Pp. 55–93 in Paul A. David et al., *Reckoning with Slavery: A Critical Study in the Quantitative History of American Negro Slavery*. New York, 1976.

Gwathmey, John H., ed. *Historical Register of Virginians in the Revolution: Soldiers, Sailors, Marines, 1775–1783*. Richmond, 1938.

Habermas, Jurgen. *The Structural Transformation of the Public Sphere: An Inquiry into a Category of Bourgeois Society*. Thomas Burger, trans. Cambridge, Mass., 1989; German ed., 1962.

——. *Theory and Practice*. John Viertel, trans. Boston, 1968.

Hacker, Louis M. *The Triumph of American Capitalism: The Development of Forces in American History to the End of the Nineteenth Century*. New York, 1940.

Hahn, Steven. *The Roots of Southern Populism: Yeoman Farmers and the Transformation of the Georgia Upcountry, 1850–1890*. New York, 1983.

Hahn, Steven, and Jonathan Prude, eds. *The Countryside in the Age of Capitalist Transformation*. Chapel Hill, N.C., 1985.

Hailes, Frances, comp. "Alabama Census Returns, 1820 and an Abstract of the Federal Census of Alabama 1830." *Alabama Historical Quarterly* 6 (1944): 333–515.

Hall, Jacqueline Dowd, et al. *Like a Family: The Making of a Southern Cotton Mill World*. Chapel Hill, N.C., 1987.

Hall, Van Beck. *Politics without Parties: Massachusetts, 1780–1791*. Pittsburgh, 1972.

Hamilton, W. B. "Mississippi 1817: A Sociological and Economic Analysis." *Journal of Mississippi History* 29 (1967): 270–92.

Handlin, Oscar. *Boston's Immigrants: A Study in Acculturation*. Rev. ed. Cambridge, Mass., 1979.

Handlin, Oscar, and Mary Flug Handlin. *Commonwealth: A Study of the Role of Government in the American Economy, Massachusetts, 1774–1861*. New York, 1947.

——. eds. *The Popular Sources of Political Authority: Documents on the Massachusetts Constitution of 1780*. Cambridge, Mass., 1966.

Hansen, Marcus Lee, and John Bartlet Brebner. *The Mingling of the Canadian and American Peoples*. New Haven, 1940.

Harris, P. M. G. "The Social Origins of American Leaders: The Demographic Foundations." *Perspectives in American History* 3 (1969): 159–344.

Harris, Richard Colebrook. *The Seigniorial System in Early Canada: A Geographical Study*. Madison, Wis., 1968.

Harrison, Joseph H. "*Sic et Non*: Thomas Jefferson and Internal Improvement." *JEarR* 7 (1987): 335–50.

Hartnett, Sean. "The Land Market on the Wisconsin Frontier: An Examination of Land Ownership Processes in Turtle and LaPrairie Townships, 1839–1890." *AgH* 65 (Fall 1991): 38–77.

Hartz, Louis. *Economic Policy and Democratic Thought: Pennsylvania, 1774–1861*. Cambridge, Mass., 1948.

Haskell, Thomas L. "Capitalism and the Origins of Humanitarian Sensibility." *AHR* 90 (1985): 339–61, 547–66.

Hast, Adele. *Loyalism in Revolutionary Virginia: The Norfolk Area and the Eastern Shore.* Ann Arbor, Mich., 1982.

Hatch, Nathan O. *The Democratization of American Christianity.* New Haven, 1989.

Hazelton, John H. *The Declaration of Independence: Its History.* 1906. Reprint. New York, 1970.

Headlee, Sue. *The Political Economy of the Family Farm: The Agrarian Roots of American Capitalism.* Westport, Conn., 1991.

Heinze, Kirk Leo. "Yeomanry Transformed: The Changing Image of the American Farmer in the Northern Agricultural Press, 1873–1893." Ph.D. diss., Michigan State, 1988.

Hening, William Waller. *The Statutes at Large; Being a Collection of all the Laws of Virginia, from the First Session of the Legislature, in the Year 1619. . . .* 13 vols. Richmond, 1819–23.

Henretta, James A. "Families and Farms: *Mentalité* in Pre-Industrial America." *WMQ* 35 (1978): 3–32.

——. "Reply [to James Lemon]." *WMQ* 37 (1980): 696–700.

——. "The Study of Social Mobility: Ideological Assumptions and Conceptual Bias." *Labor History* 18 (1977): 165–78.

——. "The Transition to Capitalism in America." Pp. 218–39 in Henretta, Kammen, and Katz, eds., *Transformation of Early American History.*

——. "The War for Independence and American Economic Development." Pp. 45–87 in Hoffman, McCusker, Menard, and Albert, eds., *Economy of Early America.*

Henretta, James A., Michael Kammen, and Stanley N. Katz, eds., *Transformation of Early American History: Society, Authority, and Ideology.* New York, 1991.

Herndon, G. Melvin. "Indian Agriculture in the Southern Colonies." *North Carolina Historical Review* 44 (1967): 283–97.

Heyrman, Christine Leigh. *Culture and Commerce: The Maritime Communities of Colonial Massachusetts, 1690–1750.* New York, 1984.

Hicks, John D. *The Populist Revolt: A History of the Farmers' Alliance and the People's Party.* Minneapolis, 1931.

Higginbotham, Don. *War and Society in Revolutionary America: The Wider Dimensions of Conflict.* Columbia, S.C., 1988.

——, ed. *Reconsiderations on the Revolutionary War: Selected Essays.* Westport, Conn., 1978.

Higgins, W. Robert. "The Geographical Origins of Negro Slaves in Colonial South Carolina." *South Atlantic Quarterly* 70 (1971): 34–47.

Higgs, Henry, ed. *Palgrave's Dictionary of Political Economy.* 3 vols. London, 1926.

Higgs, Robert. "The Growth of Cities in a Midwestern Region, 1870–1900." *Journal of Regional Science* 9 (1969): 369–75.

Higonnet, Patrice. *Sister Republics: The Origins of French and American Republicanism.* Cambridge, Mass., 1988.

Hill, C. William. *The Political Theory of John Taylor of Caroline.* Rutherford, N.J., 1974.

Hill, Christopher. "A Bourgeois Revolution?" Pp. 109–39 in J. G. A. Pocock, ed., *Three British Revolutions: 1641, 1688, 1776.* Princeton, 1980.

———. "Pottage for Freeborn Englishmen: Attitudes to Wage-Labour." Pp. 219–38 in Hill, *Change and Continuity in Seventeenth-Century England*. Cambridge, Mass., 1975.

———. *The World Turned Upside Down: Radical Ideas during the English Revolution*. Harmondsworth, Eng., 1972.

Hilliard, Sam Bowers. *Atlas of Antebellum Southern Agriculture*. Baton Rouge, 1984.

Hilton, Rodney. "Capitalism — What's in a Name?" Pp. 144–58 in Hilton, ed., *The Transition from Feudalism to Capitalism*.

———, ed. *The Transition from Feudalism to Capitalism*. London, 1976.

Hine, Robert V. *Community on the American Frontier: Separate but Not Alone*. Norman, Okla., 1980.

Hitchcock, Enos. *Farmers Friend or the History of Mr. Charles Worthy.* . . . Boston, 1793.

Hobsbawm, Eric J. Introduction. Pp. 9–65 in Marx, *Pre-Capitalist Economic Formations*.

———. Introduction: "Inventing Traditions." Pp. 1–14 in Hobsbawm and Terence Ranger, eds., *The Invention of Tradition*. Cambridge, 1983.

———. "The Making of a 'Bourgeois Revolution.'" *Social Research* 56 (1989): 5–31.

———. "Revolution." Pp. 5–46 in Roy Porter and Mikulas Teich, eds., *Revolution in History*. Cambridge, 1986.

———. "Revolution in the Theory of Karl Marx." Pp. 557–70 in Bernard Chavance, ed., *Marx en Perspective: Actes du colloque Organisé par l'Ecole des Hautes Études en Science Sociales, Paris, décembre 1983*. Paris, 1985.

Hoerder, Dirk. *Crowd Action in Revolutionary Massachusetts, 1765–1780*. New York, 1977.

Hoffman, Ronald. "The 'Disaffected' in the Revolutionary South." Pp. 273–318 in Young, ed., *American Revolution*.

Hoffman, Ronald, and Peter J. Albert, eds. *Arms and Independence: The Military Character of the American Revolution*. Charlottesville, Va., 1984.

———, eds. *Women in the Age of the American Revolution*. Charlottesville, Va., 1989.

Hoffman, Ronald, John J. McCusker, Russell R. Menard, and Peter J. Albert, eds. *The Economy of Early America: The Revolutionary Period, 1763–1790*. Charlottesville, Va., 1988.

Hofstadter, Richard. *The Age of Reform from Bryan to F.D.R.* New York, 1955.

———. *The Progressive Historians: Turner, Beard, Parrington*. New York, 1968.

Hofstadter, Richard, and Semour Martin Lipset, eds. *Turner and the Sociology of the Frontier*. New York, 1968.

Holley, Marietta. *Samantha Rastles the Woman Question*. 1873–1914. Jane Curry, ed. Urbana, Ill., 1983.

Holmes, Jack D. L. "A Spanish Province, 1779–1798." Pp. 1:158–73 in Richard Aubrey McLemore, ed., *A History of Mississippi*. 2 vols. Hattiesburg, Miss., 1973.

Hood, Andrienne Dora. "Organization and Extent of Textile Manufacture in Eighteenth-Century Rural Pennsylvania: A Case Study of Chester County." Ph.D. diss., California, San Diego, 1988.

Hooker, Richard J., ed. *The Carolina Backcountry on the Eve of the Revolution: The Journal and Other Writings of Charles Woodmason, Anglican Itinerant*. Chapel Hill, N.C., 1953.

Horlick, Stanley. *Country Boys and Merchant Princes: The Social Control of Young Men in New York*. Lewisburg, Pa., 1975.

Horn, James. "Moving On in the New World: Migration and Out-migration in the Seventeenth Century Chesapeake." Pp. 172–212 in Clark and Souden, eds., *Migration and Society*.

——. "Servant Emigration to the Chesapeake in the Seventeenth Century." Pp. 51–95 in Tate and Ammerman, eds., *Chesapeake in the Seventeenth Century*.

Horne, Thomas A. "Bourgeois Virtue: Property and Moral Virtue in America." *History of Political Thought* 4 (1983): 317–40.

Horwitz, Morton J. *The Transformation of American Law, 1780–1860*. Cambridge, Mass., 1977.

Hudson, John C. "A Location Theory for Rural Settlement." *Annals, Association of American Geographers* 59 (1968): 365–81.

——. "Migration to an American Frontier." *Annals, Association of American Geographers* 66 (1976): 242–65.

Hughes, Sarah. "Slaves for Hire: The Allocation of Black Labor in Elizabeth City County, Virginia, 1782 to 1810." *WMQ* 25 (1978): 260–86.

Hundley, Daniel R. *Social Relations in Our Southern States*. 1860. William J. Cooper, ed. Baton Rouge, 1979.

Husband, Herman. *A Fan for Fanning and Touchstone to Tryon*. . . . 1771. Pp. 341–92 in William K. Boyd, ed. *Some Eighteenth Century Tracts Concerning North Carolina*. Raleigh, N.C., 1927.

Ilsevich, Robert D. "Class Structure and Politics in Crawford County, 1800–1840." *Western Pennsylvania Historical Magazine* 63 (1980): 95–119.

Innes, Stephen. *Labor in a New Land: Economy and Society in Seventeenth-Century Springfield*. Princeton, 1983.

——, ed. *Work and Labor in Early America*. Chapel Hill, N.C., 1988.

Inter-University Consortium for Political and Social Research. "Historical, Demographic, Economic, and Social Data: The United States, 1790–1970." Data tapes ICPSR 0003.

Irwin, James R. "Farmers and Laborers: A Note on Black Occupations in the Postebellum South." *AgH* 64 (Winter 1990): 153–60.

Isaac, Rhys. *The Transformation of Virginia, 1740–1800*. Chapel Hill, N.C., 1982.

Isern, Thomas D. *Bull Threshers and Bindlestiffs: Harvesting and Threshing on the North American Plains*. Lawrence, Kan., 1990.

Jackson, Harvey H. "'American Slavery, American Freedom' and the Revolution in the Lower South: The Case of Lachlan McIntosh." *Southern Studies* 19 (1980): 81–93.

Jacob, Margaret, and James Jacob, eds. *The Origins of Anglo-American Radicalism*. London, 1984.

Jaffee, David. "Peddlers of Progress and the Transformation of the Rural North, 1760–1860." *JAH* 78 (1991): 511–35.

——. "The Village Enlightenment in New England, 1760–1820." *WMQ* 47 (1990): 327–46.

Jameson, J. Franklin. *The American Revolution Considered as a Social Movement*. Princeton, 1926.

Jaynes, David Gerald. *Branches without Roots: Genesis of the Black Working Class in the American South, 1862–1882*. New York, 1986.

Jefferson, Thomas. *Notes on the State of Virginia*. Thomas Perkins Abernethy, ed. New York, 1964.

Jeffrey, Julie Roy. "Women in the Southern Farmers' Alliance: A Reconstruction of the Role and Status of Women in the Late Nineteenth-Century South." *Feminist Sudies* 3 (1975): 72–91.

Jellison, Katherine. "Rural Technological Change and Gender Roles on Prairies and Plains, 1900–1940." Paper presented at the conference on "Rural Women and the Transition to Capitalism in Rural America," March-April 1989, DeKalb, Ill.

Jellison, Richard M., ed. *Society, Freedom, and Conscience: The American Revolution in Virginia, Massachusetts, and New York*. New York, 1976.

Jennings, Francis. *The Invasion of America: Indians, Colonialism, and the Cant of Conquest*. Chapel Hill, N.C., 1975.

Jensen, Joan M. *Loosening the Bonds: Mid-Atlantic Farm Women, 1750–1850*. New Haven, 1986.

Jensen, Merrill, and John P. Kasminski, eds. *The Documentary History of the Ratification of the Constitution*. 7 vols. Madison, Wis., 1976–90.

Jeremy, David J. *Transatlantic Industrial Revolution: The Diffusion of Textile Technologies between Britain and America, 1790–1830s*. Cambridge, Mass., 1981.

Johns, Elizabeth. "The Farmer in the Works of William Sidney Mount." *JIH* 17 (1986): 257–81.

——. "The 'Missouri Artist' as Artist." Pp. 92–139 in Schapiro, ed., *George Caleb Bingham*.

Johnson, Ellwood. "Individualism and Purtian Imagination." *AQ* 22 (1970): 230–38.

Johnson, Hildegard Binder. "The Location of German Immigrants in the Middle West." *Annals, Association of American Geographers* 41 (1951): 1–41.

Jones, Alice Hansen. *American Colonial Wealth: Documents and Records*. 2d ed. 3 vols. New York, 1978.

Jones, Douglas Lamar. "Poverty and Vagabondage: The Process of Survival in Eighteenth-Century Massachusetts," *New England Historical and Genealogical Register* 133 (1979): 243–54.

——. "The Strolling Poor: Transiency in Eighteenth-Century Massachusetts." *Journal of Social History* 8 (1975): 28–54.

——. *Village and Seaport: Migration and Society in Eighteenth-Century Massachusetts*. Hanover, N.H., 1981.

Jones, Gareth Stedman. *Languages of Class: Studies in English Working Class History, 1832–1982*. Cambridge, 1983.

Jones, Jacqueline. *Labor of Love, Labor of Sorrow: Black Women, Work, and the Family from Slavery to the Present*. New York, 1985.

Jones, Robert Leslie. *History of Agriculture in Ohio to 1880*. Kent, Ohio, 1983.

Jordan, Cynthia. "'Old Words' in 'New Circumstances': Language and Leadership in Post-Revolutionary America." *AQ* 40 (1988): 491–513.

Jordan, Terry. "Population Origins in Texas, 1850." *Geographical Review* 59 (1969): 83–103.

Jordan, Wayne. "The People of Ohio's First County." *Ohio Historical Quarterly* 49 (1940): 1–41.

Jordan, Winthrop. "Familial Politics: Thomas Paine and the Killing of the King, 1776." *JAH* 60 (1973): 294–308.

——. *White over Black: American Attitudes toward the Negro, 1550–1812*. Chapel Hill, N.C., 1968.

Justices of the Peace of Colonial Virginia 1757–1775. Bulletin of the Virginia State Library 14 (1921).

Kaestle, Carl F. *Pillars of the Republic: Common Schools and American Society, 1780–1860*. New York, 1983.

——. "Public Education in the Old Northwest: 'Necessary to Good Government and the Happiness of Mankind.'" *Indiana Magazine of History* 84 (1988): 60–74.

Kamphoefner, Walter D. *The Westfalians: From Germany to Missouri*. Princeton, 1987.

Karlsen, Carol F. *The Devil in the Shape of a Woman: Witchcraft in Colonial New England*. New York, 1987.

Kateb, George. "Walt Whitman and the Culture of Democracy." *Political Theory* 18 (1990): 545–71.

Katz, Michael B., Michael Doucet, and Mark Stern. "Migration and the Social Order in Erie County, New York: 1855." *JIH* 4 (1978): 669–702.

——. *The Social Organization of Early Capitalism*. Cambridge, Mass., 1982.

Kaufman, Polly Welts. *Woman Teachers on the Frontier*. New Haven, 1984.

Kay, Marvin L. Michael. "The North Carolina Regulation, 1766–1776: A Class Conflict." Pp. 71–123 in Young, ed., *American Revolution*.

Kay, Marvin L. Michael, and Lorin Lee Cary. "A Demographic Analysis of Colonial North Carolina with Special Emphasis upon the Slave and Black Populations." Pp. 71–121 in Jeffrey J. Crow and Flora J. Hatley, eds., *Black Americans in North Carolina and the South*. Chapel Hill, N.C., 1984.

Kaye, Frances W. "The Ladies' Department of the *Ohio Cultivator*, 1845–1855: A Feminist Forum." *AgH* 50 (1976): 414–24.

Keller, Kenneth W. "From the Rhineland to the Virginia Frontier: Flax Production as a Commercial Enterprise." *VMHB* 98 (1990): 487–511.

Kelly, Kevin P. "'In Dispers'd Country Plantations': Settlement Patterns in Seventeenth-Century Surry County, Virginia." Pp. 183–205 in Tate and Ammerman, eds., *Chesapeake in the Seventeenth Century*.

Kemp, Thomas R. "Community and War: The Civil War Experience of Two New Hampshire Towns." Pp. 31–77 in Vinovskis, ed., *Toward Social History of the American Civil War*.

Kentucky. Department of State Archives. "Lincoln County Tax Lists, 1789. *Register of the Kentucky State Historical Society* 23 (1925): 209–29.

——. "Madison County Tax Lists, 1792." *Register of the Kentucky State Historical Society* 23 (1925): 116–41.

Kephart, John E. "A Pioneer Michigan Abolitionist." *Michigan History* 45 (1961): 34–42.

Kerber, Linda K. "Can a Woman Be an Individual? The Limits of the Puritan Tradition in the Early Republic." *Texas Studies in Language and Literature* 25 (1983): 165–78.

——. *Federalists in Dissent: Imagery and Ideology in Jeffersonian America.* Ithaca, N.Y., 1970.

——. "'History Can Do It No Justice': Women and the Reinterpretation of the American Revolution." Pp. 3–42 in Hoffman and Albert, eds., *Women in Age of the American Revolution.*

——. "'I Have Don . . . Much to Carrey on the Warr': Women and the Shaping of Republican Ideology after the American Revolution." Pp. 227–58 in Applewhite and Levy, eds., *Women and Politics.*

——. "Separate Spheres, Female Worlds, Woman's Place: The Rhetoric of Women's History." *JAH* 75 (1988): 9–39.

——. *Women of the Republic: Intellect and Ideology in Revolutionary America.* Chapel Hill, N.C., 1980

Kessel, Elizabeth A. "'A Mighty Fortress Is Our God': German Religious and Educational Organizations on the Maryland Frontier, 1734–1800." *Maryland Historical Magazine* 77 (1982): 370–87.

Kettner, James H. *The Development of American Citizenship, 1608–1870.* Chapel Hill, N.C., 1978.

Kilar, Jeremy W. *Michigan's Lumbertowns: Lumbermen and Laborers in Saginaw, Bay City, and Muskegon, 1870–1905.* Detroit, 1990.

Kim, Sung Bok. *Landlord and Tenant in Colonial New York: Manorial Society, 1664–1775.* Chapel Hill, N.C., 1978.

Kirkland, W. "The West, the Paradise of the Poor." *United States Magazine and Democratic Review* 15 (1844): 182–90.

Klein, Rachel N. *Unification of a Slave State: The Rise of the Planter Class in the South Carolina Backcountry, 1760–1808.* Chapel Hill, N.C., 1990.

Klingaman, David C., and Richard K. Veddar, eds. *Essays on the Economy of the Old Northwest.* Athens, Ohio, 1987.

Kloppenberg, James T. "The Virtues of Liberalism: Christianity, Republicanism, and Ethics in Early American Political Discourse." *JAH* 74 (1987): 9–33 .

Klubes, Benjamin B. "The First Federal Congress and the First National Bank: A Case Study in Constitutional Interpretation." *JEarR* 10 (1990): 19–42.

Knights, Peter R. *Plain People of Boston, 1830–1860: A Study in City Growth.* New York, 1971.

——. "Some Characteristics of Rural Migrants to Boston in the Mid-Nineteenth Century." Paper presented at the 1986 annual meeting of the Social Science History Association.

——. *Yankee Destinies: The Lives of Ordinary Nineteenth-Century Bostonians.* Chapel Hill, N.C., 1991.

Knobel, Dale T. *Paddy and the Republic: Ethnicity and Nationality in Antebellum America.* Middletown, Conn., 1986.

Knox, Henry. "Troops, Including Militia, Furnished by the Several States during the War of the Revolution." Pp. 14–19 in Walter Lowrie and Matthew St. Clair, eds., *American State Papers: Documents, Legislative and Executive of the Congress of the United States,* Class V. Vol 1. Washington, 1832.

Konig, David Thomas. "Community Custom and the Common Law: Social Change and the Development of Land Law in Seventeenth-Century Massachusetts." *American Journal of Legal History* 17 (1974): 148–64.

——, ed. *Plymouth Court Records, 1686–1859.* 16 vols. 1978–81.

Kornblith, Gary, and John Murrin. "The Making and Unmaking of the American Ruling Class." In Young, ed., *Beyond the American Revolution.*

Kousser, Morgan. *The Shaping of Southern Politics: Suffrage Restriction and the Establishment of the One-Party South.* New Haven, 1974.

Kramnick, Isaac. *Republicanism and Bourgeois Radicalism: Political Ideology in Late Eighteenth-Century England and America.* Ithaca, N.Y., 1990.

Krooss, Herman E. "Financial Institutions." Pp. 104–38 in David T. Gilcrist, ed., *The Growth of the Seaport Cities, 1790–1825.* Charlottesville, Va., 1967.

Kross, Jessica. *The Evolution of an American Town: Newtown, New York, 1642–1775.* Philadelphia, 1983.

Kulik, Gary. "Dams, Fish, and Farmers: Defense of Public Rights in Eighteenth Century Rhode Island." Pp. 25–50 in Hahn and Prude, eds., *The Countryside in the Age of Capitalist Transformation.*

Kulikoff, Allan. "Migration and Cultural Diffusion in Early America, 1600–1860: A Review Essay." *Historical Methods* 19 (1986): 153–69.

——. "The Political Economy of Military Service in Revolution Virginia." In John Murrin, ed., *War and Society in Early America from the Aztecs to the Civil War.* Philadelphia, forthcoming.

——. "The Progress of Inequality in Revolutionary Boston." *WMQ* 28 (1971): 375–414.

——. "A 'Prolifick' People: Black Population Growth in the Chesapeake Colonies, 1700–1790." *Southern Studies* 16 (1977): 391–428.

——. *Tobacco and Slaves: The Development of Southern Cultures in the Chesapeake, 1680–1800.* Chapel Hill, N.C., 1986.

——. "Tobacco and Slaves: Population, Economy and Society in Eighteenth-Century Prince George's County, Maryland." Ph.D. diss., Brandeis, 1976.

——. "Uprooted Peoples: Black Migrants in the Age of the American Revolution, 1790–1820." Pp. 143–71 in Berlin and Hoffman, eds., *Slavery and Freedom in the Age of the American Revolution.*

——. "Why *Men* Stopped Bearing So Many Babies." Paper presented at the 1987 meeting of the Social Science History Association.

Kussmaul, Ann. *Servants in Husbandry in Early Modern England.* Cambridge, 1981.

LaChance, Paul F. "The Politics of Fear: French Louisianians and the Slave Trade, 1786–1809." *Plantation Societies* 1 (1979): 162–97.

Lachmann, Richard. *From Manor to Market: Structural Change in England, 1536–1640.* Madison, Wis., 1987.

Lamoreaux, Naomi R. "Banks, Kinship, and Economic Development: The New England Case." *JEH* 46 (1986): 647–68.

Landale, Nancy S. "Opportunity, Movement, and Marriage: U.S. Farm Sons at the Turn of the Century." *JFamH* 14 (1989): 365–86.

Landale, Nancy S., and Avery M. Guest. "Generation, Ethnicity, and Occupational Opportunity in Late 19th Century America." *American Sociological Review* 55 (1989): 280–96.

Landon, Fred. *Western Ontario and the American Frontier*. Toronto, 1941.

Landsman, Ned C. *Scotland and Its First American Colony, 1683–1765*. Princeton, 1985.

Lane, Frederick C. "Meanings of Capitalism." *JEH* 29 (1969): 5–13.

Lang, Elgrieda. "German Immigration to Dubois County, Indiana, during the Nineteenth Century." *Indiana Magazine of History* 41 (1945): 131–51.

Larson, John Lauritz. "'Bind the Republic Together': The National Union and the Struggle for a System of Internal Improvements." *JAH* 74 (1987): 363–87.

Larson, Olaf F. "Values and Beliefs of Rural People." Pp. 91–112 in Thomas R. Ford, ed., *Rural U.S.A.: Persistence and Change*. Ames, Iowa, 1978.

Lathrop, Barnes F. *Migration into East Texas, 1835–1860: A Study from the United States Census*. Austin, Tex., 1949.

Lause, Mark A. "Voting Yourself a Farm in Antebellum Iowa: Toward an Urban, Working-class Prehistory of the Post–Civil War Agrarian Insurgency." *Annals of Iowa* 49 (1988): 169–86.

Leavitt, Judith Walzer. "Under the Shadow of Maternity: American Women's Responses to Death and Debility Fears in Nineteenth-Century Childbirth." *Feminist Studies* 12 (1986): 130–54.

Lee, Jean Butendoff. "Land and Labor: Parental Bequest Practices in Charles County, Maryland, 1732–1783." Pp. 306–41 in Carr, Morgan, and Russo, eds., *Colonial Chesapeake Society*.

——. "Maryland's 'Dangerous Insurrection' of 1786.'" *Maryland Historical Magazine* 85 (1990): 329–44.

——. "The Problem of the Slave Community in the Eighteenth-Century Chesapeake." *WMQ* 43 (1986): 333–61.

Lee, Susan Previant, and Peter Passell. *A New Economic View of American History*. New York, 1979.

Leet, Don R. "The Determinants of the Fertility Transition in Antebellum Ohio." *JEH* 36 (1976): 359–78.

Lemon, James T. "Agricultural Practices of National Groups in Eighteenth-Century Southeastern Pennsylvania." *Geographical Review* 56 (1966): 467–96.

——. *The Best Poor Man's Country: A Geographical Study of Early Southeastern Pennsylvania*. Baltimore, 1972.

——. "Comment on James A. Henretta's 'Families and Farms: *Mentalité* in Pre-Industrial America.'" *WMQ* 37 (1980), 688–96.

——. "Early Americans and Their Social Environment." *Journal of Historical Geography* 6 (1980): 115–31.

Lender, Mark E. "The Social Structure of the New Jersey Brigade: The Continental Line as an American Standing Army." Pp. 27–44 in Peter Karsten, ed., *The Military in America: From the Colonial Era to the Present*. New York, 1980.

Lenin, V. I. "Capitalism and Agriculture in the United States of America," Part 1 of "New Data on the Laws Governing the Development of Capitalism in Agriculture." Pp. 115–205 in *On The United States of America*. Moscow, 1967.

Lerner, Gerda, ed. *The Female Experience: An American Documentary*. Indianapolis, 1977.

Levine, David. *Reproducing Families: The Political Economy of English Population History*. Cambridge, 1987.

Levine, Lawrence W. *Black Culture and Black Consciousness: Afro-American Folk Thought from Slavery to Freedom*. New York, 1977.

Levine, Peter. "Draft Evasion in the North during the Civil War, 1863–1865." *JAH* 67 (1981): 816–34.

——. "The Fries Rebellion: Social Violence and the Politics of the New Nation." *Pennsylvania History* 40 (1973): 241–58.

Levy, Barry. *Quakers and the American Family: British Settlement in the Delaware Valley*. New York, 1988.

Lewis, Jan. "The Republican Wife: Virtue and Seduction in the Early Republic." *WMQ* 44 (1987): 689–721.

Lewis, Jan, and Kenneth A. Lockridge. "'Sally Has Been Sick': Pregnancy and Family Limitation among Virginia Gentry Women, 1780–1830." *Journal of Social History* 22 (1988): 5–19.

Liebcap, Gary D. "Property Rights in Economic History: Implications for Research." *Explorations in Economic History* 23 (1986): 227–52.

Lightner, David L. "Construction Labor on the Illinois Central Railroad." *Journal of the Illinois State Historical Society* 66 (1973): 285–301.

Limerick, Patricia Nelson. *The Legacy of Conquest: The Unbroken Past of the American West*. New York, 1987.

Lindert, Peter H. "English Occupations, 1670–1811." *JEH* 40 (1980): 685–707.

——. "Land Scarcity and American Growth." *JEH* 34 (1974): 851–84.

Lindert, Peter H., and Jeffrey G. Williamson. "Revising England's Social Tables, 1688–1812." *Explorations in Economic History* 19 (1982): 385–408.

Lindstrom, Diane. *Economic Development in the Philadelphia Region, 1810–1850*. New York, 1978.

——. "Northeastern Migration, 1810–1860." Work in progress.

Linebaugh, Peter. "All the Atlantic Mountains Shook." *Labour–Le Travailleur* 10 (1982): 87–121.

"List of Slaves Owned or Superintended on the First Day of October 1798 within the County of Richmond [Georgia]." 1798 Federal Direct Tax List. RG 34–6–1, Georgia Department of Archives, Atlanta.

Littlefield, Daniel C. *Rice and Slaves: Ethnicity and the Slave Trade in Colonial South Carolina*. Baton Rouge, 1981.

Litwack, Leon F. *North of Slavery: The Negro in the Free States, 1790–1860*. Chicago, 1961.

Litwak, Eugene. "Geographic Mobility and Extended Family Cohesion." *American Sociological Review* 25 (1960): 385–94.

Llambi, Luis. "Small Modern Farmers: Neither Peasants nor Fully-Fledged Capitalists?" *Journal of Peasant Studies* 15 (1988): 350–72.

Lockridge, Kenneth A. *A New England Town: The First Hundred Years*. New York, 1970.

[Logan, George]. *Letters Addressed to the Yeomanry of the United States: Shewing the Necessity of Confining the Public Revenue to a Fixed Proportion of the Net Produce of the Land. . . .* Philadelphia, 1791.

Lucas, Stephen E. "The Stylistic Artistry of the Declaration of Independence." *Prologue* 22 (1990): 25–43.

Lutz, Donald S. *Popular Consent and Popular Control: Whig Political Theory in the Early State Constitutions.* Baton Rouge, 1980.

Lynd, Staughton. *Anti-Federalism in Dutchess County, New York: A Study of Democracy and Class Conflict in the Revolutionary Era.* Chicago, 1962.

——. *Class Conflict, Slavery, and the United States Constitution: Ten Essays.* Indianapolis, 1967.

——. *Intellectual Origins of American Radicalism.* New York, 1968.

McBee, May Wilson, ed. *The Natchez Court Records, 1767–1805: Abstracts of Early Records.* Ann Arbor, Mich., 1953.

McBride, John D. "The Virginia War Effort, 1775–1783: Manpower Policies and Practices." Ph.D. diss., Virginia, 1977.

McCallum John. *Unequal Beginnings: Agriculture and Economic Development in Quebec and Ontario until 1870.* Toronto, 1980.

McClelland, Peter D., and Richard J. Zeckhauser. *Demographic Dimensions of the New Republic: American Interregional Migration, Vital Statistics, and Manumissions, 1800–1860.* Cambridge, 1982.

McCusker, John J., and Russell R. Menard. *The Economy of British America, 1607–1789.* Chapel Hill, N.C., 1985.

McDermott, John Francis. *George Caleb Bingham: River Portraitist.* Norman, Okla., 1959.

McDonald, Forest. "The Constitution and Hamiltonian Capitalism." Pp. 49–74 in Robert A. Goldwin and William A. Schambra, eds., *How Capitalistic Is the Constitution?* Washington, D.C., 1982.

——. *Novus Ordo Seclorum: The Intellectual Origins of the Constitution.* Lawrence, Kans., 1985.

McDonald, Forest, and Ellen Shapiro McDonald. "The Ethnic Origins of the American People, 1790." *WMQ* 37 (1980): 179–99.

MacDonald, John S., and Leatrice A. MacDonald. "Chain Migration and Ethnic Neighborhood Formation and Social Networks." *Milbank Memorial Fund Quarterly* 42 (1964): 82–97.

McElligott, Caroll Ainsworth, comp. "1787 Census of Natchez." *Genealogical and Historical Magazine of the South* 1 (Feb. 1984): 11–32.

——. "1792 Spanish Census of Natchez, Mississippi." *Genealogical and Historical Magazine of the South* 2 (Feb. 1985): 12–48 and 2 (May 1985): 5–35.

McGettigan, James William, Jr. "Boone County Slaves: Sales, Estate Divisions, and Families, 1820–1865." *Missouri Historical Review* 72 (1978): 176–97, 271–95.

McGuire, Robert A. "Constitution Making: A Rational Choice Model of the Federal Convention of 1787." *American Journal of Political Science* 32 (1988): 482–522.

McGuire, Robert A., and Robert L. Ohsfeldt. "An Economic Model of Voting Behavior over Specific Issues at the Constitutional Convention of 1787." *JEH* 46 (1986): 79- 112.

McIlwaine, H. R., ed. *Journals of the Council of the State of Virginia.* 3 vols. Richmond, 1931.

——, ed. *Official Letters of the Governors of the State of Virginia.* 3 vols. Richmond, 1926–29.

MacLeod, Duncan J. *Slavery, Race, and the American Revolution*. Cambridge, 1974.

McMahon, Sarah F. "'Indescribable Care Devolving upon a Housewife': Gender Perceptions of the Prepraration and Consumption of Food on the Midwestern Frontier, 1790–1860." Paper presented at the conference on "Rural Women and the Transition to Capitalism in Rural America," March–April 1989, DeKalb, Ill.

McMillen, Sally G. *Motherhood in the Old South: Pregnancy, Childbirth, and Infant Rearing*. Baton Rouge, 1990.

McMurry, Sally. *Farmhouses in Nineteenth-Century America: Vernacular Design and Social Change*. New York, 1988.

McNall, Scott G. *The Road to Rebellion: Class Formation and Kansas Populism, 1865–1900*. Chicago, 1988.

McNall, Scott G., and Sally Allen McNall. *Plains Families: Exploring Sociology through Social History*. New York, 1983.

MacPherson, C. B. "Capitalism and the Changing Concept of Property." Pp. 105–24 in H. E. Hallam et al., *Feudalism, Capitalism, and Beyond*. New York, 1975.

——. *The Political Theory of Possessive Individualism: Hobbes to Locke*. Oxford, 1962.

McPherson, James M. *The Battle Cry of Freedom: The Civil War Era*. New York, 1988.

McVickar, John. *Outlines of Political Economy*. 1825. Reprint. Joseph Dorfman, ed. New York, 1966.

McWhiney, Grady. *Cracker Culture: Celtic Ways in the Old South*. Tuscaloosa, Ala., 1988.

McWilliams, Carey. *Factories in the Field: The Story of Migratory Farm Labor in California*. 1935. Reprint. Santa Barbara, Calif., 1971.

Mahon, Richard. "Wage Labor and Seasonal Migration in the Wheat Belt of the Upper Mississippi Valley, 1860–1875." Paper presented to the Chicago Area Labor History Group, December 1988.

Mahoney, Timothy R. *River Towns in the Great West: The Structure of Provincial Urbanization in the American Midwest, 1820–1870*. Cambridge, Mass., 1990.

Main, Jackson Turner. *The Antifederalists: Critics of the Constitution, 1781–1788*. Chapel Hill, N.C., 1961.

——. "Government by the People: The American Revolution and the Democratization of the Legislatures." *WMQ* 23 (1966): 391–407.

——. *Political Parties before the Constitution*. Chapel Hill, N.C., 1973.

——. *Society and Economy in Colonial Connecticut*. Princeton, 1985.

——. *The Sovereign States, 1775–1783*. New York, 1973.

Majka, Linda C., and Theo J. Majka. *Farm Workers, Agribusiness, and the State*. Philadelphia, 1982.

Mak, James. "Intraregional Trade in the Antebellum West: Ohio, a Case Study." *AgH* 46 (1972): 489–97.

Malin, James C. *History and Ecology: Studies in the Grasslands*. Robert P. Swierenga, ed. Lincoln, Neb., 1984.

Malone, Anne Patton. "Searching for the Family and Household Structure of Rural Louisiana Slaves, 1810–1864." *Louisiana History* 28 (1987): 357–79.

Mann, Susan Archer. *Agrarian Capitalism in Theory and Practice*. Chapel Hill, N.C. , 1990.

Mann, Susan Archer, and James A. Dickinson. "State and Agriculture in Two Eras of American Capitalism." Pp. 283–325 in Frederick H. Buttel and Howard Newby, eds., *The Rural Sociology of the Advanced Societies: Critical Perspectives.* Montclair, N.J., 1980.

Manning, Brian. "The Peasantry and the English Revolution." *Journal of Peasant Studies* 2 (1975): 133–58.

Manning, Roger B. *Village Revolts: Social Protest and Popular Disturbances in England, 1509–1640.* Oxford, 1988.

Mark, Irving, and Oscar Handlin. "Land Cases in Colonial New York, 1765–1767: The King v. William Prendergast." *New York University Law Quarterly Review* 19 (1942): 165–94.

Marks, Bayly Ellen. "Economics and Society in a Staple Plantation System: St. Mary's County, Maryland, 1790–1840." Ph.D. diss., Maryland, 1979.

———. "The Rage for Kentucky: Emigration from St. Mary's County 1790–1810." Pp. 108–28 in Robert D. Mitchell and Edward K. Muller, eds., *Geographic Perspectives on Maryland's Past.* University of Maryland Department of Geography Occasional Papers, no. 4, College Park, 1979.

Marshall, James M. *Land Fever: Dispossession and the Frontier Myth.* Lexington, Ky., 1986.

Marshall, T. H. *Class, Citizenship, and Social Development.* Garden City, N.Y., 1964.

Marti, Donald B. "Sisters of the Grange: Rural Feminism in the Late Nineteenth Century." *AgH* 58 (1984): 247–62.

Martin, James Kirby, and Mark Edward Lender. *A Respectable Army: The Military Origins of the Republic, 1763–1789.* Arlington Heights, Ill., 1982.

Martin, John E. *Feudalism to Capitalism: Peasant and Landlord in English Agrarian Development.* Atlantic Highlands, N.J., 1983.

Martinac, Paula. "'An Unsettled Disposition': Social Structure and Geographical Mobility in Amelia County, Virginia, 1768–1794." M.A. thesis, College of William and Mary, 1979.

Marx, Karl. *Capital: A Critique of Political Economy.* 3 vols. Ernest Mandel, ed. 1867–94. Reprint. New York, 1977–81.

———. *The Eighteenth Brumaire of Louis Bonaparte* (1849). Pp. 95–180 in *Marx and Engels: Selected Works.*

———. *Pre-Capitalist Economic Formations.* Eric J. Hobsbawm, ed. New York, 1964.

Marx, Karl, and Frederick Engels. *Karl Marx and Frederick Engels: Selected Works.* New York, 1968.

———. *Manifesto of the Communist Party* (1848). Pp. 35–63 in *Marx and Engels: Selected Works.*

Marx, Leo. *The Machine and the Garden: Technology and the Pastoral Ideal in America.* London, 1964.

Masur, Louis P. "'Age of the First Person Singular': The Vocabulary of the Self in New England, 1780–1850." *Journal of American Studies* 25 (1991): 189–211.

Mathews, Donald G. *Religion in the Old South.* Chicago, 1977.

Mathews, Lois Kimball. *The Expansion of New England: The Spread of New England Settlement and Institutions to the Mississippi River, 1620–1865.* Boston, 1909.

Matsuda, Mari J. "The West and the Legal Status of Women: Explanations of Frontier Feminism." *Journal of the West* 24 (January 1985): 47–56.

Matthews, Jean. "Race, Sex, and the Dimensions of Liberty in Antebellum America." *JEarR* 6 (1986): 275–91.

Matthews, Richard K. *The Radical Politics of Thomas Jefferson: A Revisionist View.* Lawrence, Kans., 1984.

May, Dean L. "Women, Farm Production, and the Meaning of Land in the Far West, 1860–1880." Paper presented at the conference on "Rural Women and the Transition to Capitalism in Rural America," March–April 1989, DeKalb, Ill.

Mays, David John, ed. *Letters and Papers of Edmund Pendleton, 1734–1803.* 2 vols. Charlottesville, Va., 1967.

Meinig, D. W. *The Shaping of America: A Geographical Perspective on 500 Years of History.* Vol. 1, *Atlantic America, 1492–1800.* New Haven, 1986.

Melvoin, Richard L. *New England Outpost: War and Society in Colonial Deerfield.* New York, 1989.

Menard, Russell R. "The Africanization of the Lowcountry Labor Force, 1670–1730." Pp. 81–108, 155–61 in Winthrop D. Jordan and Shelia L. Skemp, eds., *Race and Family in the Colonial South.* Jackson, Miss., 1987.

——. "British Migration to the Chesapeake Colonies in the Seventeenth Century." Pp. 99–132 in Carr, Morgan, and Russo, eds., *Colonial Chesapeake Society.*

——. "Economy and Society in Early Colonial Maryland." Ph.D. diss., Iowa, 1975.

——. "From Servant to Freeholder: Status Mobility and Property Accumulation in Seventeenth-Century Maryland." *WMQ* 30 (1973): 37–64.

——. "From Servants to Slaves: The Transformation of the Chesapeake Labor System." *Southern Studies* 16 (1977): 355–90.

Mercer, Lloyd J. "Land Grants to American Railroads: Social Cost or Social Benefit?" *Business History Review* 43 (1969): 134–51.

Merchant, Carolyn. *Ecological Revolutions: Nature, Gender, and Science in New England.* Chapel Hill, N.C., 1989.

Mercier, Laurie K. "Women's Role in Montana Agriculture: 'You Had to Make Every Minute Count.'" *Montana: Magazine of Western History* 38 (Autumn 1988): 50–61.

Merrell, James H. *The Indians' New World: Catawbas and Their Neighbors from European Contact through the Era of Removal.* Chapel Hill, N.C., 1989.

Merrill, Michael. "The Anticapitalist Origins of the United States." *Review* 13 (1990): 465–97.

——. "Cash Is Good to Eat: Self-Sufficiency and Exchange in the Rural Economy of the United States." *RHR* 4 (Winter 1977): 42–71.

——. "The Political Economy of Agrarian America." Ph.D. diss., Columbia, 1985.

——. "So What's Wrong with the 'Household Mode of Production'?" *RHR*, no. 22 (1979–80): 141–46.

——. "A Survey of the Debate over the Nature of Exchange in Early America." Paper presented at the Social Science History Association, New Orleans, 1987.

Merrill, Michael, and Sean Wilentz. "Money and Justice in Revolutionary America: The Life and Writing of William Manning, 1747–1814." In Young, ed., *Beyond the American Revolution.*

Merritt, Carole Elaine. "Slave Family and Household Arrangements in Piedmont Georgia." Ph.D. diss., Emory, 1986.

Meyer, David R. "Midwestern Industrialization and the American Manufacturing Belt in the Nineteenth Century." *JEH* 49 (1989): 921–37.

Meyer, Donald K. "Southern Illinois Migration Fields: The Shawnee Hills in 1850." *Professional Geographer* 28 (1976): 151–60.

Meyers, Marvin. *The Jacksonian Persuasion: Politics and Belief.* Stanford, Calif., 1957.

——, ed. *The Mind of the Founder: Sources of the Political Thought of James Madison.* Hanover, N.H., 1981.

Miller, Randall Martin. *The Cotton Mill Movement in Antebellum Alabama.* New York, 1978.

Miller, Zane L. "Urban Blacks in the South, 1865–1920: An Analysis of Some Quantitative Data on Richmond, Savannah, New Orleans, Louisville, and Birmingham." Pp. 184–204 in Leo F. Schnore, ed., *The New Urban History: Quantitative Explorations by American Historians.* Princeton, 1975.

Mills, David. *The Idea of Loyalty in Upper Canada, 1784–1850.* Kingston, Canada, 1988.

Millward, R. "The Emergence of Wage Labor in Early Modern England." *Explorations in Economic History* 18 (1981): 21–39.

Miner, Craig. *West of Wichita: Settling the High Plains of Kansas, 1865–1890.* Lawrence, Kans., 1986.

Mintz, Sidney W., and Richard Price. *An Anthropological Approach to the Afro-American Past: A Caribbean Perspective.* Institute for the Study of Human Issues Occasional Papers in Social Change, no. 2. Philadelphia, 1976.

Mitchell, Robert D. "American Origins and Regional Institutions: The Seventeenth-Century Chesapeake." *Annals of the Association of American Geographers* 73 (1983): 404–20.

——. *Commercialism and Frontier: Perspectives on the Early Shenandoah Valley.* Charlottesville, Va., 1977.

Modell, John. "The Peopling of a Working-Class Ward: Reading Pennsylvania, 1850." *Journal of Social History* 5 (1971): 71–95.

Mohr, James C. *Abortion in America: The Origins and Evolution of National Policy.* New York, 1978.

Moogk, Peter N. "Reluctant Exiles: Emigrants from France in Canada before 1760." *WMQ* 46 (1989): 463–505.

Moore, Barrington, Jr. *Social Origins of Dictatorship and Democracy: Lord and Peasant in the Making of the Modern World.* Boston, 1966.

Moore, Christopher. "The Disposition to Settle: The Royal Highland Emigrants and Loyalist Settlement in Upper Canada." *Ontario History* 76 (1984): 306–25.

More, Thomas, comp. *American Country Almanack.* Philadelphia and New York, 1748–67.

Morgan, Edmund S. *American Slavery, American Freedom: The Ordeal of Colonial Virginia.* New York, 1975.

——. *Inventing the People: The Rise of Popular Sovereignty in England and America.* New York, 1988.

——, ed. *Prologue to Revolution: Sources and Documents on the Stamp Act Crisis, 1764–1766.* Chapel Hill, N.C., 1959.

Morgan, George. "An Essay, exhibiting a plan for a FARM-YARD, and method of conducting the same. . . ." *Columbian Magazine* 1 (1786): 76–82.

Morgan, Madel Jacobs. "Census of Clairborne and Warren Counties, Mississippi Territory, 1810." *Journal of Mississippi History* 13 (1951): 50–63.

——. "Census of Wilkinson County, Mississippi Territory, 1805." *Journal of Mississippi History* 11 (1949): 104–11.

Morgan, Philip D. "Black Society in the Lowcountry, 1760–1810." Pp. 83–141 in Berlin and Hoffman, eds., *Slavery and Freedom in the Age of the American Revolution.*

——. "Slave Life in Piedmont Virginia, 1720–1800." Pp. 433–84 in Carr, Morgan, and Russo, eds., *Colonial Chesapeake Society.*

Morgan, Philip D., and Michael L. Nicholls. "Slaves in Piedmont Virginia, 1720–1790." *WMQ* 46 (1989): 212–51.

Morison, Samuel Eliot, ed. "William Manning's *The Key of Libberty.*" *WMQ* 13 (1956): 202–54.

Morner, Magnus. "Spanish Migration to the New World prior to 1810: A Report on the State of Research." Pp. 737–810 in Chiappelli, ed., *First Images of America.*

Morris, Richard B. "Class Struggle and the American Revolution." *WMQ* 19 (1962): 3–29.

——. "'We the People of the United States': The Bicentennial of a People's Revolution." *AHR* 82 (1977): 1–19.

Morton, Louis. *Robert Carter of Nomini Hall: A Virginia Tobacco Planter of the Eighteenth Century.* Charlottesville, Va., 1945.

Morton, W. S., comp. "Charlotte County, Va." *William and Mary Quarterly*, 2d ser., 2 (1922): 85–88.

Moynihan, Ruth Barnes. *Rebel for Rights: Abigail Scott Duniway.* New Haven, 1983.

Mullin, Gerald W. *Flight and Rebellion: Slave Resistance in Eighteenth-Century Virginia.* New York, 1972.

Murrin, John. "The Myths of Colonial Democracy and Royal Decline in Eighteenth-Century America." *Cithara* 5 (1965): 53–69.

Mutch, Robert E. "Colonial America and the Debate about the Transition to Capitalism." *Theory and Society* 9 (1980): 847–63.

——. "Yeoman and Merchant in Pre-Industrial America: Eighteenth-Century Massachusetts as a Test Case." *Societas* 7 (1977): 279–302.

Myres, Sandra L. *Westering Women and the Frontier Experience, 1800–1915.* Albuquerque, 1982.

Nannini, Michael. "The Ethnic and Regional Composition of LaSalle County, 1850–1860." Pp. 77–90 in Conzen and Morales, *Settling the Upper Illinois Valley.*

Nash, Gary B. *Forging Freedom: The Formation of Philadelphia's Black Community, 1720–1840.* Cambridge, Mass., 1988.

——. *Quakers and Politics: Pennsylvania, 1681–1726.* Princeton, 1968.

——. *Race, Class, and Politics: Essays on American Colonial and Revolutionary Society.* Urbana, Ill., 1986.

——. *Red, White, and Black: The Peoples of Early America.* 2d ed. Englewood Cliffs, N.J., 1982.

——. *The Urban Crucible: Social Change, Political Consciousness, and the Origins of the American Revolution.* Cambridge, Mass., 1979.

Nash, Gary B, and Jean R. Soderlund. *Freedom by Degrees: Emancipation in Pennsylvania and Its Aftermath.* New York, 1991.

Neale, R. S. *Class in English History, 1680–1850*. Totowa, N.J., 1981.

Nelson, John R., Jr. *Liberty and Property: Political Economy and Policymaking in the New Nation, 1789–1812*. Baltimore, 1988.

Nelson, Margaret K. "Vermont Female Schoolteachers in the Nineteenth Century." *Vermont History* 49 (1981): 5–29.

Nettels, Curtis P. *The Emergence of a National Economy, 1775–1815*. New York, 1962.

Newby, Idus A. *Plain Folk in the New South: Social Change and Cultural Persistence, 1880–1915*. Baton Rouge, 1989.

Newell, William H. "Inheritance on the Maturing Frontier: Butler County, Ohio, 1803–1865." Pp. 261–303 in Engerman and Gallman, eds., *Long-Term Factors in American Economic Growth*.

Newman, Simon. "*Principles* and not *Men*: The Political Culture of Leadership in the 1790s." Paper presented to the Philadelphia Center for Early American Studies, May 1990.

Nicholls, Michael. "Origins of the Virginia Southside, 1703–1753: A Social and Economic Study." Ph.D. Diss., College of William and Mary, 1972.

Nobles, Gregory. "Capitalism in the Countryside: The Transformation of Rural Society in the United States." *RHR*, no. 41 (1988): 163–77.

——. *Divisions throughout the Whole: Politics and Society in Hampshire County, Massachusetts, 1740–1775*. Cambridge, 1983.

——. "The Rise of Merchants in Rural Market Towns: A Case Study of Eighteenth-Century Northampton, Massachusetts." *Journal of Social History* 24 (1990): 5–23.

Nordin, D. Swen. *Rich Harvest: A History of the Grange, 1867–1900*. Jackson, Miss., 1974.

North, Douglass C. *The Economic Growth of the United States, 1790–1860*. New York, 1966.

Norton, Mary Beth. *Liberty's Daughters: The Revolutionary Experience of American Women, 1750–1800*. Boston, 1980.

——. "'What an Alarming Crisis Is This': Southern Women and the American Revolution." Pp. 203–34 in Jeffrey J. Crow and Larry E. Tise, eds., *The Southern Experience in the American Revolution*. Chapel Hill, N.C., 1978.

Norton, Mary Beth, Herbert G. Gutman, and Ira Berlin. "The Afro-American Family in the Age of Revolution." Pp. 175–91 in Berlin and Hoffman, eds., *Slavery and Freedom in the Age of the American Revolution*.

Norton, Susan L. "Marriage Migration in Essex County, Massachusetts, in the Colonial and Early Federal Periods." *Journal of Marriage and the Family* 35 (1973): 419–28.

Oakes, James. *The Ruling Race: A History of American Slaveholders*. New York, 1982.

Oates, Stephen B. *To Purge This Land with Blood: A Biography of John Brown*. New York, 1970.

Oberly, James W. *Sixty Million Acres: American Veterans and the Public Lands before the Civil War*. Kent, Ohio, 1990.

O'Brien, Michael J. "Social Dimensions of Settlement." Pp. 210–30 in O'Brien, ed., *Grassland, Forest, and Historical Settlement*.

——, ed. *Grassland, Forest, and Historical Settlement: An Analysis of Dynamics in Northeastern Missouri*. Lincoln, Neb., 1984.

Okoye, F. Nwabueze. "Chattel Slavery as the Nightmare of the American Revolution-aries." *WMQ* 38 (1980): 3–28.

Olmstead, Alan L. "Investment Constraints and New York City Mutual Savings Bank Financing of Antebellum Development." *JEH* 32 (1972): 811–40.

———. "New York Mutual Savings Bank Portfolio Management and Trustee Objectives." *JEH* 34 (1974): 815–34.

Olwell, Robert A. "'Domestick Enemies': Slavery and Political Independence in South Carolina, May 1775–March 1776." *Journal of Southern History* 45 (1989): 21–48.

Onuf, Peter S. *Statehood and Union: A History of the Northwest Ordinance.* Bloomington, Ind., 1987.

Osborne, Brian S., and Christian M. Rogerson. "Conceptualizing the Frontier Settle-ment Process: Development or Dependency?" *Comparative Frontier Studies,* no. 11 (1978): 1–3.

Osburn, Mary McMillan. "The Atacosita Census of 1826." *Texana* 1 (1963): 299–321.

Ossowski, Stanislaw. *Class Structure in the Social Consciousness.* Trans. Sheila Patterson. New York, 1963.

Ostergren, Robert C. *A Community Transplanted: The Transatlantic Experience of a Swed-ish Immigrant Settlement in the Upper Middle West, 1835–1915.* Madison, Wis., 1988.

Osterud, Nancy Grey. *Bonds of Community: The Lives of Farm Women in Nineteenth-Century New York.* Ithaca, N.Y., 1991.

Osterud, Nancy Grey, and John Fulton. "Family Limitation and Age at Marriage: Fer-tility Decline in Sturbridge, Massachusetts." *Population Studies* 30 (1976): 481–93.

Otto, John Solomon. "The Migration of Southern Plain Folk: An Interdisciplinary Synthesis." *Journal of Southern History* 51 (1985): 183–200.

Paine, Thomas. *Common Sense* (1776). Isaac Kramnick, ed. Harmondsworth, England, 1976.

Painter, Nell Irvin. *Standing at Armageddon: The United States, 1877–1919.* New York, 1987.

Palmer, Bruce. *"Man over Money": The Southern Populist Critique of American Capital-ism.* Chapel Hill, N.C., 1980.

Palmer, Bryan D. *Descent into Discourse: The Reification of Language and the Writing of Social History.* Philadelphia, 1990.

———. "Social Formation and Class Formation in North America, 1800–1900," Pp. 229–309 in David Levine, ed., *Proletarianization and Family History.* Orlando, Fla., 1984.

Palmer, William Pitt, ed. *Calendar of Virginia State Papers and Other Manuscripts Pre-served in the Capital in Richmond.* 3 vols. Richmond, 1875–83.

Pankrantz, John R. "Reading on the Ohio Frontier." Paper presented to the Philadel-phia Center for Early American Studies, 1986.

Papenfuse, Edward C., and Gregory A. Stiverson. "General Smallwood's Recruits: The Peacetime Career of the Revolutionary War Private." *WMQ* 30 (1973): 117–32.

Parenti, Michael. "The Constitution as an Elitist Document." Pp. 39–58 in Goldwin and Schambra, eds., *How Democratic Is the Constition?*

Parker, Rachel R. "Shays' Rebellion: An Episode in American State-Making." *Sociologi-cal Perspectives* 34 (1991): 95–113.

Parker, Susan R. "Men without God or King: Rural Settlers of East Florida, 1784–1790." *Florida Historical Quarterly* 59 (1990): 135–55.

Parker, William N. "The Magic of Property." *AgH* 54 (1980): 477–89.

Parker, William N., and Eric L. Jones, eds. *European Peasants and Their Markets: Essays in Agrarian Economic History*. Princeton, 1975.

Parkerson, Donald H. "How Mobile Were Nineteenth-century Americans?" *Historical Methods* 15 (1982): 99–110.

———. "Migration and the Emergence of a Commercial Agricultural Economy in New York, 1855–1865." Paper presented at the 1989 meeting of the Social Science History Association.

Parkerson, Donald H., and Jo Anne Parkerson. "'Fewer Children of Higher Spiritual Quality': Religion and the Decline of Fertility in Nineteenth-Century America." *SSH* 12 (1988): 49–70.

Paskoff, Paul F., and Daniel J. Wilson, eds. *The Cause of the South: Selections from De-Bow's Review, 1846–1867*. Baton Rouge, 1982.

Patten, John. "Patterns of Migration and Movement of Labour to Three Pre-Industrial East Anglian Towns." *Journal of Historical Geography* 2 (1976): 111–29.

Patterson, Stephen E. *Political Parties in Revolutionary Massachusetts*. Madison, Wis., 1973.

Peek, George A., Jr., ed. *The Political Writings of John Adams: Representative Selections*. New York, 1954.

Pencak, William. "The Declaration of Independence: Changing Interpretations and a New Hypothesis." *Pennsylvania History* 57 (1990): 225–35.

Perkins, Edwin J. "The Entrepreneurial Spirit in Colonial America: The Foundations of Modern Business History." *Business History Review* 63 (1989): 160–86.

Perkins, Elizabeth A. "The Consumer Frontier: Household Consumption in Early Kentucky." *JAH* 78 (1991): 486–510.

Pessen, Edward. *Most Uncommon Jacksonians: The Radical Leaders of the Early Labor Movement*. Albany, N.Y., 1970.

Peterson, Trudy Huskamp, ed. *Farmers, Bureaucrats, and Middlemen: Historical Perspectives on American Agriculture*. Washington, D.C., 1980.

Phillips, Ulrich B., ed. *Plantation and Frontier*. 2 vols. Cleveland, 1910.

Pierce, Bessie Louise. *A History of Chicago*. Vol. 1, *The Beginning of a City, 1673–1848*. Chicago, 1937.

Pole, J. R. *The Pursuit of Equality in American History*. Berkeley, Calif., 1978.

Pollack, Norman. *The Just Polity: Populism, Law, and Human Welfare*. Urbana, Ill., 1987.

Potter, David. *The Impending Crisis, 1848–1861*. New York, 1976.

Poulantzas, Nicos. *Classes in Contemporary Capitalism*. London, 1974.

Powell, William S., James K. Huhta, and Thomas J. Farnham, eds. *The Regulators in North Carolina: A Documentary History, 1759–1776*. Raleigh, N.C., 1971.

Power, Richard Lyle. *Planting Corn Belt Culture: The Impress of the Upland Southerner and Yankee in the Old Northwest*. Indianapolis, 1953.

Pred, Alan R. *Urban Growth and City Systems in the United States, 1840–1860*. Cambridge, Mass., 1980.

———. *Urban Growth and the Circulation of Information: The United States System of Cities, 1790–1840*. Cambridge, Mass., 1973.

Pritchard, Linda K. "The Burned-Over District Reconsidered: A Portent of Evolving Religious Pluralism in the United States." *SSH* 8 (1984): 243–65.

———. "Disentangling Evangelicalism, Denominationalism, and Economic Development." Paper presented before the 1986 meeting of the Social Science History Association.

Prude, Jonathan. *The Coming of Industrial Order: Town and Factory Life in Rural Massachusetts, 1810–1860.* Cambridge, 1983.

Pruitt, Bettye Hobbs. "Agriculture and Society in the Towns of Massachusetts, 1771: A Statistical Analysis." Ph.D. diss., Boston, 1981.

———. "Self-Sufficiency and the Agricultural Economy of Eighteenth-Century Massachusetts." *WMQ* 41 (1984): 333–64.

Pudup, Mary Beth. "The Boundaries of Class in Preindustrial Appalachia." *Journal of Historical Geography* 15 (1989): 139–62.

Purvis, Thomas L. "Commentary [on Akenson]." *WMQ* 41 (1984): 119–25.

———. "The European Ancestry of the United States Population, 1790." *WMQ* 41 (1984): 85–101.

———. "The European Origins of New Jersey's Eighteenth-Century Population." *New Jersey History* 100 (1982): 15–31.

———. "The National Origins of New Yorkers in 1790." *New York History* 77 (1986): 133–53.

———. "Origins and Patterns of Agrarian Unrest in New Jersey, 1735 to 1754." *WMQ* 39 (1982): 600–627.

———. "Patterns of Ethnic Settlement in Late Eighteenth-Century Pennsylvania." *Western Pennsylvania Historical Magazine* 70 (1987): 107–22.

Putnam, James William. *The Illinois and Michigan Canal: A Study in Economic History.* Chicago Historical Society's Collections, vol. 10. Chicago, 1918.

Quarles, Benjamin. *The Negro in the American Revolution.* Chapel Hill, N.C., 1961.

———. *The Negro in the Civil War.* Boston, 1969.

———. "The Revolutionary War as a Black Declaration of Independence." Pp. 283–301 in Berlin and Hoffman, eds., *Slavery and Freedom in the Age of the American Revolution.*

Rabinowitz, Howard N. *Race Relations in the Urban South, 1865–1890.* Urbana, Ill., 1980.

Raboteau, Albert J. *Slave Religion: The "Invisible Institution" in the Antebellum South.* New York, 1978.

Ranck, George W. "'The Travelling Church': An Account of the Baptist Exodus to Kentucky in 1781." *Register of the Kentucky Historical Society* 79 (1981): 240–65.

Ranking, David C. "The Tannenbaum Thesis Reconsidered: Slavery and Race Relations in Antebellum Louisiana." *Southern Studies* 18 (1979): 5–32.

Ransom, Roger L. "Interregional Canals and Economic Specialization in the Antebellum United States." *Explorations in Entrepreneurial History* 5 (1967): 12–35.

Ransom, Roger L., and Richard Sutch. *One Kind of Freedom: The Economic Consequences of Emancipation.* Cambridge, 1977.

Rash, Nancy. *The Paintings and Politics of George Caleb Bingham.* New Haven, 1991.

Ratcliffe, Donald J. "Politics in Jacksonian Ohio: Reflections on the Ethnocultural Interpretation." *Ohio History* 88 (1979): 6–36.

Rawley, James A. *Race and Politics: "Bleeding Kansas" and the Coming of the Civil War.* Lincoln, Neb., 1969.

Raymond, Daniel. *The Elements of Political Economy.* Baltimore, 1823.

Read, Colin. *The Rising in Western Upper Canada, 1837–8: The Duncombe Revolt and After.* Toronto, 1982.

Rediker, Marcus. "'Good Hands, Stout Heart, and Fast Feet': The History and Culture of Working People in Early America." *Labour–Le Travailleur* 10 (1982): 123–44.

Reed, James. *From Private Vice to Public Virtue: The Birth Control Movement and American Society since 1830.* New York, 1978.

Reid, Russell M. "Church Membership, Consanguineous Marriage, and Migration in a Scotch-Irish Frontier Population." *JFamH* 13 (1988): 397–414.

Remer, Rosalind. "Old Light and New Money: A Note on Religion, Economics, and the Social Order in 1740 Boston." *WMQ* 47 (1990): 566–73.

Revolutionary War Records, vol. 1. Virginia State Library, Richmond.

Richardson, John G. "Town versus Countryside and Systems of Common Schooling." *SSH* 11 (1987): 401–32.

Richey, Russell E. "The Four Languages of Early American Methodism." *Methodist History* 28 (1990): 155–71.

Richmond County Slave Registration Book [Augusta]. Manuscript Department, William R. Perkins Library, Duke University, Durham, N.C.

Riesman, Janet A. "Money, Credit, and Federalist Political Economy." Pp. 128–61 in Beeman, Botein, and Carter, eds., *Beyond Confederation.*

Riley, Glenda. *Frontierswomen: The Iowa Experience.* Ames, Iowa, 1981.

Risjord, Norman K. "How the 'Common Man' Voted in Jefferson's Virginia." Pp. 33–64 in John B. Boles, ed., *America, the Middle Period: Essays in Honor of Bernard Mayo.* Charlottesville, 1973.

Robbins, Roy Marvin. "Horace Greeley: Land Reform and Unemployment, 1837–1862." *AgH* 7 (1933): 18–41.

——. *Our Landed Heritage: The Public Domain, 1776–1936.* Lincoln, Neb., 1962.

Robbins, William G. "Opportunity and Persistence in the Pacific Northwest: A Quantitative Study of Roseburg, Oregon." *Pacific Historical Review* 39 (1970): 279–96.

Robertson, James Oliver. *America's Business.* New York, 1985.

Robson, David W. "'An Important Question Answered': William Graham's Defense of Slavery in Post-Revolutionary Virginia." *WMQ* 37 (1980): 644–52.

Roeber, A. G. "The Origins and Transfer of German-American Concepts of Property and Inheritance." *Perspectives in American History,* n.s., 3 (1987): 115–71.

Roemer, John E. "New Directions in the Marxian Theory of Exploitation and Class." Pp. 81–113 in Roemer, ed., *Analytical Marxism.*

——, ed. *Analytical Marxism.* Cambridge, 1986.

Rogers, Daniel T. *Contested Truths: Keywords in American Politics since Independence.* New York, 1987.

Rogers, Richard L. "Destinations of Home Missionaries: New York State, 1823–1832." Paper presented to the 1988 meeting of the Social Science History Association.

Rohrbough, Malcolm J. "Diversity and Unity in the Old Northwest, 1790–1850: Several Peoples Fashion a Single Region." Pp. 71–87 in Lloyd H. Hunter, ed., *Pathways* to the Old Northwest: An Observance of the Bicentennial of the Northwest Ordinance. Indianpolis, 1988.

Rohrer, Wayne C., and Louis H. Douglas. *The Agrarian Transition in America: Dualism and Change.* Indianapolis, 1969.

Rollins, Richard M. "Words as Social Control: Noah Webster and the Creation of the American Dictionary." *AQ* 28 (1976): 415–30.

Rome, Adam Ward. "American Farmers as Entrepreneurs." *AgH* 56 (1982): 37–49.

Rorabaugh, W. J. "Who Fought for the North in the Civil War? Concord, Massachusetts, Enlistments." *JAH* 73 (1986): 695–701.

Rose, Gregory S. "The Distribution of Indiana's Ethnic and Racial Minorities in 1850." *Indiana Magazine of History* 87 (1991): 224–60.

——. "Hoosier Origins: The Nativity of Indiana's United States-Born Population in 1850." *Indiana Magazine of History* 81 (1985): 201–32.

——. "South Central Michigan Yankees." *Michigan History* 70 (March–April 1986): 32–39.

Rosenfeld, Rachel Ann. *Farm Women: Work, Farm, and Family in the United States.* Chapel Hill, N.C., 1985.

Rosovsky, Henry, ed. *Industrialization in Two Systems: Essays in Honor of Alexander Gerschenkron by a Group of His Students.* New York, 1966.

Rossell, Daves. "Tended Images: Verbal and Visual Idolatry of Rural Life in America, 1800–1850." *New York History* 79 (1988): 425–40.

Rosswurm, Steven. *Arms, Country, and Class: The Philadelphia Militia and the "Lower Sort" during the American Revolution.* New Brunswick, N.J., 1987.

Rothenberg, Winifred. "The Bound Prometheus." *Reviews in American History* 15 (1987): 628–37.

——. "The Emergence of a Capital Market in Rural Massachusetts, 1730–1838." *JEH* 45 (1985): 781–808.

——. "The Emergence of Farm Labor Markets and the Transformation of the Rural Economy: Massachusetts, 1750–1855." *JEH* 48 (1988): 537–66.

——. "The Market and Massachusetts Farmers, 1750–1855." *JEH* 41 (1981): 283–314.

——. "The Market and Massachusetts Farmers: Reply." *JEH* 43 (1983): 479–80.

——. "Markets, Values, and Capitalism: A Discourse on Method." *JEH* 44 (1984): 174–78.

Rothstein, Morton. "'The Remotest Corner': Natchez on the American Frontier." Pp. 124–35 in Noel Polk, ed., *Natchez before 1830.* Jackson, Miss., 1989.

Royall, Ann Newport. *Letters from Alabama, 1817–1822.* Lucille Griffith, ed. 1830. Reprint. University, Ala., 1969.

Royster, Charles. *A Revolutionary People at War: The Continental Army and American Character, 1775–1783.* Chapel Hill, N.C., 1979.

Rutland, Robert A., ed. *The Papers of George Mason, 1725–1792.* 3 vols. Chapel Hill, N.C., 1970.

Rutman, Darrett B. "People in Process: The New Hampshire Towns of the Eighteenth Century." Pp. 16–37 in Tamara K. Hareven, ed., *Family and Kin in Urban Communities, 1700–1930.* New York, 1977.

Rutman, Darrett B., and Anita H. Rutman. "'More True and Perfect Lists': The Reconstruction of Censuses for Middlesex County, Virginia, 1668–1704." *VMHB* 88 (1980): 37–74.

Ryan, Dennis P. "Landholding, Opportunity, and Mobility in Revolutionary New Jersey." *WMQ* 36 (1979): 571–92.

Ryan, Mary. *The Cradle of the Middle Class: The Family in Oneida County, New York, 1790–1865*. Cambridge, 1981.

Ryerson, Stanley B. *Unequal Union: Confederation and the Roots of Conflict in the Canadas, 1815–1873*. New York, 1968.

Sachs, Carolyn E. *The Invisible Farmers: Women in Agricultural Production*. Totowa, N.J., 1983.

Sahlins, Marshall. *Stone Age Economics*. New York, 1972.

Salerno, Anthony. "The Social Background of Seventeenth-Century Emigration to America." *Journal of British Studies* 19 (1979): 31–52.

Salinger, Sharon V. *"To Serve Well and Faithfully": Labor and Indentured Servants in Pennsylvania, 1682–1800*. Cambridge, 1987.

Salmon, Marylynn. *Women and the Law of Property in Early America*. Chapel Hill, N.C. 1986.

Saloutos, Theodore. *Farmer Movements in the South, 1865–1933*. Berkeley, Calif., 1960.

Saloutos, Theodore, and John D. Hicks. *Twentieth Century Populism: Agrarian Discontent in the Middle West, 1900–1939*. Lincoln, Neb., 1951.

Sanchez-Saavedra, E. M., comp. *A Guide to Virginia Military Organizations in the American Revolution, 1774–1787*. Richmond, 1978.

Saunders, William L., ed. *The Colonial Records of North Carolina*. 10 vols. Raleigh, N.C., 1886–90.

Sawyer, Marcia R. "Surviving Freedom: Black Farm Households in Cass County, Michigan, 1832–1890." Ph.D. diss., Michigan State, 1990.

Schaefer, Donald F. "A Statistical Profile of Frontier and New South Migration: 1850–1860." *AgH* 59 (1985): 563–78.

Schafer, Joseph. *A History of Agriculture in Wisconsin*. Madison, Wis., 1922.

Schapiro, Michael Edward, ed. *George Caleb Bingham*. New York, 1990.

Scheiber, Harry N. *Ohio Canal Era: A Case Study of Government and the Economy, 1820–1861*. 1967. 2d ed., Athens, Ohio, 1987.

Schlereth, Thomas J. "The New England Presence on the Midwest Landscape." *The Old Northwest* 9 (1983): 125–42.

Schlesinger, Arthur M. *The Colonial Merchants and the American Revolution*. New York, 1917.

Schmidt, Fredricka Teute, and Barbara Ripel Wilhelm, eds. "Early Proslavery Petitions in Virginia." *WMQ* 30 (1973): 133–46.

Schob, David E. *Hired Hands and Plowboys: Farm Labor in the Midwest, 1815–60*. Urbana, Ill., 1975.

Schweitzer, Mary M. *Custom and Contract: Household, Government and the Economy in Colonial Pennsylvania*. New York, 1987.

———. "State-Issued Currency and the Ratification of the U.S. Constitution." *JEH* 49 (1989): 311–22.

Schwieder, Dorothy. "Labor and Economic Roles of Iowa Farm Wives, 1840–80." Pp. 152–68 in Peterson, ed., *Farmers, Bureaucrats, and Middlemen*.

Scranton, Philip. *Proprietary Capitalism: The Textile Manufacture at Philadelphia, 1800–1885.* Philadelphia, 1983.

Seaman, John W. "Thomas Paine: Ransom, Civil Peace, and the Natural Right to Welfare." *Political Theory* 16 (1988): 120–42.

Segal, Harvey H. "Cycles of Canal Construction." Pp. 169–215 in Carter Goodrich, ed., *Canals and American Economic Development.* New York, 1961.

Selby, John E. *The Revolution in Virginia, 1775–1783.* Williamsburg, Va., 1988.

Selesky, Harold E. *War and Society in Colonial Connecticut.* New Haven, 1990.

Sellers, John R. "The Common Soldier in the American Revolution." Pp. 151–63 in Stanley J. Underdal, ed., *Military History of the American Revolution.* Proceedings of the 6th Military History Symposium, United States Air Force Academy, 1974. Washington, D.C., 1974.

Sen, Amartya K. "Gender and Cooperative Conflicts." Pp. 123–49 in Irene Tinker, ed., *Persistent Inequalities: Women and World Development.* New York, 1990.

Sewell, William H., Jr. "How Classes Are Made: Critical Reflections on E. P. Thompson's Theory of Working Class Formation." Pp. 50–77 in Harvey J. Kaye and Keith McClelland, eds., *E. P. Thompson: Critical Perspectives.* Philadelphia, 1990.

Shade, William G. "Society and Politics in Antebellum Virginia's Southside." *Journal of Southern History* 53 (1987): 163–93.

Shalhope, Robert E. "Individualism in the Early Republic." Pp. 66–86 in Curry and Goodhart, eds. *American Chameleon.*

Shammas, Carole. "English Commercial Development and American Colonization, 1560–1620." Pp. 151–74 in K. R. Andrews, N. P. Canny, and P. E. H. Hair, eds., *The Westward Enterprise: English Acitivites in Ireland, the Atlantic, and America 1480–1650.* Detroit, 1979.

——. "The World Women Knew: Women Workers in the North of England during the Late Seventeenth Century." Pp. 99–115 in Richard S. Dunn, and Mary Maples Dunn, eds., *The World of William Penn.* Philadelphia, 1986.

Shammas, Carole, Marylynn Salmon, and Michel Dahlin. *Inheritance in America from Colonial Times to the Present.* New Brunswick, N.J., 1987.

Shannon, Fred A. *The Farmer's Last Frontier: Agriculture, 1860–1897.* New York, 1945.

Sharp, Buchanan. *In Contempt of All Authority: Rural Artisans and Riot in the West of England, 1586–1660.* Berkeley, Calif., 1980.

Sharp, James Rogers. *The Jacksonians versus the Banks: Politics in the States after the Panic of 1837.* New York, 1970.

Shelton, Cynthia J. *The Mills of Manayunk: Industrialization and Social Conflict in the Philadelphia Region, 1787–1837.* Baltimore, 1986.

Shenton, James P. *Robert John Walker: A Politician from Jackson to Lincoln.* New York, 1961.

Shepherd, Rebecca A. "Restless Americans: The Geographic Mobility of Farm Laborers in the Old Midwest, 1850–1870." *Ohio History* 89 (1980): 25–45.

Shirley, Michael. "The Market and Community Culture in Antebellum Salem, North Carolina." *JEarR* 11 (1991): 219–48.

Shover, John L. *First Majority—Last Minority: The Transformation of Rural Life in America.* DeKalb, Ill., 1976.

Shy, John W. "The Legacy of the American Revolutionary War." Pp. 43–60 in Larry R.

Gerlach, James A. Dolph, and Michael L. Nicholls, eds., *Legacies of the American Revolution*. Logan, Utah, 1978.

——. *A People Numerous and Armed: Reflections on the Military Struggle for American Independence*. Rev. ed. Ann Arbor, Mich., 1990.

Silverman, Jason H. "Roots Revisited: The Anglicization of America." *Georgia Historical Quarterly* 74 (1990): 254–68.

Simler, Lucy. "The Landless Worker: An Index of Economic and Social Change in Chester County, Pennsylvania, 1750–1820." *Pennsylvania Magazine of History and Biography* 114 (1990): 163–99.

——. "Tenancy in Colonial Pennsylvania: The Case of Chester County." *WMQ* 43 (1986): 542–69.

Simpson, David. *The Politics of American English, 1776–1850*. New York, 1986.

Siracusa, Carl. *A Mechanical People: Perceptions of the Industrial Order in Massachusetts, 1815–1880*. Middletown, Conn., 1979.

Skaggs, David Curtis. *Roots of Maryland Democracy 1753–1776*. Westport, Conn., 1973.

Sklar, Martin J. *The Corporate Reconstruction of American Capitalism, 1890–1916: The Market, the Law, and Politics*. Cambridge, 1988.

Slack, Paul. "Vagrants and Vagrancy in England, 1598–1664." *Economic History Review*, 2d ser., 27 (1974): 360–79.

Slaughter, Thomas P. "Crowds in Eighteenth-Century America: Reflections and New Directions." *Pennsylvania Magazine of History and Biography* 105 (1991): 3–34.

——. *The Whiskey Rebellion: Frontier Epilogue to the American Revolution*. New York, 1986.

Smith, A. Hassell. "Labourers in Late Sixteenth-Century England: A Case Study from North Norfolk." *Continuity and Change* 4 (1989): 11–52, 367–94.

Smith, Abbot Emerson. *Colonists in Bondage: White Servitude and Convict Labor in America, 1607–1776*. Chapel Hill, N.C., 1947.

Smith, Adam. *An Inquiry into the Nature and Causes of the Wealth of Nations*. 5th. ed., 1789. Reprint. Edwin Cannon, ed. New York, 1937.

Smith, Billy G. *The "Lower Sort": Philadelphia's Laboring People, 1750–1800*. Ithaca, N.Y., 1990.

Smith, Daniel Scott. "'Early' Fertility Decline in America: A Problem in Family History." *JFamH* 12 (1987): 73–84.

——. Family Limitation, Sexual Control, and Domestic Feminism in Victorian America." Pp. 222–45 in Nancy F. Cott and Elizabeth H. Pleck, eds., *A Heritage of Her Own: Toward a New Social History of American Women*. New York, 1979.

——. "A Malthusian-Frontier Interpretation of United States Demographic History before c. 1815." Pp. 15–24 in Woodrow Borah, Jorge Hardoy, and Gilbert A. Stelter, eds., *Urbanization in the Americas: The Background in Comparative Perspective*. Ottawa, 1980.

——. "Process, Event, Process: The Federalist-Republican Division in the First Parish of Hingham, Massachusetts, in 1806 in Long-Run Perspective." Unpublished paper.

Smith, Henry Nash. *Virgin Land: The American West as Symbol and Myth*. Cambridge, Mass., 1950.

Smith, Paul. *Discerning the Subject*. Minneapolis, 1988.

Smith, Warren. "Land Patterns in Ante-Bellum Montgomery County, Alabama." *Alabama Review* 8 (1955): 196–208.

Smuksta, Michael. "Work, Family, and Community: Rural Women in Illinois, 1830–1900." Ph.D. diss., Northern Illinois, 1991.

So, Alvin Y. "Class Struggle Analysis: A Critique of Class Structure Analysis." *Sociological Perspectives* 34 (1991): 39–59.

So, Alvin Y., and Muhammad Hikam. "'Class' in the Writings of Wallerstein and Thompson." *Sociological Perspectives* 32 (1989): 453–67.

Sobel, Mechal. *Trabelin' On: The Slave Journey to an Afro-Bapitist Faith.* New York, 1979.

——. *The World They Made Together: Black and White Values in Eighteenth-Century Virginia.* Princeton, 1987.

Soderlund, Jean R. *Quakers and Slavery: A Divided Spirit.* Princeton, 1985.

Sokoloff, Kenneth L. "Inventive Activity in Early Industrial America: Evidence from Patent Records, 1790–1846." *JEH* 48 (1988): 813–50.

Soltow, Lee. "America's First Progressive Tax." *National Tax Journal* 30 (1977): 53–58.

——. "Inequality amidst Abundance: Land Ownership in Early Nineteenth Century Ohio." *Ohio History* 88 (1979): 133–47.

——. "Kentucky Wealth at the End of the Eighteenth Century." *JEH* 43 (1983): 617–34.

——. "Land Inequality on the Frontier: The Distribution of Land in East Tennessee at the Beginning of the Nineteenth Century." *SSH* 5 (1981): 275–92.

——. "Progress and Mobility among Ohio Propertyholders, 1810–1825." *SSH* 7 (1983): 405–27.

——. *Wealth and Income in the United States in 1798.* Pittsburgh, 1989.

Soltow, Lee, and Kenneth W. Keller. "Rural Pennsylvania in 1800: A Portrait from the Septennial Census." *Pennsylvania History* 49 (1982): 25–47.

Soltow, Lee, and Edward Stevens. *The Rise of Literacy in the United States: A Socioeconomic Analysis to 1870.* Chicago, 1981.

Souden, David. "'Rogues, Whores and Vagabonds'? Indentured Servant Emigrants to North America, and the Case of Mid-Seventeenth-Century Bristol." *Social History* 3 (1978): 23–41.

South Carolina Legislative Petitions, 1817. South Carolina Department of Archives and History, Columbia.

Spaulding, Thomas W. "The Maryland Catholic Diaspora." *U.S. Catholic Historian* 8 (1989): 163–72.

Stagg, J. C. A. "Enlisted Men in the United States Army, 1812–1815: A Preliminary Survey." *WMQ* 43 (1986): 615–45.

Standing, Guy. "Migration and Modes of Explanation: Social Origins of Immobility and Mobility." *Journal of Peasant Studies* 8 (1980–81): 173–211.

Stansell, Christine. *City of Women: Sex and Class in New York, 1789–1860.* New York, 1986.

"A State of the Inspector's Accounts from Oct 1786 to Oct 1787." Auditors Item 49. Virginia State Library, Richmond.

Statom, Thomas R. "Negro Slavery in Eighteenth-Century Georgia." Ph.D. diss., Alabama, 1982.

Steckel, Richard H. "Antebellum Southern White Fertility: A Demographic and Economic Analysis." *JEH* 40 (1980): 331–50.

——. "The Economic Foundations of East-West Migration during the 19th Century." *Explorations in Economic History* 20 (1983): 14–36.

——. "Household Migration and Rural Settlement in the United States, 1850–1860." *Explorations in Economic History* 26 (1989): 190–218.

——. "Household Migration, Urban Growth, and Industrialization: The United States, 1850–1860." National Bureau of Economic Research, Working Paper no. 2281.

Steinfeld, Robert J. "Property and Suffrage in the Early American Republic." *Stanford Law Review* 41 (1989): 335–76.

Stern, Mark J. *Society and Family Strategy: Erie County, New York, 1850–1920.* Albany, N.Y., 1987.

Stern, Steve J. "Feudalism, Capitalism, and the World-System in the Perspective of Latin America and the Caribbean." *AHR* 93 (1988): 829–72.

Stevens, Edward W., Jr. "Relationship of Social Library Membership, Wealth, and Literary Culture in Early Ohio." *Journal of Library History* 16 (1981): 574–94.

——. "Structural and Ideological Dimensions of Literacy and Education in the Old Northwest." Pp. 157–86 in Klingaman and Vedder, eds., *Essays on the Economy of Old Northwest.*

Stevens, Harry R. "Bank Enterprisers in a Western Town." *Business History Review* 29 (1955): 139–56.

Stewart, Roma Jones. "The Migration of a Free People: Cass County's Free Black Settlers from North Carolina." *Michigan History* 71 (1987): 34–38.

Stilgoe, John R. *Borderland: Origins of the American Suburb, 1820–1939.* New Haven, 1988.

Still, Bayard, ed. *Urban America: A History with Documents.* Boston, 1974.

Stiverson, Gregory A. *Poverty in a Land of Plenty: Tenancy in Eighteenth-Century Maryland.* Baltimore, 1981.

Storing, Herbert J., ed. *The Complete Anti-Federalist.* 7 vols. Chicago, 1981.

Stoutt, Richard. "Hinterland Development and Differences in Work Setting: The New York City Region, 1820–1870." Pp. 45–71 in William Pencak and Conrad Edick Wright, eds., *New York and the Rise of American Capitalism: Economic Development and the Social and Political History of an American State, 1780–1870.* New York, 1989.

Stuart, Reginald C. *United States Expansionism and British North America, 1775–1871.* Chapel Hill, N.C., 1988.

Sundstrom, William A., and Paul A. David. "Old-Age Security Motives, Labor Markets, and Farm Family Fertility in Antebellum America." *Explorations in Economic History* 25 (1988): 164–97.

Swaney, James A. "Common Rights, Reciprocity, and Community." *Journal of Economic Issues* 24 (1990): 541–61.

Sweet, Leonard I. *The Minister's Wife: Her Role in Nineteenth-Century American Evangelicalism.* Philadelphia, 1983.

Sweezy, Paul. "A Critique." Pp. 33–56 in Hilton, ed., *The Transition from Feudalism to Capitalism.*

Swierenga, Robert P. *Pioneers and Profits: Land Speculation on the Iowa Frontier.* Ames, Iowa, 1968.

——. "Quantitative Measures in Rural Landholding." *JIH* 13 (1983): 761–86.

——. "The Settlement of the Old Northwest: Ethnic Pluralism in a Featureless Plain." *JEarR* 9 (1989): 73–105.

Sydnor, Charles S. *Gentlemen Freeholders: Political Practices in Washington's Virginia.* Chapel Hill, N.C., 1952.

——. *Slavery in Mississippi.* New York, 1933.

Szatmary, David P. *Shays' Rebellion: The Making of an Agrarian Insurrection.* Amherst, Mass., 1981.

Tadman, Michael. *Speculators and Slaves: Masters, Traders, and Slaves in the Old South.* Madison, Wis., 1989.

Tate, Thad W., and David L. Ammerman, eds. *The Chesapeake in the Seventeenth Century: Essays on Anglo-American Society.* Chapel Hill, N.C., 1979.

Taylor, Alan. "The Backcountry Conclusion to the American Revolution: Agrarian Unrest in the Northeast, 1750–1820. In Young, ed., *Beyond the American Revolution.*

——. *Liberty Men and Great Proprietors: The Revolutionary Settlement on the Maine Frontier, 1760–1820.* Chapel Hill, N.C., 1990.

Taylor, Carl C. *The Farmers' Movement, 1620–1920.* New York, 1953.

Taylor, George Rogers. *The Transportation Revolution, 1815–1860.* New York, 1951.

Taylor, Joe G. "The Foreign Slave Trade in Louisiana after 1808." *Louisiana History* 1 (1960): 36–43.

Taylor, John. *Arator, Being a Series of Agricultural Essays, Practical and Political: In Sixty-Four Numbers.* M. E. Bradford, ed. 1818. Reprint. Indianapolis, 1977.

——. *Construction Construed and Constitutions Vindicated.* Richmond, 1820.

Taylor, Paul S. "Colonizing Georgia, 1732–1752: A Statistical Note." *WMQ* 22 (1965): 119–27.

Temkin-Greener, H., and A. C. Swedlund. "Fertility Transition in the Connecticut Valley, 1740–1850." *Population Studies* 32 (1978): 27–41.

Thayer, Theodore. *Pennsylvania Politics and the Growth of Democracy, 1740–1776.* Harrisburg, Pa., 1953.

Thirsk, Joan, and J. P. Cooper, eds. *Seventeenth-Century Economic Documents.* Oxford, 1972.

Thomas, Brinley. *Migration and Economic Growth: A Study of Great Britain and the Atlantic Economy.* 2d. ed. Cambridge, Eng., 1973.

Thomas, William H. B. *Patriots of the Upcountry: Orange County, Virginia, in the Revolution.* Orange, Va., 1976.

Thompson, E. P. "Eighteenth-Century English Society: Class Struggle without Class?" *Social History* 3 (1978): 133–65.

——. "E. P. Thompson." Interview with Michael Merrill. Pp. 3–25 in MAHRO, The Radical Historians' Association, eds., *Visions of History.* New York, 1984.

——. *The Making of the English Working Class.* New York, 1963.

Thompson, Roger. "Early Modern Migration." *Journal of American Studies* 25 (1991): 59–69.

Thornton, J. Mills. *Politics and Power in a Slave Society: Alabama, 1800–1860.* Baton Rouge, 1978.

Thornton, Tamara Plakins. "Between Generations: Boston Agricultural Reform and the Aging of New England, 1815–1830." *New England Quarterly* 59 (1988): 189–211.

Thorp, Daniel B. "Assimilation in North Carolina's Moravian Community." *Journal of Southern History* 52 (1986): 19–42.

Tibebu, Teshale. "On the Question of Feudalism, Absolutism, and the Bourgeois Revolution." *Review* 13 (1990): 49–152.

Tise, Larry E. *Proslavery: A History of the Defense of Slavery in America, 1701–1840*. Athens, Ga., 1987.

"Tobacco Exports, from Octo 1782 to Octo 1799." Auditor's Item 49, Virginia State Library, Richmond.

Tobin, Catherine. "The Lowly Muscular Digger: Irish Canal Workers in Nineteenth Century America." Ph.D. diss., Notre Dame, 1987.

Tocqueville, Alexis de. *Democracy in America*. Henry Reeve and Francis Bowen, trans., Phillips Bradley, ed. 2 vols. 1834–41. New York, 1945.

Tolles, Frederick B. "The American Revolution Considered as a Social Movement: A Re-Evaluation." *AHR* 60 (1954): 1–12.

——. *George Logan of Philadelphia*. New York, 1953.

Tryon, Rolla M. *Household Manufactures in the United States, 1640–1860*. Chicago, 1917.

Tully, Alan. "Englishmen and Germans: National Group Contact in Colonial Pennsylvania, 1700–1755." *Pennsylvania History* 45 (1978): 237–56.

Turner, Frederick Jackson. *The Frontier in American History*. New York, 1921.

Tyler, Alice Felt. *Freedom's Ferment: Phases of American Social History from the Colonial Period to the Outbreak of the Civil War*. 1944. Reprint. New York, 1962.

Tyler, Ron. "George Caleb Bingham: The Native Talent." Pp. 25–49 in Alan Alexrod, ed., *American Frontier Life: Early Western Painting and Prints*.

Ulrich, Laurel Thatcher. "'Daughters of Liberty': Religious Women in Revolutionary New England." Pp. 211–43 in Hoffman and Albert, eds., *Women in the Age of the American Revolution*.

——. *Good Wives: Image and Reality in the Lives of Women in Northern New England, 1650–1750*. New York, 1982.

——. "Housewife and Gadder: Themes of Self-Sufficiency and Community in Eighteenth-Century New England." Pp. 21–34 in Carol Groneman and Mary Beth Norton, eds., *"To Toil the Livelong Day": America's Women at Work, 1780–1980*. Ithaca, N.Y., 1987.

Underdown, David. *Revel, Riot, and Rebellion: Popular Politics and Culture in England, 1603–1660*. Oxford, 1987.

U.S. Bureau of the Census. *Heads of Families at the First Census of the United States Taken in the Year 1790, Records of the State Enumerations: 1782–1785, Virginia*. Washington, D.C., 1908.

——. *Historical Statistics of the United States, Colonial Times to 1970, Bicentennial Edition*. 2 vols. Washington, D.C. , 1975.

Unser, Daniel. "Food Marketing and Interethnic Exchange in the Eighteenth-Century Lower Mississippi Valley." *Food and Foodways* 1 (1986): 279–310.

Van Atta, John R. "Conscription in Revolutionary Virginia: The Case of Culpeper County, 1780–1781." *VMHB* 92 (1984): 263–81.

Van Schreeven, William J., et al., eds. *Revolutionary Virginia: The Road to Independence*. 8 vols. Charlottesville, Va., 1973–83.

Van Vugt, William E. "Running from Ruin? The Emigration of British Farmers to the U.S.A. in the Wake of the Repeal of the Corn Laws." *Economic History Review* 41 (1988): 411–28.

Vassberg, David E. *Land and Society in Golden Age Castille*. Cambridge, 1984.

Vickers, Daniel. "Competency and Competition: Economic Culture in Early America." *WMQ* 47 (1990): 3–29.

——. "Working the Fields in a Developing Economy: Essex County, Massachusetts, 1630–1675." Pp. 49–69 in Innes, ed., *Work and Labor in Early America*.

Villaflor, Georgia C., and Kenneth L. Sokoloff. "Migration in Colonial America: Evidence from the Militia Rolls." *SSH* 6 (1982): 539–70.

Vinovskis, Maris A. *Fertility in Massachusetts from the Revolution to the Civil War*. New York, 1981.

——. "Have Social Historians Lost the Civil War? Some Preliminary Demographic Speculations." Pp. 1–30 in Vinovskis, ed., *Toward a Social History of the Civil War*.

——, ed. *Toward a Social History of the American Civil War: Exploratory Essays*. Cambridge, 1990.

Vogeler, Ingolf. *The Myth of the Family Farm: Agribusiness Dominance of U.S. Agriculture*. Boulder, Colo., 1981.

Volpe, Vernon L. *Forlorn Hope of Freedom: The Liberty Party in the Old Northwest, 1838–1848*. Kent, Ohio, 1990.

Von Ende, Eleanor, and Thomas Weiss. "Labor Force Changes in the Old Northwest." Pp. 103–30 in Klingaman and Veddar, eds., *Essays on the Economy of Old Northwest*.

Waciega, Lisa Wilson. "A 'Man of Business': The Widow of Means in Southeastern Pennsylvania, 1750–1850." *WMQ* 44 (1987): 40–64.

Wahl, Jenny Bourne. "New Results on the Decline of Fertility in the United States from 1750 to 1900." Pp. 391–437 in Engerman and Gallman, eds., *Long-Term Factors in American Economic Growth*.

Walker, James W. St. G. *The Black Loyalists: The Search for a Promised Land in Nova Scotia and Sierra Leone, 1783–1870*. London, 1976.

Wallenstein, Peter. *From Slave South to New South: Public Policy in Nineteenth-Century Georgia*. Chapel Hill, N.C., 1987.

Wallerstein, Immanuel. *Historical Capitalism*. London, 1983.

——. *The Modern World-System I: Capitalist Agriculture and the Origins of the European World Economy in the Sixteenth Century*. New York, 1974.

Walsh, Lorena S. "Staying Put or Getting Out: Findings for Charles County, Maryland, 1650–1720." *WMQ* 44 (1987): 89–103.

Walton, Gary M., and James F. Shepherd. *The Economic Rise of Early America*. Cambridge, 1979.

Ward, Christopher. *The War of the Revolution*. John Richard Alden, ed. New York, 1952.

Ward, David. *Cities and Immigrants: A Geography of Change in Nineteenth-Century America*. New York, 1971.

Ward, Harry M. *Duty, Honor or Country: General George Weedon and the American Revolution*. Philadelphia, 1979.

Wareing, John. "Migration to London and Transatlantic Emigration to Indentured Servants, 1683–1775." *Journal of Historical Geography* 7 (1981): 356–78.

Warner, Sam Bass. *The Private City: Philadelphia in Three Periods of Its Growth.* Philadelphia, 1968.

Warren, Robert E., and Michael J. O'Brien. "A Model of Frontier Settlement." Pp. 22–57 in O'Brien, ed., *Grassland, Forest, Historical Settlement.*

Washburn, Wilcomb E. *The Governor and the Rebel: A History of Bacon's Rebellion in Virginia.* Chapel Hill, N.C., 1957.

Watson, Harry L. *Jacksonian Politics and Community Conflict: The Emergence of the Second Party System in Cumberland County, North Carolina.* Chapel Hill, N.C., 1981.

Watts, Steven. "The Idiocy of American Studies: Poststructuralism, Language, and Politics in the Age of Self-Fulfillment." *AQ* 43 (1991): 625–60.

Wax, Darrold D. "'New Negroes Are Always in Demand': The Slave Trade in Eighteenth-Century Georgia." *Georgia Historical Quarterly* 68 (1984): 193–220.

Wayland, Francis. *The Elements of Political Economy.* New York, 1837.

Webb, Stephen Saunders. *1676: The End of American Independence.* New York, 1984.

Webb, Walter Prescott. *The Great Plains.* Boston, 1931.

Weber, Adna Ferrin. *The Growth of Cities in the Nineteenth Century: A Study in Statistics.* New York, 1899.

Weber, Max. "Capitalism and Rural Society in Germany," Pp. 363–85 in *From Max Weber: Essays in Sociology.* Trans. and ed. by H. H. Gerth and C. Wright Mills. New York: 1946.

Weiman, David F. "The Economic Emancipation of the Non-Slaveholding Class: Upcountry Farmers in the Georgia Cotton Economy." *JEH* 45 (1985): 71–94.

——. "Families, Farms, and Rural Society in Pre-Industrial America." Pp. 255–77 in George Grantham and Carol S. Leonard, eds., *Agrarian Organization in the Century of Industrialization: Europe, Russia and North America.* Supplement 5 of *Research in Economic History.* Greenwich, Conn., 1989.

——. "Farmers and the Market in Antebellum America: A View from the Georgia Upcountry." *JEH* 37 (1987): 627–48.

——. "Peopling the Land by Lottery: The Market in Public Lands and the Regional Differentiation of Territory on the Georgia Frontier." *JEH* 51 (1991): 835–60.

——. "Slavery, Plantation Settlement, and Regional Development in the Antebellum Cotton South." Paper presented at the 1985 meeting of the Economic History Association.

Weiss, Rona. "The Market and Massachusetts Farmers, 1750–1850: Comment." *JEH* 43 (1983): 475–78.

Wellman, Judith. "The Seneca Falls Women's Rights Convention: A Study of Social Networks." *Journal of Women's History* 3 (1991): 9–37.

——. "Women and Radical Reform in Antebellum Upstate New York: A Profile of Grassroots Female Abolitionists." Pp. 113–27 in Deutrich and Purdy, eds., *Clio Was a Woman.*

——. "Women's Rights, Republicanism, and Revolutionary Rhetoric in Antebellum New York State." *New York History* 69 (1988): 353–84.

Wells, Tom Henderson. "Moving a Plantation to Louisiana." *Louisiana Studies* 6 (1967): 280–89.

Wessman, James W. "A Household Mode of Production—Another Comment." *RHR*, no. 22 (1979–80): 129–39.

Westbury, Susan. "Slaves of Colonial Virginia: Where They Came From." *WMQ* 42 (1985): 228–37.

Weston, Jack. *The Real American Cowboy*. New York, 1985.

Whartenby, Franklee Gilbert. "Land and Labor Productivity in United States Cotton Production, 1800–1840." Ph.D. diss., North Carolina, 1963.

White, Shane. *Somewhat More Independent: The End of Slavery in New York City, 1770–1810*. Athens, Ga., 1991.

——. "'We Dwell in Safety and Pursue Our Honest Callings': Free Blacks in New York City, 1783–1810." *JAH* 75 (1988): 445–70.

Whittenberg, James P. "Planters, Merchants, and Lawyers: Social Change and the Origins of the North Carolina Regulation." *WMQ* 34 (1977): 215–38.

Wilentz, Sean. *Chants Democratic: New York City and the Rise of the American Working Class, 1788–1850*. New York, 1984.

——. "On Class and Politics in Jacksonian America." *Reviews in American History* 10 (1982): 45–63.

——. "Many Democracies: On Tocqueville and Jacksonian America." Pp. 207–28 in Abraham S. Eisenstadt, ed., *Reconsidering Tocqueville's Democracy in America*. New Brunswick, N.J., 1988.

Williams, E. Russ, ed. *Records of Marion County, Mississippi: 1850 Federal Census, 1816 Territorial Census*. 3 vols. Bogalusa, La., 1965.

——. *Resource Records of Pike/Walthnall Counties, 1798–1910*. Easley, S.C., 1978.

Williams, Raymond. *The Country and the City*. New York, 1973.

——. *Keywords: A Vocabulary of Culture and Society*. Glasgow, 1976.

——. *Marxism and Literature*. Oxford, 1977.

Williamson, Jeffrey G. "Greasing the Wheels of Sputtering Export Engines: Midwestern Grains and American Growth." *Explorations in Economic History* 17 (1980): 189–217.

Winkel, Kenneth J. *The Politics of Community: Migration and Politics in Antebellum Ohio*. Cambridge, 1988.

Winters, Donald L. "The Agricultural Ladder in Southern Agriculture: Tennessee, 1850–1870." *AgH* 61 (Summer 1987): 36–52.

——. "Tenancy as an Economic Institution: The Growth and Distribution of Agricultural Tenancy in Iowa, 1850–1900." *JEH* 37 (1977): 382–408.

Wokeck, Marianne. "The Flow and the Composition of German Immigration to Philadelphia, 1727–1775." *Pennsylvania Magazine of History and Biography* 105 (1981): 249–78.

Wolf, Stephanie Grauman. *Urban Village: Population, Community, and Family Structure in Germantown, Pennsylvania, 1683–1800*. Princeton, 1976.

Wood, Ellen Meiksins. "The Politics of Theory and the Concept of Class: E. P. Thompson and His Critics." *Studies in Political Economy* 9 (1982): 45–75.

Wood, Gordon S. *The Creation of the American Republic, 1776–1787*. Chapel Hill, N.C., 1969.

——. "Interests and Disinterestedness in the Making of the Constitution." Pp. 66–109 in Beeman, Botein, and Carter, eds., *Beyond Confederation*.

Wood, J. S. "Elaboration of a Settlement System: The New England Village in the Federal Period." *Journal of Historical Geography* 10 (1984): 331–56.

Wood, Peter. *Black Majority: Negroes in Colonial South Carolina from 1670 through the Stono Rebellion.* New York, 1974.

Woodman, Harold D. "Post-Civil War Agriculture and the Law." *AgH* 53 (1979): 319–37.

Wooten, Hugh Hill. "Westward Migration from Iredell County, 1800–1850." *North Carolina Historical Review* 30 (1953): 61–71.

Wordie, J. R. "The Chronology of English Enclosure, 1500–1914." *Economic History Review* 36 (1983): 483–505.

Worster, Donald. *Dust Bowl: The Southern Plains in the 1930s.* New York, 1979.

——. "Transformations of the Earth: Toward an Agroecological Perspective in History." *JAH* 76 (1990): 1087–1106.

——. "The Vulnerable Earth: Toward a Planetary History," Pp. 3–20 in Worster, ed., *The Ends of the Earth: Perspectives on Modern Environmental History.* Cambridge, 1988.

Wright, Erik Olin. *Classes.* London, 1985.

Wright, Gavin. "American Agriculture and the Labor Market: What Happened to Proletarianization?" *AgH* 62 (Summer 1988): 182–210.

——. *Old South, New South: Revolutions in the Southern Economy since the Civil War.* New York, 1986.

——. *The Political Economy of the Cotton South: Households, Markets, and Wealth in the Nineteenth Century.* New York, 1978.

Wrightson, Keith. *English Society, 1580–1680.* New Brunswick, N.J., 1982.

Wrigley Edward A. "A Simple Model of London's Importance in Changing English Economy and Society 1650–1750." *Past and Present,* no. 37 (1967): 44–70.

Wrigley Edward A., and Roger S. Schofield. *The Population History of England, 1541–1871: A Reconstruction.* Cambridge, Mass., 1981.

Wyatt-Brown, Bertram. *Southern Honor: Ethics and Behavior in the Old South.* New York, 1982.

Wyckoff, William. *The Developer's Frontier: The Making of the Western New York Landscape.* New Haven, 1988.

Wyman, Mark. *Immigrants in the Valley: Irish, Germans, and Americans in the Upper Mississippi Valley, 1830–1860.* Chicago, 1984.

Yasuba, Yasukichi. *Birth Rates of the White Population of the United States, 1800–1860.* Baltimore, 1962.

Young, Alfred F. "Afterword." Pp. 449–62 in Young, ed., *American Revolution.*

——. "Conservatives, the Constitution, and the 'Spirit of Accommodation.'" Pp. 117–47 in Goldwin and Schambra, eds., *How Democratic Is the Constitution?*

——. *The Democratic Republicans of New York: The Origins, 1763–1797.* Chapel Hill, N.C., 1967.

——. "English Plebian Culture and Eighteenth-Century American Radicalism." Pp. 185–212 in Jacob and Jacob, eds., *Origins of Anglo-American Radicalism.*

——. "The Women of Boston: 'Persons of Consequence' in the Making of the American Revolution, 1765–76." Pp. 181–226 in Applewhite and Levy, eds., *Women and Poltics.*

——, ed. *The American Revolution: Explorations in the History of American Radicalism.* DeKalb, Ill., 1976.

——, ed. *Beyond the American Revolution: Further Explorations in Radicalism.* DeKalb, Ill., forthcoming.

——. ed., *The Debate over the Constitution, 1787–1789.* Chicago, Ill., 1965.

Young, James Sterling. *The Washington Community, 1800–1828.* New York, 1966.

Young, Mary E. "Congress Looks West: Liberal Ideology and Public Land Policy in the Nineteenth Century." Pp. 74–112 in Ellis, ed., *Frontier in American Development.*

Yuasa, Shigehiro. "The Commercial Pattern of the Illinois and Michigan Canal, 1848–1860." Pp. 9–21 in Conzen and Morales, eds., *Settling the Upper Illinois Valley.*

Zahler, Helene Sara. *Eastern Workingmen and National Land Policy, 1829–1862.* New York, 1941.

Zelinsky, Wilbur. "The Hypothesis of the Mobility Transition." *Geographic Review* 61 (1971): 219–49.

Zevin, Robert Brooke. "The Growth of Cotton Textile Production after 1815." Pp. 122–47 in Robert W. Fogel and Stanley L. Engerman, eds., *The Reinterpretation of American Economic History.* New York, 1971.

Zilversmit, Arthur. *The First Emancipation: The Abolition of Slavery in the North.* Chicago, 1967.

Zuckerman, Michael. "The Fabrication of Identity in Early America." *WMQ* 34 (1977): 183–214.

——. *Peaceable Kingdoms: New England Towns in the Eighteenth Century.* New York, 1970.

Index